DAILY LIGHT is the most widely read Christian inspirational guide in the world. These readings were selected and compiled over a century ago, yet they remain as relevant now as when they were first published.

DAILY LIGHT is made up entirely of selected Scripture verses, with the devot for ach day, both the morning and eve a single theme. This give to the meaning of

Daily Light
From
The Bible

Morning & Evening

A BARBOUR BOOK

Leatherette Edition ISBN 0-916441-62-8
Bonded Leather Edition ISBN 0-916441-68-7

Published by Barbour and Company, Inc.
P.O. Box 719
Uhrichsville, OH 44683

EVANGELICAL CHRISTIAN PUBLISHERS ASSOCIATION ecpa MEMBER

Printed in the United States of America

Daily Light
From
The Bible

**This one thing I do, forgetting those things which are behind, . . .
I press toward the mark for the prize of the high calling of God
in Christ Jesus.**

Father, I will that they . . . whom thou hast given me, be with
me where I am; that they may behold my glory, which thou hast
given me.—I know whom I have believed, and am persuaded that
he is able to keep that which I have committed unto him against
that day.—He which hath begun a good work in you will perform
it until the day of Jesus Christ.

Know ye not that they which run in a race run all, but one receiveth the prize? So run, that ye may obtain. And every man that
striveth for the mastery is temperate in all things. Now they do
it to obtain a corruptible crown; but we an incorruptible.—Let
us lay aside every weight, and the sin which doth so easily beset
us, and let us run with patience the race that is set before us, looking unto Jesus.

PHI. 3. 13, 14. *Jno.* 17. 24.—2 *Ti.* 1. 12.—*Phi.* 1. 6. 1 *Co.* 9. 24, 25.—
He. 12. 1, 2.

**The Lord, he it is that doth go before thee; he will be with thee,
he will not fail thee.**

If thy presence go not with me, carry us not up hence.— O
Lord, I know that the way of man is not in himself: it is not in
man that walketh to direct his steps.

The steps of a good man are ordered by the Lord: and he delighteth in his way. Though he fall, he shall not be utterly cast
down: for the Lord upholdeth him with his hand.

I am continually with thee: thou hast holden me by my right
hand. Thou shalt guide me with thy counsel, and afterward receive me to glory.—I am persuaded, that neither death, nor life,
nor angels, nor principalities, nor powers, nor things present, nor
things to come, nor height, nor depth, nor any other creature,
shall be able to separate us from the love of God, which is in
Christ Jesus our Lord.

DEUT. 31. 8. *Ex.* 33. 15.—*Je.* 10. 23. *Ps.* 37. 23, 24. *Ps.* 73. 23, 24.—
Ro. 8. 38, 39.

Sing unto the Lord a new song.

Sing aloud unto God our strength; make a joyful noise unto the God of Jacob. Take a psalm, and bring hither the timbrel, the pleasant harp with the psaltery.—He hath put a new song in my mouth, even praise unto our God: many shall see it, and fear, and shall trust in the LORD.

Be strong and of a good courage; be not afraid, neither be thou dismayed: for the LORD thy God is with thee whithersoever thou goest.—The joy of the Lord is your strength.—Paul . . . thanked God, and took courage.

Knowing the time, that now it is high time to awake out of sleep: for now is our salvation nearer than when we believed. The night is far spent, the day is at hand: let us therefore cast off the works of darkness, and let us put on the armour of light. Let us walk honestly, as in the day; not in rioting and drunkenness, not in chambering and wantonness, not in strife and envying. But put ye on the Lord Jesus Christ, and make not provision for the flesh, to fulfil the lusts thereof.

ISA. 42. 10. *Ps.* 81. 1, 2.—*Ps.* 40, 3. *Jos.* 1. 9.—*Ne.* 8. 10.—*Acts* 28.15.
Ro. 13. 11-14.

Let my prayer be set forth before thee as incense; and the lifting up of my hands as the evening sacrifice.

Thou shalt make an altar to burn incense upon: . . . and thou shalt put it before the vail that is by the ark of the testimony, before the mercy seat that is over the testimony, where I will meet with thee. And Aaron shall burn thereon sweet incense every morning: . . . and when Aaron lighteth the lamps at even, he shall burn incense upon it, a perpetual incense before the LORD throughout your generations.

[Jesus] is able to save them to the uttermost that come unto God by him, seeing he ever liveth to make intercession for them. —The smoke of the incense, which came with the prayers of the saints, ascended up before God out of the angel's hand.

Ye also, as lively stones, are built up a spiritual house, an holy priesthood, to offer up spiritual sacrifices, acceptable to God by Jesus Christ.

Pray without ceasing.

PSA. 141.2. *Ex.* 30. 1, 6-8. *Heb.* 7.25.—*Re.* 8.4. 1 *Pe.* 2.5. 1 *Thes.* 5.17.

He led them forth by the right way.

He found [Jacob] in a desert land, and in the waste howling wilderness; he led him about, he instructed him, he kept him as the apple of his eye. As an eagle stirreth up her nest, fluttereth over her young, spreadeth abroad her wings, taketh them, beareth them on her wings: so the LORD alone did lead him.—Even to your old age I am he; and even to hoar hairs will I carry you: I have made, and I will bear; even I will carry, and will deliver you.

He restoreth my soul: he leadeth me in the paths of righteousness for his name's sake. Yea, though I walk through the valley of the shadow of death, I will fear no evil: for thou art with me; thy rod and thy staff they comfort me.

The LORD shall guide thee continually, and satisfy thy soul in drought, and make fat thy bones: and thou shalt be like a watered garden, and like a spring of water, whose waters fail not. —For this GOD is our GOD for ever and ever: he will be our guide even unto death. Who teacheth like him?

PSA. 107. 7. *De.* 32. 10-12.—*Is.* 46. 4. *Ps.* 23. 3, 4. *Is.* 58. 11.—*Ps.* 48. 14. *Job* 36. 22.

What wilt thou that I shall do unto thee? . . . Lord, that I may receive my sight.

Open thou mine eyes, that I may behold wondrous things out of thy law.

Then opened he their understanding, that they might understand the scriptures.—The Comforter, which is the Holy Ghost, whom the Father will send in my name, . . . shall teach you all things.—Every good gift and every perfect gift is from above, and cometh down from the Father of lights.

The God of our Lord Jesus Christ, the Father of glory, . . . give unto you the spirit of wisdom and revelation in the knowledge of him: the eyes of your understanding being enlightened; that ye may know what is the hope of his calling, and what the riches of the glory of his inheritance in the saints, and what is the exceeding greatness of his power to us-ward who believe, according to the working of his mighty power.

LUKE 18. 41. *Ps.* 119. 18. *Lu.* 24. 45.—*Jno.* 14. 26.—*Ja.* 1. 17. *Ep.* 1. 17-19.

Ye are not as yet come to the rest and to the inheritance, which the Lord your God giveth you.

This is not your rest.—There remaineth therefore a rest to the people of God.—Within the veil; whither the forerunner is for us entered, even Jesus.

In my Father's house are many mansions: if it were not so, I would have told you. I go to prepare a place for you. And if I go and prepare a place for you, I will come again, and receive you unto myself; that where I am, there ye may be also.—With Christ; which is far better.

God shall wipe away all tears from their eyes; and there shall be no more death, neither sorrow, nor crying, neither shall there be any more pain; for the former things are passed away.—There the wicked cease from troubling: and there the weary be at rest.

Lay up for yourselves treasures in heaven. For where your treasure is, there will your heart be also.—Set your affection on things above, not on things on the earth.

DEUT. 12. 9.—*Mi.* 2. 10.—*He.* 4. 9.—*He.* 6. 19, 20. *Jno.* 14. 2, 3.— *Phi.* 1. 23. *Re.* 21. 4.—*Job* 3. 17. *Mat.* 6. 20, 21.—*Col.* 3. 2.

O death, where is thy sting? O grave, where is thy victory?

The sting of death is sin.—But now once in the end of the world hath he appeared to put away sin by the sacrifice of himself. And as it is appointed unto men once to die, but after this the judgment: so Christ was once offered to bear the sins of many; and unto them that look for him shall he appear the second time without sin unto salvation.

As the children are partakers of flesh and blood, he also himself likewise took part of the same; that through death he might destroy him that had the power of death, that is, the devil; and deliver them who through fear of death were all their lifetime subject to bondage.

I am now ready to be offered, and the time of my departure is at hand. I have fought a good fight, I have finished my course, I have kept the faith: henceforth there is laid up for me a crown of righteousness.

1 *COR.* 15. 55. 1 *Co.* 15. 56.—*Heb.* 9. 26-28. *Heb.* 2. 14, 15. 2 *Ti.* 4. 6-8.

We which have believed do enter into rest.

They weary themselves to commit iniquity.—I see another law in my members, warring against the law of my mind, and bringing me into captivity to the law of sin which is in my members. O wretched man that I am! who shall deliver me from the body of this death?

Come unto me, all ye that labour and are heavy laden, and I will give you rest.—Being justified by faith, we have peace with God through our Lord Jesus Christ: by whom also we have access by faith into this grace wherein we stand, and rejoice in hope of the glory of God.

He that is entered into his rest, he also hath ceased from his own works.—Not having mine own righteousness, which is of the law, but that which is through the faith of Christ, the righteousness which is of God by faith.—This is the rest wherewith ye may cause the weary to rest; and this is the refreshing.

HEB. 4. 3. —*Je.* 9. 5.—*Ro.* 7. 23, 24. *Mat.* 11. 28.—*Ro.* 5. 1, 2. *He.* 4. 10. *Phi.* 3. 9.—*Is.* 28. 12.

Set a watch, O Lord, before my mouth; keep the door of my lips.

If thou, LORD, shouldest mark iniquities, O Lord, who shall stand?—They provoked his spirit, so that he spake unadvisedly with his lips.

Not that which goeth into the mouth defileth a man; but that which cometh out of the mouth, this defileth a man.

A whisperer separateth chief friends.—There is that speaketh like the piercings of a sword: but the tongue of the wise is health. The lip of truth shall be established for ever: but a lying tongue is but for a moment.—The tongue can no man tame; it is an unruly evil, full of deadly poison. Out of the same mouth proceedeth blessing and cursing. My brethren, these things ought not so to be.

Put off . . . anger, wrath, malice, blasphemy, filthy communication out of your mouth. Lie not one to another, seeing that ye have put off the old man with his deeds.—This is the will of God, even your sanctification.—In their mouth was found no guile.

PSA. 141. 3. *Ps.* 130. 3.—*Ps.* 106. 33. *Mat.* 15. 11. *Pr.* 16. 28.— *Pr.* 12. 18, 19.—*Ja.* 3. 8, 10. *Col.* 3. 8, 9.—1 *Th.* 4. 3.—*Re.* 14. 5.

Let the beauty of the Lord our God be upon us: and establish thou the work of our hands.

Thy renown went forth among the heathen for thy beauty: for it was perfect through my comeliness, which I had put upon thee, saith the Lord GOD.—We all, with open face beholding as in a glass the glory of the Lord, are changed into the same image from glory to glory, even as by the Spirit of the Lord.—The Spirit of glory and of God resteth upon us.

Blessed is every one that feareth the LORD; that walketh in his ways. For thou shalt eat the labour of thine hands: happy shalt thou be, and it shall be well with thee.—Commit thy works unto the LORD, and thy thoughts shall be established.

Work out your own salvation with fear and trembling. For it is God which worketh in you both to will and to do of his good pleasure.—Our Lord Jesus Christ himself, and God, even our Father, which hath loved us, and hath given us everlasting consolation and good hope through grace, comfort your hearts, and stablish you in every good word and work.

PSA. 90. 17. *Eze.* 16. 14.—2 *Co.* 3. 18.—1 *Pe.* 4. 14. *Ps.* 128. 1, 2.—*Pr.* 16. 3. *Phi.* 2. 12, 13.—2 *Th.* 2. 16, 17.

The apostles gathered themselves together unto Jesus, and told him all things they had done.

There is a friend that sticketh closer than a brother.—The LORD spake unto Moses face to face, as a man speaketh unto his friend.—Ye are my friends, if ye do whatsoever I command you. Henceforth I call you not servants; for the servant knoweth not what his lord doeth: but I have called you friends; for all things that I have heard of my Father I have made known unto you.

When ye shall have done all those things which are commanded you, say, We are unprofitable servants.

Ye have not received the spirit of bondage again to fear; but ye have received the Spirit of adoption, whereby we cry, Abba, Father.

In every thing by prayer and supplication with thanksgiving let your requests be made known unto God.—The prayer of the upright is his delight.

MARK 6. 30. *Pr.* 18. 24.—*Ex.* 33. 11.—*Jno.* 15. 14, 15. *Lu.* 17. 10. *Ro.* 8. 15. *Phi.* 4. 6.—*Pr.* 15. 8.

Think upon me, my God, for good.

Thus saith the LORD; I remember thee, the kindness of thy youth, the love of thine espousals, when thou wentest after me in the wilderness.—I will remember my covenant with thee in the days of thy youth, and I will establish unto thee an everlasting covenant.—I will visit you, and perform my good word toward you.—For I know the thoughts that I think toward you, saith the LORD, thoughts of peace, and not of evil, to give you an expected end.

As the heavens are higher than the earth, so are my ways higher than your ways, and my thoughts than your thoughts.—I would seek unto God, and unto God would I commit my cause: which doeth great things and unsearchable; marvellous things without number.—Many, O LORD my God, are thy wonderful works which thou hast done, and thy thoughts which are to us-ward: they cannot be reckoned up in order unto thee: if I would declare and speak of them they are more than can be numbered.

NEH. 5. 19. *Je.* 2. 2.—*Eze.* 16. 60.—*Je.* 29. 10, 11. *Is.* 55. 9.—*Job.* 5. 8, 9. —*Ps.* 40. 5.

I will not fail thee, nor forsake thee.

There failed not ought of any good thing which the LORD had spoken unto the house of Israel; all came to pass.—God is not a man, that he should lie; neither the son of man, that he should repent: hath he said, and shall he not do it? or hath he spoken, and shall he not make it good?

The LORD thy God, he is God, the faithful God, which keepeth covenant and mercy with them that love him.—He will ever be mindful of his covenant.

Can a woman forget her sucking child, that she should not have compassion on the son of her womb? yea, they may forget, yet will I not forget thee. Behold, I have graven thee upon the palms of my hands.

The LORD thy God in the midst of thee is mighty; he will save, he will rejoice over thee with joy; he will rest in his love, he will joy over thee with singing.

JOSH. 1. 5. *Jos.* 21. 45.—*Nu.* 23. 19. *De.* 7. 9.—*Ps.* 111. 5. *Is.* 49. 15. 16. *Zep.* 3. 17.

They that know thy name will put their trust in thee: for thou, Lord, hast not forsaken them that seek thee.

The name of the LORD is a strong tower: the righteous runneth into it, and is safe.—I will trust, and not be afraid: for the LORD JEHOVAH is my strength and my song; he also is become my salvation.

I have been young, and now am old; yet have I not seen the righteous forsaken, nor his seed begging bread.—For the LORD loveth judgment, and forsaketh not his saints, they are preserved for ever: but the seed of the wicked shall be cut off.—The LORD will not forsake his people for his great name's sake: because it hath pleased the LORD to make you his people.—Who delivered us from so great a death, and doth deliver: in whom we trust that he will yet deliver us.

Be content with such things as ye have: for he hath said, I will never leave thee, nor forsake thee. So that we may boldly say, The Lord is my helper, I will not fear what man shall do unto me.

PSA. 9. 10. *Pr.* 18. 10.—*Is.* 12. 2. *Ps.* 37. 25.—*Ps.* 37. 28.—1 *Sa.* 12. 22.— 2 *Co.* 1. 10.—*He.* 13. 5, 6.

They are without fault before the throne of God.

The iniquity of Israel shall be sought for, and there shall be none; and the sins of Judah, and they shall not be found: for I will pardon them whom I reserve.—Who is a God like unto thee, that pardoneth iniquity, and passeth by the transgression of the remnant of his heritage? he retaineth not his anger for ever, because he delighteth in mercy. He will turn again, he will have compassion upon us; he will subdue our iniquities; and thou wilt cast all their sins into the depths of the sea.

He hath made us accepted in the beloved.—To present you holy and unblameable and unreproveable in his sight.

Now unto him that is able to keep you from falling, and to present you faultless before the presence of his glory with exceeding joy, to the only wise God our Saviour, be glory and majesty, dominion and power, both now and ever. Amen.

REV. 14. 5. *Je.* 50. 20.—*Mi.* 7. 18, 19. *Ep.* 1. 6.—*Col.* 1. 22. *Jude* 24, 25.

Thou hast given a banner to them that fear thee, that it may be displayed because of the truth.

Jehovah Nissi (The LORD my banner).—When the enemy shall come in like a flood, the Spirit of the LORD shall lift up a standard against him.

We will rejoice in thy salvation, and in the name of our God we will set up our banners.—The LORD hath brought forth our right-eousness: come, and let us declare in Zion the work of the LORD our God.—We are more than conquerors through him that loved us.—Thanks be to God, which giveth us the victory through our Lord Jesus Christ.—The captain of our salvation.

My brethren, be strong in the Lord, and in the power of his might.—Valiant for the truth.—Fight the LORD's battles.—Be strong, all ye people of the land, saith the LORD, and work: . . . fear ye not.—Lift up your eyes, and look on the fields; for they are white already to harvest.—Yet a little while, and he that shall come will come, and will not tarry.

PSA. 60. 4. *Ex.* 17. 15.—*Is.* 59. 19. *Ps.* 20. 5.—*Je.* 51. 10.—*Ro.* 8. 37.— 1 *Co.* 15. 57.—*He.* 2. 10. *Ep.* 6. 10.—*Je.* 9. 3.—1 *Sa.* 18. 17.—*Hag.* 2. 4, 5. —*Jno.* 4. 35.—*He.* 10. 37.

One thing is needful.

There be many that say, Who will shew us any good? LORD, lift thou up the light of thy countenance upon us. Thou hast put gladness in my heart, more than in the time that their corn and their wine increased.

As the hart panteth after the water brooks, so panteth my soul after thee, O God. My soul thirsteth for God, for the living God.— O God, thou art my God; early will I seek thee: my soul thirsteth for thee, my flesh longeth for thee in a dry and thirsty land, where no water is.

I am the bread of life: he that cometh to me shall never hunger; and he that believeth on me shall never thirst. Lord, evermore give us this bread.—Mary . . . sat at Jesus' feet, and heard his word.—One thing have I desired of the LORD, that will I seek after; that I may dwell in the house of the LORD all the days of my life, to behold the beauty of the LORD, and to enquire in his temple.

LUKE 10. 42. *Ps.* 4. 6, 7. *Ps.* 42. 1, 2.—*Ps.* 63. 1. *Jno.* 6. 35, 34.— *Lu.* 10. 39.—*Ps.* 27. 4.

I pray God your whole spirit and soul and body be preserved blameless unto the coming of our Lord Jesus Christ.

Christ loved the church, and gave himself for it; that he might present it to himself a glorious church, not having spot, or wrinkle, or any such thing; but that it should be holy and without blemish. —Whom we preach, warning every man, and teaching every man in all wisdom; that we may present every man perfect in Christ Jesus.

The peace of God . . . passeth all understanding.—Let the peace of God rule in your hearts, to the which also ye are called in one body.

Our Lord Jesus Christ himself, and God, even our Father, which hath loved us, and hath given us everlasting consolation and good hope through grace, comfort your hearts, and stablish you in every good word and work.—Who shall also confirm you unto the end, that ye may be blameless in the day of our Lord Jesus Christ.

1 *THES.* 5. 23. *Ep.* 5. 25, 27.—*Col.* 1. 28. *Phi.* 4. 7.—*Col.* 3. 15.
2 *Th.* 2. 16, 17.—1 *Co.* 1. 8.

Will God in very deed dwell with men on the earth?

Let them make me a sanctuary; that I may dwell among them. —I will meet with the children of Israel, and the tabernacle shall be sanctified by my glory. And I will dwell among the children of Israel, and will be their God.

Thou hast ascended on high, thou hast led captivity captive: thou hast received gifts for men; yea, for the rebellious also, that the LORD God might dwell among them.

Ye are the temple of the living God; as God hath said, I will dwell in them, and walk in them; and I will be their God, and they shall be my people.—Your body is the temple of the Holy Ghost which is in you.—Ye . . . are builded together for an habitation of God through the Spirit.

The heathen shall know that I the LORD do sanctify Israel, when my sanctuary shall be in the midst of them for evermore.

2 *CHRON.* 6. 18. *Ex.* 25. 8.—*Ex.* 29. 43, 45. *Ps.* 68. 18. 2 *Co.* 6. 16.—
1 *Co.* 6. 19.—*Eph.* 2. 22. *Eze.* 37. 28.

Praise waiteth for thee, O God, in Sion.

To us there is but one God, the Father, of whom are all things, and we in him; and one Lord Jesus Christ, by whom are all things, and we by him.—All men should honour the Son, even as they honour the Father. He that honoureth not the Son honoureth not the Father which hath sent him.—By him therefore let us offer the sacrifice of praise to God continually, that is, the fruit of our lips giving thanks to his name.—Whoso offereth praise glorifieth me: and to him that ordereth his conversation aright will I shew the salvation of God.

I beheld, and, lo, a great multitude, which no man could number, of all nations, and kindreds, and people, and tongues, stood before the throne, and before the Lamb, clothed with white robes, and palms in their hands; and cried with a loud voice, saying, Salvation to our God which sitteth upon the throne, and unto the Lamb. Amen: Blessing, and glory, and wisdom, and thanksgiving, and honour, and power, and might, be unto our God for ever and ever. Amen.

PSA. 65. 1. 1 Co. 8. 6.—Jno. 5. 23.—He. 13. 15.—Ps. 50. 23.
Re. 7. 9, 10, 12.

Who redeemeth thy life from destruction.

Their Redeemer is strong; the LORD of hosts is his name.—I will ransom them from the power of the grave; I will redeem them from death: O death, I will be thy plagues; O grave, I will be thy destruction.

As the children are partakers of flesh and blood, he also himself likewise took part of the same; that through death he might destroy him that had the power of death, that is, the devil; and deliver them who through fear of death were all their lifetime subject to bondage.

He that believeth on the Son hath everlasting life: and he that believeth not the Son shall not see life; but the wrath of God abideth on him.

Ye are dead, and your life is hid with Christ in God. When Christ, who is our life, shall appear, then shall ye also appear with him in glory.—When he shall come to be glorified in his saints, and to be admired in all them that believe.

PSA. 103. 4. Jer. 50. 34.—Hos. 13. 14. Heb. 2. 14, 15. Jno. 3. 36.
Col. 3. 3, 4.—2 Th. 1. 10.

The only wise God our Saviour

Christ Jesus, who of God is made unto us wisdom, and right-eousness, and sanctification, and redemption.—Canst thou by searching find out God? canst thou find out the Almighty unto perfection? It is as high as heaven; what canst thou do? deeper than hell; what canst thou know?

We speak the wisdom of God in a mystery, even the hidden wisdom, which God ordained before the world unto our glory.— The mystery, which from the beginning of the world hath been hid in God, who created all things by Jesus Christ: to the intent that now unto the principalities and powers in heavenly places might be known, by the church, the manifold wisdom of God.

If any of you lack wisdom, let him ask of God, that giveth to all men liberally, and upbraideth not; and it shall be given him.— The wisdom that is from above is first pure, then peaceable, gentle, and easy to be intreated, full of mercy and good fruits, without partiality, and without hypocrisy.

JUDE 25. 1 *Co.* 1. 30.—*Job* 11. 7, 8. 1 *Co.* 2. 7.—*Ep.* 3. 9, 10. *Ja.* 1. 5.— *Ja.* 3. 17.

When shall I arise, and the night be gone?

Watchman, what of the night? The watchman said, The morning cometh.

Yet a little while, and he that shall come will come, and will not tarry.—He shall be as the light of the morning, when the sun riseth, even a morning without clouds.

I go to prepare a place for you. And if I go and prepare a place for you, I will come again, and receive you unto myself; that where I am, there ye may be also. Let not your heart be troubled, neither let it be afraid. Ye have heard how I said unto you, I go away, and come again unto you.

Let all thine enemies perish, O Lord; but let them that love him be as the sun when he goeth forth in his might.—Ye are all the children of light, and the children of the day: we are not of the night, nor of darkness.

There shall be no night there.

JOB 7. 4. *Is.* 21. 11, 12. *Heb.* 10. 37.—2 *Sa.* 23. 4. *Jno.* 14. 2, 3, 27, 28. *Ju.* 5. 31.—1 *Th.* 5. 5. *Re.* 21. 25.

Thou wilt keep him in perfect peace, whose mind is stayed on thee.

Cast thy burden upon the LORD, and he shall sustain thee; he shall never suffer the righteous to be moved.—I will trust, and not be afraid: for the LORD JEHOVAH is my strength and my song; he also is become my salvation.

Why are ye fearful, O ye of little faith?—Be careful for nothing; but in every thing by prayer and supplication with thanksgiving let your requests be made known unto God. And the peace of God, which passeth all understanding, shall keep your hearts and minds through Christ Jesus.—In quietness and in confidence shall be your strength.

The effect of righteousness [shall be] quietness and assurance for ever.—Peace I leave with you, my peace I give unto you: not as the world giveth, give I unto you. Let not your heart be troubled, neither let it be afraid.—Peace, from him which is, and which was, and which is to come.

ISA. 26. 3. Ps. 55. 22.—Is. 12. 2. Mat. 8. 26.—Phi. 4. 6, 7.—Is. 30. 15. Is. 32. 17.—Jno. 14. 27.—Rev. 1. 4.

Let not the sun go down upon your wrath.

If thy brother shall trespass against thee, go and tell him his fault between thee and him alone: if he shall hear thee, thou hast gained thy brother. . . . Lord, how oft shall my brother sin against me, and I forgive him? till seven times? Jesus saith unto him, I say not unto thee, Until seven times: but, Until seventy times seven.—When ye stand praying, forgive, if ye have ought against any: that your Father also which is in heaven may forgive you your trespasses.

Put on, therefore, as the elect of God, holy and beloved, bowels of mercies, kindness, humbleness of mind, meekness, longsuffering; forbearing one another, and forgiving one another, if any man have a quarrel against any: even as Christ forgave you, so also do ye.—Be ye kind one to another, tenderhearted, forgiving one another, even as God for Christ's sake hath forgiven you.

The apostles said unto the Lord, Increase our faith.

EPH. 4. 26. Mat. 18. 15, 21, 22.—Mar. 11. 25. Col. 3. 12, 13.—Eph. 4. 32. Lu. 17. 5.

My Father is greater than I.

When ye pray, say, Our Father which art in heaven.—My Father, and your Father; . . . my God and your God.

As the Father gave me commandment, even so I do.—The words that I speak unto you I speak not of myself: but the Father that dwelleth in me, he doeth the works.

The Father loveth the Son, and hath given all things into his hand.—Thou hast given him power over all flesh, that he should give eternal life to as many as thou hast given him.

Lord, shew us the Father, and it sufficeth us. Jesus saith unto him, Have I been so long time with you, and yet hast thou not known me, Philip? he that hath seen me hath seen the Father; and how sayest thou then, Shew us the Father? Believest thou not that I am in the Father, and the Father in me?—I and my Father are one.—As the Father hath loved me, so have I loved you: continue ye in my love. If ye keep my commandments, ye shall abide in my love; even as I have kept my Father's commandments, and abide in his love.

JOHN 14. 28. *Lu.* 11. 2.—*Jno.* 20. 17. *Jno.* 14. 31.—*Jno.* 14. 10. *Jno.* 3. 35.—*Jno.* 17. 2. *Jno.* 14. 8-10.—*Jno.* 10. 30.—*Jno.* 15. 9, 10.

[The woman's seed] shall bruise thy head, and thou shalt bruise his heel.

His visage was so marred more than any man, and his form more than the sons of men.—He was wounded for our transgressions, he was bruised for our iniquities: the chastisement of our peace was upon him; and with his stripes we are healed.

This is your hour, and the power of darkness.—Thou couldest have no power at all against me, except it were given thee from above.

The Son of God was manifested, that he might destroy the works of the devil.—He cast out many devils; and suffered not the devils to speak, because they knew him.

All power is given unto me in heaven and in earth.—In my name shall they cast out devils.

The God of peace shall bruise Satan under your feet shortly.

GEN. 3. 15. *Is.* 52. 14.—*Is.* 53. 5. *Lu.* 22. 53.—*Jno.* 19. 11. 1 *Jno.* 3. 8.—*Mar.* 1. 34. *Mat.* 28. 18.—*Mar.* 16. 17. *Ro.* 16. 20.

My soul cleaveth unto the dust: quicken thou me according to thy word.

If ye . . . be risen with Christ, seek those things which are above, where Christ sitteth on the right hand of God. Set your affection on things above, not on things on the earth. For . . . your life is hid with Christ in God.—Our conversation is in heaven; from whence also we look for the Saviour, the Lord Jesus Christ: who shall change our vile body, that it may be fashioned like unto his glorious body, according to the working whereby he is able even to subdue all things unto himself.

The flesh lusteth against the Spirit, and the Spirit against the flesh; and these are contrary the one to the other: so that ye cannot do the things that ye would.—Brethren, we are debtors, not to the flesh, to live after the flesh. For if ye live after the flesh, ye shall die: but if ye through the Spirit do mortify the deeds of the body, ye shall live.—Dearly beloved, I beseech you as strangers and pilgrims, abstain from fleshly lusts, which war against the soul.

PSA. 119. 25. *Col.* 3. 1-3.—*Phi.* 3. 20, 21. *Gal.* 5. 17.—*Ro.* 8. 12, 13.—
1 *Pe.* 2. 11.

The measure of faith.

Him that is weak in the faith.—Strong in faith, giving to God.

O thou of little faith, wherefore didst thou doubt?—Great is thy faith: be it unto thee even as thou wilt.

Believe ye that I am able to do this? They said unto him, Yea, Lord. . . . According to your faith be it unto you.

Lord, increase our faith.—Building up yourselves on your most holy faith.—Rooted and built up in him, and established in the faith.—He which stablisheth us with you in Christ, . . . is God.—The God of all grace . . . after that ye have suffered a while, make you perfect, stablish, strengthen, settle you.

We . . . that are strong ought to bear the infirmities of the weak, and not to please ourselves.—Let us not . . . judge one another : . . . but judge this rather, that no man put a stumblingblock or an occasion to fall in his brother's way.

ROM. 12. 3. *Ro.* 14.1.—*Ro.* 4. 20. *Mat.* 14. 31.—*Mat.* 15. 28. *Mat.* 9. 28, 29. *Lu.* 17. 5.—*Jude* 20.—*Col.* 2. 7.—2 *Co.* 1. 21.—1 *Pe.* 5. 10.
Ro. 15. 1.—*Ro.* 14. 13.

It pleased the Father, that in him should all fulness dwell.

The Father loveth the Son, and hath given all things into his hand.—God hath highly exalted him, and given him a name which is above every name: that at the name of Jesus every knee should bow, of things in heaven, and things in earth, and things under the earth; and that every tongue should confess that Jesus Christ is Lord, to the glory of God the Father.—Far above all principality, and power, and might, and dominion, and every name that is named, not only in this world, but also in that which is to come.—By him were all things created, that are in heaven, and that are in earth, visible and invisible, whether they be thrones, or dominions, or principalities, or powers: all things were created by him, and for him.

Christ both died, and rose, and revived, that he might be Lord both of the dead and living.—And ye are complete in him, which is the head of all principality and power.—Of his fulness have all we received.

COL. 1. 19. *Jno.* 3. 35.—*Phi.* 2. 9-11.—*Ep.* 1. 21.—*Col.* 1. 16. *Rom.* 14. 9.
—*Col.* 2. 10.—*Jno.* 1. 16.

Write the things which thou hast seen, and the things which are, and the things which shall be hereafter.

Holy men of God spake as they were moved by the Holy Ghost.
—That which we have seen and heard declare we unto you, that ye also may have fellowship with us: and truly our fellowship is with the Father, and with his Son Jesus Christ.

Behold my hands and my feet, that it is I myself: handle me, and see; for a spirit hath not flesh and bones, as ye see me have. And when he had thus spoken, he shewed them his hands and his feet.—He that saw it bare record, and his record is true: and he knoweth that he saith true, that ye might believe.

We have not followed cunningly devised fables, when we made known unto you the power and coming of our Lord Jesus Christ, but were eyewitnesses of his majesty.—That your faith should not stand in the wisdom of men, but in the power of God.

REV. 1. 19. 2 *Pe.* 1. 21.—1 *Jno.* 1. 3. *Lu.* 24. 39, 40.—*Jno.* 19. 35.
2 *Pe.* 1. 16.—1 *Co.* 2. 5.

Thou hast in love to my soul delivered it from the pit of corruption.

God sent his only begotten Son into the world, that we might live through him. Herein is love, not that we loved God, but that he loved us, and sent his Son to be the propitiation for our sins.

Who is a God like unto thee, that pardoneth iniquity, and passeth by the transgression of the remnant of his heritage? he retaineth not his anger for ever, because he delighteth in mercy. He will turn again, he will have compassion upon us; he will subdue our iniquities; and thou wilt cast all their sins into the depths of the sea.—O LORD my God, I cried unto thee, and thou hast healed me. O LORD, thou hast brought up my soul from the grave: thou hast kept me alive, that I should not go down to the pit.—When my soul fainted within me I remembered the LORD: and my prayer came in unto thee, into thine holy temple.—I waited patiently for the LORD. He brought me up . . . out of an horrible pit, out of the miry clay, and set my feet upon a rock.

ISA. 38. 17. 1 *Jno.* 4. 9, 10. *Mi.* 7. 18, 19.—*Ps.* 30. 2, 3.—*Jon.* 2. 7.
—*Ps.* 40. 1, 2.

The things which are.

Now we see through a glass, darkly.—Now we see not yet all things put under him.

We have . . . a more sure word of prophecy; whereunto ye do well that ye take heed, as unto a light that shineth in a dark place, until the day dawn, and the day star arise in your hearts.—Thy word is a lamp unto my feet, and a light unto my path.

Beloved, remember ye the words which were spoken before of the apostles of our Lord Jesus Christ; how that they told you there should be mockers in the last time, who should walk after their own ungodly lusts.—The Spirit speaketh expressly, that in the latter times some shall depart from the faith, giving heed to seducing spirits, and doctrines of devils.

Little children, it is the last time.—The night is far spent, the day is at hand: let us therefore cast off the works of darkness, and let us put on the armour of light.

REV. 1. 19. 1 *Co.* 13. 12.—*He.* 2. 8. 2 *Pe.* 1. 19.—*Ps.* 119. 105.
Jude 17, 18.—1 *Ti.* 4. 1. 1 *Jno.* 2. 18.—*Ro.* 13. 12.

Him that was to come.

Jesus . . . made a little lower than the angels for the suffering of death, . . . that he by the grace of God should taste death for every man.—One died for all.—As by one man's disobedience many were made sinners, so by the obedience of one shall many be made righteous.

The first man Adam was made a living soul; the last Adam was made a quickening spirit.—That was not first which is spiritual, but that which is natural; and afterward that which is spiritual.— God said, Let us make man in our image, after our likeness. So God created man in his own image, in the image of God created he him.—God . . . hath in these last days spoken unto us by his Son, . . . the brightness of his glory, and the express image of his person.—Thou hast given him power over all flesh.

The first man is of the earth, earthy: the second man is the Lord from heaven. As is the earthy, such are they also that are earthy: and as is the heavenly, such are they also that are heavenly.

ROM. 5. 14. He. 2. 9.—2 Co. 5. 14.—Ro. 5. 19. 1 Co. 15. 45, 46.—
—Ge. 1. 26, 27.—He. 1. 1-3.—Jno. 17. 2. 1 Co. 15. 47, 48.

Things which shall be hereafter.

It is written, Eye hath not seen, nor ear heard, neither have entered into the heart of man, the things which God hath prepared for them that love him. But God hath revealed them unto us by his Spirit.—The Spirit of truth . . . will shew you things to come.

Behold, he cometh with clouds; and every eye shall see him, and they also which pierced him: and all kindreds of the earth shall wail because of him. Even so, Amen.

I would not have you to be ignorant, brethren, concerning them which are asleep, that ye sorrow not, even as others which have no hope. For if we believe that Jesus died and rose again, even so them also which sleep in Jesus will God bring with him. For the Lord himself shall descend from heaven, with a shout, with the voice of the archangel, and with the trump of God: and the dead in Christ shall rise first: then we which are alive and remain shall be caught up together with them in the clouds, to meet the Lord in the air: and so shall we ever be with the Lord.

REV. 1. 19. 1 Co. 2. 9, 10.—Jno. 16. 13. Re. 1. 7. 1 Th. 4. 13, 14, 16, 17.

Serving the Lord with all humility of mind.

Whosoever will be great among you, let him be your minister; and whosoever will be chief among you, let him be your servant: even as the Son of man came not to be ministered unto, but to minister, and to give his life a ransom for many.

If a man think himself to be something, when he is nothing, he deceiveth himself.—I say, through the grace given unto me, to every man, . . . not to think of himself more highly than he ought to think; but to think soberly, according as God hath dealt to every man the measure of faith.—When ye shall have done all those things which are commanded you, say, We are unprofitable servants: we have done that which was our duty to do.

Our rejoicing is this, . . . that in simplicity and godly sincerity, not with fleshly wisdom, but by the grace of God, we have had our conversation in the world.—We have this treasure in earthen vessels, that the excellency of the power may be of God, and not of us.

ACTS 20. 19. *Mat.* 20. 26-28. *Gal.* 6. 3.—*Ro.* 12. 3.—*Lu.* 17. 10.
2 *Co.* 1. 12.—2 *Co.* 4. 7.

We have turned every one to his own way.

Noah . . . planted a vineyard: and he drank of the wine, and was drunken.—Abram . . . said unto Sarai his wife, . . . Say, I pray thee, thou art my sister: that it may be well with me for thy sake. —Isaac said unto Jacob, . . . Art thou my very son Esau? And he said, I am.—Moses . . . spake unadvisedly with his lips.—The men took of their victuals, and asked not counsel at the mouth of the LORD. And Joshua made peace with them.—David did that which was right in the eyes of the LORD, and turned not aside from any thing that he commanded him all the days of his life, save only in the matter of Uriah the Hittite.

These all . . . obtained a good report through faith.—Being justified freely by his grace through the redemption that is in Christ Jesus.—The LORD hath laid on him the iniquity of us all.

Not for your sakes do I this, saith the Lord GOD, be it known unto you: be ashamed and confounded for your own ways.

ISA. 53. 6. *Ge.* 9. 20, 21.—*Ge.* 12. 11, 13.—*Ge.* 27. 21, 24.—
Ps. 106. 32, 33.—*Jos.* 9. 14, 15.—1 *Ki.* 15. 5. *He.* 11. 39.—
Ro. 3. 24.—*Is.* 53. 8. *Eze.* 36. 32.

His name shall be called Wonderful.

The Word was made flesh, and dwelt among us, (and we beheld his glory, the glory as of the only begotten of the Father,) full of grace and truth.—Thou hast magnified thy word above all thy name.

They shall call his name Emmanuel, which being interpreted is, God with us.—JESUS: for he shall save his people from their sins.

All men should honour the Son, even as they honour the Father. —God . . . hath highly exalted him, and given him a name which is above every name.—Far above all principality, and power, and might, and dominion, and every name that is named, not only in this world, but also in that which is to come; and hath put all things under his feet.—He had a name written, that no man knew, but he himself . . . KING OF KINGS, AND LORD OF LORDS.

Touching the Almighty, we cannot find him out.—What is his name, and what is his son's name, if thou canst tell?

ISA. 9. 6. *Jno.* 1. 14.—*Ps.* 138. 2. *Mat.* 1. 23.—*Mat.* 1. 21. *Jno.* 5. 23.— *Phi.* 2. 9. *Ep.* 1. 21, 22.—*Re.* 19. 12, 16. *Job* 37. 23.—*Pr.* 30. 4.

The Lord's portion is his people.

Ye are Christ's; and Christ is God's.—I am my beloved's, and his desire is toward me.—I am his.—The Son of God . . . loved me, and gave himself for me.

Ye are not your own, ye are bought with a price: therefore glorify God in your body, and in your spirit, which are God's.— The LORD hath taken you, and brought you forth out of the iron furnace, even out of Egypt, to be unto him a people of inheritance, as ye are this day.

Ye are God's husbandry, ye are God's building.—Christ as a son over his own house; whose house are we, if we hold fast the confidence and the rejoicing of the hope firm unto the end.—A spiritual house, an holy priesthood.

They shall be mine, saith the LORD of hosts, in that day when I make up my jewels.—All mine are thine, and thine are mine; and I am glorified in them.—The glory of his inheritance in the saints.

DEUT. 32. 9. 1 *Co.* 3. 23.—*Ca.* 7. 10.—*Ca.* 2. 16.—*Ga.* 2. 20. 1 *Co.* 6. 19, 20.—*De.* 4. 20. 1 *Co.* 3. 9.—*He.* 3. 6.—1 *Pe.* 2. 5. *Mal.* 3. 17.— *Jno.* 17. 10. *Ep.* 1, 18.

Every branch that beareth fruit, he purgeth it.

He is like a refiner's fire, and like fullers' soap: and he shall sit as a refiner and purifier of silver: and he shall purify the sons of Levi, and purge them as gold and silver, that they may offer unto the LORD an offering in righteousness.

We glory in tribulations: knowing that tribulation worketh patience; and patience, experience; and experience, hope: and hope maketh not ashamed; because the love of God is shed abroad in our hearts by the Holy Ghost which is given unto us.—If ye endure chastening, God dealeth with you as with sons, for what son is he whom the Father chasteneth not? But if ye be without chastisement, whereof all are partakers, then are ye bastards, and not sons. Now no chastening for the present seemeth to be joyous, but grievous: nevertheless afterward it yieldeth the peaceable fruit of righteousness unto them which are exercised thereby. Wherefore lift up the hands which hang down, and the feeble knees.

JOHN 15. 2. *Mal.* 3. 2, 3. *Ro.* 5. 3-5. *He.* 12. 7, 8, 11, 12.

Now we call the proud happy.

Thus saith the high and lofty One that inhabiteth eternity, whose name is Holy; I dwell in the high and holy place, with him also that is of a contrite and humble spirit, to revive the spirit of the humble, and to revive the heart of the contrite ones.

Better it is to be of an humble spirit with the lowly, than to divide the spoil with the proud.—Blessed are the poor in spirit: for their's is the kingdom of heaven.

These six things doth the LORD hate: yea, seven are an abomination unto him: a proud look, etc.—Every one that is proud in heart is an abomination to the LORD.

Search me, O God, and know my heart: try me, and know my thoughts: and see if there be any wicked way in me, and lead me in the way everlasting.

Grace be unto you, and peace, from God our Father, and from the Lord Jesus Christ. I thank my God upon every remembrance of you.—Blessed are the meek: for they shall inherit the earth.

MAL. 3. 15. *Is.* 57. 15. *Pr.* 16. 19.—*Mat.* 5. 3. *Pr.* 6. 16, 17.—*Pr.* 16. 5. *Ps.* 139. 23, 24. *Phi.* 1. 2, 3.—*Mat.* 5. 5.

This God is our God for ever and ever: he will be our guide even unto death.

O LORD, thou art my God; I will exalt thee, I will praise thy name; for thou hast done wonderful things; thy counsels of old are faithfulness and truth.—The LORD is the portion of mine inheritance, and of my cup.

He leadeth me in the paths of righteousness, for his name's sake. Yea, though I walk through the valley of the shadow of death, I will fear no evil: for thou art with me; thy rod and thy staff they comfort me.—Thou hast holden me by my right hand. Thou shalt guide me with thy counsel, and afterward receive me to glory. Whom have I in heaven but thee? and there is none upon earth that I desire beside thee. My flesh and my heart faileth: but God is the strength of my heart, and my portion for ever.—Our heart shall rejoice in him, because we have trusted in his holy name.— The LORD will perfect that which concerneth me: thy mercy, O LORD, endureth for ever: forsake not the works of thine own hands.

PSA. 48. 14. Is. 25. 1.—Ps. 16. 5. Ps. 23. 3, 4.—Ps. 73. 23-26.— Ps. 33. 21.—Ps. 138. 8.

In the multitude of my thoughts within me thy comforts delight my soul.

When my heart is overwhelmed: lead me to the rock that is higher than I.

O LORD, I am oppressed; undertake for me.—Cast thy burden upon the LORD, and he shall sustain thee.

I am but a little child: I know not how to go out or come in.— If any of you lack wisdom, let him ask of God, . . . and it shall be given him.

Who is sufficient for these things?—I know that in me (that is, in my flesh,) dwelleth no good thing.—My grace is sufficient for thee: for my strength is made perfect in weakness.

Son, be of good cheer; thy sins be forgiven thee. . . . Daughter, be of good comfort; thy faith hath made thee whole.

My soul shall be satisfied as with marrow and fatness; . . . when I remember thee upon my bed, and meditate on thee in the night watches.

PSA. 94. 19. Ps. 61. 2. Is. 38. 14.—Ps. 55. 22. 1 Ki. 3. 7.—Ja. 1. 5. 2 Co. 2. 16.—Ro. 7. 18.—2 Co. 12. 9. Mat. 9. 2, 22. Ps. 63. 5, 6.

Hope maketh not ashamed.

I am the LORD: . . . they shall not be ashamed that wait for me.
—Blessed is the man that trusteth in the LORD, and whose hope
the LORD is.—Thou wilt keep him in perfect peace, whose mind is
stayed on thee: because he trusteth in thee. Trust ye in the LORD
for ever: for in the LORD JEHOVAH is everlasting strength.—
My soul, wait thou only upon God; for my expectation is from
him. He only is my rock and my salvation: he is my defence; I
shall not be moved.—I am not ashamed, for I know whom I have
believed.

God, willing more abundantly to shew unto the heirs of promise
the immutability of his counsel, confirmed it by an oath: that by
two immutable things, in which it was impossible for God to lie,
we might have a strong consolation, who have fled for refuge to
lay hold upon the hope set before us; which hope we have as an
anchor of the soul, both sure and stedfast, and which entereth into that within the veil; whither the forerunner is for us entered,
even Jesus.

ROM. 5. 5. Is. 49. 23.—Je. 17. 7.—Is. 26. 3, 4.—Ps. 62. 5, 6. 2 Ti. 1. 12.
He. 6. 17-20.

The offence of the cross.

If any man will come after me, let him deny himself, and take
up his cross, and follow me.

Know ye not that the friendship of the world is enmity with
God? whosoever therefore will be a friend of the world is the
enemy of God.—We must through much tribulation enter into the
kingdom of God.

Whosoever believeth on him shall not be ashamed.—Unto you
therefore which believe he is precious: but unto them which be
disobedient, the stone which the builders disallowed, the same is
made the head of the corner, and a stone of stumbling, and a rock
of offence.

God forbid that I should glory, save in the cross of our Lord
Jesus Christ, by whom the world is crucified unto me, and I unto
the world.—I am crucified with Christ.—They that are Christ's
have crucified the flesh with the affections and lusts.

If we suffer, we shall also reign with him: if we deny him, he
also will deny us.

GAL. 5. 11. Mat. 16. 24. Ja. 4. 4.—Ac. 14. 22. Ro. 9. 33.—1 Pe. 2. 7, 8.
Gal. 6. 14.—Gal. 2. 20.—Gal. 5. 24. 2 Ti. 2. 12.

The Lord is at hand.

The Lord himself shall descend from heaven with a shout, with the voice of the archangel, and with the trump of God: and the dead in Christ shall rise first: then we which are alive and remain, shall be caught up together with them in the clouds, to meet the Lord in the air: and so shall we ever be with the Lord. Wherefore comfort one another with these words.—He which testifieth these things saith, Surely I come quickly; Amen. Even so, come, Lord Jesus.

Wherefore, beloved, seeing that ye look for such things, be diligent that ye may be found of him in peace, without spot, and blameless.—Abstain from all appearance of evil. And the very God of peace sanctify you wholly; and I pray God your whole spirit and soul and body be preserved blameless unto the coming of our Lord Jesus Christ. Faithful is he that calleth you, who also will do it.

Be ye also patient; stablish your hearts; for the coming of the Lord draweth nigh.

PHI. 4. 5. *1 Thes.* 4. 16-18.—*Re.* 22. 20. *2 Pe.* 3. 14.—*1 Thes.* 5. 22-24. *Ja.* 5. 8.

The choice vine.

My wellbeloved hath a vineyard in a very fruitful hill: and he fenced it, and gathered out the stones thereof, and planted it with the choicest vine, . . . and he looked that it should bring forth grapes, and it brought forth wild grapes.—Yet I had planted thee a noble vine, wholly a right seed: how then art thou turned into the degenerate plant of a strange vine unto me.

The works of the flesh are manifest, which are these; Adultery, fornication, uncleanness, . . . envyings, murders, drunkenness, revellings, and such like: . . . but the fruit of the Spirit is love, joy, peace, longsuffering, gentleness, goodness, faith, meekness, temperance.

I am the true vine, and my Father is the husbandman. Every branch in me that beareth not fruit he taketh away: and every branch that beareth fruit, he purgeth it, that it may bring forth more fruit. Abide in me, and I in you. . . . Herein is my Father glorified, that ye bear much fruit; so shall ye be my disciples.

GEN. 49. 11. *Is.* 5. 1, 2.—*Je.* 2. 21. *Gal.* 5. 19, 21-23. *Jno.* 15. 1, 2, 4, 8.

**The righteousness of God which is by faith of Jesus Christ unto all
and upon all them that believe.**

He hath made him to be sin for us, who knew no sin; that we
might be made the righteousness of God in him.—Christ hath redeemed us from the curse of the law, being made a curse for us.—
Who of God is made unto us wisdom, and righteousness, and sanctification, and redemption.—Not by works of righteousness which
we have done, but according to his mercy he saved us, by the washing of regeneration, and renewing of the Holy Ghost; which he
shed on us abundantly through Jesus Christ our Saviour.

I count all things but loss for the excellency of the knowledge
of Christ Jesus my Lord: for whom I have suffered the loss of
all things, and do count them but dung, that I may win Christ, and
be found in him, not having mine own righteousness, which is of
the law, but that which is through the faith of Christ, the righteousness which is of God by faith.

ROM. 3. 22. *2 Co.* 5. 21.—*Gal.* 3. 13.—1 *Co.* 1. 30.—*Tit.* 3. 5, 6.
Phi. 3. 8, 9.

The spirit of adoption, whereby we cry, Abba, Father.

Jesus . . . lifted up his eyes to heaven, and said, Father, . . . Holy
Father, . . . O righteous Father.—He said, Abba, Father.—Because ye are sons, God hath sent forth the Spirit of his Son into
your hearts, crying, Abba, Father.—For through him we both have
access by one Spirit unto the Father. Now therefore ye are no
more strangers and foreigners, but fellowcitizens with the saints,
and of the household of God.

Doubtless thou art our father, . . . thou, O LORD, art our father,
our redeemer; thy name is from everlasting.

I will arise and go to my father, and will say unto him, Father,
I have sinned against heaven, and before thee, and am no more
worthy to be called thy son: make me as one of thy hired servants.
And he arose, and came to his father.

Be ye therefore followers of God, as dear children.

ROM. 8. 15. *Jno.* 17. 1, 11, 25.—*Mar.* 14. 36.—*Gal.* 4. 6.—*Ep.* 2. 18, 19.
Is. 63. 16. *Lu.* 15. 18-20. *Ep.* 5. 1.

Let us go forth unto him without the camp, bearing his reproach. For here have we no continuing city, but we seek one to come.

Beloved, think it not strange concerning the fiery trial which is to try you, as though some strange thing happened unto you: but rejoice, inasmuch as ye are partakers of Christ's sufferings; that, when his glory shall be revealed, ye may be glad also with exceeding joy.—As ye are partakers of the sufferings, so shall ye be also of the consolation.

If ye be reproached for the name of Christ, happy are ye; for the Spirit of glory and of God resteth upon you: on their part he is evil spoken of, but on your part he is glorified.

They departed from the presence of the council, rejoicing that they were counted worthy to suffer shame for his name.—Choosing rather to suffer affliction with the people of God, than to enjoy the pleasures of sin for a season; esteeming the reproach of Christ greater riches than the treasures in Egypt: for he had respect unto the recompence of the reward.

HEB. 13. 13, 14. *1 Pe.* 4. 12, 13.—*2 Co.* 1. 7. *1 Pe.* 4. 14. *Ac.* 5. 41.—
He. 11. 25, 26.

The Lord Jesus Christ . . . shall change our vile body, that it may be fashioned like unto his glorious body.

Upon the likeness of the throne was the likeness as the appearance of a man above upon it. And I saw as the colour of amber, as the appearance of fire round about within it, from the appearance of his loins even upward, and from the appearance of his loins even downward, I saw as it were the appearance of fire, and it had brightness round about. This was the appearance of the likeness of the glory of the LORD.

We all, with open face, beholding as in a glass the glory of the Lord, are changed into the same image from glory to glory, even as by the Spirit of the Lord.—It doth not yet appear what we shall be: but we know that, when he shall appear, we shall be like him; for we shall see him as he is.

They shall hunger no more, neither thirst any more.—They sing the song of Moses the servant of God, and the song of the Lamb.

PHIL. 3. 20, 21. *Eze.* 1. 26-28. *2 Co.* 3. 18.—*1 Jno.* 3. 2. *Re.* 7. 16.—
Re. 15. 3.

Ye know that he was manifested to take away our sins: and in him is no sin.

God, . . . hath in these last days spoken unto us by his Son, . . . who being the brightness of his glory, and the express image of his person, and upholding all things by the word of his power, when he had by himself purged our sins, sat down on the right hand of the Majesty on high.—He hath made him to be sin for us, who knew no sin; that we might be made the righteousness of God in him.

Pass the time of your sojourning here in fear: forasmuch as ye know that ye were not redeemed with corruptible things, as silver and gold; . . . but with the precious blood of Christ, as of a lamb without blemish and without spot: who verily was foreordained before the foundation of the world, but was manifest in these last times for you.—The love of Christ constraineth us; because we thus judge, that if one died for all, then were all dead: and that he died for all, that they which live should not henceforth live unto themselves, but unto him which died for them, and rose again.

1 JOHN 3. 5. He. 1. 1-3.—2 Co. 5. 21. 1 Pe. 1. 17-20,—2 Co. 5. 14, 15.

I have set before you life and death, blessing and cursing: therefore choose life.

For I have no pleasure in the death of him that dieth, saith the Lord GOD: wherefore turn yourselves, and live ye.

If I had not come and spoken unto them, they had not had sin: but now they have no cloke for their sin.

That servant, which knew his lord's will, and prepared not himself, neither did according to his will, shall be beaten with many stripes.

The wages of sin is death; but the gift of God is eternal life through Jesus Christ our Lord.—He that believeth on the Son hath everlasting life: and he that believeth not the Son shall not see life; but the wrath of God abideth on him.—Know ye not, that to whom ye yield yourselves servants to obey, his servants ye are to whom ye obey; whether of sin unto death, or of obedience unto righteousness?

If any man serve me, let him follow me; and where I am, there shall also my servant be: if any man serve me, him will my Father honour.

DEUT. 30. 19. Eze. 18. 32. Jno. 15. 22. Lu. 12. 47. Ro. 6. 23.— Jno. 3. 36.—Ro. 6. 16. Jno. 12. 26.

As thy days, so shall thy strength be.

When they shall lead you, and deliver you up, take no thought beforehand what ye shall speak, neither do ye premeditate: but whatsoever shall be given you in that hour, that speak ye: for it is not ye that speak, but the Holy Ghost.—Take no thought for the morrow: for the morrow shall take thought for the things of itself. Sufficient unto the day is the evil thereof.

The God of Israel is he that giveth strength and power unto his people. Blessed be God.—He giveth power to the faint; and to them that have no might he increaseth strength.

My grace is sufficient for thee: for my strength is made perfect in weakness. Most gladly therefore will I rather glory in my infirmities, that the power of Christ may rest upon me. Therefore I take pleasure in infirmities, in reproaches, in necessities, in persecutions, in distresses for Christ's sake: for when I am weak, then am I strong.—I can do all things through Christ which strengtheneth me.—O my soul, thou hast trodden down strength.

DEUT. 33. 25. *Mar.* 13. 11.—*Mat.* 6. 34. *Ps.* 68. 35.—*Is.* 40. 29.
2 *Co.* 12. 9, 10.—*Phi.* 4. 13.—*Ju.* 5. 21.

Awake, O north wind, and . . . blow upon my garden, that the spices thereof may flow out.

No chastening for the present seemeth to be joyous, but grievous: nevertheless afterward it yieldeth the peaceable fruit of righteousness unto them which are exercised thereby.—The fruit of the Spirit.

He stayeth his rough wind in the day of the east wind.

Like as a father pitieth his children, so the LORD pitieth them that fear him.

Though our outward man perish, yet the inward man is renewed day by day. For our light affliction, which is but for a moment, worketh for us a far more exceeding and eternal weight of glory; while we look not at the things which are seen, but at the things which are not seen.

Though [Jesus] were a Son, yet learned he obedience by the things which he suffered.—In all points tempted like as we are, yet without sin.

CANT. 4. 16. *He.* 12. 11.—*Gal.* 5. 22. *Is.* 27. 8. *Ps.* 103. 13. 2 *Co.* 4. 16-18.
He. 5. 8.—*He.* 4. 15.

Thou God seest me.

O LORD, thou hast searched me, and known me. Thou knowest my downsitting and mine uprising, thou understandest my thought afar off. Thou compassest my path and my lying down, and art acquainted with all my ways. For there is not a word in my tongue, but, lo, O LORD, thou knowest it altogether. . . . Such knowledge is too wonderful for me: it is high, I cannot attain unto it.

The eyes of the LORD are in every place, beholding the evil and the good.—The ways of man are before the eyes of the LORD, and he pondereth all his goings.—God knoweth your hearts: for that which is highly esteemed among men is abomination in the sight of God.—The eyes of the LORD run to and fro throughout the whole earth, to shew himself strong in the behalf of them whose heart is perfect toward him.

Jesus . . . knew all men, and needed not that any should testify of man; for he knew what was in man.—Lord, thou knowest all things; thou knowest that I love thee.

GEN. 16. 13. *Ps.* 139. 1-4, 6. *Pr.* 15. 3.—*Pr.* 5. 21.—*Lu.* 16. 15.—
2 *Ch.* 16. 9. *Jno.* 2. 24, 25.—*Jno.* 21. 17.

I will praise thee, O Lord my God, with all my heart : and I will glorify thy name for evermore.

Whoso offereth praise glorifieth me.—It is a good thing to give thanks unto the LORD, and to sing praises unto thy name, O most High: to shew forth thy lovingkindness in the morning, and thy faithfulness every night.

Let every thing that hath breath praise the LORD.

I beseech you, . . . brethren, by the mercies of God, that ye present your bodies a living sacrifice, holy, acceptable unto God, which is your reasonable service.—Jesus, . . . that he might sanctify the people with his own blood, suffered without the gate. By him therefore let us offer the sacrifice of praise to God continually, that is, the fruit of our lips giving thanks to his name.—Giving thanks always for all things unto God and the Father in the name of our Lord Jesus Christ.

Worthy is the Lamb that was slain to receive power, and riches, and wisdom, and strength, and honour, and glory, and blessing.

PSA. 86. 12. *Ps.* 50. 23.—*Ps.* 92. 1, 2. *Ps.* 150. 6. *Ro.* 12. 1.—
He. 13. 12, 15.—*Ep.* 5. 20. *Re.* 5. 12.

**Let us run with patience the race that is set before us, looking unto
Jesus the author and finisher of our faith.**

If any man will come after me, let him deny himself, and take
up his cross daily, and follow me.—Whosoever he be of you that
forsaketh not all that he hath, he cannot be my disciple.—Let
us therefore cast off the works of darkness.

Every man that striveth for the mastery is temperate in all
things. Now they do it to obtain a corruptible crown; but we an
incorruptible. I therefore so run, not as uncertainly; so fight I,
not as one that beateth the air: but I keep under my body, and
bring it into subjection: lest that by any means, when I have
preached to others, I myself should be a castaway.—Brethren, I
count not myself to have apprehended: but this one thing I do,
forgetting those things which are behind, and reaching forth unto
those things which are before, I press toward the mark for the
prize of the high calling of God in Christ Jesus.—Then shall we
know, if we follow on to know the LORD.

HEB. 12. 1, 2. *Lu.* 9. 23.—*Lu.* 14. 33.—*Ro.* 13. 12. 1 *Co.* 9. 25, 27.—
Phi. 3. 13, 14.—*Ho.* 6. 3.

It is good for a man that he bear the yoke in his youth.

Train up a child in the way he should go: and when he is old,
he will not depart from it.

We have had fathers of our flesh, which corrected us; and we
gave them reverence: shall we not much rather be in subjection
unto the Father of spirits, and live? For they verily for a few days
chastened us after their own pleasure; but he for our profit, that
we might be partakers of his holiness.

Before I was afflicted I went astray: but now have I kept thy
word. It is good for me that I have been afflicted; that I might
learn thy statutes.

I know the thoughts that I think toward you, saith the LORD,
thoughts of peace, and not of evil, to give you an expected end.
—Humble yourselves therefore under the mighty hand of God,
that he may exalt you in due time.

LAM. 3. 27. *Pr.* 22. 6. *He.* 12. 9, 10. *Ps.* 119. 67, 71. *Je.* 29. 11.—1 *Pe.* 5. 6.

If ye will not drive out the inhabitants of the land from before you; . . . those which ye let remain of them shall be pricks in your eyes, and thorns in your sides, and shall vex you in the land wherein ye dwell.

Fight the good fight of faith.—The weapons of our warfare are not carnal, but mighty through God to the pulling down of strong holds; casting down imaginations, . . . and bringing into captivity every thought to the obedience of Christ.

Brethren, we are debtors, not to the flesh, to live after the flesh. For if ye live after the flesh, ye shall die; but if ye through the Spirit do mortify the deeds of the body, ye shall live.

The flesh lusteth against the Spirit, and the Spirit against the flesh; and these are contrary the one to the other: so that ye cannot do the things that ye would.—I see another law in my members, warring against the law of my mind, and bringing me into captivity to the law of sin which is in my members.—We are more than conquerors through him that loved us.

NUM. 33. 55. 1 *Ti.* 6. 12.—2 *Co.* 10. 4, 5. *Ro.* 8. 12, 13. *Gal.* 5. 17.— *Ro.* 7. 23.—*Ro.* 8. 37.

If a man sin against the Lord, who shall intreat for him?

If any man sin, we have an advocate with the Father, Jesus Christ the righteous: and he is the propitiation for our sins: and not for our's only, but also for the sins of the whole world.—Whom God hath set forth to be a propitiation through faith in his blood, to declare his righteousness for the remission of sins that are past, through the forbearance of God; to declare, I say, at this time his righteousness: that he might be just, and the justifier of him which believeth in Jesus.

He is gracious unto him, and saith, Deliver him from going down to the pit: I have found a ransom.

What shall we then say to these things? If God be for us, who can be against us? It is God that justifieth. Who is he that condemneth? It is Christ that died, yea, rather, that is risen again, who is even at the right hand of God, who also maketh intercession for us.

1 *SAM.* 2. 25. 1 *Jno.* 2. 1, 2.—*Ro.* 3. 25, 26. *Job* 33. 24. *Ro.* 8. 31, 33, 34.

Whom having not seen, ye love.

We walk by faith, not by sight.—We love him, because he first loved us.—And we have known and believed the love that God hath to us. God is love; and he that dwelleth in love dwelleth in God, and God in him.—In whom ye trusted, after that ye heard the word of truth, the gospel of your salvation: in whom also after that ye believed, ye were sealed with that holy Spirit of promise.—God would make known what is the riches of the glory of this mystery among the Gentiles; which is Christ in you, the hope of glory.

If a man say, I love God, and hateth his brother, he is a liar: for he that loveth not his brother whom he hath seen, how can he love God whom he hath not seen?

Jesus saith unto him, Thomas, because thou hast seen me, thou hast believed: blessed are they that have not seen, and yet have believed.—Blessed are all they that put their trust in him.

1 *PETER* 1. 8. 2 *Co.* 5. 7.—1 *Jno.* 4. 19.—1 *Jno.* 4. 16. *Ep.* 1. 13. *Col.* 1. 27. 1 *Jno.* 4. 20. *Jno.* 20. 29.—*Ps.* 2. 12.

THE LORD OUR RIGHTEOUSNESS.

We are all as an unclean thing, and all our righteousnesses are as filthy rags.

I will go in the strength of the Lord GOD: I will make mention of thy righteousness, even of thine only.—I will greatly rejoice in the LORD, my soul shall be joyful in my God; for he hath clothed me with the garments of salvation, he hath covered me with the robe of righteousness, as a bridegroom decketh himself with ornaments, and as a bride adorneth herself with her jewels.

Bring forth the best robe, and put it on him.—To her was granted that she should be arrayed in fine linen, clean and white: for the fine linen is the righteousness of saints.

I count all things but loss for the excellency of the knowledge of Christ Jesus my Lord . . . that I may win Christ, and be found in him, not having mine own righteousness, which is of the law, but that which is through the faith of Christ, the righteousness which is of God by faith.

JER. 23. 6. *Is.* 64. 6. *Ps.* 71. 16.—*Is.* 61. 10. *Lu.* 15. 22.—*Re.* 19. 8. *Phi.* 3. 8, 9.

Oh that thou wouldest keep me from evil.

Why sleep ye? rise and pray, lest ye enter into temptation.—
The spirit indeed is willing, but the flesh is weak.

Two things have I required of thee; deny me them not before I
die: remove far from me vanity and lies: give me neither poverty
nor riches, feed me with food convenient for me: lest I be full,
and deny thee, and say, Who is the LORD? or lest I be poor, and
steal, and take the name of my God in vain.

The LORD shall preserve thee from all evil: he shall preserve
thy soul.—I will deliver thee out of the hand of the wicked, and
I will redeem thee out of the hand of the terrible.—He that is
begotten of God keepeth himself, and that wicked one toucheth
him not.

Because thou hast kept the word of my patience, I also will
keep thee from the hour of temptation, which shall come upon all
the world, to try them that dwell upon the earth.—The LORD
knoweth how to deliver the godly out of temptations.

1 *CHR.* 4. 10. *Lu.* 22. 46.—*Mat.* 26. 41. *Pr.* 30. 7-9. *Ps.* 121. 7.—
Je. 15. 21.—1 *Jno.* 5. 18. *Re.* 3. 10.—2 *Pe.* 2. 9.

One star differeth from another star in glory.

By the way they had disputed among themselves, who should be
the greatest. And he sat down, and called the twelve, and saith
unto them, If any man desire to be first, the same shall be last of
all.—Be clothed with humility: for God resisteth the proud, and
giveth grace to the humble. Humble yourselves therefore under the
mighty hand of God, that he may exalt you in due time.

Let this mind be in you, which was also in Christ Jesus: who
... made himself of no reputation, and took upon him the form of
a servant, and was made in the likeness of men. Wherefore God
also hath highly exalted him, and given him a name which is
above every name: that at the name of Jesus every knee should
bow.

They that be wise shall shine as the brightness of the firmament;
and they that turn many to righteousness as the stars for ever
and ever.

1 *COR.* 15. 41. *Mar.* 9. 34, 35.—1 *Pe.* 5. 5, 6. *Phi.* 2. 5-7, 9, 10. *Da.* 12. 3.

Be strong, and work ; for I am with you, saith the Lord of hosts.

I am the vine, ye are the branches: he that abideth in me, and I in him, the same bringeth forth much fruit: for without me ye can do nothing.—I can do all things through Christ which strengtheneth me.—Strong in the Lord, and in the power of his might.—The joy of the Lord is your strength.

Thus said the Lord of hosts; Let your hands be strong, ye that hear in these days these words by the mouth of the prophets.—Strengthen ye the weak hands, and confirm the feeble knees. Say to them that are of a fearful heart, Be strong, fear not.—The Lord looked upon him, and said, Go in this thy might.

If God be for us, who can be against us?—Therefore seeing we have this ministry, as we have received mercy, we faint not.

Let us not be weary in well doing: for in due season we shall reap, if we faint not.—Thanks be to God, which giveth us the victory through our Lord Jesus Christ.

HAG. 2. 4. *Jno.* 15. 5.—*Phi.* 4. 13.—*Ep.* 6. 10.—*Ne.* 8. 10. *Zec.* 8. 9.—
Is. 35. 3, 4.—*Ju.* 6. 14. *Ro.* 8. 31.—*2 Co.* 4. 1. *Gal.* 6. 9.—*1 Co.* 15. 57.

The darkness hideth not from thee.

His eyes are upon the ways of man, and he seeth all his goings. There is no darkness, nor shadow of death, where the workers of iniquity may hide themselves.—Can any hide himself in secret places that I shall not see him? . . . Do not I fill heaven and earth? saith the Lord.

Thou shalt not be afraid for the terror by night; . . . nor for the pestilence that walketh in darkness. . . . Because thou hast made the Lord, which is my refuge, even the most High, thy habitation; there shall no evil befall thee, neither shall any plague come nigh thy dwelling.—He that keepeth thee will not slumber. The Lord is thy keeper: the Lord is thy shade upon thy right hand. The sun shall not smite thee by day, nor the moon by night. The Lord shall preserve thee from all evil.

Yea, though I walk through the valley of the shadow of death, I will fear no evil: for thou art with me.

PSA. 139. 12. *Job* 34. 21, 22.—*Je.* 23. 24. *Ps.* 91. 5, 6, 9, 10.—
Ps. 121. 3, 5-7. *Ps.* 23. 4.

The Lord hath said unto you, Ye shall henceforth return no more that way.

Truly if they had been mindful of that country from whence they came out, they might have had opportunity to have returned. But now they desire a better country, that is a heavenly. Choosing rather to suffer affliction with the people of God, than to enjoy the pleasures of sin for a season; esteeming the reproach of Christ greater riches than the treasures in Egypt.—The just shall live by faith: but if any man draw back, my soul shall have no pleasure in him. But we are not of them who draw back unto perdition, but of them that believe to the saving of the soul.—No man, having put his hand to the plough, and looking back, is fit for the kingdom of God.

God forbid that I should glory, save in the cross of our Lord Jesus Christ, by whom the world is crucified unto me, and I unto the world.—Come out from among them, and be ye separate, saith the Lord, and touch not the unclean thing; and I will receive you.

He which hath begun a good work in you, will perform it until the day of Jesus Christ.

DEUT. 17. 16. *He.* 11. 15, 16, 25, 26.—*He.* 10. 38, 39.—*Lu.* 9. 62.
Gal. 6. 14.—2 *Co.* 6. 17. *Phi.* 1. 6.

They talk to the grief of those whom thou hast wounded.

I was but a little displeased, and they helped forward the affliction.

Brethren, if a man be overtaken in a fault, ye which are spiritual, restore such an one in the spirit of meekness; considering thyself, lest thou also be tempted.

He which converteth the sinner from the error of his way shall save a soul from death, and shall hide a multitude of sins.—Comfort the feeble-minded, support the weak, be patient toward all men.

Let us not . . . judge one another any more: but judge this rather, that no man put a stumblingblock or an occasion to fall in his brother's way.—We . . . that are strong ought to bear the infirmities of the weak, and not to please ourselves.

Charity . . . rejoiceth not in iniquity.—Let him that thinketh he standeth take heed lest he fall.

PSA. 69. 26. *Zec.* 1. 15. *Gal.* 6. 1. *Ja.* 5. 20.—1 *Th.* 5. 14.
Ro. 14. 13.—*Ro.* 15. 1. 1 *Co.* 13. 4, 6.—1 *Co.* 10. 12.

I am come that they might have life, and that they might have it more abundantly.

In the day that thou eatest thereof thou shalt surely die.—She took of the fruit thereof, and did eat, and gave also unto her husband with her; and he did eat.

The wages of sin is death; but the gift of God is eternal life through Jesus Christ our Lord.—If by one man's offence death reigned by one; much more they which receive abundance of grace and of the gift of righteousness shall reign in life by one, Jesus Christ.—Since by man came death, by man came also the resurrection of the dead. For as in Adam all die, even so in Christ shall all be made alive.—Our Saviour Jesus Christ, . . . hath abolished death, and hath brought life and immortality to light through the gospel.

God hath given to us eternal life, and this life is in his Son. He that hath the Son hath life; and he that hath not the Son of God hath not life. For God sent not his Son into the world to condemn the world; but that the world through him might be saved.

JOHN 10. 10. *Ge.* 2. 17.—*Ge.* 3. 6. *Ro.* 6. 23.—*Ro.* 5. 17.—
1 *Co.* 15. 21, 22.—2 *Ti.* 1. 10. 1 *Jno.* 5. 11, 12. *Jno.* 3. 17.

The judgment-seat.

We are sure that the judgment of God is according to truth.—When the Son of man shall come in his glory, and all the holy angels with him, then shall he sit upon the throne of his glory: and before him shall be gathered all nations: and he shall separate them one from another, as a shepherd divideth his sheep from the goats.

Then shall the righteous shine forth as the sun, in the kingdom of their Father.—Who shall lay any thing to the charge of God's elect? It is God that justifieth. Who is he that condemneth? It is Christ that died, yea, rather, that is risen again, who is even at the right hand of God, who also maketh intercession for us.—There is therefore now no condemnation to them which are in Christ Jesus.

We are chastened of the Lord, that we should not be condemned with the world.

2 *COR.* 5. 10. *Ro.* 2. 2.—*Mat.* 25. 31, 32. *Mat.* 13. 43.—*Ro.* 8. 33, 34.—
Ro. 8. 1. 1 *Co.* 11. 32.

The grace of our Lord was exceeding abundant with faith and love which is in Christ Jesus.

Ye know the grace of our Lord Jesus Christ, that, though he was rich, yet for your sakes he became poor, that ye through his poverty might be rich.—Where sin abounded, grace did much more abound.

That in the ages to come he might shew the exceeding riches of his grace in his kindness toward us through Christ Jesus. For by grace are ye saved through faith; and that not of yourselves: it is the gift of God: not of works, lest any man should boast.— Knowing that a man is not justified by the works of the law, but by the faith of Jesus Christ, even we have believed in Jesus Christ, that we might be justified by the faith of Christ, and not by the works of the law: for by the works of the law shall no flesh be justified.—According to his mercy he saved us, by the washing of regeneration, and renewing of the Holy Ghost; which he shed on us abundantly through Jesus Christ our Saviour.

1 *TIM*. 1. 14. 2 *Co*. 8. 9.—*Ro*. 5. 20. *Ep*. 2. 7, 9.—*Gal*. 2. 16.—*Tit*. 3. 5, 6.

I am . . . the bright and morning Star.

There shall come a star out of Jacob.

The night is far spent, the day is at hand: let us therefore cast off the works of darkness, and let us put on the armour of light.— Until the day break, and the shadows flee away, turn, my beloved, and be thou like a roe or a young hart upon the mountains of Bether.

Watchman, what of the night? The watchman said, The morning cometh, and also the night: if ye will enquire, enquire ye: return, come.

I am the light of the world.—I will give him the morning star.

Take ye heed, watch and pray: for ye know not when the time is. For the Son of man is as a man taking a far journey, who left his house, and gave authority to his servants, and to every man his work, and commanded the porter to watch. Watch ye therefore: . . . lest coming suddenly he find you sleeping. And what I say unto you I say unto all, Watch.

REV. 22. 16. *Nu*. 24. 17. *Ro*. 13. 12.—*Ca*. 2. 17. *Is*. 21. 11, 12. *Jno*. 8. 12.
—*Re*. 2. 28. *Mar*. 13. 33-37.

When thou has eaten and are full, . . . thou shalt bless the Lord thy God for the good land which he hath given thee.

Beware that thou forget not the LORD thy God.—One of them, when he saw that he was healed, turned back, and with a loud voice glorified God, and fell down on his face at his feet, giving him thanks: and he was a Samaritan. And Jesus answering said, Were there not ten cleansed? but where are the nine? There are not found that returned to give glory to God, save this stranger.

Every creature of God is good, and nothing to be refused, if it be received with thanksgiving: for it is sanctified by the word of God and prayer.—He that eateth, eateth to the Lord, for he giveth God thanks.—The blessing of the LORD, it maketh rich, and he addeth no sorrow with it.

Bless the LORD, O my soul: and all that is within me, bless his holy name. Bless the LORD, O my soul, . . . who forgiveth all thine iniquities; . . . who crowneth thee with loving-kindness and tender mercies.

DEUT. 8. 10. *De.* 8. 11.—*Lu.* 17. 15-18. 1 *Ti.* 4. 4, 5.—*Ro.* 14. 6.—
Pr. 10. 22. *Ps.* 103. 1-4.

Jesus . . . was moved with compassion toward them.

Jesus Christ the same yesterday, and today, and for ever.—We have not an high priest which cannot be touched with the feeling of our infirmities; but was in all points tempted like as we are, yet without sin.—Who can have compassion on the ignorant, and on them that are out of the way.—He cometh, and findeth them sleeping, and saith unto Peter, Simon, sleepest thou? couldest not thou watch one hour? Watch ye and pray, lest ye enter into temptation. The spirit truly is ready, but the flesh is weak.

Like as a father pitieth his children, so the LORD pitieth them that fear him. For he knoweth our frame; he remembereth that we are dust.

Thou, O LORD, art a God full of compassion, and gracious, longsuffering, and plenteous in mercy and truth. O turn unto me, and have mercy upon me; give thy strength unto thy servant, and save the son of thine handmaid.

MAT. 14. 14. *He.* 13. 8.—*He.* 4. 15.—*He.* 5. 2.—*Mar.* 14. 37, 38.
Ps. 103. 13, 14. *Ps.* 86. 15, 16.

Henceforth I call you not servants ; for the servant knoweth not what his lord doeth : but I have called you friends.

The LORD said, shall I hide from Abraham that thing which I do?—It is given unto you to know the mysteries of the kingdom of heaven.—God hath revealed them unto us by his Spirit: for the Spirit searcheth all things, yea, the deep things of God.—Even the hidden wisdom, which God ordained before the world unto our glory.

Blessed is the man whom thou choosest, and causest to approach unto thee, that he may dwell in thy courts: we shall be satisfied with the goodness of thy house, even of thy holy temple.— The secret of the LORD is with them that fear him; and he will shew them his covenant.—I have given unto them the words which thou gavest me; and they have received them, and have known surely that I came out from thee, and they have believed that thou didst send me.

Ye are my friends, if ye do whatsoever I command you.

JOHN 15. 15. *Ge.* 18. 17.—*Mat.* 13. 11.—1 *Co.* 2. 10.—1 *Co.* 2. 7. *Ps.* 65. 4.—*Ps.* 25. 14.—*Jno.* 17. 8. *Jno.* 15. 14.

Thou shalt call thy walls Salvation, and thy gates Praise.

The wall of the city had twelve foundations, and in them the names of the twelve apostles of the Lamb.

Ye are no more strangers and foreigners, but fellowcitizens with the saints, and of the household of God; and are built upon the foundation of the apostles and prophets, Jesus Christ himself being the chief corner stone; in whom all the building fitly framed together groweth unto an holy temple in the Lord: in whom ye also are builded together for an habitation of God through the Spirit.—If so be ye have tasted that the Lord is gracious. To whom coming, as unto a living stone, disallowed indeed of men, but chosen of God, and precious, ye also, as lively stones, are built up a spiritual house, an holy priesthood, to offer up spiritual sacrifices, acceptable to God by Jesus Christ.

Praise waiteth for thee, O God, in Zion.

ISA. 60. 18. *Re.* 21. 14. *Ep.* 2. 19-22.—1 *Pe.* 2. 3-5. *Ps.* 65. 1.

Now he is comforted.

Thy sun shall no more go down; neither shall thy moon withdraw itself: for the LORD shall be thine everlasting light, and the days of thy mourning shall be ended.—He will swallow up death in victory; and the LORD God will wipe away tears from off all faces; and the rebuke of his people shall he take away from off all the earth.—These are they which came out of great tribulation, and have washed their robes, and made them white in the blood of the Lamb. Therefore are they before the throne of God, and serve him day and night in his temple: and he that sitteth on the throne shall dwell among them. They shall hunger no more, neither thirst any more; neither shall the sun light on them, nor any heat. For the Lamb which is in the midst of the throne shall feed them, and shall lead them unto living fountains of waters.— God shall wipe away all tears from their eyes; and there shall be no more death, neither sorrow, nor crying, neither shall there be any more pain: for the former things are passed away.

LUKE 16. 25. *Is.* 60. 20.—*Is.* 25. 8.—*Re.* 7. 14-17.—*Re.* 21. 4.

The night cometh when no man can work.

Blessed are the dead which die in the Lord, . . . they . . . rest from their labours; and their works do follow them.—There the wicked cease from troubling; and there the weary be at rest.— Samuel said to Saul, Why hast thou disquieted me, to bring me up?

Whatsoever thy hand findeth to do, do it with thy might; for there is no work, nor device, nor knowledge, nor wisdom, in the grave, whither thou goest.—The dead praise not the LORD, neither any that go down into silence.

I am now ready to be offered, and the time of my departure is at hand. I have fought a good fight, I have finished my course, I have kept the faith: henceforth there is laid up for me a crown of righteousness, which the Lord, the righteous judge, shall give me at that day.

There remaineth therefore a rest to the people of God. For he that is entered into his rest, he also hath ceased from his own works, as God did from his.

JNO. 9. 4. *Re.* 14. 13.—*Job* 3. 17.—1 *Sa.* 28. 15. *Ec.* 9. 10.—*Ps.* 115. 17. 2 *Ti.* 4. 6-8. *He.* 4. 9, 10.

The light of the body is the eye: therefore when thine eye is single, thy whole body also is full of light.

The natural man receiveth not the things of the Spirit of God: for they are foolishness unto him: neither can he know them, because they are spiritually discerned.—Open thou mine eyes, that I may behold wondrous things out of thy law.

I am the light of the world: he that followeth me shall not walk in darkness, but shall have the light of life.—We all, with open face beholding as in a glass the glory of the Lord, are changed into the same image . . . even as by the Spirit of the Lord.—God, who commanded the light to shine out of darkness, hath shined in our hearts, to give the light of the knowledge of the glory of God in the face of Jesus Christ.

The God of our Lord Jesus Christ, the Father of glory, . . . give unto you the spirit of wisdom and revelation in the knowledge of him: . . . that ye may know what is the hope of his calling, and what the riches of the glory of his inheritance in the saints.

LUKE 11. 34. 1 *Co*. 2. 14.—*Ps*. 119. 18. *Jno*. 8. 12.—2 *Co*. 3. 18.—
2 *Co*. 4. 6. *Ep*. 1. 17, 18.

He smote the rock, that the waters gushed out, and the streams overflowed.

All our fathers were under the cloud, and all passed through the sea; and were all baptized unto Moses in the cloud and in the sea; and did all eat the same spiritual meat; and did all drink the same spiritual drink: for they drank of that spiritual Rock that followed them: and that rock was Christ.—One of the soldiers with a spear pierced his side, and forthwith came there out blood and water.—He was wounded for our transgressions, he was bruised for our iniquities: the chastisement of our peace was upon him; and with his stripes we are healed.

Ye will not come to me, that ye might have life.—My people have committed two evils; they have forsaken me the fountain of living waters, and hewed them out cisterns, broken cisterns, that can hold no water.

If any man thirst, let him come unto me, and drink.—Whosoever will, let him take the water of life freely.

PSA. 78. 20. 1 *Co*. 10. 1-4.—*Jno*. 19. 34.—*Is*. 53. 5. *Jno*. 5. 40.—*Je*. 2. 13.
Jno. 7. 37.—*Re*. 22. 17.

They that feared the Lord spake often one to another: and the Lord hearkened, and heard it, and a book of remembrance was written before him for them that feared the Lord, and that thought upon his name.

It came to pass, that, while they communed together and reasoned, Jesus himself drew near, and went with them.—Where two or three are gathered together in my name, there am I in the midst of them.—My fellowlabourers, whose names are in the book of life.

Let the word of Christ dwell in you richly in all wisdom; teaching and admonishing one another in psalms and hymns and spiritual songs, singing with grace in your hearts to the Lord.—Exhort one another daily, while it is called to day; lest any of you be hardened through the deceitfulness of sin.

Every idle word that men shall speak, they shall give account thereof in the day of judgment. For by thy words thou shalt be justified, and by thy words thou shalt be condemned.—Behold, it is written before me.

MAL. 3. 16. *Lu.* 24. 15.—*Mat.* 18. 20.—*Phi.* 4. 3. *Col.* 3. 16.—*He.* 3. 13.
Mat. 12. 36, 37.—*Is.* 65. 6.

The trees of the Lord are full of sap.

I will be as the dew unto Israel: he shall grow as the lily, and cast forth his roots as Lebanon. His branches shall spread, and his beauty shall be as the olive tree, and his smell as Lebanon.—Blessed is the man that trusteth in the LORD, and whose hope the LORD is. For he shall be as a tree planted by the waters, and that spreadeth out her roots by the river, and shall not see when heat cometh, but her leaf shall be green; and shall not be careful in the year of drought, neither shall cease from yielding fruit.

I the LORD have brought down the high tree, have exalted the low tree, have dried up the green tree, and have made the dry tree to flourish.

The righteous shall flourish like the palm tree: he shall grow like a cedar in Lebanon. Those that be planted in the house of the LORD shall flourish in the courts of our God. They shall still bring forth fruit in old age; they shall be fat and flourishing.

PSA. 104. 16. *Ho.* 14. 5, 6.—*Je.* 17. 7, 8. *Eze.* 17. 24. *Ps.* 92. 12-14.

They shall be mine, saith the Lord of hosts, in that day when I make up my jewels.

I have manifested thy name unto the men which thou gavest me out of the world: thine they were, and thou gavest them me; and they have kept thy word. I pray for them: I pray not for the world, but for them which thou hast given me; for they are thine. And all mine are thine, and thine are mine; and I am glorified in them. Father, I will that they also, whom thou hast given me, be with me where I am: that they may behold my glory, which thou hast given me: for thou lovedst me before the foundation of the world.

I will come again, and receive you unto myself.—He shall come to be glorified in his saints, and to be admired in all them that believe . . . in that day.—We which are alive and remain shall be caught up together with them in the clouds, to meet the Lord in the air: and so shall we ever be with the Lord.—Thou shalt also be a crown of glory in the hand of the Lord, and a royal diadem in the hand of thy God.

MAL. 3. 17. *Jno.* 17. 6, 9, 10, 24. *Jno.* 14. 3.—2 *Th.* 1. 10.—1 *Th.* 4. 17.—*Is.* 62. 3.

I beseech thee, shew me thy glory.

God, who commanded the light to shine out of darkness, hath shined in our hearts, to give the light of the knowledge of the glory of God in the face of Jesus Christ.—The Word was made flesh, and dwelt among us, (and we beheld his glory, the glory as of the only begotten of the Father,) full of grace and truth. . . . No man hath seen God at any time ; the only begotten Son, which is in the bosom of the Father, he hath declared him.

My soul thirsteth for God, for the living God: when shall I come and appear before God?—When thou saidst, Seek ye my face; my heart said unto thee, Thy face, LORD, will I seek.

We all, with open face beholding as in a glass the glory of the Lord, are changed into the same image from glory to glory, even as by the Spirit of the Lord.—Father, I will that they also, whom thou hast given me, be with me where I am; that they may behold my glory, which thou hast given me: for thou lovedst me before the foundation of the world.

EXOD. 33. 18. 2 *Co.* 4. 6.—*Jno.* 1. 14, 18. *Ps.* 42. 2.—*Ps.* 27. 8. 2 *Co.* 3. 18.—*Jno.* 17. 24.

Upon the likeness of the throne was the likeness as the appearance of a man above upon it.

The man Christ Jesus.—Made in the likeness of men . . . found in fashion as a man.—Forasmuch . . . as the children are partakers of flesh and blood, he also himself likewise took part of the same; that through death he might destroy him that had the power of death.

I am he that liveth, and was dead; and, behold, I am alive for evermore.—Christ being raised from the dead dieth no more; death hath no more dominion over him. For in that he died, he died unto sin once: but in that he liveth, he liveth unto God.—What and if ye shall see the Son of Man ascend up where he was before?—He raised him from the dead, and set him at his own right hand in the heavenly places.—In him dwelleth all the fulness of the Godhead bodily.

Though he was crucified through weakness, yet he liveth by the power of God. For we also are weak in him, but we shall live with him by the power of God.

EZEK. 1. 26. 1 *Ti.* 2. 5.—*Phi.* 2. 7, 8.—*He.* 2. 14. *Re.* 1. 18.—*Ro.* 6. 9. *Jno.* 6. 62.—*Ep.* 1. 20.—*Col.* 2. 9. 2 *Co.* 13. 4.

Thy word hath quickened me.

The first man Adam was made a living soul; the last Adam was made a quickening spirit.

As the Father hath life in himself; so hath he given to the Son to have life in himself.—I am the resurrection, and the life: he that believeth in me, though he were dead, yet shall he live: and whosoever liveth and believeth in me shall never die.

In him was life; and the life was the light of men. . . . As many as received him, to them gave he power to become the sons of God, even to them that believe on his name: which were born, not of blood, nor of the will of the flesh, nor of the will of man, but of God.

It is the spirit that quickeneth; the flesh profiteth nothing: the words that I speak unto you, they are spirit, and they are life.—The word of God is quick, and powerful, and sharper than any two-edged sword, piercing even to the dividing asunder of soul and spirit, and of the joints and marrow, and is a discerner of the thoughts and intents of the heart.

PSA. 119. 50. 1 *Co.* 15. 45. *Jno.* 5. 26.—*Jno.* 11. 25, 26. *Jno.* 1. 4, 12, 13. *Jno.* 6. 63.—*He.* 4. 12.

Suffer it to be so now: for thus it becometh us to fulfil all righteousness.

I delight to do thy will, O my God: yea, thy law is within my heart.

Think not that I am come to destroy the law, or the prophets: I am not come to destroy, but to fulfil. For verily I say unto you, Till heaven and earth pass, one jot or one tittle shall in no wise pass from the law, till all be fulfilled.—The Lord is well pleased for his righteousness' sake; he will magnify the law, and make it honourable.—Except your righteousness shall exceed the righteousness of the scribes and Pharisees, ye shall in no case enter into the kingdom of heaven.

What the law could not do, in that it was weak through the flesh, God sending his own Son in the likeness of sinful flesh, and for sin, condemned sin in the flesh: that the righteousness of the law might be fulfilled in us, who walk not after the flesh, but after the Spirit.—Christ is the end of the law for righteousness to every one that believeth.

MATT. 3. 15. *Ps.* 40. 8. *Mat.* 5. 17, 18.—*Is.* 42. 21.—*Mat.* 5. 20.
Ro. 8. 3, 4.—*Ro.* 10. 4.

FEBRUARY 14   EVENING

I am thy part and thine inheritance.

Whom have I in heaven but thee! and there is none upon earth that I desire beside thee. My flesh and my heart faileth: but God is the strength of my heart, and my portion for ever.—The LORD is the portion of mine inheritance and of my cup: thou maintainest my lot. The lines are fallen unto me in pleasant places; yea, I have a goodly heritage.

The LORD is my portion, saith my soul; therefore will I hope in him.

Thy testimonies have I taken as an heritage for ever: for they are the rejoicing of my heart.

O God, thou art my God; early will I seek thee: my soul thirsteth for thee, my flesh longeth for thee in a dry and thirsty land, where no water is. . . . Because thou hast been my help, therefore in the shadow of thy wings will I rejoice.

My beloved is mine, and I am his.

NUM. 18. 20. *Ps.* 73. 25, 26.—*Ps.* 16. 5, 6. *La.* 3. 24. *Ps.* 119. 111.
Ps. 63. 1, 7. *Ca.* 2. 16.

Who can say, I have made my heart clean?

The LORD looked down from heaven upon the children of men, to see if there were any that did understand, and seek God. They are all gone aside, they are all together become filthy: there is none that doeth good, no, not one.—They that are in the flesh cannot please God.

To will is present with me; but how to perform that which is good I find not. For the good that I would I do not: but the evil which I would not, that I do.—We are all as an unclean thing, and all our righteousnesses are as filthy rags: and we all do fade as a leaf: and our iniquities, like the wind, have taken us away.

The scripture hath concluded all under sin, that the promise by faith of Jesus Christ might be given to them that believe.—God was in Christ, reconciling the world unto himself, not imputing their trespasses unto them.

If we say that we have no sin, we deceive ourselves, and the truth is not in us. If we confess our sins, he is faithful and just to forgive us our sins, and to cleanse us from all unrighteousness.

PROV. 20. 9. *Ps.* 14. 2, 3.—*Ro.* 8. 8. *Ro.* 7. 18, 19.—*Is.* 64. 6. *Gal.* 3. 22.— 2 *Co.* 5. 19. 1 *Jno.* 1. 8, 9.

The floods lift up their waves.

The LORD on high is mightier than the noise of many waters, yea, than the mighty waves of the sea.—O LORD God of hosts, who is a strong LORD like unto thee? or to thy faithfulness round about thee? thou rulest the raging of the sea: when the waves thereof arise, thou stillest them.

Fear ye not me? saith the LORD: will ye not tremble at my presence, which have placed the sand for the bound of the sea by a perpetual decree, that it cannot pass it?

When thou passest through the waters, I will be with thee; and through the rivers, they shall not overflow thee.

Peter . . . walked on the water, to go to Jesus. But when he saw the wind boisterous, he was afraid; and beginning to sink, he cried, saying, Lord, save me. And immediately Jesus stretched forth his hand, and caught him, and said unto him, O thou of little faith, wherefore didst thou doubt?

What time I am afraid, I will trust in thee.

PSA. 93. 3. *Ps.* 93. 4.—*Ps.* 89. 8, 9. *Je.* 5. 22. *Is.* 43. 2. *Mat.* 14. 29-31. *Ps.* 56. 3.

Thy name is as ointment poured forth.

Christ . . . hath loved us, and hath given himself for us, an offering and a sacrifice to God for a sweetsmelling savour.—Unto you therefore which believe he is precious.—God also hath highly exalted him, and given him a name which is above every name : that at the name of Jesus every knee should bow.—In him dwelleth all the fulness of the Godhead bodily.

If ye love me, keep my commandments.—The love of God is shed abroad in our hearts by the Holy Ghost which is given unto us.—The house was filled with the odour of the ointment.—They took knowledge of them, that they had been with Jesus.

O LORD our Lord, how excellent is thy name in all the earth! who hast set thy glory above the heavens.—Emmanuel . . . God with us.—His name shall be called Wonderful, Counsellor, The mighty God, The everlasting Father, The Prince of Peace.—The name of the LORD is a strong tower: the righteous runneth into it, and is safe.

CANT. 1. 3. *Ep.* 5. 2.—1 *Pe.* 2. 7.—*Phi.* 2. 9, 10.—*Col.* 2. 9. *Jno.* 14. 15.—
Ro. 5. 5.—*Jno.* 12. 3.—*Acts* 4. 13. *Ps.* 8. 1.—*Mat.* 1. 23.—*Is.* 9. 6.—
Pr. 18. 10.

We that are in this tabernacle do groan, being burdened.

Lord, all my desire is before thee; and my groaning is not hid from thee. . . . Mine iniquities are gone over mine head: as an heavy burden they are too heavy for me—O wretched man that I am! who shall deliver me from the body of this death?

The whole creation groaneth and travaileth in pain together until now. And not only they, but ourselves, . . . which have the first-fruits of the Spirit, . . . groan within ourselves, waiting for the adoption, to wit, the redemption of our body.—Now for a season, if need be, ye are in heaviness through manifold temptations.

Shortly I must put off this my tabernacle.—For this corruptible must put on incorruption, and this mortal must put on immortality. So when this corruptible shall have put on incorruption, and this mortal shall have put on immortality, then shall be brought to pass the saying that is written, Death is swallowed up in victory.

2 COR. 5. 4. *Ps.* 38. 9, 4.—*Ro.* 7. 24. *Ro.* 8. 22, 23.—1 *Pe.* 1. 6.
2 Pe. 1. 14.—1 *Co.* 15. 53, 54.

The whole bullock shall he carry forth without the camp unto a clean place, where the ashes are poured out, and burn him on the wood with fire.

They took Jesus, and led him away. And he bearing his cross went forth into a place called the place of a skull, which is called in the Hebrew Golgotha: where they crucified him.—The bodies of those beasts, whose blood is brought into the sanctuary by the high priest for sin, are burned without the camp. Wherefore Jesus also, that he might sanctify the people with his own blood, suffered without the gate. Let us go forth therefore unto him without the camp, bearing his reproach.—The fellowship of his sufferings.

Rejoice, inasmuch as ye are partakers of Christ's sufferings: that, when his glory shall be revealed, ye may be glad also with exceeding joy.—Our light affliction, which is but for a moment, worketh for us a far more exceeding and eternal weight of glory.

LEV. 4. 12. *Jno.* 19. 16, 18.—*He.* 13. 11-13.—*Phi.* 3. 10. 1 *Pe.* 4. 13.—
2 *Co.* 4. 17.

God created man in his own image.

Forasmuch then as we are the offspring of God, we ought not to think that the Godhead is like unto gold, or silver, or stone, graven by art and man's device.

God, who is rich in mercy, for his great love wherewith he loved us, even when we were dead in sins, hath quickened us together with Christ. We are his workmanship, created in Christ Jesus unto good works, which God hath before ordained that we should walk in them.—For whom he did foreknow, he also did predestinate to be conformed to the image of his Son, that he might be the firstborn among many brethren.

We know that, when he shall appear, we shall be like him; for we shall see him as he is.—I shall be satisfied, when I awake, with thy likeness.

He that overcometh shall inherit all things; and I will be his God, and he shall be my son.—If children, then heirs; heirs of God, and joint-heirs with Christ.

GEN. 1. 27. *Ac.* 17. 29. *Ep.* 2. 4, 5, 10.—*Ro.* 8. 29. 1 *Jno.* 3. 2.—*Ps.* 17. 15.
Re. 21. 7.—*Ro.* 8. 17.

Thou art my hope in the day of evil.

There be many that say, Who will shew us any good? LORD, lift thou up the light of thy countenance upon us.—I will sing of thy power; yea, I will sing aloud of thy mercy in the morning: for thou hast been my defence and refuge in the day of my trouble.

In my prosperity I said, I shall never be moved. Thou didst hide thy face, and I was troubled. I cried to thee, O LORD: and unto the LORD I made supplication. What profit is there in my blood, when I go down to the pit? Shall the dust praise thee? shall it declare thy truth? Hear, O LORD, and have mercy upon me: LORD, be thou my helper.

For a small moment have I forsaken thee; but with great mercies will I gather thee. In a little wrath I hid my face from thee for a moment; but with everlasting kindness will I have mercy on thee, saith the LORD thy Redeemer.—Sorrow shall be turned into joy.—Weeping may endure for a night, but joy cometh in the morning.

JER. 17. 17. *Ps.* 4. 6.—*Ps.* 59. 16. *Ps.* 30. 6, 8-10. *Is.* 54. 7, 8.— *Jno.* 16. 20.—*Ps.* 30. 5.

Adam ... begat a son in his own likeness.

Who can bring a clean thing out of an unclean?—Behold, I was shapen in iniquity; and in sin did my mother conceive me.

Dead in trespasses and sins; . . . by nature the children of wrath, even as others.—I am carnal, sold under sin. That which I do I allow not; for what I would, that do I not; but what I hate, that do I. I know that in me (that is, in my flesh,) dwelleth no good thing.

By one man sin entered into the world, . . . by one man's disobedience many were made sinners.—If through the offence of one many be dead, much more the grace of God, and the gift by grace, which is by one man, Jesus Christ, hath abounded unto many.

The law of the Spirit of life in Christ Jesus hath made me free from the law of sin and death.

Thanks be to God, which giveth us the victory through our Lord Jesus Christ.

GEN. 5. 3. *Job* 14. 4.—*Ps.* 51. 5. *Ep.* 2. 1, 3.—*Ro.* 7. 14, 15, 18. *Ro.* 5. 12, 19.—*Ro* 5. 15. *Ro.* 8. 2. 1 *Co.* 15. 57.

The Lord giveth wisdom : out of his mouth cometh knowledge and understanding.

Trust in the LORD with all thine heart; and lean not unto thine own understanding.—If any of you lack wisdom, let him ask of God, that giveth to all men liberally, and upbraideth not; and it shall be given him.—The foolishness of God is wiser than men; and the weakness of God is stronger than men.—God hath chosen the foolish things of the world to confound the wise. That no flesh should glory in his presence.

The entrance of thy words giveth light; it giveth understanding unto the simple.—Thy word have I hid in my heart, that I might not sin against thee.

All bare him witness, and wondered at the gracious words which proceeded out of his mouth.—Never man spake like this man.— Of him are ye in Christ Jesus, who of God is made unto us wisdom, and righteousness, and sanctification, and redemption.

PROV. 2. 6. *Pr.* 3. 5.—*Ja.* 1. 5.—1 *Co.* 1. 25.—1 *Co.* 1. 27, 29. *Ps.* 119. 130. —*Ps.* 119. 11. *Lu.* 4. 22.—*Jno.* 7. 46.—1 *Co.* 1. 30.

The year of my redeemed is come.

Ye shall hallow the fiftieth year, and proclaim liberty throughout all the land unto all the inhabitants thereof: it shall be a jubilee unto you; and ye shall return every man unto his possession, . . . and unto his family.

Thy dead men shall live, together with my dead body shall they arise. Awake and sing, ye that dwell in dust: for thy dew is as the dew of herbs, and the earth shall cast out the dead.

The Lord himself shall descend from heaven with a shout, with the voice of the archangel, and with the trump of God: and the dead in Christ shall rise first: then we which are alive and remain shall be caught up together with them in the clouds, to meet the Lord in the air: and so shall we ever be with the Lord.

I will ransom them from the power of the grave; I will redeem them from death: O death, I will be thy plagues; O grave, I will be thy destruction.

Their Redeemer is strong; the LORD of hosts is his name.

ISA. 63. 4. *Le.* 25. 10. *Is.* 26. 19. 1 *Th.* 4. 16, 17. *Hos.* 13. 14. *Je.* 50. 34.

He shall see of the travail of his soul, and shall be satisfied.

Jesus . . . said, It is finished: and he bowed his head, and gave up the ghost.—He hath made him to be sin for us, who knew no sin; that we might be made the righteousness of God in him.

This people have I formed for myself; they shall shew forth my praise.—To the intent that now unto the principalities and powers in heavenly places might be known by the church the manifold wisdom of God, according to the eternal purpose which he purposed in Christ Jesus our Lord.—That in the ages to come he might shew the exceeding riches of his grace in his kindness toward us through Christ Jesus.

After that ye believed, ye were sealed with that holy Spirit of promise, which is the earnest of our inheritance until the redemption of the purchased possession, unto the praise of his glory.— Ye are a chosen generation, a royal priesthood, a holy nation, a peculiar people; that ye should shew forth the praises of him who hath called you out of darkness into his marvellous light.

ISA. 53. 11. *Jno.* 19. 30.—2 *Co.* 5. 21. *Is.* 43. 21.—*Ep.* 3. 10, 11.—*Ep.* 2. 7.
Ep. 1. 13, 14.—1 *Pe.* 2. 9.

The day of temptation in the wilderness.

Let no man say when he is tempted, I am tempted of God: for God cannot be tempted with evil, neither tempteth he any man: but every man is tempted, when he is drawn away of his own lust, and enticed. Then when lust hath conceived, it bringeth forth sin.

They lusted exceedingly in the wilderness, and tempted God in the desert.

Jesus being full of the Holy Ghost . . . was led by the Spirit into the wilderness, being forty days tempted of the devil. And in those days he did eat nothing: and when they were ended, he afterward hungered. And the devil said unto him, If thou be the Son of God, command this stone that it be made bread.

He himself hath suffered being tempted, he is able to succour them that are tempted.—Simon, Simon, . . . Satan hath desired to have you, that he may sift you as wheat: but I have prayed for thee, that thy faith fail not.

HEB. 3. 8. *Ja.* 1. 13-15. *Ps.* 106. 14. *Lu.* 4. 1-3. *He.* 2. 18.—*Lu.* 22. 31, 32

I am the Lord which sanctify you.

I am the LORD your God, which have separated you from other people. And ye shall be holy unto me: for I the LORD am holy, and have severed you from other people, that ye should be mine.

Sanctified by God the Father.—Sanctify them through thy truth: thy word is truth.—The very God of peace sanctify you wholly; and I pray God your whole spirit and soul and body be preserved blameless unto the coming of our Lord Jesus Christ.

Jesus . . . that he might sanctify the people with his own blood, suffered without the gate.—Our Saviour Jesus Christ . . . gave himself for us, that he might redeem us from all iniquity, and purify unto himself a peculiar people, zealous of good works.— Both he that sanctifieth and they who are sanctified are all of one: for which cause he is not ashamed to call them brethren.—For their sakes I sanctify myself, that they also might be sanctified through the truth. Through sanctification of the Spirit, unto obedience, and sprinkling of the blood of Jesus Christ.

LEV. 20. 8. *Le.* 20. 24, 26. *Jude* 1.—*Jno.* 17. 17.—1 *Thes.* 5. 23.
He. 13. 12.—*Tit.* 2. 13, 14.—*He.* 2. 11.—*Jno.* 17. 19—1 *Pe.* 1. 2.

Light is sown for the righteous, and gladness for the upright in heart.

They that sow in tears shall reap in joy. He that goeth forth and weepeth, bearing precious seed, shall doubtless come again with rejoicing, bringing his sheaves with him.

That which thou sowest, thou sowest not that body that shall be.

Blessed be the God and Father of our Lord Jesus Christ, which according to his abundant mercy hath begotten us again unto a lively hope by the resurrection of Jesus Christ from the dead. Wherein ye greatly rejoice, though now for a season, if need be, ye are in heaviness through manifold temptations: that the trial of your faith, being much more precious than of gold that perisheth, though it be tried with fire, might be found unto praise and honour and glory at the appearing of Jesus Christ.

PSA. 97. 11. *Ps.* 126. 5, 6. 1 *Co.* 15. 27. 1 *Pe.* 1. 3, 6, 7.

What man is he that feareth the Lord ? him shall he teach in the way that he shall choose.

The light of the body is the eye: if therefore thine eye be single, thy whole body shall be full of light.

Thy word is a lamp unto my feet, and a light unto my path.—Thine ears shall hear a word behind thee, saying, This is the way, walk ye in it, when ye turn to the right hand, and when ye turn to the left.—I will instruct thee and teach thee in the way which thou shalt go: I will guide thee with mine eye. Be ye not as the horse, or as the mule, which have no understanding: whose mouth must be held in with bit and bridle, lest they come near unto thee. Many sorrows shall be to the wicked: but he that trusteth in the LORD, mercy shall compass him about. Be glad in the LORD, and rejoice, ye righteous: and shout for joy, all ye that are upright in heart.

O LORD, I know that the way of man is not in himself : it is not in man that walketh to direct his steps.

PSA. 25. 12. *Mat.* 6. 22. *Ps.* 119. 105.—*Is.* 30. 21.—*Ps.* 32. 8-11. *Je.* 10. 23.

When thou liest down, thou shall not be afraid : yea, thou shalt lie down, and thy sleep shall be sweet.

There arose a great storm of wind, and the waves beat into the ship, so that it was now full. And he was in the hinder part of the ship, asleep on a pillow.

Be careful for nothing; but in every thing by prayer and supplication with thanksgiving let your requests be made known unto God. And the peace of God, which passeth all understanding, shall keep your hearts and minds through Christ Jesus.

I will both lay me down in peace, and sleep: for thou, LORD, only makest me dwell in safety.—He giveth his beloved sleep.

They stoned Stephen, calling upon God, and saying, Lord Jesus, receive my spirit. And he kneeled down, and cried with a loud voice, Lord, lay not this sin to their charge. And when he had said this, he fell asleep.—Absent from the body, . . . present with the Lord.

PRO. 3. 24. *Mar.* 4. 37, 38. *Phi.* 4. 6, 7. *Ps.* 4. 8.—*Ps.* 127. 2. *Ac.* 7. 59, 60.
—2 *Co.* 5. 8.

The blood of sprinkling, that speaketh better things than that of Abel.

Behold the Lamb of God, which taketh away the sin of the world.—The Lamb slain from the foundation of the world.—It is not possible that the blood of bulls and of goats should take away sins. Wherefore when he cometh into the world, he saith, Sacrifice and offering thou wouldest not, but a body hast thou prepared me. By the which will we are sanctified through the offering of the body of Jesus Christ once for all.

Abel . . . brought of the firstlings of his flock and of the fat thereof. . . . The LORD had respect unto Abel and to his offering.— Christ . . . hath loved us, and hath given himself for us, an offering and a sacrifice to God for a sweet-smelling savour.

Let us draw near with a true heart in full assurance of faith, having our hearts sprinkled from an evil conscience, and our bodies washed with pure water.—Having . . . boldness to enter into the holiest by the blood of Jesus.

HEB. 12. 24. Jno. 1. 29.—Re. 13. 8.—He. 10. 4, 5, 10. Ge. 4. 4.—Ep. 5. 2.
He. 10. 22.—He. 10. 19.

Who knoweth the power of thine anger?

From the sixth hour there was darkness over all the land unto the ninth hour. And about the ninth hour Jesus cried with a loud voice, saying, Eli, Eli, lama sabachthani? that is to say, My God, my God, why hast thou forsaken me?—The LORD hath laid on him the iniquity of us all.

There is therefore now no condemnation to them which are in Christ Jesus.—Being justified by faith, we have peace with God through our Lord Jesus Christ.—Christ hath redeemed us from the curse of the law, being made a curse for us.

God sent his only begotten Son into the world, that we might live through him. Herein is love, not that we loved God, but that he loved us, and sent his Son to be the propitiation for our sins.— That he might be just, and the justifier of him which believeth in Jesus.

PSA. 90. 11. Mat. 27. 45, 46.—Is. 53. 6. Ro. 8. 1.—Ro. 5. 1.—Ga. 3. 13.
1 Jno. 4. 9, 10.—Ro. 3. 26.

Thus saith the Lord God, I will yet for this be enquired of.

Ye have not, because ye ask not.

Ask, and it shall be given you; seek, and ye shall find; knock, and it shall be opened unto you: for every one that asketh receiveth; and he that seeketh findeth; and to him that knocketh it shall be opened.—This is the confidence that we have in him, that, if we ask any thing according to his will, he heareth us: and if we know that he hear us, whatsoever we ask, we know that we have the petitions that we desired of him.—If any of you lack wisdom, let him ask of God, that giveth to all men liberally, and upbraideth not; and it shall be given him.—Open thy mouth wide, and I will fill it.—Men ought always to pray, and not to faint.

The eyes of the LORD are upon the righteous, and his ears are open unto their cry. The LORD heareth, and delivereth them out of all their troubles.—Ye shall ask in my name; and I say not unto you, that I will pray the Father for you: for the Father himself loveth you, because ye have loved me. Ask, and ye shall receive, that your joy may be full.

EZEK. 36. 37. *Ja.* 4. 2. *Mat.* 7. 7, 8.—1 *Jno.* 5. 14, 15.—*Ja.* 1. 5.—
Ps. 81. 10.—*Lu.* 18, 1. *Ps.* 34. 15, 17.—*Jno.* 16. 26, 27, 24.

Shall we receive good at the hand of God, and shall we not receive evil?

I know, O LORD, that thy judgments are right, and that thou in faithfulness hast afflicted me.—O LORD, thou art our father; we are the clay, and thou our potter; and we all are the work of thy hand.—It is the LORD: let him do what seemeth him good.

Righteous art thou, O LORD, when I plead with thee: yet let me talk with thee of thy judgments.

He shall sit as a refiner and purifier of silver.—Whom the Lord loveth he chasteneth, and scourgeth every son whom he receiveth.—It is enough for the disciple that he be as his master, and the servant as his lord.—Though he were a Son, yet learned he obedience by the things which he suffered.

Rejoice, inasmuch as ye are partakers of Christ's sufferings; that, when his glory shall be revealed, ye may be glad also with exceeding joy.—These are they which came out of great tribulation, and have washed their robes, and made them white in the blood of the Lamb.

JOB 2. 10. *Ps.* 119. 75.—*Is.* 64. 8.—1 *Sa.* 3. 18. *Je.* 12. 1. *Mal.* 3. 3.—
He. 12. 6.—*Mat.* 10. 25.—*He.* 5. 8. 1 *Pe.* 4. 13.—*Re.* 7. 14.

Resist the devil, and he will flee from you.

When the enemy shall come in like a flood, the Spirit of the LORD shall lift up a standard against him.—Get thee hence, Satan: for it is written, Thou shalt worship the Lord thy God, and him only shalt thou serve. Then the devil leaveth him, and, behold, angels came and ministered unto him.

Be strong in the Lord, and in the power of his might. Put on the whole armour of God, that ye may be able to stand against the wiles of the devil.—And have no fellowship with the unfruitful works of darkness, but rather reprove them.—Lest Satan should get an advantage of us: for we are not ignorant of his devices.—Be sober, be vigilant; because your adversary the devil, as a roaring lion, walketh about, seeking whom he may devour; whom resist stedfast in the faith, knowing that the same afflictions are accomplished in your brethren that are in the world.—This is the victory that overcometh the world, even our faith.

Who shall lay any thing to the charge of God's elect? It is God that justifieth.

JAMES 4. 7. *Is.* 59. 19.—*Mat.* 4. 10, 11. *Ep.* 6. 10, 11.—*Ep.* 5. 11.—
2 *Co.* 2. 11.—1 *Pe.* 5. 8, 9.—1 *Jno.* 5. 4. *Ro.* 8. 33.

Oh that I knew where I might find him!

Who is among you that feareth the LORD, that obeyeth the voice of his servant, that walketh in darkness, and hath no light? let him trust in the name of the LORD, and stay upon his God.

Ye shall seek me, and find me, when ye shall search for me with all your heart.—Seek, and ye shall find; knock, and it shall be opened unto you. For every one that asketh receiveth; and he that seeketh findeth; and to him that knocketh it shall be opened.

Truly our fellowship is with the Father, and with his Son Jesus Christ.—Now in Christ Jesus ye who sometime were far off are made nigh by the blood of Christ. For through him we both have access by one Spirit unto the Father.

If we say that we have fellowship with him, and walk in darkness, we lie, and do not the truth.

Lo, I am with you alway.—I will never leave thee, nor forsake thee.—The Comforter . . . dwelleth with you, and shall be in you.

JOB 23. 3. *Is.* 50. 10. *Je.* 29. 13.—*Lu.* 11. 9, 10. 1 *Jno.* 1. 3.—*Ep.* 2. 13, 18.
1 *Jno.* 1. 6. *Mat.* 28. 20.—*He.* 13. 5.—*Jno.* 14. 16, 17.

Let us search and try our ways, and turn again to the Lord.

Examine me, O LORD, and prove me; try my reins and my heart.—Behold, thou desirest truth in the inward parts: and in the hidden part thou shalt make me to know wisdom.—I thought on my ways, and turned my feet unto thy testimonies. I made haste, and delayed not to keep thy commandments.—Let a man examine himself, and so let him eat of that bread, and drink of that cup.

If we confess our sins, he is faithful and just to forgive us our sins, and to cleanse us from all unrighteousness.—We have an advocate with the Father, Jesus Christ the righteous: and he is the propitiation for our sins.—Having therefore, brethren, boldness to enter into the holiest by the blood of Jesus, by a new and living way which he hath consecrated for us, through the veil, that is to say, his flesh: and having a high priest over the house of God; let us draw near with a true heart, in full assurance of faith, having our hearts sprinkled from an evil conscience, and our bodies washed with pure water.

LAM. 3. 40. *Ps.* 26. 2.—*Ps.* 51. 6.—*Ps.* 119. 59, 60.—1 *Co.* 11. 28.
1 *Jno.* 1. 9.—1 *Jno.* 2. 1.—*He.* 10. 19-22.

There was a rainbow round about the throne, in sight like unto an emerald.

This is the token of the covenant which I make between me and you and every living creature that is with you, for perpetual generations: I do set my bow in the cloud, . . . and I will look upon it, that I may remember the everlasting covenant between God and every living creature of all flesh that is upon the earth.—An everlasting covenant, ordered in all things, and sure.—That by two immutable things, in which it was impossible for God to lie, we might have a strong consolation, who have fled for refuge to lay hold upon the hope set before us.

We declare unto you glad tidings, how that the promise which was made unto the fathers, God hath fulfilled the same unto us their children, in that he hath raised up Jesus again.

Jesus Christ the same yesterday, and to-day, and for ever.

REV. 4. 3. *Ge.* 9. 12, 13, 16.—2 *Sa.* 23. 5.—*He.* 6. 18. *Ac.* 13. 32, 33.
He. 13. 8.

Reckon ye yourselves to be dead indeed unto sin, but alive unto God through Jesus Christ our Lord.

He that heareth my word, and believeth on him that sent me, hath everlasting life, and shall not come into condemnation; but is passed from death unto life.—I through the law am dead to the law, that I might live unto God. I am crucified with Christ; nevertheless I live; yet not I, but Christ liveth in me: and the life which I now live in the flesh I live by the faith of the Son of God, who loved me, and gave himself for me.

Because I live, ye shall live also.—I give unto them eternal life: and they shall never perish, neither shall any man pluck them out of my hand. My Father, which gave them me, is greater than all; and no man is able to pluck them out of my Father's hand. I and my Father are one.

If ye then be risen with Christ, seek those things which are above, where Christ sitteth on the right hand of God . . . For ye are dead, and your life is hid with Christ in God.

ROM. 6. 11. *Jno.* 5. 24.—*Ga.* 2. 19, 20. *Jno.* 14. 19.—*Jno.* 10. 28-30. *Col.* 3. 1, 3.

God . . . giveth . . . liberally, and upbraideth not.

Woman, where are those thine accusers? hath no man condemned thee? She said, No man, Lord. And Jesus said unto her, Neither do I condemn thee: go, and sin no more.

The grace of God, and the gift by grace, which is by one man, Jesus Christ, hath abounded unto many. . . . The free gift is of many offences unto justification.

God, who is rich in mercy, for his great love wherewith he loved us, even when we were dead in sins, hath quickened us together with Christ, (by grace ye are saved;) and hath raised us up together, and made us sit together in heavenly places in Christ Jesus: that in the ages to come he might shew the exceeding riches of his grace in his kindness toward us through Christ Jesus.

He that spared not his own Son, but delivered him up for us all, how shall he not with him also freely give us all things?

JAM. 1. 5. *Jno.* 8. 10, 11. *Ro.* 5. 15, 16. *Ep.* 2. 4-7. *Ro.* 8. 32.

God so loved the world, that he gave his only begotten Son, that whosoever believeth in him should not perish, but have everlasting life.

God . . . hath reconciled us to himself by Jesus Christ, and hath given to us the ministry of reconciliation; to wit, that God was in Christ, reconciling the world unto himself, not imputing their trespasses unto them; and hath committed unto us the word of reconciliation. Now then we are ambassadors for Christ, as though God did beseech you by us: we pray you in Christ's stead, be ye reconciled to God. For he hath made him to be sin for us, who knew no sin; that we might be made the righteousness of God in him.—God is love. In this was manifested the love of God toward us, because that God sent his only begotten Son into the world, that we might live through him. Herein is love, not that we loved God, but that he loved us, and sent his Son to be the propitiation for our sins. Beloved, if God so loved us, we ought also to love one another.

JOHN 3. 16. 2 *Co.* 5. 18-21.—1 *Jno.* 4. 8-11.

The spirit of man is the candle of the Lord.

He that is without sin among you, let him first cast a stone at her. . . . And they which heard it, being convicted by their own conscience, went out one by one, beginning at the eldest, even unto the last.

Who told thee that thou wast naked? Hast thou eaten of the tree, whereof I commanded thee that thou shouldest not eat?

To him that knoweth to do good, and doeth it not, to him it is sin.—If our heart condemn us, God is greater than our heart, and knoweth all things. Beloved, if our heart condemn us not, then have we confidence toward God.

All things indeed are pure; but it is evil for that man who eateth with offence. Happy is he that condemneth not himself in that thing which he alloweth.

Search me, O God, and know my heart: try me, and know my thoughts: and see if there be any wicked way in me, and lead me in the way everlasting.

PRO. 20. 27. *Jno.* 8. 7, 9. *Ge.* 3. 11. *Ja.* 4. 17.—1 *Jno.* 3. 20, 21.
Ro. 14. 20, 22. *Ps.* 139. 23, 24.

Boast not thyself of to-morrow; for thou knowest not what a day may bring forth.

Behold, now is the accepted time; behold, now is the day of salvation.—Yet a little while is the light with you. Walk while ye have the light, lest darkness come upon you: for he that walketh in darkness knoweth not whither he goeth. While ye have light, believe in the light, that ye may be the children of light.

Whatsoever thy hand findeth to do, do it with thy might; for there is no work, nor device, nor knowledge, nor wisdom, in the grave, whither thou goest.

Soul, thou hast much goods laid up for many years; take thine ease, eat, drink, and be merry. . . . Thou fool, this night thy soul shall be required of thee: then whose shall those things be, which thou hast provided? So is he that layeth up treasure for himself, and is not rich toward God.

What is your life? It is even a vapour, that appeareth for a little time, and then vanisheth away.—The world passeth away, and the lust thereof: but he that doeth the will of God abideth for ever.

PROV. 27. 1.   2 *Co.* 6. 2.—*Jno.* 12. 35, 36.   *Ec.* 9. 10.
Lu. 12. 19-21. *Ja.* 4. 14.—1 *Jno.* 2. 17.

Thou art the same, and thy years shall have no end.

Before the mountains were brought forth, or ever thou hadst formed the earth and the world, even from everlasting to everlasting, thou art God.

I am the LORD, I change not; therefore ye sons of Jacob are not consumed.—The same yesterday, and to day, and for ever.

Every good gift and every perfect gift is from above, and cometh down from the Father of lights, with whom is no variableness, neither shadow of turning.—The gifts and calling of God are without repentance.

God is not a man, that he should lie: neither the son of man, that he should repent.—It is of the LORD's mercies that we are not consumed, because his compassions fail not.

This man, because he continueth ever, hath an unchangeable priesthood. Wherefore he is able also to save them to the uttermost that come unto God by him, seeing he ever liveth to make intercession for them.—Fear not; I am the first and the last.

PSA. 102. 27. *Ps.* 90. 2. *Mal.* 3. 6.—*He.* 13. 8. *Ja.* 1. 17.—*Ro.* 11. 29.
Nu. 23. 19.—*La.* 3. 22. *He.* 7. 24, 25.—*Re.* 1. 17.

The fruit of the Spirit is love.

God is love: and he that dwelleth in love dwelleth in God, and God in him.—The love of God is shed abroad in our hearts by the Holy Ghost which is given unto us.—Unto you . . . which believe he is precious.—We love him, because he first loved us.—The love of Christ constraineth us; because we thus judge, that if one died for all, then were all dead: and that he died for all, that they which live should not henceforth live unto themselves, but unto him which died for them, and rose again.

Ye yourselves are taught of God to love one another.—This is my commandment, That ye love one another, as I have loved you. —Above all things have fervent charity among yourselves: for charity shall cover the multitude of sins.—Walk in love, as Christ also hath loved us, and hath given himself for us, an offering and a sacrifice to God for a sweet-smelling savour.

GAL. 5. 22. 1 *Jno.* 4. 16.—*Ro.* 5. 5.—1 *Pe.* 2. 7.—1 *Jno.* 4. 19.— 2 *Co.* 5. 14, 15. 1 *Th.* 4. 9.—*Jno.* 15. 12.—1 *Pe.* 4. 8.—*Ep.* 5. 2.

Jehovah-nissi: The Lord my banner.

If God be for us, who can be against us?—The LORD is on my side; I will not fear: what can man do unto me?

Thou hast given a banner to them that fear thee.

The LORD is my light and my salvation; whom shall I fear? the LORD is the strength of my life; of whom shall I be afraid? Though an host should encamp against me, my heart shall not fear: though war should rise against me, in this will I be confident.

Behold, God himself is with us for our captain.—The LORD of hosts is with us; the God of Jacob is our refuge.

These shall make war with the Lamb, and the Lamb shall overcome them.

Why do the heathen rage, and the people imagine a vain thing? He that sitteth in the heavens shall laugh: the LORD shall have them in derision.—Take counsel together, and it shall come to nought; speak the word, and it shall not stand: for God is with us.

EX. 17. 15. *Ro.* 8. 31.—*Ps.* 118. 6. *Ps.* 60. 4. *Ps.* 27. 1, 3. 2 *Ch.* 13. 12.— *Ps.* 46. 7. *Re.* 17. 14. *Ps.* 2. 1, 4.—*Is.* 8. 10.

God hath caused me to be fruitful in the land of my affliction.

Blessed be God, even the Father of our Lord Jesus Christ, the Father of mercies, and the God of all comfort; who comforteth us in all our tribulation, that we may be able to comfort them which are in any trouble, by the comfort wherewith we ourselves are comforted of God. For as the sufferings of Christ abound in us, so our consolation also aboundeth by Christ.

Now for a season, if need be, ye are in heaviness through manifold temptations: that the trial of your faith, being much more precious than of gold that perisheth, though it be tried with fire, might be found unto praise and honour and glory at the appearing of Jesus Christ.—The Lord stood with me, and strengthened me.

Let them that suffer according to the will of God commit the keeping of their souls to him in well doing, as unto a faithful Creator.

GEN. 41. 52.   2 *Co.* 1. 3-5.   1 *Pe.* 1. 6, 7.—2. *Tl.* 4. 17.   1 *Pe.* 4. 19.

There remaineth therefore a rest to the people of God.

There the wicked cease from troubling; and there the weary be at rest. There the prisoners rest together; they hear not the voice of the oppressor.

Blessed are the dead which die in the Lord from henceforth; . . . they . . . rest from their labours; and their works do follow them.

Our friend Lazarus sleepeth. . . . Jesus spake of his death: but they thought that he had spoken of taking of rest in sleep.

We that are in this tabernacle do groan, being burdened.—Ourselves also, which have the firstfruits of the Spirit, even we ourselves groan within ourselves, waiting for the adoption, to wit, the redemption of our body. For we are saved by hope: but hope that is seen is not hope. . . . But if we hope for that we see not, then do we with patience wait for it.

HEB. 4. 9.   *Job* 3. 17, 18.   *Re.* 14. 13.   *Jno.* 11. 11, 13.   2 *Co.* 5. 4.—
Ro. 8. 23-25.

Trust in the Lord with all thine heart; and lean not unto thine own understanding. In all thy ways acknowledge him, and he shall direct thy paths.

Trust in him at all times; ye people, pour out your heart before him: God is a refuge for us.

I will instruct thee and teach thee in the way which thou shalt go: I will guide thee with mine eye. Be ye not as the horse, or as the mule, which have no understanding: whose mouth must be held in with bit and bridle, lest they come near unto thee. Many sorrows shall be to the wicked: but he that trusteth in the LORD, mercy shall compass him about.—Thine ears shall hear a word behind thee, saying, This is the way, walk ye in it, when ye turn to the right hand, and when ye turn to the left.

If thy presence go not with me, carry us not up hence. For wherein shall it be known here that I and thy people have found grace in thy sight? is it not in that thou goest with us? so shall we be separated, I and thy people, from all the people that are upon the face of the earth.

PROV. 3. 5, 6. Ps. 62. 8. Ps. 32. 8-10.—Is. 30. 21. Ex. 33. 15, 16.

The prize of the high calling of God in Christ Jesus.

Thou shalt have treasure in heaven: . . . come and follow me.— I am . . . thy exceeding great reward.

Well done, thou good and faithful servant: thou hast been faithful over a few things, I will make thee ruler over many things: enter thou into the joy of thy lord.—They shall reign for ever and ever.

Ye shall receive a crown of glory that fadeth not away.—The crown of life.—A crown of righteousness.—An incorruptible crown.

Father, I will that they also, whom thou hast given me, be with me where I am; that they may behold my glory, which thou hast given me.—So shall we ever be with the Lord.

I reckon that the sufferings of this present time are not worthy to be compared with the glory which shall be revealed in us.

PHI. 3. 14. Mat. 19. 21.—Ge. 15. 1. Mat. 25. 21.—Re. 22. 5. 1 Pe. 5. 4.— Ja. 1. 12.—2 Ti. 4. 8.—1 Co. 9. 25. Jno. 17. 24.—1 Th. 4. 17. Ro. 8. 18.

Set your affection on things above, not on things on the earth.

Love not the world, neither the things that are in the world. If any man love the world, the love of the Father is not in him.— Lay not up for yourselves treasures upon earth, where moth and rust doth corrupt, and where thieves break through and steal: but lay up for yourselves treasures in heaven, where neither moth nor rust doth corrupt, and where thieves do not break through nor steal: for where your treasure is, there will your heart be also.

We walk by faith, not by sight.—We faint not; but though our outward man perish, yet the inward man is renewed day by day. For our light affliction which is but for a moment, worketh for us a far more exceeding and eternal weight of glory: while we look not at the things which are seen, but at the things which are not seen: for the things which are seen are temporal; but the things which are not seen are eternal.—An inheritance incorruptible, and undefiled, and that fadeth not away, reserved in heaven for you.

COL. 3. 2. 1 *Jno.* 2. 15.—*Mat.* 6. 19-21. 2 *Co.* 5. 7.—2 *Co.* 4. 16-18.— 1 *Pe.* 1. 4.

He bowed his shoulder to bear.

Take, my brethren, the prophets, who have spoken in the name of the Lord, for an example of suffering affliction, and of patience. —Now all these things happened unto them for ensamples: and they are written for our admonition, upon whom the ends of the world are come.

Shall we receive good at the hand of God, and shall we not receive evil? In all this did not Job sin with his lips.—Aaron held his peace.—It is the LORD; let him do what seemeth him good.

Cast thy burden upon the LORD, and he shall sustain thee.— Surely he hath borne our griefs, and carried our sorrows.

Come unto me, all ye that labour and are heavy laden, and I will give you rest. Take my yoke upon you, and learn of me; for I am meek and lowly in heart: and ye shall find rest unto your souls. For my yoke is easy, and my burden is light.

GEN. 49. 15. *Ja.* 5. 10.—1 *Co.* 10, 11. *Job* 2. 10.—*Le.* 10. 3.—1 *Sa.* 3. 18. *Ps.* 55. 22.—*Is.* 53. 4. *Mat.* 11. 28-30.

O Lord, I am oppressed; undertake for me.

Unto thee lift I up mine eyes, O thou that dwellest in the heavens. Behold, as the eyes of servants look unto the hand of their masters, and as the eyes of a maiden unto the hand of her mistress; so our eyes wait upon the LORD our God.—Hear my cry, O God; attend unto my prayer. From the end of the earth will I cry unto thee, when my heart is overwhelmed: lead me to the rock that is higher than I. For thou hast been a shelter for me, and a strong tower from the enemy. I will abide in thy tabernacle for ever: I will trust in the covert of thy wings.—Thou hast been a strength to the poor, a strength to the needy in his distress, a refuge from the storms.

Christ . . . suffered for us, leaving us an example, that ye should follow his steps: who did no sin, neither was guile found in his mouth: who, when he was reviled, reviled not again; when he suffered, he threatened not; but committed himself to him that judgeth righteously.

ISA. 38. 14. *Ps*. 123. 1, 2.—*Ps*. 61. 1-4.—*Is*. 25. 4. 1 *Pe*. 2. 21-23.

Fight the good fight of faith.

We were troubled on every side; without were fightings, within were fears.—Fear not: for they that be with us are more than they that be with them.—Strong in the Lord, and in the power of his might.

Thou comest to me with a sword, and with a spear, and with a shield: but I come to thee in the name of the LORD of hosts, the God of the armies of Israel, whom thou hast defied.—God is my strength and power: . . . he teacheth my hands to war; so that a bow of steel is broken by mine arms.—Our sufficiency is of God.

The angel of the LORD encampeth round about them that fear him, and delivereth them.—Behold, the mountain was full of horses and chariots of fire round about Elisha.

The time would fail me to tell of [those] who through faith subdued kingdoms, . . . out of weakness were made strong, waxed valiant in fight, turned to flight the armies of the aliens.

1 *TIM*. 6. 12. 2 *Co*. 7. 5.—2 *Ki*. 6. 16.—*Ep*. 6. 10. 1 *Sa*. 17. 45.—
2 *Sa*. 22. 33, 35.—2 *Co*. 3. 5. *Ps*. 34. 7.—2 *Ki*. 6. 17. *He*. 11. 32-34.

He preserveth the way of his saints.

The LORD your God . . . went in the way before you, to search you out a place to pitch your tents in, in fire by night, to shew you by what way ye should go, and in a cloud by day.—As an eagle stirreth up her nest, fluttereth over her young, spreadeth abroad her wings, taketh them, beareth them on her wings: so the LORD alone did lead him.—The steps of a good man are ordered by the LORD: and he delighteth in his way. Though he fall, he shall not be utterly cast down: for the LORD upholdeth him with his hand.—Many are the afflictions of the righteous: but the LORD delivereth him out of them all.—For the LORD knoweth the way of the righteous; but the way of the ungodly shall perish.—We know that all things work together for good to them that love God, to them who are the called according to his purpose.—With us is the LORD our God to help us, and to fight our battles.

The LORD thy God in the midst of thee is mighty; he will save, he will rejoice over thee with joy.

PROV. 2. 8. *De.* 1. 32, 33.—*De.* 32. 11, 12.—*Ps.* 37. 23, 24.—*Ps.* 34. 19.—
Ps. 1. 6.—*Ro.* 8. 28.—2 *Ch.* 32. 8. *Zep.* 3. 17.

My God, my God, why hast thou forsaken me?

He was wounded for our transgressions, he was bruised for our iniquities: the chastisement of our peace was upon him; . . . the LORD hath laid on him the iniquity of us all. . . . For the transgression of my people was he stricken. . . . It pleased the LORD to bruise him; he hath put him to grief.

Jesus our Lord . . . was delivered for our offences.—Christ . . . hath once suffered for sins, the just for the unjust, that he might bring us to God.—Who his own self bare our sins in his own body on the tree, that we, being dead to sins, should live unto righteousness: by whose stripes ye were healed.

He hath made him to be sin for us, who knew no sin; that we might be made the righteousness of God in him.

Christ hath redeemed us from the curse of the law, being made a curse for us.

MAT. 27. 46. *Is.* 53. 5, 6, 8, 10. *Ro.* 4. 24, 25.—1 *Pe.* 3. 18.—1 *Pe.* 2. 24.
2 *Co.* 5. 21. *Ga.* 3. 13.

Thy Maker is thine husband; the Lord of hosts is his name.

This is a great mystery: but I speak concerning Christ and the church.

Thou shalt no more be termed Forsaken . . . but thou shalt be called Hephzi-bah, . . . for the LORD delighteth in thee. And as the bridegroom rejoiceth over the bride, so shall thy God rejoice over thee.—He hath sent me . . . to comfort all that mourn; to appoint unto them that mourn in Zion, to give unto them beauty for ashes, the oil of joy for mourning, the garment of praise for the spirit of heaviness.

I will greatly rejoice in the LORD, my soul shall be joyful in my God; for he hath clothed me with the garments of salvation, . . . as a bridegroom decketh himself with ornaments, and as a bride adorneth herself with her jewels.

I will betroth thee unto me for ever; yea, I will betroth thee unto me in righteousness, and in judgment, and in lovingkindness, and in mercies.

Who shall separate us from the love of Christ?

ISA. 54. 5. *Ep.* 5. 32. *Is.* 62. 4, 5.—*Is.* 61. 1-3. *Is.* 61. 10. *Ho.* 2. 19. *Ro.* 8. 35.

My times are in thy hand.

All his saints are in thy hand.—The word of the LORD came unto [Elijah], saying, Get thee hence, and turn thee eastward, and hide thyself by the brook Cherith, that is before Jordan. And it shall be, that thou shalt drink of the brook; and I have commanded the ravens to feed thee there. And the word of the LORD came unto him, saying, Arise, get thee to Zarephath, which belongeth to Zidon, and dwell there: behold, I have commanded a widow woman there to sustain thee.

Take no thought for your life, what ye shall eat, or what ye shall drink; nor yet for your body, what ye shall put on. Your heavenly Father knoweth that ye have need of all these things.

Trust in the LORD with all thine heart; and lean not unto thine own understanding. In all thy ways acknowledge him, and he shall direct thy paths.—Casting all your care upon him; for he careth for you.

PSA. 31. 15. *De.* 33. 3.—1 *Ki.* 17. 2-4, 8, 9. *Mat.* 6. 25, 32. *Pr.* 3. 5, 6.— 1 *Pe.* 5. 7.

Thou hast cast all my sins behind thy back.

Who is a God like unto thee, that pardoneth iniquity, and passeth by the transgression of the remnant of his heritage? he retaineth not his anger for ever, because he delighteth in mercy. He will turn again, he will have compassion upon us; he will subdue our iniquities; and thou wilt cast all their sins into the depths of the sea.

For a small moment have I forsaken thee; but with great mercies will I gather thee. In a little wrath I hid my face from thee for a moment; but with everlasting kindness will I have mercy on thee, saith the LORD thy Redeemer.—I will forgive their iniquity, and I will remember their sin no more.

Blessed is he whose transgression is forgiven, whose sin is covered. Blessed is the man unto whom the LORD imputeth not iniquity, and in whose spirit there is no guile.—The blood of Jesus Christ his Son cleanseth us from all sin.

ISA. 38. 17. *Mi.* 7. 18, 19. *Is.* 54. 7, 8.—*Je.* 31. 34. *Ps.* 32. 1, 2.—1 *Jno.* 1. 7.

I know whom I have believed, and am persuaded that he is able.

Able to do exceeding abundantly above all that we ask or think.

Able to make all grace abound toward you; that ye, always having all sufficiency in all things, may abound to every good work.

Able to succour them that are tempted.

Able . . . to save them to the uttermost that come unto God by him, seeing he ever liveth to make intercession for them.

Able to keep you from falling, and to present you faultless before the presence of his glory with exceeding joy.

Able to keep that which I have committed unto him against that day.

Who shall change our vile body, that it may be fashioned like unto his glorious body, according to the working whereby he is able even to subdue all things unto himself.

Believe ye that I am able to do this? . . . Yea, Lord. According to your faith be it unto you.

2 *TIM.* 1. 12. *Ep.* 3. 20. 2 *Co.* 9, 8. *He.* 2. 18. *He.* 7. 25. *Jude* 24.
2 Ti. 1. 12. *Phi.* 3. 21. *Mat.* 9. 28, 29.

The living God giveth us richly all things to enjoy.

Beware that thou forget not the LORD thy God, in not keeping his commandments, and his judgments, and his statutes, which I command thee this day: lest when thou hast eaten and art full, and hast built goodly houses, and dwelt therein; . . . then thine heart be lifted up, and thou forget the LORD thy God: . . . for it is he that giveth thee power to get wealth.

Except the LORD build the house, they labour in vain that build it: except the LORD keep the city, the watchman waketh but in vain. It is vain for you to rise up early, to sit up late, to eat the bread of sorrows: for so he giveth his beloved sleep.—They got not the land in possession by their own sword, neither did their own arm save them: but thy right hand, and thine arm, and the light of thy countenance, because thou hadst a favour unto them.— There be many that say, Who will shew us any good? LORD, lift thou up the light of thy countenance upon us.

1 *TIM.* 6. 17. *De.* 8. 11, 12, 14, 18. *Ps.* 127. 1, 2.—*Ps.* 44. 3.—*Ps.* 4. 6.

They sung as it were a new song.

A new and living way, which he hath consecrated for us.—Not by works of righteousness which we have done, but according to his mercy he saved us, by the washing of regeneration, and renewing of the Holy Ghost; which he shed on us abundantly through Jesus Christ our Saviour.—By grace are ye saved through faith; and that not of yourselves: it is the gift of God; not of works, lest any man should boast.

Not unto us, O LORD, not unto us, but unto thy name give glory. —Unto him that loved us, and washed us from our sins in his own blood, and hath made us kings and priests unto God and his Father; to him be glory and dominion for ever and ever. Amen.— Thou wast slain, and hast redeemed us to God by thy blood out of every kindred, and tongue, and people, and nation.—I beheld, and, lo, a great multitude, which no man could number, . . cried, . . saying, Salvation to our God which sitteth upon the throne, and unto the Lamb.

REV. 14. 3. *He.* 10. 20.—*Ti.* 3. 5, 6.—*Ep.* 2. 8. 9. *Ps.* 115. 1.—*Re.* 1. 5, 6.
—*Re.* 5. 9.—*Re.* 7. 9, 10.

The Lord will provide.

God will provide himself a lamb for a burnt offering.

Behold, the LORD's hand is not shortened, that it cannot save; neither his ear heavy, that it cannot hear.—There shall come out of Sion the Deliverer, and shall turn away ungodliness from Jacob.

Happy is he that hath the God of Jacob for his help, whose hope is in the LORD his God.—Behold, the eye of the LORD is upon them that fear him, upon them that hope in his mercy; to deliver their soul from death.

My God shall supply all your need, according to his riches in glory by Christ Jesus.—He hath said, I will never leave thee, nor forsake thee. So that we may boldly say, The Lord is my helper, and I will not fear what man shall do unto me.—The LORD is my strength and my shield; my heart trusteth in him, and I am helped: therefore my heart greatly rejoiceth: and with my song will I praise him.

GEN. 22. 14 (*marg.*). *Ge.* 22. 8. *Is.* 59. 1.—*Ro.* 11. 26. *Ps.* 146. 5.— *Ps.* 33. 18, 19. *Phi.* 4. 19.—*He.* 13. 5, 6.—*Ps.* 28. 7.

He feedeth among the lilies.

Where two or three are gathered together in my name, there am I in the midst of them.—If a man love me, he will keep my words: and my Father will love him, and we will come unto him, and make our abode with him.

If ye keep my commandments, ye shall abide in my love; even as I have kept my Father's commandments, and abide in his love.

Let my beloved come into his garden, and eat his pleasant fruits.—I am come into my garden, my sister, my spouse: I have gathered my myrrh with my spice; I have eaten my honeycomb with my honey.—The fruit of the Spirit is love, joy, peace, long-suffering, gentleness, goodness, faith, meekness, temperance.

Herein is my Father glorified, that ye bear much fruit; so shall ye be my disciples.—Every branch that beareth fruit, he purgeth it, that it may bring forth more fruit.—Being filled with the fruits of righteousness, which are by Jesus Christ, unto the glory and praise of God.

CANT. 2. 16. *Mat.* 18. 20.—*Jno.* 14. 23. *Jno.* 15. 10. *Ca.* 4. 16.—5. 1.— *Ga.* 5. 22, 23. *Jno.* 15. 8.—*Jno.* 15. 2.—*Phi.* 1. 11.

The Lord bless thee, and keep thee.

The blessing of the LORD, it maketh rich, and he addeth no sorrow with it.—Thou, LORD, wilt bless the righteous; with favour wilt thou compass him as with a shield.

He will not suffer thy foot to be moved: he that keepeth thee will not slumber. Behold, he that keepeth Israel shall neither slumber nor sleep. The LORD is thy keeper: the LORD is thy shade upon thy right hand. The LORD shall preserve thee from all evil: he shall preserve thy soul. The LORD shall preserve thy going out and thy coming in from this time forth, and even for evermore.— I the LORD do keep it; I will water it every moment: lest any hurt it, I will keep it night and day.

Holy Father, keep through thine own name those whom thou hast given me. While I was with them in the world, I kept them in thy name: those that thou gavest me I have kept.

The Lord shall deliver me from every evil work, and will preserve me unto his heavenly kingdom: to whom be glory for ever and ever. Amen.

NUM. 6. 24. *Pr.* 10. 22.—*Ps.* 5. 12. *Ps.* 121. 3-5, 7, 8.—*Is.* 27. 3. *Jno.* 17. 11, 12. 2 *Ti.* 4. 18.

Jesus wept.

A man of sorrows, and acquainted with grief.—We have not an high priest which cannot be touched with the feeling of our infirmities.—It became him, for whom are all things, and by whom are all things, in bringing many sons unto glory, to make the captain of their salvation perfect through sufferings.—Though he were a Son, yet learned he obedience by the things which he suffered.

I was not rebellious, neither turned away back. I gave my back to the smiters, and my cheeks to them that plucked off the hair: I hid not my face from shame and spitting.

Behold how he loved.—He took not on him the nature of angels; but he took on him the seed of Abraham. In all things it behooved him to be made like unto his brethren, that he might be a merciful and faithful high priest in things pertaining to God, to make reconciliation for the sins of the people.

JNO. 11. 35. *Is.* 53. 3.—*He.* 4. 15.—*He.* 2 .10.—*He.* 5. 8. *Is.* 50. 5. 6. *Jno.* 11. 36.—*He.* 2. 16, 17.

The Lord make his face shine upon thee, and be gracious unto thee. The Lord lift up his countenance upon thee, and give thee peace.

No man hath seen God at any time; the only begotten Son, which is in the bosom of the Father, he hath declared him.—The brightness of his glory, and the express image of his person.—The god of this world hath blinded the minds of them which believe not, lest the light of the glorious gospel of Christ, who is the image of God, should shine unto them.

Make thy face to shine upon thy servant: save me for thy mercies' sake. Let me not be ashamed, O LORD; for I have called upon thee.—LORD, by thy favour thou hast made my mountain to stand strong: thou didst hide thy face, and I was troubled.—Blessed is the people that know the joyful sound: they shall walk, O LORD, in the light of thy countenance.

The LORD will give strength unto his people; the LORD will bless his people with peace.

Be of good cheer; it is I; be not afraid.

NUM. 6. 25, 26. *Jno.* 1. 18.—*He.* 1. 3.—2 *Co.* 4. 4. *Ps.* 31. 16, 17.—
Ps. 30. 7.—*Ps.* 89. 15. *Ps.* 29. 11. *Mat.* 14. 27.

Things that are pleasing in his sight.

Without faith it is impossible to please him.—So then they that are in the flesh cannot please God.—The LORD taketh pleasure in his people.

This is thankworthy, if a man for conscience toward God endure grief, suffering wrongfully. If, when ye do well, and suffer for it, ye take it patiently, this is acceptable with God.—The ornament of a meek and quiet spirit, . . . is in the sight of God of great price.

Whoso offereth praise glorifieth me: and to him that ordereth his conversation aright will I shew the salvation of God.—I will praise the name of God with a song, and will magnify him with thanksgiving. This also shall please the LORD better than an ox or bullock that hath horns and hoofs.

I beseech you, . . . brethren, by the mercies of God, that ye present your bodies a living sacrifice, holy, acceptable unto God, which is your reasonable service.

1 *JNO.* 3. 22. *He.* 11. 6.—*Ro.* 8. 8.—*Ps.* 149. 4. 1 *Pe.* 2. 19, 20.—
1 *Pe.* 3. 4. *Ps.* 50. 23.—*Ps.* 69. 30, 31. *Ro.* 12. 1.

There is one God, and one mediator between God and men, the man Christ Jesus.

Forasmuch . . . as the children are partakers of flesh and blood, he also himself likewise took part of the same.

Look unto me, and be ye saved, all the ends of the earth: for I am God, and there is none else.

We have an advocate with the Father, Jesus Christ the righteous.—In Christ Jesus, ye who sometime were far off, are made nigh by the blood of Christ. For he is our peace.—By his own blood he entered in once into the holy place, having obtained eternal redemption for us. And for this cause he is the mediator of the new testament, that by means of death, for the redemption of the transgressions that were under the first testament, they which are called might receive the promise of eternal inheritance.—He is able also to save them to the uttermost that come unto God by him, seeing he ever liveth to make intercession for them.

1 *TIM.* 2. 5. *He.* 2. 14. *Is.* 45. 22. 1 *Jno.* 2. 1.—*Ep.* 2. 13, 14.—
He. 9. 12, 15.—*He.* 7. 25.

O my God, my soul is cast down within me.

Thou wilt keep him in perfect peace, whose mind is stayed on thee: because he trusteth in thee. Trust ye in the LORD for ever: for in the LORD JEHOVAH is everlasting strength.

Cast thy burden upon the LORD, and he shall sustain thee.—He hath not despised nor abhorred the affliction of the afflicted; neither hath he hid his face from him; but when he cried unto him, he heard.—Is any among you afflicted? let him pray.

Let not your heart be troubled, neither let it be afraid.—Take no thought for your life, what ye shall eat, or what ye shall drink; nor yet for your body, what ye shall put on. Behold the fowls of the air: for they sow not, neither do they reap, nor gather into barns; yet your heavenly Father feedeth them. Are ye not much better than they?—Be not faithless, but believing.—Lo, I am with you alway.

PSA. 42. 6. *Is.* 26. 3, 4. *Ps.* 55. 22.—*Ps.* 22. 24.—*Ja.* 5. 13. *Jno.* 14. 27.—
Mat. 6. 25, 26.—*Jno.* 20. 27.—*Mat.* 28. 20.

Adorn the doctrine of God our Saviour in all things.

Let your conversation be as it becometh the gospel of Christ.—Abstain from all appearance of evil.—If ye be reproached for the name of Christ, happy are ye. But let none of you suffer as a murderer, or as a thief, or as an evildoer, or as a busybody in other men's matters.—Be blameless and harmless, the sons of God, without rebuke, in the midst of a crooked and perverse nation, among whom ye shine as lights in the world.—Let your light so shine before men, that they may see your good works, and glorify your Father which is in heaven.

Let not mercy and truth forsake thee: bind them about thy neck; write them upon the table of thine heart; so shalt thou find favour and good understanding in the sight of God and man.—Brethren, whatsoever things are true, whatsoever things are honest, whatsoever things are just, whatsoever things are pure, whatsoever things are lovely, whatsoever things are of good report; if there be any virtue, and if there be any praise, think on these things.

TITUS 2. 10. *Phi.* 1. 27.—1 *Thes.* 5. 22.—1 *Pe.* 4. 14, 15.—*Phi.* 2. 15.—*Mat.* 5. 16. *Pr.* 3. 3, 4.—*Phi.* 4. 8.

The words that I speak unto you, they are spirit, and they are life.

Of his own will begat he us with the word of truth.—The letter killeth, but the spirit giveth life.

Christ . . . loved the church, and gave himself for it; that he might sanctify and cleanse it with the washing of water by the word, that he might present it to himself a glorious church, not having spot, or wrinkle, or any such thing.

Wherewithal shall a young man cleanse his way? by taking heed thereto according to thy word. Thy word hath quickened me. Thy word have I hid in mine heart, that I might not sin against thee. I will not forget thy word. I trust in thy word. The law of thy mouth is better unto me than thousands of gold and silver. I will never forget thy precepts: for with them thou hast quickened me. How sweet are thy words unto my taste! yea, sweeter than honey to my mouth! Through thy precepts I get understanding: therefore I hate every false way.

JNO. 6. 63. *Ja.* 1. 18.—2 *Co.* 3. 6. *Ep.* 5. 25-27. *Ps.* 119. 9, 50, 11, 16, 42, 72, 93, 103, 104.

Perfect through sufferings.

My soul is exceeding sorrowful, even unto death: tarry ye here, and watch with me. And he went a little farther, and fell on his face, and prayed, saying, O my Father, if it be possible, let this cup pass from me: nevertheless not as I will, but as thou wilt.— And being in an agony he prayed more earnestly: and his sweat was as it were great drops of blood falling down to the ground.

The sorrows of death compassed me, and the pains of hell gat hold upon me: I found trouble and sorrow.—Reproach hath broken my heart; and I am full of heaviness: and I looked for some to take pity, but there was none; and for comforters, but I found none.—I looked on my right hand, and behold, but there was no man that would know me: refuge failed me; no man cared for my soul.

He is despised and rejected of men; a man of sorrows, and acquainted with grief: and we hid as it were our faces from him; he was despised, and we esteemed him not.

HEB. 2. 10. *Mat.* 26. 38, 39.—*Lu.* 22. 44. *Ps.* 116. 3.—*Ps.* 69. 20.—
Ps. 142. 4. *Is.* 53. 3.

The Lord made heaven and earth, the sea, and all that in them is.

The heavens declare the glory of God; and the firmament sheweth his handywork.—By the word of the LORD were the heavens made; and all the host of them by the breath of his mouth. For he spake, and it was done; he commanded, and it stood fast.— Behold, the nations are as a drop of a bucket, and are counted as the small dust of the balance: behold, he taketh up the isles as a very little thing.

Through faith we understand that the worlds were framed by the word of God, so that things which are seen were not made of things which do appear.

When I consider thy heavens, the work of thy fingers, the moon and the stars, which thou hast ordained; what is man, that thou art mindful of him? and the son of man, that thou visitest him?

EX. 20. 11. *Ps.* 19. 1.—*Ps.* 33. 6, 9.—*Is.* 40. 15. *He.* 11. 3. *Ps.* 8. 3, 4.

What is your life? It is even a vapour, that appeareth for a little time, and then vanisheth away.

My days are swifter than a post: they flee away, they see no good. They are passed away as the swift ships: as the eagle that hasteth to the prey.—Thou carriest them away as with a flood; they are as a sleep: in the morning they are like grass which groweth up. In the morning it flourisheth, and groweth up: in the evening it is cut down, and withereth.—Man that is born of a woman is of few days, and full of trouble. He cometh forth like a flower, and is cut down.

The world passeth away, and the lust thereof: but he that doeth the will of God abideth for ever.—They shall perish, but thou shalt endure: yea, all of them shall wax old like a garment; as a vesture shalt thou change them, and they shall be changed: but thou art the same, and thy years shall have no end.—Jesus Christ, the same yesterday, and to day, and for ever.

JAMES 4. 14. *Job* 9. 25, 26.—*Ps.* 90. 5, 6.—*Job* 14. 2. 1 *Jno.* 2. 17.—
Ps. 102. 26, 27.—*He.* 13. 8.

I will sing with the spirit, and I will sing with the understanding also.

Be filled with the Spirit, speaking to yourselves in psalms and hymns and spiritual songs, singing and making melody in your heart to the Lord.—Let the word of Christ dwell in you richly in all wisdom; teaching and admonishing one another in psalms and hymns and spiritual songs, singing with grace in your hearts to the Lord.

My mouth shall speak the praise of the LORD: and let all flesh bless his holy name for ever and ever.

Praise ye the LORD: for it is good to sing praises unto our God; for it is pleasant; and praise is comely. Sing unto the LORD with thanksgiving; sing praise upon the harp unto our God.

I heard a voice from heaven, as the voice of many waters, and as the voice of a great thunder; and I heard the voice of harpers harping with their harps.

1 *COR.* 14. 15. *Ep.* 5. 18, 19.—*Col.* 3. 16. *Ps.* 145. 21. *Ps.* 147. 1, 7.
Re. 14. 2.

He shall put his hand upon the head of the burnt offering ; and it shall be accepted for him to make atonement for him.

Ye know that ye were not redeemed with corruptible things, as silver and gold, from your vain conversation received by tradition from your fathers; but with the precious blood of Christ, as of a lamb without blemish and without spot.—Who his own self bare our sins in his own body on the tree.

He hath made us accepted in the Beloved.

As lively stones, . . . built up a spiritual house, a holy priesthood, to offer up spiritual sacrifices, acceptable to God by Jesus Christ.—I beseech you therefore, brethren, by the mercies of God, that ye present your bodies a living sacrifice, holy, acceptable unto God, which is your reasonable service.

Now unto him that is able to keep you from falling, and to present you faultless before the presence of his glory with exceeding joy, to the only wise God our Saviour, be glory and majesty, dominion and power, both now and ever.

LEV. 1. 4. 1 *Pe.* 1. 18, 19.—1 *Pe.* 2. 24. *Ep.* 1. 6. 1 *Pe.* 2. 5.—*Ro.* 12. 1.
Jude 24, 25.

In all points tempted like as we are, yet without sin.

When the woman saw that the tree was good for food (the lust of the flesh), and that it was pleasant to the eyes (the lust of the eyes), and a tree to be desired to make one wise (the pride of life), she took of the fruit thereof, and did eat, and gave also unto her husband with her ; and he did eat.

When the tempter came to [Jesus], he said, If thou be the Son of God, command that these stones be made bread (the lust of the flesh). But he answered, . . . Man shall not live by bread alone, but by every word that proceedeth out of the mouth of God. The devil . . . sheweth him all the kingdoms of the world, and the glory of them (the lust of the eyes, and the pride of life). Then saith Jesus unto him, Get thee hence, Satan.

In that he himself hath suffered being tempted, he is able to succour them that are tempted.

Blessed is the man that endureth temptation.

HEB. 4. 15. *Ge.* 3. 6. 1 *Jno.* 2. 16. *Mat.* 4. 3, 4, 8-10.—1 *Jno.* 2. 16.
He. 2. 18. *Ja.* 1. 12.

Mine eyes fail with looking upward.

Have mercy upon me, O LORD; for I am weak: O LORD, heal me; for my bones are vexed. My soul is also sore vexed: but thou, O LORD, how long? Return, O LORD, deliver my soul: oh save me for thy mercies' sake.—My heart is sore pained within me: and the terrors of death are fallen upon me. Fearfulness and trembling are come upon me, and horror hath overwhelmed me. And I said, Oh that I had wings like a dove! for then would I fly away, and be at rest.

Ye have need of patience.

While they looked stedfastly toward heaven as he went up, behold, two men stood by them in white apparel; which also said, Ye men of Galilee, why stand ye gazing up into heaven? this same Jesus, which is taken up from you into heaven, shall so come in like manner as ye have seen him go into heaven.—Our conversation is in heaven; from whence also we look for the Saviour, the Lord Jesus Christ.—That blessed hope, . . . the glorious appearing of the great God and our Saviour Jesus Christ.

ISA. 38. 14. *Ps.* 6. 2-4.—*Ps.* 55. 4-6. *He.* 10. 36.—*Ac.* 1. 10, 11.—
Phi. 3. 20.—*Tit.* 2. 13.

His name shall be in their foreheads.

I am the good shepherd, and know my sheep.—The foundation of God standeth sure, having this seal, The Lord knoweth them that are his. And, Let every one that nameth the name of Christ depart from iniquity.

The LORD is good, a strong hold in the day of trouble; and he knoweth them that trust in him.—Hurt not the earth, neither the sea, nor the trees, till we have sealed the servants of our God in their foreheads.

After that ye believed, ye were sealed with that holy Spirit of promise, which is the earnest of our inheritance.—Now he which stablisheth us with you in Christ, and hath anointed us, is God; who hath also sealed us, and given the earnest of the Spirit in our hearts.

I will write upon him the name of my God, and the name of the city of my God, which is new Jerusalem, which cometh down out of heaven from my God: and I will write upon him my new name.—This is the name wherewith she shall be called, The LORD our righteousness.

REV. 22. 4. *Jno.* 10. 14.—2 *Ti.* 2. 19. *Na.* 1. 7.—*Re.* 7. 3. *Ep.* 1. 13, 14.—
2 *Co.* 1. 21, 22. *Re.* 3. 12.—*Je.* 33. 16.

God, having raised up his Son Jesus, sent him to bless you, in turning away every one of you from his iniquities.

Blessed be the God and Father of our Lord Jesus Christ, which according to his abundant mercy hath begotten us again unto a lively hope by the resurrection of Jesus Christ from the dead.—Saved by his life.

Our Saviour Jesus Christ, . . . who gave himself for us that he might redeem us from all iniquity, and purify unto himself a peculiar people, zealous of good works.—As he which hath called you is holy, so be ye holy in all manner of conversation; because it is written, Be ye holy; for I am holy.

The God and Father of our Lord Jesus Christ, . . . hath blessed us with all spiritual blessings in heavenly places in Christ.—In him dwelleth all the fulness of the Godhead bodily. And ye are complete in him.—Of his fulness have all we received, and grace for grace.

He that spared not his own Son, but delivered him up for us all, how shall he not with him also freely give us all things?

ACTS 3. 26. 1 Pe. 1. 3.—Ro. 5. 10. Tit. 2. 13, 14.—1 Pe. 1. 15, 16. Ep. 1. 3.
—Col. 2. 9, 10.—Jno. 1. 16. Ro. 8. 32.

Strengthen thou me according unto thy word.

Remember the word unto thy servant, upon which thou hast caused me to hope.—O LORD, I am oppressed; undertake for me.

Heaven and earth shall pass away: but my words shall not pass away.—Ye know in all your hearts and in all your souls, that not one thing hath failed of all the good things which the LORD your God spake concerning you; all are come to pass unto you, and not one thing hath failed thereof.

Fear not: peace be unto thee, be strong, yea, be strong. And when he had spoken unto me, I was strengthened, and said, Let my lord speak ; for thou hast strengthened me.—Be strong, . . . and work: for I am with you, saith the LORD of hosts.—Not by might, nor by power, but by my spirit, saith the LORD of hosts.

Be strong in the Lord, and in the power of his might.

PSA. 119. 28. Ps. 119. 49.—Is. 38. 14. Lu. 21. 33.—Jos. 23. 14. Da. 10. 19.
—Hag. 2. 4.—Zec. 4. 6. Ep. 6. 10.

The entrance of thy words giveth light.

This . . . is the message which we have heard of him, and declare unto you, that God is light, and in him is no darkness at all.—God, who commanded the light to shine out of darkness, hath shined in our hearts, to give the light of the knowledge of the glory of God in the face of Jesus Christ.—The Word was God. In him was life; and the life was the light of men.—If we walk in the light, as he is in the light, we have fellowship one with another, and the blood of Jesus Christ his Son cleanseth us from all sin.

Thy word have I hid in mine heart, that I might not sin against thee.—Ye are clean through the word which I have spoken unto you.

Ye were sometimes darkness, but now are ye light in the Lord: walk as children of light.—Ye are a chosen generation, a royal priesthood, a holy nation, a peculiar people; that ye should shew forth the praises of him who hath called you out of darkness into his marvellous light.

PSA. 119. 130.   1 *Jno.* 1. 5.—2 *Co.* 4. 6.—*Jno.* 1. 1, 4.—1 *Jno.* 1. 7.
Ps. 119. 11.—*Jno.* 15. 3.   *Ep.* 5. 8.—1 *Pe.* 2. 9.

Noah was a just man.

The just shall live by faith.—Noah builded an altar unto the Lord; and took of every clean beast, and of every clean fowl, and offered burnt offerings on the altar. And the Lord smelled a sweet savour.—The Lamb slain from the foundation of the world.

Being justified by faith, we have peace with God through our Lord Jesus Christ.

By the deeds of the law there shall no flesh be justified in his sight: for by the law is the knowledge of sin. But now the righteousness of God without the law is manifested, being witnessed by the law and the prophets; even the righteousness of God which is by faith of Jesus Christ unto all and upon all them that believe: for there is no difference.

We . . . joy in God, through our Lord Jesus Christ, by whom we have now received the atonement.

Who shall lay any thing to the charge of God's elect? It is God that justifieth.—Whom he did predestinate, them he also called: and whom he called, them he also justified.

GEN. 6. 9.   *Ga.* 3. 11.—*Ge.* 8. 20, 21.—*Re.* 13. 8.   *Ro.* 5. 1.   *Ro.* 3. 20-22.
Ro. 5. 11.   *Ro.* 8. 33, 30.

Be watchful, and strengthen the things which remain, that are ready to die.

The end of all things is at hand: be ye therefore sober, and watch unto prayer.—Be sober, be vigilant; because your adversary the devil, as a roaring lion, walketh about, seeking whom he may devour.—Take heed to thyself, and keep thy soul diligently, lest thou forget the things which thine eyes have seen, and lest they depart from thy heart all the days of thy life.—The just shall live by faith: but if any man draw back, my soul shall have no pleasure in him. But we are not of them who draw back unto perdition; but of them that believe to the saving of the soul.

What I say unto you I say unto all, Watch.

Fear thou not; for I am with thee: be not dismayed; for I am thy God: I will strengthen thee; yea, I will help thee; yea, I will uphold thee with the right hand of my righteousness. I the LORD thy God will hold thy right hand.

REV. 3. 2. 1 *Pe.* 4. 7. 1 *Pe.* 5. 8.—*De.* 4. 9.—*He.* 10. 38, 39. *Mark* 13. 37. *Is.* 41. 10, 13.

Is his mercy clean gone for ever?

His mercy endureth for ever.—The LORD is longsuffering, and of great mercy.—Who is a God like unto thee, that pardoneth iniquity? . . . he retaineth not his anger for ever, because he delighteth in mercy. He will turn again, he will have compassion upon us; he will subdue our iniquities; and thou wilt cast all their sins into the depths of the sea.—Not by works of righteousness which we have done, but according to his mercy he saved us.

Blessed be God, even the Father of our Lord Jesus Christ, the Father of mercies, and the God of all comfort; who comforteth us in all our tribulation, that we may be able to comfort them which are in any trouble, by the comfort wherewith we ourselves are comforted of God.

A merciful and faithful high priest in things pertaining to God, to make reconciliation for the sins of the people. For in that he himself hath suffered being tempted, he is able to succour them that are tempted.

PSA. 77. 8. *Ps.* 136. 23.—*Nu.* 14. 18.—*Mi.* 7. 18, 19.—*Tit.* 3. 5. 2 *Co.* 1. 3, 4. *He.* 2. 17, 18.

Lot lifted up his eyes, and beheld all the plain of Jordan, that it was well watered every where, before the Lord destroyed Sodom and Gomorrah, even as the garden of the Lord. Then Lot chose him all the plain of Jordan.

Just Lot . . . that righteous man.

Be not deceived; God is not mocked: for whatsoever a man soweth, that shall he also reap.—Remember Lot's wife.

Be ye not unequally yoked together with unbelievers: for what fellowship hath righteousness with unrighteousness? and what communion hath light with darkness? Wherefore come out from among them, and be ye separate, saith the Lord, and touch not the unclean thing.—Be not ye . . . partakers with them. For ye were sometime darkness, but now are ye light in the Lord: walk as children of light: proving what is acceptable unto the Lord. And have no fellowship with the unfruitful works of darkness, but rather reprove them.

GEN. 13. 10, 11. 2 *Pe.* 2. 7, 8. *Gal.* 6. 7.—*Lu.* 17. 32. 2 *Co.* 6. 14, 17.—
Ep. 5. 7, 8, 10, 11.

If so be the Lord will be with me, then I shall be able to drive them out, as the Lord said.

He hath said, I will never leave thee, nor forsake thee. So that we may boldly say, The Lord is my helper, and I will not fear what man shall do unto me.—I will go in the strength of the LORD GOD: I will make mention of thy righteousness, even of thine only.

The work of righteousness shall be peace; and the effect of righteousness quietness and assurance for ever.

Stand . . . having your loins girt about with truth, and having on the breastplate of righteousness. For we wrestle not against flesh and blood, but against principalities, against powers, against the rulers of the darkness of this world, against spiritual wickedness in high places. Wherefore take unto you the whole armour of God, that ye may be able to withstand in the evil day, and having done all, to stand.—The LORD is with thee, . . . Go in this thy might.

JOS. 14. 12. *He.* 13. 5, 6.—*Ps.* 71. 16. *Is.* 32. 17. *Ep.* 6. 14, 12, 13.—
Ju. 6. 12, 14.

Holy, holy, holy, Lord God Almighty.

Thou art holy, O thou that inhabitest the praises of Israel.—Draw not nigh hither; put off thy shoes from off thy feet, for the place whereon thou standest is holy ground. . . . I am the God of thy father, the God of Abraham, the God of Isaac, and the God of Jacob. And Moses hid his face; for he was afraid to look upon God.—To whom then will ye liken me, or shall I be equal? saith the Holy One.—I am the LORD thy God, the Holy One of Israel, thy Saviour. I, even I, am the LORD; and beside me there is no saviour.

As he which hath called you is holy, so be ye holy in all manner of conversation; because it is written, Be ye holy; for I am holy.—Know ye not that your body is the temple of the Holy Ghost which is in you, which ye have of God, and ye are not your own.—Ye are the temple of the living God; as God hath said, I will dwell in them, and walk in them; and I will be their God, and they shall be my people.—Can two walk together, except they be agreed?

REV. 4. 8. *Ps.* 22. 3.—*Ex.* 3. 5, 6.—*Is.* 40. 25.—*Is.* 43. 3, 11. **1** *Pe.* **1.** 15, 16. —1 *Co.* 6. 19.—2 *Co.* 6. 16.—*Amos* 3. 3.

They constrained him, saying, Abide with us.

Behold, I stand at the door, and knock: if any man hear my voice, and open the door, I will come in to him, and will sup with him, and he with me.—Tell me, O thou whom my soul loveth, where thou feedest, where thou makest thy flock to rest at noon: for why should I be as one that turneth aside by the flocks of thy companions?—I found him whom my soul loveth: I held him, and would not let him go.

Let my beloved come into his garden, and eat his pleasant fruits.—I am come into my garden.—I said not unto the seed of Jacob, Seek ye me in vain.

Lo, I am with you alway, even unto the end of the world.—I will never leave thee, nor forsake thee.—Where two or three are gathered together in my name, there am I in the midst of them.—The world seeth me no more; but ye see me.

LUKE 24. 29. *Re.* 3. 20.—*Ca.* 1. 7.—*Ca.* 3. 4. *Ca.* 4. 16.—*Ca.* 5. 1.— *Is.* 45. 19.—*Mat.* 28. 20.—*He.* 13. 5.—*Mat.* 18. 20.—*Jno.* 14. 19.

Abraham believed in the Lord; and he counted it to him for righteousness.

He staggered not at the promise of God through unbelief; but was strong in faith, giving glory to God; and being fully persuaded that, what he had promised, he was able also to perform. And therefore it was imputed to him for righteousness. Now it was not written for his sake alone, that it was imputed to him: but for us also, to whom it shall be imputed, if we believe on him that raised up Jesus our Lord from the dead.

The promise, that he should be the heir of the world, was not to Abraham, or to his seed, through the law, but through the righteousness of faith.

The just shall live by faith.—Let us hold fast the profession of our faith without wavering; (for he is faithful that promised).— Our God is in the heavens; he hath done whatsoever he hath pleased.—With God nothing shall be impossible. And blessed is she that believed: for there shall be a performance of those things which were told her from the Lord.

GEN. 15. 6. *Ro.* 4. 20-24. *Ro.* 4. 13. *Ro.* 1. 17.—*He.* 10. 23.—*Ps.* 115. 3.— *Lu.* 1. 37, 45.

God hath called you unto his kingdom and glory.

My kingdom is not of this world: if my kingdom were of this world, then would my servants fight, . . . but now is my kingdom not from hence.—Expecting till his enemies be made his footstool.

The kingdoms of this world are become the kingdoms of our Lord, and of his Christ; and he shall reign for ever and ever.— Thou hast made us unto our God kings and priests: and we shall reign on the earth.—I saw thrones, and they sat upon them, and judgment was given unto them; . . . and they lived and reigned with Christ a thousand years.—Then shall the righteous shine forth as the sun in the kingdom of their Father.—Fear not, little flock; for it is your Father's good pleasure to give you the kingdom.

I appoint unto you a kingdom, as my Father hath appointed unto me; that ye may eat and drink at my table in my kingdom, and sit on thrones judging the twelve tribes of Israel.

Thy kingdom come.

1 *THES.* 2. 12. *Jno.* 18. 36.—*He.* 10. 13. *Re.* 11. 15.—*Re.* 5. 10.—*Re.* 20. 4. —*Mat.* 13. 43.—*Lu.* 12. 32. *Lu.* 22. 29, 30. *Mat.* 6. 10.

I will never leave thee, nor forsake thee.

So that we may boldly say, The Lord is my helper, and I will not fear what man shall do unto me.

Behold, I am with thee, and will keep thee in all places whither thou goest, and will bring thee again into this land; for I will not leave thee, until I have done that which I have spoken to thee of.—Be strong and of a good courage, fear not, nor be afraid of them: for the LORD thy God, he it is that doth go with thee; he will not fail thee, nor forsake thee.

Demas hath forsaken me, having loved this present world. At my first answer no man stood with me, but all men forsook me: I pray God that it may not be laid to their charge. Notwithstanding the Lord stood with me, and strengthened me.—When my father and my mother forsake me, then the Lord will take me up.

Lo, I am with you alway, even unto the end of the world.—I am he that liveth, and was dead; and, behold, I am alive for evermore.—I will not leave you comfortless; I will come to you.— My peace I give unto you.

HEB. 13. 5. *He.* 13. 6. *Ge.* 28. 15.—*De.* 31. 6. 2 *Ti.* 4. 10, 16, 17.— *Ps.* 27. 10. *Mat.* 28. 20.—*Re.* 1. 18.—*Jno.* 14. 18.—*Jno.* 14. 27.

Master, we have toiled all the night, and have taken nothing; nevertheless at thy word I will let down the net.

All power is give unto me in heaven and in earth. Go ye therefore, and teach all nations, baptizing them in the name of the Father, and of the Son, and of the Holy Ghost: . . . and, lo, I am with you alway, even unto the end of the world.

The kingdom of heaven is like unto a net, that was cast into the sea.

Though I preach the gospel, I have nothing to glory of: for necessity is laid upon me; yea, woe is unto me, if I preach not the gospel! I am made all things to all men, that I might by all means save some.

Let us not be weary in well doing: for in due season we shall reap, if we faint not.—My word . . . shall not return unto me void, but it shall accomplish that which I please.—So then neither is he that planteth any thing, neither he that watereth; but God that giveth the increase.

LUKE 5. 5. *Mat.* 28. 18-20. *Mat.* 13. 47. 1 *Co.* 9. 16, 22. *Ga.* 6. 9.— *Is.* 55. 11.—1 *Co.* 3. 7.

The kingdom of heaven is as a man travelling into a far country, who called his own servants, and delivered unto them his goods ... to every man according to his several ability.

Know ye not, that to whom ye yield yourselves servants to obey, his servants ye are to whom ye obey?

All these worketh that one and the selfsame Spirit, dividing to every man severally as he will. The manifestation of the Spirit is given to every man to profit withal.—As every man hath received the gift, even so minister the same one to another, as good stewards of the manifold grace of God.—It is required in stewards, that a man be found faithful.—Unto whomsoever much is given, of him shall be much required: and to whom men have committed much, of him they will ask the more.

Who is sufficient for these things? — I can do all things through Christ which strengtheneth me.

MAT. 25. 14, 15. *Ro.* 6. 16. 1 *Co.* 12. 11, 7.—1 *Pe.* 4. 10.—1 *Co.* 4. 2.—
Lu. 12. 48. 2 *Co.* 2. 16.—*Phi.* 4. 13.

Distributing to the necessity of saints.

David said, Is there yet any that is left ... of the house of Saul, that I may shew him kindness for Jonathan's sake?

Come, ye blessed of my Father, inherit the kingdom prepared for you from the foundation of the world : for I was an hungered, and ye gave me meat: I was thirsty, and ye gave me drink: I was a stranger, and ye took me in: naked, and ye clothed me: I was sick, and ye visited me: I was in prison, and ye came unto me. Inasmuch as ye have done it unto one of the least of these my brethren, ye have done it unto me.—Whosoever shall give to drink unto one of these little ones a cup of cold water only in the name of a disciple, verily I say unto you, he shall in no wise lose his reward.

To do good and to communicate forget not: for with such sacrifices God is well pleased.—God is not unrighteous to forget your work and labour of love, which ye have shewed toward his name, in that ye have ministered to the saints, and do minister.

ROM. 12. 13. 2 *Sa.* 9. 1. *Mat.* 25. 34-36, 40.—*Mat.* 10. 42. *He.* 13. 16.—
He. 6. 10.

To him that soweth righteousness shall be a sure reward.

After a long time the lord of those servants cometh, and reckoneth with them. And so he that had received five talents came and brought other five talents, saying, Lord, thou deliveredst unto me five talents: behold, I have gained beside them five talents more. His lord said unto him, Well done, thou good and faithful servant: thou hast been faithful over a few things, I will make thee ruler over many things; enter thou into the joy of thy lord.

We must all appear before the judgment seat of Christ; that every one may receive the things done in his body, according to that he hath done, whether it be good or bad.

I have fought a good fight, I have finished my course, I have kept the faith: henceforth there is laid up for me a crown of righteousness, which the Lord, the righteous judge, shall give me at that day: and not to me only, but unto all them also that love his appearing.

Behold, I come quickly: hold that fast which thou hast, that no man take thy crown.

PROV. 11. 18. *Mat.* 25. 19-21. *2 Co.* 5. 10. *2 Ti.* 4. 7, 8. *Re.* 3. 11.

God is faithful.

God is not a man that he should lie; neither the Son of man that he should repent: hath he said, and shall he not do it? or hath he spoken, and shall he not make it good?—The Lord sware and will not repent.

God, willing more abundantly to shew unto the heirs of promise the immutability of his counsel, confirmed it by an oath: that by two immutable things, in which it was impossible for God to lie, we might have a strong consolation, who have fled for refuge to lay hold upon the hope set before us.—Wherefore let them that suffer according to the will of God commit the keeping of their souls to him in well doing, as unto a faithful Creator.

I know whom I have believed, and am persuaded that he is able to keep that which I have committed unto him against that day. —Faithful is he that calleth you, who also will do it.—All the promises of God in him are yea, and in him Amen, unto the glory of God by us.

1 COR. 10. 13. *Nu.* 23. 19.—*He.* 7. 21. *He.* 6. 17, 18.—*1 Pe.* 4. 19. *2 Ti.* 1. 12.—*1 Th.* 5. 24.—*2 Co.* 1. 20.

Be strong and of a good courage.

The LORD is my light and my salvation: whom shall I fear? the LORD is the strength of my life: of whom shall I be afraid?— He giveth power to the faint; and to them that have no might he increaseth strength. Even the youths shall faint and be weary, and the young men shall utterly fall: but they that wait upon the LORD shall renew their strength; they shall mount up with wings as eagles; they shall run, and not be weary; and they shall walk, and not faint.—My flesh and my heart faileth: but God is the strength of my heart, and my portion for ever.

If God be for us, who can be against us?—The LORD is on my side; I will not fear: what can man do unto me?—Through thee will we push down our enemies: through thy name will we tread them under that rise up against us.—We are more than conquerors through him that loved us.

Arise therefore, and be doing, and the LORD be with thee.

JOS. 1. 18. *Ps.* 27. 1.—*Is.* 40. 29-31.—*Ps.* 73. 26. *Ro.* 8. 31.—*Ps.* 118. 6.— *Ps.* 44. 5.—*Ro.* 8. 37. 1 *Ch.* 22. 16.

Our friend sleepeth.

I would not have you to be ignorant, brethren, concerning them which are asleep, that ye sorrow not, even as others which have no hope. For if we believe that Jesus died and rose again, even so them also which sleep in Jesus will God bring with him.

If the dead rise not, then is not Christ raised: and if Christ be not raised, your faith is vain; ye are yet in your sins. Then they also which are fallen asleep in Christ are perished. But now is Christ risen from the dead, and become the firstfruits of them that slept.

It came to pass, when all the people were clean passed over Jordan, that the LORD spake unto Joshua, saying, Take you hence out of the midst of Jordan, out of the place where the priests' feet stood firm, twelve stones, . . . and these stones shall be for a memorial· unto the children of Israel for ever.—This Jesus hath God raised up, whereof we all are witnesses.—Witnesses chosen before of God, . . . who did eat and drink with him after he rose from the dead.

JNO. 11. 11. 1 *Th.* 4. 13, 14. 1 *Co.* 15. 16-18, 20. *Jos.* 4. 1, 3, 7.—*Ac.* 2. 32. —*Ac.* 10. 41.

Come, ye blessed of my Father, inherit the kingdom prepared for you from the foundation of the world.

Fear not, little flock; for it is your Father's good pleasure to give you the kingdom.—Hath not God chosen the poor of this world rich in faith, and heirs of the kingdom which he hath promised to them that love him?—Heirs of God, and joint-heirs with Christ; if so be that we suffer with him, that we may be also glorified together.

The Father himself loveth you, because ye have loved me.—God is not ashamed to be called their God: for he hath prepared for them a city.

He that overcometh shall inherit all things; and I will be his God, and he shall be my son.—There is laid up for me a crown of righteousness, which the Lord, the righteous judge, shall give me at that day: and not to me only, but unto all them also that love his appearing.—He which hath begun a good work in you will perform it until the day of Jesus Christ.

MAT. 25. 34. *Lu.* 12. 32.—*Ja.* 2. 5.—*Ro.* 8. 17. *Jno.* 16. 27.—*He.* 11. 16.
　　　Re. 21. 7.—2 *Ti.* 4. 8.—*Phi.* 1. 6.

Riches are not for ever; and doth the crown endure to every generation?

Surely every man walketh in a vain shew: surely they are disquieted in vain: he heapeth up riches, and knoweth not who shall gather them.—Set your affection on things above, not on things on the earth.—Lay not up for yourselves treasures upon earth, where moth and rust doth corrupt, and where thieves break through and steal: but lay up for yourselves treasures in heaven. For where your treasure is, there will your heart be also.

They do it to obtain a corruptible crown, but we an incorruptible.—We look not at the things which are seen but at the things which are not seen.—To him that soweth righteousness shall be a sure reward.—There is laid up for me a crown of righteousness, which the Lord, the righteous judge, shall give me at that day: and not to me only, but unto all them also that love his appearing.—A crown of glory that fadeth not away.

PRO. 27. 24. *Ps.* 39. 6.—*Col.* 3. 2.—*Mat.* 6. 19-21. 1 *Co.* 9. 25.—
　　　2 *Co.* 4. 18.—*Pr.* 11. 18.—2 *Ti.* 4. 8.—1 *Pe.* 5. 4.

Isaac went out to meditate in the field at the eventide.

Let the words of my mouth, and the meditation of my heart, be acceptable in thy sight, O LORD, my strength, and my redeemer.

When I consider thy heavens, the work of thy fingers, the moon and the stars, which thou hast ordained ; what is man, that thou art mindful of him? and the son of man, that thou visitest him?—The works of the LORD are great, sought out of all them that have pleasure therein.

Blessed is the man that walketh not in the counsel of the ungodly, nor standeth in the way of sinners, nor sitteth in the seat of the scornful. But his delight is in the law of the LORD; and in his law doth he meditate day and night.—This book of the law shall not depart out of thy mouth; but thou shalt meditate therein day and night.—My soul shall be satisfied as with marrow and fatness; and my mouth shall praise thee with joyful lips: when I remember thee upon my bed, and meditate on thee in the night watches.

GEN. 24. 63. *Ps.* 19. 14. *Ps.* 8. 3, 4.—*Ps.* 111. 2. *Ps.* 1. 1, 2.—*Jos.* 1. 8.— *Ps.* 63. 5, 6.

How long wilt thou forget me, O Lord ! for ever ? how long wilt thou hide thy face from me ?

Every good gift, and every perfect gift is from above, and cometh down from the Father of lights, with whom is no variableness, neither shadow of turning.—But Zion said, The LORD hath forsaken me, and my Lord hath forgotten me. Can a woman forget her suckling child, that she should not have compassion on the son of her womb? yea, they may forget, yet will I not forget thee.

Thou shalt not be forgotten of me. I have blotted out, as a thick cloud, thy transgressions, and, as a cloud, thy sins.

Jesus loved Martha, and her sister, and Lazarus. When he had heard therefore that he was sick, he abode two days still in the same place where he was.—A woman . . . cried unto him, saying, Have mercy on me, O Lord, thou son of David! But he answered her not a word.

The trial of your faith, being much more precious than of gold that perisheth.

PSA. 13. 1. *Ja.* 1. 17.—*Is.* 49. 14, 15. *Is.* 44. 21, 22. *Jno.* 11. 5, 6.— *Mat.* 15. 22, 23. 1 *Pe.* 1. 7.

My God shall supply all your need according to his riches in glory by Christ Jesus.

Seek ye first the kingdom of God, and his righteousness; and all . . . things shall be added unto you.—He that spared not his own Son, but delivered him up for us all, how shall he not with him also freely give us all things?—All things are your's: whether Paul, or Apollos, or Cephas, or the world, or life, or death, or things present, or things to come: all are your's: and ye are Christ's; and Christ is God's.—As having nothing, and yet possessing all things.

The LORD is my shepherd; I shall not want.—The LORD GOD is a sun and shield: the LORD will give grace and glory: no good thing will be withheld from them that walk uprightly.—The living God, . . . giveth us richly all things to enjoy.—God is able to make all grace abound toward you; that ye, always having all sufficiency in all things, may abound to every good work.

PHIL. 4. 19. *Mat.* 6. 33.—*Ro.* 8. 32.—1 *Co.* 3. 21-23.—2 *Co.* 6. 10. *Ps.* 23. 1.—*Ps.* 84. 11.—1 *Ti.* 6. 17.—2 *Co.* 9. 8.

What communion hath light with darkness?

Men loved darkness rather than light, because their deeds were evil.—Ye are all the children of light, and the children of the day: we are not of the night, nor of darkness.

Darkness hath blinded his eyes.—Thy word is a lamp unto my feet, and a light unto my path.

The dark places of the earth are full of the habitations of cruelty.—Love is of God; and every one that loveth is born of God, and knoweth God. He that loveth not knoweth not God; for God is love.

The way of the wicked is as darkness: they know not at what they stumble. The path of the just is as the shining light, that shineth more and more unto the perfect day.

I am come a light into the world, that whosoever believeth on me should not abide in darkness . . .

Ye were sometime darkness, but now are ye light in the Lord: walk as children of light.

2 *COR.* 6. 14. *Jno.* 3. 19.—1 *Th.* 5. 5. 1 *Jno.* 2. 11.—*Ps.* 119. 105. *Ps.* 74. 20.—1 *Jno.* 4. 7, 8. *Pr.* 4. 19, 18. *Jno.* 12. 46.—*Ep.* 5. 8.

The fruit of the Spirit is joy.

Joy in the Holy Ghost.—Unspeakable and full of glory.

Sorrowful, yet alway rejoicing ; . . . exceeding joyful in all our tribulation.—We glory in tribulations.

Jesus the author and finisher of our faith ; . . . for the joy that was set before him, endured the cross, despising the shame.—These things have I spoken unto you, that my joy might remain in you, and that your joy might be full.—As the sufferings of Christ abound in us, so our consolation also aboundeth by Christ.

Rejoice in the Lord alway: and again I say, Rejoice.—The joy of the LORD is your strength.

In thy presence is fulness of joy: at thy right hand there are pleasures for evermore.—For the Lamb which is in the midst of the throne shall feed them, and shall lead them unto living fountains of waters: and God shall wipe away all tears from their eyes.

GAL. 5. 22. *Ro.* 14. 17.—1 *Pe.* 1. 8. 2 *Co.* 6. 10; 7, 4.—*Ro.* 5. 3. *He.* 12. 2. *Jno.* 15. 11.—2 *Co.* 1. 5. *Phi.* 4. 4. *Ne.* 8. 10. *Ps.* 16. 11.—*Re.* 7. 17.

Jehovah-shalom: (The Lord send peace.)

Behold, a son shall be born to thee, who shall be a man of rest; and I will give him rest from all his enemies round about: for his name shall be Solomon, and I will give peace and quietness unto Israel in his days.

Behold, a greater than Solomon is here.—Unto us a child is born, unto us a son is given; and the government shall be upon his shoulder, and his name shall be called Wonderful, Counsellor, the mighty God, the everlasting Father, the Prince of Peace.—My people shall dwell in a peaceable habitation, and in sure dwellings, and in quiet resting places; when it shall hail, coming down on the forest ; and the city shall be low in a low place.

He is our peace.—This man shall be the peace when the Assyrian shall come into our land.

These shall make war with the Lamb, and the Lamb shall overcome them: for he is Lord of lords, and King of kings.

Peace I leave with you, my peace I give unto you.

JUDGES 6. 24. 1 *Ch.* 22. 9. *Mat.* 12. 42.—*Is.* 9. 6.—*Is.* 32. 18, 19. *Ep.* 2. 14.—*Mi.* 5. 5. *Re.* 17. 14. *Jno.* 14. 27.

If ye do return unto the Lord with all your hearts, then put away the strange gods and Ashtaroth from among you, and prepare your hearts unto the Lord, and serve him only.

Little children, keep yourselves from idols.—Come out from among them, and be ye separate, saith the Lord, and touch not the unclean thing; and I will receive you, and will be a Father unto you, and ye shall be my sons and daughters, saith the Lord Almighty.—Ye cannot serve God and Mammon.

Thou shalt worship no other god: for the LORD, whose name is Jealous, is a jealous God.—Serve him with a perfect heart and with a willing mind: for the LORD searcheth all hearts, and understandeth all the imaginations of the thoughts.

Behold, thou desireth truth in the inward parts: and in the hidden part thou shalt make me to know wisdom.—Man looketh on the outward appearance, but the LORD looketh on the heart.—Beloved, if our heart condemn us not, then have we confidence toward God.

1 *SAM.* 7. 3. 1 *Jno.* 5. 21.—2 *Co.* 6. 17, 18.—*Mat.* 6. 24. *Ex.* 34. 14.—
1 *Ch.* 28. 9. *Ps.* 51. 6.—1 *Sa.* 16. 7.—1 *Jno.* 3. 21.

When the Son of man cometh, shall he find faith on the earth?

He came unto his own, and his own received him not.—The Spirit speaketh expressly, that in the latter times some shall depart from the faith.

Preach the word; be instant in season, out of season; reprove, rebuke, exhort with all longsuffering and doctrine. For the time will come when they will not endure sound doctrine; but after their own lusts shall they heap to themselves teachers, having itching ears; and they shall turn away their ears from the truth, and shall be turned unto fables.

Of that day and that hour knoweth no man, no, not the angels which are in heaven, neither the Son, but the Father. Take ye heed, watch and pray: for ye know not when the time is.—Blessed are those servants, whom the lord when he cometh shall find watching.—Looking for that blessed hope, . . . the glorious appearing of the great God, and our Saviour Jesus Christ.

LUKE 18. 8. *Jno.* 1. 11.—1 *Ti.* 4. 1. 2 *Ti.* 4. 2-4. *Mar.* 13. 32, 33.—
Lu. 12. 37.—*Tit.* 2. 13.

Beloved, be not ignorant of this one thing, that one day is with the Lord as a thousand years, and a thousand years as one day. The Lord is not slack concerning his promise, as some men count slackness.

My thoughts are not your thoughts, neither are your ways my ways, saith the LORD. For as the heavens are higher than the earth, so are my ways higher than your ways, and my thoughts than your thoughts. For as the rain cometh down, and the snow from heaven, and returneth not thither, but watereth the earth, . . . so shall my word be that goeth forth out of my mouth: it shall not return unto me void, but it shall acomplish that which I please, and it shall prosper in the thing whereto I sent it.

God hath concluded them all in unbelief, that he might have mercy upon all. O the depth of the riches both of the wisdom and knowledge of God! how unsearchable are his judgments, and his ways past finding out!

2 *PET.* 3. 8, 9. *Is.* 55. 8-11. *Ro.* 11. 32, 33.

Ye were as a firebrand plucked out of the burning.

The sinners in Zion are afraid; fearfulness hath surprised the hypocrites. Who among us shall dwell with the devouring fire? who among us shall dwell with everlasting burnings?—We had the sentence of death in ourselves, that we should not trust in ourselves, but in God which raiseth the dead: who delivered us from so great a death, and doth deliver: in whom we trust that he will yet deliver us.—The wages of sin is death; but the gift of God is eternal life through Jesus Christ our Lord.

It is a fearful thing to fall into the hands of the living God.— Knowing therefore the terror of the Lord, we persuade men.

Be instant in season, out of season.—Others save with fear, pulling them out of the fire.

Not by might, nor by power, but by my Spirit, saith the LORD of hosts.—Who will have all men to be saved, and to come unto the knowledge of the truth.

AMOS 4. 11. *Is.* 33. 14.—2 *Co.* 1. 9, 10.—*Ro.* 6. 23. *He.* 10. 31.— 2 *Co.* 5. 11. 2 *Ti.* 4. 2.—*Jude* 23. *Zec.* 4. 6.—1 *Ti.* 2. 4.

Fear not; I am the first and the last.

Ye are not come unto the mount that might be touched, and that burned with fire, nor unto blackness, and darkness, and tempest, ... but ye are come unto mount Sion, ... to God the Judge of all, and to the spirits of just men made perfect, and to Jesus the mediator of the new covenant.—Jesus the author and finisher of our faith.—We have not a high priest which cannot be touched with the feeling of our infirmities; but was in all points tempted like as we are, yet without sin. Let us therefore come boldly unto the throne of grace, that we may obtain mercy, and find grace to help in time of need.

Thus saith the LORD the King of Israel, and his redeemer the LORD of hosts; I am the first, and I am the last; and beside me there is no God.—The mighty God, The everlasting Father, The Prince of Peace.

Art thou not from everlasting, O LORD my God, mine Holy One?—Who is God, save the LORD? and who is a rock, save our God?

REV. 1. 17. *He.* 12. 18, 22-24.—*He.* 12. 2.—*He.* 4. 15, 16. *Is.* 44. 6.—
Is. 9. 6. *Ha.* 1. 12.—2 *Sa.* 22. 32.

Lead me to the rock that is higher than I.

Be careful for nothing; but in every thing by prayer and supplication with thanksgiving let your requests be made known unto God. And the peace of God, which passeth all understanding, shall keep your hearts and minds through Christ Jesus.

When my spirit was overwhelmed within me, then thou knewest my path.—He knoweth the way that I take: when he hath tried me, I shall come forth as gold.—LORD, thou hast been our dwelling place in all generations.—Thou hast been a strength to the poor, a strength to the needy in his distress, a refuge from the storm, a shadow from the heat.

Who is a rock save our God?—They shall never perish, neither shall any man pluck them out of my hand.—Uphold me according unto thy word, that I may live: and let me not be ashamed of my hope.—Which hope we have as an anchor of the soul, both sure and stedfast, and which entereth into that within the veil.

PSA. 61. 2. *Phi.* 4. 6, 7. *Ps.* 142. 3.—*Job* 23. 10.—*Ps.* 90. 1.—*Is.* 25. 4.
Ps. 18. 31.—*Jno.* 10. 28.—*Ps.* 119. 116.—*He.* 6. 19.

I will not let thee go, except thou bless me.

Let him take hold of my strength, that he may make peace with me; and he shall make peace with me.

O woman, great is thy faith; be it unto thee even as thou wilt.—According to your faith be it unto you.—Let him ask in faith, nothing wavering. For he that wavereth is like a wave of the sea driven with the wind and tossed. For let not that man think that he shall receive any thing of the Lord.

They drew nigh unto the village, whither they went: and [Jesus] made as though he would have gone further. But they constrained him, saying, Abide with us: . . . he vanished out of their sight. And they said one to another, Did not our heart burn within us, while he talked with us by the way, and while he opened to us the scriptures?—I pray thee, if I have found grace in thy sight, shew me now thy way, that I may know thee, that I may find grace in thy sight.—My presence shall go with thee, and I will give thee rest.

GEN. 32. 26. *Is.* 27. 5. *Mat.* 15. 28.—*Mat.* 9. 29.—*Ja.* **1. 6, 7.**
Luke 24. 28, 29, 31, 32.—*Ex.* 33. 13, 14.

Jesus the author and finisher of our faith.

I am Alpha and Omega, the beginning and the ending, saith the Lord, which is, and which was, and which is to come, the Almighty.—Who hath wrought and done it, calling the generations from the beginning? I the LORD, the first, and with the last: I am he.

Sanctified by God the Father, and preserved in Jesus Christ. The very God of peace sanctify you wholly: and I pray God your whole spirit and soul and body be preserved blameless unto the coming of our Lord Jesus Christ. Faithful is he that calleth you, who also will do it.—He which hath begun a good work in you will perform it until the day of Jesus Christ.—Are ye so foolish? having begun in the Spirit, are ye now made perfect by the flesh? —The LORD will perfect that which concerneth me.

It is God which worketh in you both to will and to do of his good pleasure.

HEB. 12. 2. *Re.* **1.** 8.—*Is.* 41. 4 *Jude* 1. 1 *Th.* 5. 23, 24.—*Phi.* **1.** 6.—
Ga. 3. 3.—*Ps.* 138. 8. *Phi.* 2. 13.

He ever liveth to make intercession.

Who is he that condemneth? It is Christ that died . . . who also maketh intercession for us.—Christ is not entered into the holy places made with hands, which are the figures of the true; but into heaven itself, now to appear in the presence of God for us.

If any man sin, we have an advocate with the Father, Jesus Christ the righteous.—There is one God, and one mediator between God and men, the man Christ Jesus.

Seeing . . . that we have a great high priest, that is passed into the heavens, Jesus the Son of God, let us hold fast our profession. For we have not an high priest which cannot be touched with the feeling of our infirmities; but was in all points tempted like as we are, yet without sin. Let us therefore come boldly unto the throne of grace, that we may obtain mercy, and find grace to help in time of need.—Through him we . . . have access by one Spirit unto the Father.

HEB. 7. 25. *Ro.* 8. 34.—*He* 9. 24. 1 *Jno.* 2. 1.—1 *Ti.* 2. 5.
He. 4. 14-16.—*Ep.* 2. 18.

They that know thy name will put their trust in thee.

This is his name whereby he shall be called, THE LORD OUR RIGHTEOUSNESS.—I will go in the strength of the Lord God: I will make mention of thy righteousness, even of thine only.

His name shall be called Wonderful, Counsellor.—O LORD, I know that the way of man is not in himself: it is not in man that walketh to direct his steps.

The mighty God, The everlasting Father.— I know whom I have believed, and am persuaded that he is able to keep that which I have committed unto him against that day.

The Prince of Peace.—He is our peace.—Being justified by faith, we have peace with God through our Lord Jesus Christ.

The name of the LORD is a strong tower: the righteous runneth into it, and is safe.—Woe to them that go down to Egypt for help.—As birds flying, so will the LORD of hosts defend Jerusalem; defending also he will deliver it; and passing over he will preserve it.

PSA. 9. 10. *Je.* 23. 6.—*Ps.* 71. 16. *Is.* 9. 6.—*Je.* 10. 23. *Is.* 9. 6.—2 *Ti.* 1. 12.
Isa. 9. 6.—*Ep.* 2. 14.—*Ro.* 5. 1. *Pr.* 18. 10.—*Is.* 31. 1.—*Is.* 31. 5.

As sorrowful, yet always rejoicing; as poor, yet making many rich; as having nothing, and yet possessing all things.

We . . . rejoice in hope of the glory of God. And not only so, but we glory in tribulations also.—I am filled with comfort, I am exceeding joyful in all our tribulation.—Believing, ye rejoice with joy unspeakable and full of glory.

In a great trial of affliction the abundance of their joy and their deep poverty abounded unto the riches of their liberality.—Unto me, who am less than the least of all saints, is this grace given, that I should preach among the Gentiles the unsearchable riches of Christ; and to make all men see what is the fellowship of the mystery, which from the beginning of the world hath been hid in God, who created all things by Jesus Christ.

Hath not God chosen the poor of this world rich in faith, and heirs of the kingdom which he hath promised to them that love him?—God is able to make all grace abound toward you; that ye, always having all sufficiency in all things, may abound to every good work.

2 COR. 6. 10. *Ro.* 5. 2, 3.—2 *Co.* 7. 4.—1 *Pe.* 1. 8. 2 *Co.* 8. 2.—
Ep. 3. 8, 9. *Ja.* 2. 5.—2 *Co.* 9. 8.

The Lord strengthen him upon the bed of languishing: thou wilt make all his bed in his sickness.

In all their affliction he was afflicted, and the angel of his presence saved them: in his love and in his pity he redeemed them; and he bare them, and carried them.—He whom thou lovest is sick.—My grace is sufficient for thee: for my strength is made perfect in weakness.

Most gladly therefore will I rather glory in my infirmities, that the power of Christ may rest upon me.—I can do all things through Christ which strengtheneth me.

We faint not; . . . though our outward man perish, yet the inward man is renewed day by day.

In him we live, and move, and have our being.—He giveth power to the faint; and to them that have no might he increaseth strength. Even the youths shall faint and be weary, and the young men shall utterly fall: but they that wait upon the LORD shall renew their strength.—The eternal God is thy refuge, and underneath are the everlasting arms.

PSA. 41. 3. *Is.* 63. 9.—*Jno.* 11. 3.—2 *Co.* 12. 9.—*Phi.* 4. 13. 2 *Co.* 4. 16.
Ac. 17. 28.—*Is.* 40. 29-31.—*De.* 33. 27.

In everything ye are enriched by him.

When we were yet without strength, in due time Christ died for the ungodly.—He that spared not his own Son, but delivered him up for us all, how shall he not with him also freely give us all things?

In him dwelleth all the fulness of the Godhead bodily. And ye are complete in him, which is the head of all principality and power.

Abide in me, and I in you. As the branch cannot bear fruit of itself, except it abide in the vine; no more can ye, except ye abide in me. I am the vine, ye are the branches: he that abideth in me, and I in him, the same bringeth forth much fruit: for without me ye can do nothing.—To will is present with me; but how to perform that which is good I find not.—Unto every one of us is given grace according to the measure of the gift of Christ.

If ye abide in me, and my words abide in you, ye shall ask what ye will, and it shall be done unto you.—Let the word of Christ dwell in you richly in all wisdom.

1 COR. 1. 5. Ro. 5. 6.—Ro. 8. 32. Col. 2. 9, 10. Jno. 15. 4, 5.—Ro. 7. 18.— Ep. 4. 7. Jno. 15. 7.—Col. 3. 16.

They shall see his face.

I beseech thee shew me thy glory. And he said, Thou canst not see my face: for there shall no man see me, and live.—No man hath seen God at any time; the only begotten Son, which is in the bosom of the Father, he hath declared him.

Every eye shall see him, and they also which pierced him: and all kindreds of the earth shall wail because of him.—I shall see him, but not now: I shall behold him, but not nigh.

I know that my Redeemer liveth, and that he shall stand at the latter day upon the earth: and though after my skin worms destroy this body, yet in my flesh shall I see God.—I will behold thy face in righteousness: I shall be satisfied, when I awake, with thy likeness.—We shall be like him; for we shall see him as he is.— The Lord himself shall descend from heaven . . . the dead in Christ shall rise first: then we which are alive and remain shall be caught up together with them in the clouds, to meet the Lord in the air: and so shall we ever be with the Lord.

REV. 22. 4. Ex. 33. 18, 20.—Jno. 1. 18. Re. 1. 7.—Nu. 24. 17. Job 19. 25, 26.—Ps. 17. 15.—1 Jno. 3. 2.—1 Th. 4. 16, 17.

Fear not; for I have redeemed thee.

Fear not; for thou shalt not be ashamed: neither be thou confounded; for thou shalt not be put to shame: for thou shalt forget the shame of thy youth, and shalt not remember the reproach of thy widowhood any more.—For thy Maker is thine husband; the LORD of hosts is his name; and thy Redeemer the Holy One of Israel.—I have blotted out, as a thick cloud, thy transgressions, and, as a cloud, thy sins: return unto me; for I have redeemed thee.—With the precious blood of Christ, as of a lamb without blemish and without spot.

Their Redeemer is strong; the LORD of hosts is his name: he shall throughly plead their cause.—My Father, which gave them me, is greater than all; and no man is able to pluck them out of my Father's hand.

Grace be to you and peace from God the Father, and from our Lord Jesus Christ, who gave himself for our sins, that he might deliver us from this present evil world, according to the will of God and our Father: to whom be glory for ever and ever. Amen.

*ISA. 43. 1. Is. 54. 4, 5.—Is. 44. 22.—1 Pe. 1. 19. Je. 50. 34.—Jno. 10. 29.
Gal. 1. 3-5.*

I will mention the lovingkindnesses of the Lord, and the praises of the Lord, according to all that the Lord hath bestowed on us.

He brought me up . . . out of an horrible pit, out of the miry clay, and set my feet upon a rock, and established my goings.—The Son of God . . . loved me, and gave himself for me.—He that spared not his own Son, but delivered him up for us all, how shall he not with him also freely give us all things?—God commendeth his love toward us, in that, while we were yet sinners, Christ died for us.

Who hath also sealed us, and given the earnest of the Spirit in our hearts.—Which is the earnest of our inheritance until the redemption of the purchased possession, unto the praise of his glory.

God, who is rich in mercy, for his great love wherewith he loved us, even when we were dead in sins, hath quickened us together with Christ, (by grace ye are saved;) and hath raised us up together, and made us sit together in heavenly places in Christ Jesus.

*ISA. 63. 7. Ps. 40. 2.—Ga. 2. 20.—Ro. 8. 32.—Ro. 5. 8. 2 Co. 1. 22.—
Ep. 1. 14. Ep. 2. 4-6.*

I am black, but comely.

Behold, I was shapen in iniquity; and in sin did my mother conceive me.—Thy renown went forth among the heathen for thy beauty: for it was perfect through my comeliness, which I had put upon thee, saith the Lord God.

I am a sinful man, O Lord.—Behold, thou art fair, my love; behold, thou art fair.

I abhor myself, and repent in dust and ashes.—Thou art all fair, my love; there is no spot in thee.

When I would do good, evil is present with me.—Be of good cheer; thy sins be forgiven thee.

I know that in me (that is, in my flesh,) dwelleth no good thing.—Ye are complete in him.—Perfect in Christ Jesus.

Ye are washed, . . . ye are sanctified, . . . ye are justified in the name of the Lord Jesus, and by the Spirit of our God.—That ye should shew forth the praises of him who hath called you out of darkness into his marvellous light.

CANT. 1. 5. *Ps.* 51. 5.—*Eze.* 16. 14. *Lu.* 5. 8.—*Ca.* 4. 1. *Job* 42. 6.—
Ca. 4. 7. *Ro.* 7. 21.—*Mat.* 9. 2. *Ro.* 7. 18.—*Col.* 2. 10; 1. 28.
1 *Co.* 6. 11.—1 *Pe.* 2. 9.

All that will live godly in Christ Jesus shall suffer persecution.

I am come to set a man at variance against his father, and the daughter against her mother and the daughter-in-law against her mother-in-law. And a man's foes shall be they of his own household.—Whosoever . . . will be a friend of the world is the enemy of God.—Love not the world, neither the things that are in the world. If any man love the world the love of the Father is not in him. For all that is in the world, the lust of the flesh, and the lust of the eyes, and the pride of life, is not of the Father, but is of the world.

If the world hate you, ye know that it hated me before it hated you. If ye were of the world, the world would love his own: but because ye are not of the world, but I have chosen you out of the world, therefore the world hateth you. The servant is not greater than his lord.—I have given them thy word; and the world hath hated them, because they are not of the world, even as I am not of the world.

2 *TIM.* 3. 12. *Mat.* 10. 35, 36.—*Ja.* 4. 4.—1 *Jno.* 2. 15, 16. *Jno.* 15. 18-20.—
Jno. 17. 14.

In the multitude of words there wanteth not sin: but he that refraineth his lips is wise.

My beloved brethren, let every man be swift to hear, slow to speak, slow to wrath.—He that is slow to anger is better than the mighty: and he that ruleth his spirit than he that taketh a city.— If any man offend not in word, the same is a perfect man, and able also to bridle the whole body.—By thy words thou shalt be justified, and by thy words thou shalt be condemned.—Set a watch, O LORD, before my mouth; keep the door of my lips.

Christ . . . suffered for us, leaving us an example, that ye should follow his steps: who did no sin, neither was guile found in his mouth: who when he was reviled, reviled not again; when he suffered, he threatened not; but committed himself to him that judgeth righteously.—Consider him that endured such contradiction of sinners against himself, lest ye be wearied and faint in your minds.

In their mouth was found no guile: for they are without fault before the throne of God.

PROV. 10. 19. *Ja.* 1. 19.—*Pr.* 16. 32.—*Ja.* 3. 2.—*Mat.* 12. 37.—*Ps.* 141. 3.
1 Pe. 2. 21-23.—*He.* 12. 3. *Re.* 14. 5.

Teach me thy way, O Lord.

I will instruct thee and teach thee in the way which thou shalt go: I will guide thee with mine eye.—Good and upright is the LORD: therefore will he teach sinners in the way. The meek will he guide in judgment: and the meek will he teach his way.

I am the door: by me if any man enter in, he shall be saved, and shall go in and out, and find pasture.

Jesus saith unto him, I am the way, the truth, and the life: no man cometh unto the Father, but by me.—Having . . . boldness to enter into the holiest by the blood of Jesus, by a new and living way, which he hath consecrated for us, through the veil, that is to say, his flesh; and having an high priest over the house of God; let us draw near with a true heart in full assurance of faith.

Then shall we know, if we follow on to know the LORD.—All the paths of the LORD are mercy and truth unto such as keep his covenant and his testimonies.

PSA. 27. 11. *Ps.* 32. 8. *Ps.* 25. 8, 9. *Jno.* 10. 9. *Jno.* 14. 6.—*He.* 10. 19-22.
Ho. 6. 3.—*Ps.* 25. 10.

What the law could not do, in that it was weak through the flesh,
God sending his own Son in the likeness of sinful flesh, and for
sin, condemned sin in the flesh.

The law having a shadow of good things to come, and not the
very image of the things, can never with those sacrifices which they
offered year by year continually make the comers thereunto perfect.
For then would they not have ceased to be offered?—By him all
that believe are justified from all things, from which ye could not
be justified by the law of Moses.

Forasmuch . . . as the children are partakers of flesh and blood,
he also himself likewise took part of the same; that through death
he might destroy him that had the power of death, that is the devil;
and deliver them who through fear of death were all their lifetime
subject to bondage. For verily he took not on him the nature of
angels; but he took on him the seed of Abraham. Wherefore in
all things it behoved him to be made like unto his brethren.

ROM. 8. 3. *He.* 10. 1, 2.—*Ac.* 13. 39. *He.* 2. 14-17.

All have sinned, and come short of the glory of God.

There is none righteous, no, not one: there is none that doeth
good, no, not one.—There is not a just man upon earth, that doeth
good, and sinneth not.—How can he be clean that is born of a
woman?

Let us therefore fear, lest a promise being left us of entering
into his rest, any of you should seem to come short of it.

I acknowledge my transgressions: and my sin is ever before me.
Behold, I was shapen in iniquity; and in sin did my mother conceive me.

The LORD . . . hath put away thy sin; thou shalt not die.—
Whom he justified, them he also glorified.—We all, with open face
beholding as in a glass the glory of the Lord, are changed into the
same image from glory to glory, even as by the Spirit of the Lord.
—If ye continue in the faith grounded and settled, and be not
moved away from the hope of the gospel.

Walk worthy of God, who hath called you unto his kingdom
and glory.

ROM. 3. 23. *Ro.* 3. 10, 12.—*Ec.* 7. 20.—*Job* 25. 4. *He.* 4. 1. *Ps.* 51. 3, 5.
2 *Sa.* 12. 13.—*Ro.* 8. 30.—2 *Co.* 3. 18.—*Col.* 1. 23. 1 *Th.* 2. 12.

Honour the Lord with thy substance, and with the firstfruits of all thine increase.

He which soweth sparingly shall reap also sparingly; and he which soweth bountifully shall reap also bountifully.—Upon the first day of the week let every one of you lay by him in store, as God hath prospered him.

God is not unrighteous to forget your work and labour of love, which ye have shewed toward his name, in that ye have ministered to the saints and do minister.

I beseech you, . . . brethren, by the mercies of God, that ye present your bodies a living sacrifice, holy, acceptable unto God, which is your reasonable service.—The love of Christ constraineth us; because we thus judge, that if one died for all, then were all dead: and that he died for all, that they which live should not henceforth live unto themselves, but unto him which died for them, and rose again.—Whether therefore ye eat, or drink, or whatsoever ye do, do all to the glory of God.

PROV. 3. 9. *2 Co.* 9. 6.—1 *Co.* 16. 2. *He.* 6. 10. *Ro.* 12. 1.—2 *Co.* 5. 14, 15. —1 *Co.* 10. 31.

There shall be no night there.

The LORD shall be unto thee an everlasting light, and thy God thy glory.

The city had no need of the sun, neither of the moon, to shine in it: for the glory of God did lighten it, and the Lamb is the light thereof.—They need no candle, neither light of the sun; for the Lord God giveth them light.

Ye are a chosen generation, a royal priesthood, an holy nation, a peculiar people; that ye should shew forth the praises of him who hath called you out of darkness into his marvellous light.—Giving thanks unto the Father, which hath made us meet to be partakers of the inheritance of the saints in light: who hath delivered us from the power of darkness, and hath translated us into the kingdom of his dear Son.—Ye were sometime darkness, but now are ye light in the Lord: walk as children of light.

We are not of the night, nor of darkness.

The path of the just is as the shining light, that shineth more and more unto the perfect day.

REV. 21. 25. *Is.* 60. 19. *Re.* 21. 24.—*Re.* 22. 5. 1 *Pe.* 2. 9.—*Col.* 1. 12, 13. —*Ep.* 5. 8. 1 *Th.* 5. 5. *Pr.* 4. 18.

My soul shall be satisfied as with marrow and fatness; and my mouth shall praise thee with joyful lips: when I remember thee upon my bed, and meditate on thee in the night watches.

How precious . . . are thy thoughts unto me, O God! how great is the sum of them! If I should count them, they are more in number than the sand: when I awake, I am still with thee.—How sweet are thy words unto my taste! yea, sweeter than honey to my mouth!—Thy love is better than wine.

Whom have I in heaven but thee? and there is none upon earth that I desire beside thee.—Thou art fairer than the children of men.

As the apple tree among the trees of the wood, so is my beloved among the sons. I sat down under his shadow with great delight, and his fruit was sweet to my taste. He brought me to the banqueting house, and his banner over me was love.—His countenance is as Lebanon, excellent as the cedars. His mouth is most sweet: yea, he is altogether lovely. This is my beloved, and this is my friend.

PSA. 63. 5, 6. *Ps.* 139. 17, 18.—*Ps.* 119. 103.—*Ca.* 1. 2. *Ps.* 73. 25.— *Ps.* 45. 2. *Ca.* 2. 3, 4.—*Ca.* 5. 15, 16.

Restore unto me the joy of thy salvation.

I have seen his ways, and will heal him: I will lead him also, and restore comforts unto him and to his mourners.

Come now, and let us reason together, saith the LORD: though your sins be as scarlet, they shall be as white as snow; though they be red like crimson, they shall be as wool.—Return, ye backsliding children, and I will heal your backslidings. Behold, we come unto thee; for thou art the LORD our God.—I will hear what God the LORD will speak: for he will speak peace unto his people, and to his saints: but let them not turn again to folly.

Bless the LORD, O my soul, and forget not all his benefits: who forgiveth all thine iniquities; who healeth all thy diseases.—He restoreth my soul.—O LORD, I will praise thee: though thou wast angry with me, thine anger is turned away, and thou comfortedst me.

Hold thou me up, and I shall be safe.

I, even I, am he that blotteth out thy transgressions for mine own sake, and will not remember thy sins.

PSA. 51. 12. *Is.* 57. 18. *Is.* 1. 18.—*Je.* 3. 22.—*Ps.* 85. 8. *Ps.* 103. 2, 3.— *Ps.* 23. 3.—*Is.* 12. 1. *Ps.* 119. 117. *Is.* 43. 25.

Their Redeemer is strong.

I know your manifold transgressions and your mighty sins.—I have laid help upon one that is mighty.—The LORD . . . thy Saviour and thy Redeemer, the mighty one of Jacob. Mighty to save.—Able to keep you from falling.—Where sin abounded, grace did much more abound.

He that believeth on him is not condemned: but he that believeth not is condemned already, because he hath not believed in the name of the only begotten Son of God.—He is able . . . to save them to the uttermost that come unto God by him.

Is my hand shortened at all, that it cannot redeem?

Who shall separate us from the love of Christ? . . . I am persuaded, that neither death, nor life, nor angels, nor principalities, nor powers, nor things present, nor things to come, nor height, nor depth, nor any other creature, shall be able to separate us from the love of God, which is in Christ Jesus our Lord.

JER. 50. 34. *Amos* 5. 12.—*Ps.* 89. 19.—*Is.* 49. 26. *Is.* 63. 1.—*Jude* 24.—
Ro. 5. 20. *Jno.* 3. 18.—*He.* 7. 25. *Is.* 50. 2. *Ro.* 8, 35, 38, 39.

Seekest thou great things for thyself? seek them not.

Take my yoke upon you, and learn of me; for I am meek and lowly in heart: and ye shall find rest unto your souls.—Let this mind be in you, which was also in Christ Jesus; who, being in the form of God, thought it not robbery to be equal with God: but made himself of no reputation, and took upon him the form of a servant, and was made in the likeness of men: and being found in fashion as a man, he humbled himself, and became obedient unto death, even the death of the cross.

He that taketh not his cross, and followeth after me, is not worthy of me.—Christ . . . suffered for us, leaving us an example, that ye should follow his steps.

Godliness with contentment is great gain. For we brought nothing into this world, and it is certain we can carry nothing out. And having food and raiment let us be therewith content.

I have learned, in whatsoever state I am, therewith to be content.

JER. 45. 5. *Mat.* 11. 29.—*Phi.* 2. 5-8. *Mat.* 10. 38.—*1 Pe.* 2. 21.
1 Ti. 6. 6-8. *Phi.* 4. 11.

I said in my haste, I am cut off from before thine eyes: nevertheless thou heardest the voice of my supplications when I cried unto thee.

I sink in deep mire, where there is no standing: I am come into deep waters, where the floods overflow me.—Waters flowed over mine head; then I said, I am cut off. I called upon thy name, O LORD, out of the low dungeon. Thou hast heard my voice: hide not thine ear at my breathing, at my cry. Thou drewest near in the day that I called upon thee: thou saidst, Fear not.

Will the LORD cast off for ever? and will he be favourable no more? Is his mercy clean gone for ever? doth his promise fail for evermore? Hath God forgotten to be gracious? hath he in anger shut up his tender mercies? And I said, This is my infirmity: but I will remember the years of the right hand of the most High. I will remember the works of the LORD: surely I will remember thy wonders of old—I had fainted, unless I had believed to see the goodness of the LORD in the land of the living.

PSA. 31. 32. *Ps.* 69. 2.—*La.* 3. 54-57. *Ps.* 77. 7-11. *Ps.* 27. 13.

He shall call upon me, and I will answer him: I will be with him in trouble, I will deliver him.

And Jabez called on the God of Israel, saying, Oh that thou wouldest bless me indeed, and enlarge my coast, and that thine hand might be with me, and that thou wouldest keep me from evil, that it may not grieve me! And God granted him that which he requested.—Ask what I shall give thee. And Solomon said unto God, . . . Give me now wisdom and knowledge, that I may go out and come in before this people.—And God gave Solomon wisdom and understanding exceeding much, and largeness of heart, even as the sand that is on the sea shore.

Asa cried unto the LORD his God, and said, LORD, it is nothing with thee to help, whether with many, or with them that have no power. . . . O LORD, thou art our God; let not man prevail against thee. So the LORD smote the Ethiopians before Asa.

O thou that hearest prayer, unto thee shall all flesh come.

PSA. 91. 15. 1 *Ch.* 4. 10.—2 *Ch.* 1. 7, 8, 10.—1 *Ki.* 4. 29. 2 *Ch.* 14. 11, 12.
—*Ps.* 65. 2.

Whoso offereth praise glorifieth me.

Let the word of Christ dwell in you richly in all wisdom; teaching and admonishing one another in psalms and hymns and spiritual songs, singing with grace in your hearts to the Lord. And whatsoever ye do in word or deed, do all in the name of the Lord Jesus, giving thanks to God and the Father by him.—Glorify God in your body, and in your spirit, which are God's.

Ye are a royal priesthood, . . . that ye should shew forth the praises of him who hath called you out of darkness into his marvellous light.—Ye . . . as lively stones, are built up a spiritual house, a holy priesthood, to offer up spiritual sacrifices, acceptable to God by Jesus Christ.—By him . . . let us offer the sacrifice of praise to God continually, that is, the fruit of our lips, giving thanks to his name.

My soul shall make her boast in the LORD: the humble shall hear thereof, and be glad. O magnify the LORD with me, and let us exalt his name together.

PSA. 50. 23. *Col.* 3. 16, 17.—1 *Co.* 6. 20. 1 *Pe.* 2. 9.—1 *Pe.* 2. 5.—
He. 13. 15. *Ps.* 34. 2, 3.

Draw me, we will run after thee.

I have loved thee with an everlasting love: therefore with lovingkindness have I drawn thee.—I drew them with cords of a man, with bands of love.—I, if I be lifted up from the earth, will draw all men unto me.—Behold the Lamb of God !—As Moses lifted up the serpent in the wilderness, even so must the Son of man be lifted up: that whosoever believeth in him should not perish, but have eternal life.

Whom have I in heaven but thee? and there is none upon earth that I desire beside thee.—We love him, because he first loved us.

My beloved spake, and said unto me, Rise up, my love, my fair one, and come away. For, lo, the winter is past, the rain is over and gone; the flowers appear on the earth; the time of the singing of birds is come, and the voice of the turtle is heard in our land; the fig tree putteth forth her green figs, and the vines with the tender grape give a good smell. Arise, my love, my fair one, and come away.

CANT. 1. 4. *Je.* 31. 3.—*Ho.* 11. 4.—*Jno.* 12. 32.—*Jno.* 1. 36.—
Jno. 3. 14, 15. *Ps.* 73. 25.—1 *Jno.* 4. 19. *Ca.* 2. 10-13.

I will raise them up a Prophet from among their brethren, like unto thee.

[Moses] stood between the LORD and you at that time, to shew you the word of the LORD: for ye were afraid.—There is one God, and one mediator between God and men, the man Christ Jesus.

Now the man Moses was very meek, above all the men which were upon the face of the earth.—Take my yoke upon you, and learn of me; for I am meek and lowly in heart: and ye shall find rest unto your souls.—Let this mind be in you, which was also in Christ Jesus: who, being in the form of God, thought it not robbery to be equal with God: but made himself of no reputation, and took upon him the form of a servant, and was made in the likeness of men.

Moses verily was faithful in all his house, as a servant, for a testimony of those things which were to be spoken after; but Christ as a son over his own house; whose house are we, if we hold fast the confidence and the rejoicing of the hope firm unto the end.

DEUT. 18. 18. *De.* 5. 5.—1 *Ti.* 2. 5. *Nu.* 12. 3.—*Mat.* 11. 29.—*Phi.* 2. 5-7. *He.* 3. 5, 6.

Everlasting consolation.

I will remember my covenant with thee in the days of thy youth, and I will establish unto thee an everlasting covenant.

By one offering he hath perfected for ever them that are sanctified.—He is able to save them to the uttermost that come unto God by him, seeing he ever liveth to make intercession for them.—I know whom I have believed, and am persuaded that he is able to keep that which I have committed unto him against that day.

The gifts and calling of God are without repentance.—Who shall separate us from the love of Christ?—The Lamb which is in the midst of the throne shall feed them, and shall lead them unto living fountains of waters: and God shall wipe away all tears from their eyes.—So shall we ever be with the Lord. Wherefore comfort one another with these words.

This is not your rest.—Here have we no continuing city, but we seek one to come.

2 *THES.* 2. 16. *Eze.* 16. 60. *He.* 10. 14.—*He.* 7. 25.—2 *Ti.* 1. 12. *Ro.* 11. 29.—*Ro.* 8. 35.—*Re.* 7. 17.—1 *Th.* 4. 17. 18. *Mi.* 2. 10.— *He.* 13. 14.

Verily, verily, I say unto you, I am the door of the sheep.

The veil of the temple was rent in twain from the top to the bottom.—Christ . . . hath once suffered for sins, the just for the unjust, that he might bring us to God.—The way into the holiest of all was not yet made manifest, while as the first tabernacle was yet standing.

I am the door: by me if any man enter in, he shall be saved, and shall go in and out, and find pasture.

No man cometh unto the Father, but by me.—Through him we . . . have access by one Spirit unto the Father. Now therefore ye are no more strangers and foreigners, but fellowcitizens with the saints, and of the household of God.—Having . . . boldness to enter into the holiest by the blood of Jesus, by a new and living way, which he hath consecrated for us, through the veil, that is to say, his flesh.—We have peace with God through our Lord Jesus Christ: by whom also we have access by faith into this grace wherein we stand, and rejoice in hope of the glory of God.

JNO. 10. 7. *Mat.* 27. 51.—1 *Pe.* 3. 18.—*He.* 9. 8. *Jno.* 10. 9. *Jno.* 14. 6.—
Ep. 2. 18, 19.—*He.* 10. 19, 20.—*Ro.* 5. 1, 2.

His word was in mine heart as a burning fire shut up in my bones, and I was weary with forbearing, and I could not stay.

Necessity is laid upon me; yea woe is unto me, if I preach not the gospel! What is my reward then? Verily that, when I preach the gospel, I may make the gospel of Christ without charge, that I abuse not my power in the gospel.—They called them, and commanded them not to speak at all nor teach in the name of Jesus. But Peter and John answered and said unto them, . . . We cannot but speak the things which we have seen and heard.—The love of Christ constraineth us.

I was afraid, and went and hid thy talent in the earth. . . . Thou wicked and slothful servant, . . . thou oughtest . . . to have put my money to the exchangers, and then at my coming I should have received mine own with usury.

Go . . . to thy friends, and tell them how great things the Lord hath done for thee.

JER. 20. 9. 1 *Co.* 9. 16, 18.—*Ac.* 4. 18-20.—2 *Co.* 5. 14. *Mat.* 25. 25-27.
Mar. 5. 19.

There shall cleave nought of the cursed thing to thine hand.

Come out from among them, and be ye separate, saith the Lord, and touch not the unclean thing.—Dearly beloved, I beseech you as strangers and pilgrims, abstain from fleshly lusts, which war against the soul.—Hating even the garment spotted by the flesh.

Beloved, now are we the sons of God, and it doth not yet appear what we shall be: but we know that, when he shall appear, we shall be like him; for we shall see him as he is. And every man that hath this hope in him purifieth himself, even as he is pure.—The grace of God that bringeth salvation hath appeared to all men, teaching us that, denying ungodliness and worldly lusts, we should live soberly, righteously, and godly, in this present world; looking for that blessed hope, and the glorious appearing of the great God and our Saviour Jesus Christ: who gave himself for us, that he might redeem us from all iniquity, and purify unto himself a peculiar people, zealous of good works.

DEUT. 13. 17. 2 *Co.* 6. 17.—*1 Pe.* 2. 11.—*Jude* 23. 1 *Jno.* 3. 2, 3.—
Tit. 2. 11-14.

Who art thou, Lord? I am Jesus.

It is I; be not afraid.—When thou passest through the waters, I will be with thee; and through the rivers, they shall not overflow thee: when thou walkest through the fire, thou shalt not be burned; neither shall the flame kindle upon thee. For I am the LORD thy God, . . . thy Saviour.

Though I walk through the valley of the shadow of death, I will fear no evil: for thou art with me; thy rod and thy staff they comfort me.—Emmanuel, God with us.

Thou shalt call his name JESUS: for he shall save his people from their sins.—If any man sin, we have an advocate with the Father, Jesus Christ the righteous.—Who is he that condemneth? It is Christ that died, yea rather, that is risen again, who is even at the right hand of God, who also maketh intercession for us. Who shall separate us from the love of Christ? shall tribulation, or distress, or persecution, or famine, or nakedness, or peril, or sword?

ACTS 26. 15. *Mat.* 14. 27.—*Is.* 43. 2, 3. *Ps.* 23. 4.—*Mat.* 1. 23. *Mat.* 1. 21.
—1 *Jno.* 2. 1.—*Ro.* 8. 34, 35.

Stand fast in the Lord.

My foot hath held his steps, his way have I kept, and not declined.

The LORD loveth judgment, and forsaketh not his saints; they are preserved for ever.—The LORD shall preserve thee from all evil: he shall preserve thy soul.

The just shall live by faith: but if any man draw back, my soul shall have no pleasure in him. But we are not of them who draw back into perdition; but of them that believe to the saving of the soul.—If they had been of us, they would no doubt have continued with us: but they went out, that they might be made manifest that they were not all of us.

If ye continue in my word then are ye my disciples indeed.— He that shall endure unto the end, the same shall be saved.— Watch ye, stand fast in the faith, quit you like men, be strong.— Hold that fast which thou hast, that no man take thy crown.—He that overcometh, the same shall be clothed in white raiment; and I will not blot out his name out of the book of life.

PHIL. 4. 1. *Job* 23. 11. *Ps.* 37. 28.—*Ps.* 121. 7. *He.* 10. 38, 39.—1 *Jno.* 2. 19. *Jno.* 8. 31.—*Mat.* 24. 13.—1 *Co.* 16. 13.—*Re.* 3. 11.—*Re.* 3. 5.

Enoch walked with God.

Can two walk together, except they be agreed?

Having made peace through the blood of his cross. . . . You, that were sometimes alienated and enemies in your mind by wicked works, yet now hath he reconciled in the body of his flesh through death, to present you holy and unblameable and unreproveable in his sight.—In Christ Jesus ye who sometimes were far off are made nigh by the blood of Christ.

If, when we were enemies, we were reconciled to God by the death of his Son, much more, being reconciled, we shall be saved by his life. And not only so, but we also joy in God through our Lord Jesus Christ.

Our fellowship is with the Father, and with his Son Jesus Christ.

The grace of the Lord Jesus Christ, and the love of God, and the communion of the Holy Ghost, be with you all. Amen.

GEN. 5. 22. *Am.* 3. 3. *Col.* 1. 20-22.—*Ep.* 2. 13. *Ro.* 5. 10, 11. 1 *Jno.* 1. 3. 2 *Co.* 13. 14.

If his offering be a burnt sacrifice of the herd, let him offer a male without blemish: he shall offer it of his own voluntary will. And he shall put his hand upon the head of the burnt offering; and it shall be accepted for him to make atonement for him.

God will provide himself a lamb for a burnt offering.—Behold the Lamb of God, which taketh away the sin of the world.—We are sanctified through the offering of the body of Jesus Christ once for all.—A ransom for many.

No man taketh it from me, but I lay it down of myself. I have power to lay it down, and I have power to take it again.—I will love them freely.—The Son of God . . . loved me and gave himself for me.

He hath made him to be sin for us, who knew no sin; that we might be made the righteousness of God in him.—He hath made us accepted in the beloved.

LEV. 1. 3, 4. *Ge.* 22. 8.—*Jno.* 1. 29.—*He.* 10. 10.—*Mat.* 20. 28. *Jno.* 10. 18.
—*Ho.* 14. 4.—*Gal.* 2. 20. 2 *Co.* 5. 21.—*Ep.* 1. 6.

Great is thy mercy toward me: and thou hast delivered my soul from the lowest hell.

Fear him which is able to destroy both soul and body in hell.

Fear not: for I have redeemed thee, I have called thee by thy name; thou art mine. I, even I, am the LORD; and beside me there is no saviour. I, even I, am he that blotteth out thy transgressions for mine own sake, and will not remember thy sins.— They that trust in their wealth, and boast themselves in the multitude of their riches; none of them can by any means redeem his brother, nor give to God a ransom for him: for the redemption of their soul is precious.—I have found a ransom.—God, who is rich in mercy, for his great love wherewith he loved us, even when we were dead in sins, hath quickened us together with Christ.

Neither is there salvation in any other: for there is none other name under heaven given among men, whereby we must be saved.

PSA. 86. 13. *Mat.* 10. 28. *Is.* 43. 1, 11, 25.—*Ps.* 49. 6-8. *Job* 33. 24.—
Ep. 2. 4, 5. *Ac.* 4. 12.

The Lord was my stay.

Truly in vain is salvation hoped for from the hills, and from the multitude of mountains: truly in the LORD our God is the salvation of Israel.—The LORD is my rock, and my fortress, and my deliverer; my God, my strength, in whom I will trust; my buckler, and the horn of my salvation, and my high tower.—Cry out and shout, thou inhabitant of Zion; for great is the Holy One of Israel in the midst of thee.

The angel of the LORD encampeth round about them that fear him, and delivereth them. The righteous cry, and the LORD heareth, and delivereth them out of all their troubles.—The eternal God is thy refuge, and underneath are the everlasting arms.—So that we may boldly say, The Lord is my helper, and I will not fear what man shall do unto me.—For who is God save the LORD? or who is a rock save our God? It is God that girdeth me with strength, and maketh my way perfect.

By the grace of God I am what I am.

PSA. 18. 18. *Je.* 3. 23.—*Ps.* 18. 2.—*Is.* 12. 6.—*Ps.* 34. 7, 17. *De.* 33. 27.— *He.* 13. 6.—*Ps.* 18. 31, 32. 1 *Co.* 15. 10.

All we like sheep have gone astray.

If we say that we have no sin, we deceive ourselves, and the truth is not in us.—There is none righteous, no, not one: there is none that understandeth. They are all gone out of the way, they are together become unprofitable.

Ye were as sheep going astray; but are now returned unto the Shepherd and Bishop of your souls.—I have gone astray like a lost sheep; seek thy servant; for I do not forget thy commandments.

He restoreth my soul: he leadeth me in the paths of righteousness for his name's sake.

My sheep hear my voice, and I know them, and they follow me: and I give unto them eternal life; and they shall never perish, neither shall any man pluck them out of my hand.

What man of you, having an hundred sheep, if he lose one of them, doth not leave the ninety and nine in the wilderness, and go after that which is lost, until he find it?

ISA. 53. 6. 1 *Jno.* 1. 8.—*Ro.* 3. 10-12. 1 *Pe.* 2. 25.—*Ps.* 119. 176. *Ps.* 23. 3. *Jno.* 10. 27, 28. *Lu.* 15. 4.

The Lord visited Sarah as he had said, and the Lord did unto Sarah as he had spoken.

Trust in him at all times; ye people, pour out your heart before him: God is a refuge for us.—David encouraged himself in the Lord his God.—God will surely visit you, and bring you out of this land unto the land which he sware to Abraham, to Isaac, and to Jacob.—I have seen, I have seen the affliction of my people which is in Egypt, and I have heard their groaning, and am come down to deliver them. He brought them out, after that he had shewed wonders and signs in the land of Egypt, and in the Red sea, and in the wilderness forty years.—There failed not ought of any good thing which the Lord had spoken unto the house of Israel; all came to pass.

He is faithful that promised.—Hath he said, and shall he not do it? or hath he spoken, and shall he not make it good?— Heaven and earth shall pass away, but my words shall not pass away.—The grass withereth, the flower fadeth: but the word of our God shall stand for ever.

GEN. 21. 1. *Ps.* 62. 8.—1 *Sa.* 30. 6.—*Ge.* 50. 24.—*Ac.* 7. 34, 36.— *Jos.* 21. 45. *He.* 10. 23.—*Nu.* 23. 19.—*Mat.* 24. 35.—*Is.* 40. 8.

The eyes of all wait upon thee.

He giveth to all life, and breath, and all things.—The Lord is good to all: and his tender mercies are over all his works.—Behold the fowls of the air: for they sow not, neither do they reap, nor gather into barns; yet your heavenly Father feedeth them.

The same Lord over all is rich unto all that call upon him.

I will lift up mine eyes unto the hills, from whence cometh my help.—Behold, as the eyes of servants look unto the hand of their masters, and as the eyes of a maiden unto the hand of her mistress; so our eyes wait upon the Lord our God.

The Lord is a God of judgment: blessed are all they that wait for him.—And it shall be said in that day, Lo, this is our God; we have waited for him, and he will save us: this is the Lord; we have waited for him, we will be glad and rejoice in his salvation.—If we hope for that we see not, then do we with patience wait for it.

PSA. 145. 15. *Ac.* 17. 25.—*Ps.* 145. 9.—*Mat.* 6. 26. *Ro.* 10. 12. *Ps.* 121. 1. —*Ps.* 123. 2. *Is.* 30. 18.—*Is.* 25. 9.—*Ro.* 8. 25.

Thou shalt call his name JESUS: for he shall save his people from their sins.

Ye know that he was manifested to take away our sins.—That we, being dead to sins, should live unto righteousness.—He is able also to save them to the uttermost that come unto God by him.

He was wounded for our transgressions, he was bruised for our iniquities: the chastisement of our peace was upon him; and with his stripes we are healed. The LORD hath laid on him the iniquity of us all.—Thus it behoved Christ to suffer, . . . that repentance and remission of sins should be preached in his name among all nations.—He appeared to put away sin by the sacrifice of himself.

Him hath God exalted with his right hand to be a Prince and a Saviour, . . . to give repentance.—Through this man is preached unto you the forgiveness of sins: and by him all that believe are justified from all things, from which ye could not be justified by the law of Moses.—Your sins are forgiven you for his name's sake.

MAT. 1. 21. 1 *Jno.* 3. 5.—1 *Pe.* 2. 24.—*He.* 7. 25. *Is.* 53. 5, 6.— *Lu.* 24. 46, 47. *He.* 9. 26. *Ac.* 5. 31.—*Ac.* 13. 38, 39.—1 *Jno.* 2. 12.

Our Lord Jesus Christ, . . . though he was rich, yet for your sakes . . . became poor, that ye through his poverty might be rich.

It pleased the Father that in him should all fulness dwell.—The brightness of his glory, and the express image of his person, and upholding all things by the word of his power, when he had by himself purged our sins, sat down on the right hand of the Majesty on high; being made so much better than the angels, as he hath by inheritance obtained a more excellent name than they.—Who, being in the form of God, thought it not robbery to be equal with God: but made himself of no reputation.

The foxes have holes, and the birds of the air have nests; but the Son of man hath not where to lay his head.

All things are yours; whether Paul, or Apollos, or Cephas, or the world, or life, or death, or things present, or things to come; all are yours; and ye are Christ's; and Christ is God's.

2 *COR.* 8. 9. *Col.* 1. 19.—*He.* 1. 3, 4.—*Phi.* 2. 6, 7. *Mat.* 8. 20. 1 *Co.* 3. 21-23.

His left hand is under my head, and his right hand doth embrace me.

Underneath are the everlasting arms.—When [Peter] saw the wind boisterous, he was afraid; and beginning to sink, he cried, saying, Lord, save me. And immediately Jesus stretched forth his hand, and caught him, and said unto him, O thou of little faith, wherefore didst thou doubt?—The steps of a good man are ordered by the LORD: and he delighteth in his way. Though he fall, he shall not be utterly cast down: for the LORD upholdeth him with his hand.

The beloved of the LORD shall dwell in safety by him; and the LORD shall cover him all the day long, and he shall dwell between his shoulders.—Casting all your care upon Him, for he careth for you.—He that toucheth you, toucheth the apple of his eye.

They shall never perish, neither shall any man pluck them out of my hand. My Father, which gave them me, is greater than all.

CANT. 2. 6. *De.* 33. 27.—*Mat.* 14. 30. 31.—*Ps.* 37. 23, 24. *De.* 33. 12.— 1 *Pe.* 5. 7.—*Zec.* 2. 8. *Jno.* 10. 28, 29.

Who is she that looketh forth as the morning, fair as the moon, clear as the sun, and terrible as an army with banners?

The church of God, which he hath purchased with his own blood.

Christ loved the church, and gave himself for it; that he might sanctify and cleanse it with the washing of water by the word, that he might present it to himself a glorious church, not having spot, or wrinkle, or any such thing; but that it should be holy and without blemish.

There appeared a great wonder in heaven; a woman clothed with the sun.—The marriage of the Lamb is come, and his wife hath made herself ready. And to her was granted that she should be arrayed in fine linen, clean and white: for the fine linen is the righteousness of saints.—The righteousness of God which is by faith of Jesus Christ unto all and upon all them that believe.

The glory which thou gavest me I have given them.

CANT. 6. 10. *Ac.* 20. 28. *Ep.* 5. 25-27. *Re.* 12. 1.—*Re.* 19. 7, 8.— *Ro.* 3. 22. *Jno.* 17. 22.

Brethren, the time is short.

Man that is born of a woman is of few days, and full of trouble. He cometh forth like a flower, and is cut down: he fleeth also as a shadow, and continueth not.—The world passeth away, and the lust thereof: but he that doeth the will of God abideth for ever.—As in Adam all die, even so in Christ shall all be made alive. Death is swallowed up in victory.—Whether we live, we live unto the Lord; and whether we die, we die unto the Lord: whether we live therefore, or die, we are the Lord's.—To live is Christ, and to die is gain.

Cast not away . . . your confidence, which hath great recompence of reward. For ye have need of patience, that, after ye have done the will of God, ye might receive the promise. For yet a little while, and he that shall come will come, and will not tarry.— The night is far spent, the day is at hand: let us therefore cast off the works of darkness, and let us put on the armour of light.— The end of all things is at hand: be ye therefore sober, and watch unto prayer.

1 *COR.* 7. 29. *Job* 14. 1, 2.—1 *Jno.* 2. 17.—1 *Co.* 15. 22, 54.—*Ro.* 14. 8.— *Phi.* 1. 21. *He.* 10. 35-37. *Ro.* 13. 12.—1 *Pe.* 4. 7.

A new name.

The disciples were called Christians first in Antioch.—Let every one that nameth the name of Christ depart from iniquity.— They that are Christ's have crucified the flesh with the affections and lusts.—Ye are bought with a price: therefore glorify God in your body, and in your spirit, which are God's.

God forbid that I should glory, save in the cross of our Lord Jesus Christ, by whom the world is crucified unto me, and I unto the world. For in Christ Jesus neither circumcision availeth any thing, nor uncircumcision, but a new creature.

Be ye . . . followers of God, as dear children; and walk in love, as Christ also hath loved us, and hath given himself for us an offering and a sacrifice to God for a sweetsmelling savour. But fornication, and all uncleanness, or covetousness, let it not be once named among you, as becometh saints. Now are ye light in the Lord: walk as children of light.

REV. 2. 17. *Ac.* 11. 26.—2 *Ti.* 2. 19.—*Ga.* 5. 24. 1 *Co.* 6. 20. *Ga.* 6. 14, 15. *Ep.* 5. 1-3, 8.

Behold the Lamb of God.

It is not possible that the blood of bulls and of goats should take away sins. Wherefore when he cometh into the world, he saith, Sacrifice and offering thou wouldest not, but a body hast thou prepared me: in burnt offerings and sacrifices for sin thou hast had no pleasure. Then said I, Lo, I come (in the volume of the book it is written of me,) to do thy will, O God.—He was oppressed, and he was afflicted, yet he opened not his mouth: he is brought as a lamb to the slaughter, and as a sheep before her shearers is dumb, so he openeth not his mouth.

Ye were not redeemed with corruptible things, as silver and gold, . . . but with the precious blood of Christ, as of a lamb without blemish and without spot: . . . manifest in these last times for you who by him do believe in God . . . that your faith and hope might be in God.

Worthy is the Lamb that was slain to receive power, and riches, and wisdom, and strength, and honour, and glory, and blessing.

JOHN 1. 29. *He.* 10. 4-7.—*Is.* 53. 7. 1 *Pe.* 1. 18-21. *Re.* 5. 12.

I will hope continually, and will yet praise thee more and more.

Not as though I had already attained, either were already perfect.—Leaving the principles of the doctrine of Christ, let us go on unto perfection; not laying again the foundation of repentance from dead works, and of faith toward God.—The path of the just is as the shining light, that shineth more and more unto the perfect day.

I love the LORD, because he hath heard my voice and my supplications. Because he hath inclined his ear unto me, therefore will I call upon him as long as I live.—I will bless the LORD at all times: his praise shall continually be in my mouth.

Praise waiteth for thee, O God, in Sion.—They rest not day and night, saying, Holy, holy, holy, Lord God Almighty.—Whoso offereth praise glorifieth me.—Rejoice evermore. Pray without ceasing. In every thing give thanks: for this is the will of God in Christ Jesus concerning you.—Rejoice in the Lord, always; and again I say, Rejoice.

PSA. 71. 14. *Phi.* 3. 12.—*He.* 6. 1.—*Pr.* 4. 18. *Ps.* 116. 1, 2.—*Ps.* 34. 1. *Ps.* 65. 1.—*Re.* 4. 8.—*Ps.* 50. 23.—1 *Th.* 5. 16-18.—*Phi.* 4. 4.

Consider how great things He hath done for you.

Thou shalt remember all the way which the LORD thy God led thee these forty years in the wilderness, to humble thee, and to prove thee, to know what was in thine heart, whether thou wouldest keep his commandments, or no. Thou shalt also consider in thine heart, that, as a man chasteneth his son, so the LORD thy God chasteneth thee.

I know, O LORD, that thy judgments are right, and that thou in faithfulness hast afflicted me. It is good for me that I have been afflicted; that I might learn thy statutes. Before I was afflicted I went astray: but now have I kept thy word.—The LORD hath chastened me sore: but he hath not given me over unto death.— He hath not dealt with us after our sins, nor rewarded us according to our iniquities. For as the heaven is high above the earth, so great is his mercy toward them that fear him. He knoweth our frame; he remembereth that we are dust.

1 *SAM.* 12. 24. *De.* 8. 2, 5.—*Ps.* 119. 75, 71, 67. *Ps.* 118. 18.— *Ps.* 103. 10, 11, 14.

That blessed hope, . . . the glorious appearing of the great God and our Saviour Jesus Christ.

Which hope we have as an anchor of the soul, both sure and stedfast, and which entereth into that within the veil: whither the forerunner is for us entered, even Jesus.—Whom the heaven must receive until the times of restitution of all things.—When he shall come to be glorified in his saints, and to be admired in all them that believe.

The whole creation groaneth and travaileth in pain together until now. And not only they, but ourselves also, . . . groan within ourselves, waiting for the adoption, to wit, the redemption of our body.—Beloved, now are we the sons of God, and it doth not yet appear what we shall be: but we know that, when he shall appear, we shall be like him; for we shall see him as he is.—When Christ, who is our life, shall appear, then shall ye also appear with him in glory.

Surely I come quickly. Amen. Even so, come, Lord Jesus.

TIT. 2. 13.—*He.* 6. 19, 20.—*Ac.* 3. 21.—2 *Th.* 1. 10. *Ro.* 8. 22, 23.— 1 *Jno.* 3. 2.—*Col.* 3. 4. *Re.* 22. 20.

Whoso keepeth his word, in him verily is the love of God perfected.

The God of peace, that brought again from the dead our Lord Jesus, that great shepherd of the sheep, through the blood of the everlasting covenant, make you perfect in every good work to do his will, working in you that which is well pleasing in his sight, through Jesus Christ; to whom be glory for ever and ever. Amen.

Hereby we do know that we know him, if we keep his commandments.—If a man love me, he will keep my words: and my Father will love him, and we will come unto him, and make our abode with him.—Whosoever abideth in him sinneth not: whosoever sinneth hath not seen him, neither known him. Little children, let no man deceive you: he that doeth righteousness is righteous, even as he is righteous.—Herein is our love made perfect, that we may have boldness in the day of judgment: because as he is, so are we in this world.

1 *JOHN* 2. 5. *He.* 13. 20, 21. 1 *Jno.* 2. 3.—*Jno.* 14. 23.—1 *Jno.* 3. 6, 7.—
1 *Jno.* 4. 17.

He that is slow to wrath is of great understanding.

The LORD passed by before him, and proclaimed, The LORD, The LORD God, merciful and gracious, longsuffering.—The Lord is not slack concerning his promise, as some men count slackness; but is longsuffering to us-ward, not willing that any should perish, but that all should come to repentance.

Be ye . . . followers of God, as dear children; and walk in love. —The fruit of the Spirit is love, joy, peace, longsuffering, gentleness, goodness, faith, meekness, temperance: against such there is no law.—This is thankworthy, if a man for conscience toward God endure grief, suffering wrongfully. If, when ye do well, and suffer for it, ye take it patiently, this is acceptable with God. Christ . . . suffered for us, leaving us an example, that ye should follow his steps: who, when he was reviled, reviled not again; when he suffered, he threatened not; but committed himself to him that judgeth righteously.

Be ye angry, and sin not.

PRO. 14. 29. *Ex.* 34. 6.—*2 Pe.* 3. 9. *Ep.* 5. 1.—*Ga.* 5. 22, 23.—
1 *Pe.* 2. 19-21, 23. *Ep.* 4. 26.

The fruit of the Spirit is peace.

To be spiritually minded is life and peace.

God hath called us to peace.—Peace I leave with you, my peace I give unto you: not as the world giveth, give I unto you. Let not your heart be troubled, neither let it be afraid.—The God of hope fill you with all joy and peace in believing, that ye may abound in hope, through the power of the Holy Ghost.

I know whom I have believed, and am persuaded that he is able to keep that which I have committed unto him against that day.—Thou wilt keep him in perfect peace, whose mind is stayed on thee: because he trusteth in thee.

The work of righteousness shall be peace; and the effect of righteousness quietness and assurance for ever. And my people shall dwell in a peaceable habitation, and in sure dwellings, and in quiet resting places.—Whoso hearkeneth unto me shall dwell safely, and shall be quiet from fear of evil.

Great peace have they which love thy law.

GAL. 5. 22. *Ro.* 8. 6. 1 *Co.* 7. 15.—*Jno.* 14. 27.—*Ro.* 15. 13. 2 *Ti.* 1. 12.— *Is.* 26. 3. *Is.* 32. 17, 18.—*Pr.* 1. 33. *Ps.* 119. 165.

Jehovah-shammah (The Lord is there.)

Behold, the tabernacle of God is with men, and he will dwell with them, and they shall be his people, and God himself shall be with them, and be their God.

I saw no temple: . . . for the Lord God Almighty and the Lamb are the temple. The city had no need of the sun, neither of the moon, to shine in it: for the glory of God did lighten it, and the Lamb is the light thereof.

I shall be satisfied, when I awake, with thy likeness.—Whom have I in heaven but thee? and there is none upon earth that I desire beside thee.

Judah shall dwell for ever, and Jerusalem from generation to generation. For I will cleanse their blood that I have not cleansed: for the LORD dwelleth in Zion.—Sing and rejoice, O daughter of Zion; for, lo, I come, and I will dwell in the midst of thee, saith the LORD.—There shall be no more curse: but the throne of God and of the Lamb shall be in it; and his servants shall serve him.

EZE. 48. 35. *Re.* 21. 3. *Re.* 21. 22, 23. *Ps.* 17. 15.—*Ps.* 73. 25. *Joel* 3. 20, 21.—*Zec.* 2. 10.—*Re.* 22. 3.

Surely the Lord is in this place; and I knew it not.

Where two or three are gathered together in my name, there am I in the midst of them.—Lo, I am with you alway, even unto the end of the world.—My presence shall go with thee, and I will give thee rest.

Whither shall I go from thy spirit? or whither shall I flee from thy presence? If I ascend up into heaven, thou art there: if I make my bed in hell, behold, thou art there.—Am I a God at hand, saith the LORD, and not a God afar off? Can any hide himself in secret places that I shall not see him? saith the LORD. Do not I fill heaven and earth? saith the LORD.

Behold, the heaven and heaven of heavens cannot contain thee; how much less this house that I have builded?—Thus saith the high and lofty One that inhabiteth eternity, whose name is Holy: I dwell in the high and holy place, with him also that is of a contrite and humble spirit, to revive the spirit of the humble, and to revive the heart of the contrite ones.—Ye are the temple of the living God.

GEN. 28. 16. *Mat.* 18. 20.—*Mat.* 28. 20.—*Ex.* 33. 14. *Ps.* 139. 7, 8.—
Je. 23. 23, 24. 1 *Ki.* 8. 27.—*Is.* 57. 15.—2 *Co.* 6. 16.

Keep yourselves from idols.

My son, give me thine heart.—Set your affection on things above, not on things on the earth.

Son of man, these men have set up their idols in their heart, and put the stumblingblock of their iniquity before their face: should I be enquired of at all by them?—Mortify . . . your members which are upon the earth; fornication, uncleanness, inordinate affection, evil concupiscence, and covetousness, which is idolatry.—They that will be rich fall into temptation and a snare. For the love of money is the root of all evil: which while some coveted after, they have erred from the faith, and pierced themselves through with many sorrows. But thou, O man of God, flee these things.

If riches increase, set not your heart upon them.—My fruit is better than gold, yea, than fine gold; and my revenue than choice silver.

Where your treasure is, there will your heart be also.—The LORD looketh on the heart.

1 *JNO.* 5. 21. *Pr.* 23. 26.—*Col.* 3. 2. *Eze.* 14. 3.—*Col.* 3. 5.—1 *Ti.* 6. 9-11.
Ps. 62. 10.—*Pr.* 8. 19. *Mat.* 6. 21.—1 *Sa.* 16. 7.

Be ye perfect, even as your Father which is in heaven is perfect.

I am the Almighty God; walk before me, and be thou perfect. —Ye shall be holy unto me: for I the LORD am holy, and have severed you from other people, that ye should be mine.

Ye are bought with a price: therefore glorify God in your body, and in your spirit, which are God's.

Ye are complete in him, which is the head of all principality and power.—Who gave himself for us, that he might redeem us from all iniquity.—Be diligent that ye may be found of him in peace, without spot, and blameless.

Blessed are the undefiled in the way, who walk in the law of the LORD.—Whoso looketh into the perfect law of liberty, and continueth therein, he being not a forgetful hearer, but a doer of the work, this man shall be blessed in his deed.—Search me, O God, and know my heart: try me, and know my thoughts: and see if there be any wicked way in me, and lead me in the way everlasting.

MAT. 5. 48. *Ge.* 17. 1.—*Le.* 20. 26. 1 *Co.* 6. 20. *Col.* 2. 10.—*Tit.* 2. 14.— 2 *Pe.* 3. 14. *Ps.* 119. 1.—*Ja.* 1. 25.—*Ps.* 139. 23, 24.

Perfecting holiness in the fear of God.

Dearly beloved, let us cleanse ourselves from all filthiness of the flesh and spirit.

Behold, thou desirest truth in the inward parts: and in the hidden part thou shalt make me to know wisdom.—Teaching us that denying ungodliness and wordly lusts, we should live soberly, righteously, and godly, in this present world.—Let your light so shine before men, that they may see your good works, and glorify your Father which is in heaven.—Not as though I had already attained, either were already perfect.

Every man that hath this hope in him purifieth himself, even as he is pure.

Now he that hath wrought us for the selfsame thing is God, who also hath given unto us the earnest of the Spirit.—For the perfecting of the saints, for the work of the ministry, for the edifying of the body of Christ: till we all come in the unity of the faith, and of the knowledge of the Son of God, unto a perfect man, unto the measure of the stature of the fulness of Christ.

2 *COR.* 7. 1. 2 *Co.* 7. 1. *Ps.* 51. 6.—*Tit.* 2. 12.—*Mat.* 5. 16.—*Phi.* 3. 12. 1 *Jno.* 3. 3. 2 *Co.* 5. 5.—*Eph.* 4. 12, 13.

Behold, the Lord's hand is not shortened, that it cannot save; neither is his ear heavy, that it cannot hear.

In the day when I cried thou answeredst me, and strengthenedst me with strength in my soul.—While I was speaking in prayer, even the man Gabriel, whom I had seen in the vision at the beginning, being caused to fly swiftly, touched me about the time of the evening oblation.

Hide not thy face far from me; put not thy servant away in anger: thou hast been my help, leave me not, neither forsake me, O God of my salvation.—Be not thou far from me, O LORD: O my strength, haste thee to help me.

Ah Lord God! behold, thou hast made the heaven and the earth by thy great power and stretched out arm, and there is nothing too hard for thee.—Who delivered us from so great a death, and doth deliver: in whom we trust that he will yet deliver us.—Shall not God avenge his own elect, which cry day and night unto him, though he bear long with them? I tell you that he will avenge them speedily.

ISA. 59. 1. *Ps.* 138. 3.—*Da.* 9. 21. *Ps.* 27. 9.—*Ps.* 22. 19. *Je.* 32. 17.
2 *Co.* 1. 10.—*Lu.* 18. 7, 8.

I have glorified thee on the earth.

My meat is to do the will of him that sent me, and to finish his work.—I must work the works of him that sent me, while it is day: the night cometh, when no man can work.

Wist ye not that I must be about my Father's business? And they understood not the saying which he spake unto them.—This sickness is not unto death, but for the glory of God, that the Son of God might be glorified thereby. Said I not unto thee, that, if thou wouldest believe, thou shouldest see the glory of God?

Jesus increased in wisdom and stature, and in favour with God and man.—Thou art my beloved Son; in thee I am well pleased. —All bare him witness, and wondered at the gracious words which proceeded out of his mouth.

Thou art worthy . . . for thou wast slain, and hast redeemed us to God by thy blood, out of every kindred, and tongue, and people, and nation; and hast made us unto our God kings and priests: and we shall reign on the earth.

JOHN 17. 4. *Jno.* 4. 34.—*Jno.* 9. 4. *Lu.* 2. 49, 50.—*Jno.* 11. 4, 40.
Lu. 2. 52.—*Lu.* 3. 22.—*Lu.* 4. 22. *Rev.* 5. 9, 10.

Take no thought, saying, What shall we eat? or, What shall we drink? or, Wherewithal shall we be clothed? for your heavenly Father knoweth that ye have need of all these things.

O fear the LORD, ye his saints: for there is no want to them that fear him. The young lions do lack, and suffer hunger: but they that seek the LORD shall not want any good thing.—No good thing will he withhold from them that walk uprightly. O LORD of hosts, blessed is the man that trusteth in thee.

I would have you without carefulness.—Be careful for nothing; but in every thing by prayer and supplication with thanksgiving let your requests be made known unto God.

Are not two sparrows sold for a farthing? and one of them shall not fall on the ground without your Father. The very hairs of your head are all numbered. Fear ye not therefore, ye are of more value than many sparrows.—Why are ye so fearful? how is it that ye have no faith?—Have faith in God.

MAT. 6. 31, 32. *Ps.* 34. 9, 10.—*Ps.* 84. 11, 12.—1 *Co.* 7. 32.—*Phi.* 4. 6.
Mat. 10. 29-31.—*Mar.* 4. 40.—*Mar.* 11. 22.

He spread a cloud for a covering; and fire to give light in the night.

Like as a father pitieth his children, so the LORD pitieth them that fear him. For he knoweth our frame; he remembereth that we are dust.

The sun shall not smite thee by day, nor the moon by night.— There shall be a tabernacle for a shadow in the daytime from the heat, and for a place of refuge, and for a covert from storm and from rain.

The LORD is thy keeper: the LORD is thy shade upon thy right hand. The LORD shall preserve thy going out and thy coming in from this time forth, and even for evermore.—The LORD went before them by day in a pillar of a cloud, to lead them the way; and by night in a pillar of fire, to give them light; to go by day and night: he took not away the pillar of the cloud by day, nor the pillar of fire by night, from before the people.

Jesus Christ the same yesterday, and to day, and for ever.

PSA. 105. 39. *Ps.* 103. 13, 14. *Ps.* 121. 6.—*Is.* 4. 6. *Ps.* 121. 5, 8.—
Ex. 13. 21, 22. *He.* 13. 8.

Mercy and truth are met together; righteousness and peace have kissed each other.

A just God and a Saviour.

The LORD is well pleased for his righteousness' sake; he will magnify the law, and make it honourable.

God was in Christ, reconciling the world unto himself, not imputing their trespasses unto them.—Whom God hath set forth to be a propitiation through faith in his blood, to declare his righteousness for the remission of sins that are past, through the forbearance of God; to declare I say at this time his righteousness: that he might be just, and the justifier of him which believeth in Jesus.—He was wounded for our transgressions, he was bruised for our iniquities: the chastisement of our peace was upon him; and with his stripes we are healed.—Who shall lay any thing to the charge of God's elect? It is God that justifieth.—To him that worketh not, but believeth on him that justifieth the ungodly; his faith is counted for righteousness.

PSA. 85. 10. *Is.* 45. 21. *Is.* 42. 21. 2 *Co.* 5. 19.—*Ro.* 3. 25, 26.—*Is.* 53. 5.—
Ro. 8. 33.—*Ro.* 4. 5.

How are the dead raised up? and with what body do they come?

Beloved, now are we the Sons of God; . . . it doth not yet appear what we shall be: but we know that, when he shall appear, we shall be like him; for we shall see him as he is.—As we have borne the image of the earthy, we shall also bear the image of the heavenly.

The Saviour, the Lord Jesus Christ; . . . shall change our vile body, that it may be fashioned like unto his glorious body, according to the working whereby he is able even to subdue all things unto himself.

Jesus himself stood in the midst of them, and saith unto them, Peace be unto you. But they were terrified and affrighted, and supposed that they had seen a spirit.—He was seen of Cephas, then of the twelve : after that he was seen of above five hundred brethren at once.

If the Spirit of him that raised up Jesus from the dead dwell in you, he that raised up Christ from the dead shall also quicken your mortal bodies by his Spirit that dwelleth in you.

1 *COR.* 15. 35. 1 *Jno.* 3. 2.—1 *Co.* 15. 49. *Phi.* 3. 20, 21. *Lu.* 24. 36, 37.—
1 *Co.* 15. 5, 6.—*Ro.* 8. 11.

Ye shall hear of wars and rumours of wars: see that ye be not troubled.

God is our refuge and strength, a very present help in trouble. Therefore will not we fear, though the earth be removed, and though the mountains be carried into the midst of the sea; though the waters thereof roar and be troubled, though the mountains shake with the swelling thereof.—Come, my people, enter thou into thy chambers, and shut thy doors about thee: hide thyself as it were for a little moment, until the indignation be overpast. For, behold, the LORD cometh out of his place to punish the inhabitants of the earth for their iniquity.—In the shadow of thy wings will I make my refuge, until these calamities be overpast.— Your life is hid with Christ in God.

He shall not be afraid of evil tidings: his heart is fixed, trusting in the LORD.

These things I have spoken unto you, that in me ye might have peace. In the world ye shall have tribulation: but be of good cheer; I have overcome the world.

MAT. 24. 6. *Ps.* 46. 1-3.—*Is.* 26. 20, 21.—*Ps.* 57. 1.—*Col.* 3. 3. *Ps.* 112. 7.
Jno. 16. 33.

They persecute him whom thou hast smitten.

It is impossible but that offences will come: but woe unto him, through whom they come!—Him, being delivered by the determinate counsel and foreknowledge of God, ye have taken, and by wicked hands have crucified and slain.—They did spit in his face, and buffeted him; and others smote him with the palms of their hands, saying, Prophesy unto us, thou Christ, Who is he that smote thee?—Likewise also the chief priests mocking him, with the scribes and elders, said, He saved others; himself he cannot save. If he be the King of Israel, let him now come down from the cross.—Of a truth against thy holy child Jesus, whom thou hast anointed, both Herod, and Pontius Pilate, with the Gentiles, and the people of Israel, were gathered together, to do whatsoever thy hand and thy counsel determined before to be done.

Surely he hath borne our griefs, and carried our sorrows: yet we did esteem him stricken, smitten of God, and afflicted.

PSA. 69. 26. *Lu.* 17. 1.—*Ac.* 2. 23.—*Mat.* 26. 67, 68.—*Mat.* 27. 41, 42.
Ac. 4. 27, 28. *Is.* 53. 4.

It pleased the Lord to bruise him; he hath put him to grief.

Now is my soul troubled; and what shall I say? Father, save me from this hour: but for this cause came I unto this hour. Father, glorify thy name. Then came there a voice from heaven, saying, I have both glorified it, and will glorify it again.—Father, if thou be willing, remove this cup from me: nevertheless not my will, but thine, be done. And there appeared an angel unto him from heaven, strengthening him.

Being found in fashion as a man, he humbled himself, and became obedient unto death, even the death of the cross.—Therefore doth my Father love me, because I lay down my life, that I might take it again.—For I came down from heaven, not to do mine own will, but the will of him that sent me.—The cup which my Father hath given me, shall I not drink it?

The Father hath not left me alone; for I do always those things that please him—My beloved Son, in whom I am well pleased.—Mine elect, in whom my soul delighteth.

ISA. 53. 10. *Jno.* 12. 27, 28. *Lu.* 22. 42, 43. *Phi.* 2. 8.—*Jno.* 10. 17.—
Jno. 6. 38.—*Jno.* 18. 11. *Jno.* 8. 29.—*Mat.* 3. 17.—*Is.* 42. 1.

Ye that are the Lord's remembrancers, keep not silence.

Thou . . hast made us unto our God kings and priests.—The sons of Aaron, the priests, shall blow with the trumpets; and they shall be to you for an ordinance for ever throughout your generations. And if ye go to war in your land against the enemy that oppresseth you, then ye shall blow an alarm with the trumpets; and ye shall be remembered before the LORD your God, and ye shall be saved from your enemies.

I said not unto the seed of Jacob, Seek ye me in vain.—Their voice was heard, and their prayer came up to his holy dwelling place, even unto heaven.—The eyes of the LORD are upon the righteous, and his ears are open unto their cry.—Pray one for another: the effectual fervent prayer of a righteous man availeth much.

Come, Lord Jesus.—Make no tarrying, O my God.—Looking for and hasting unto the coming of the day of God.

ISA. 62. 6. *Re.* 5. 9, 10.—*Nu.* 10. 8, 9. *Is.* 45. 19.—2 *Ch.* 30. 27.—
Ps. 34. 15.—*Ja.* 5. 16. *Re.* 22. 20.—*Ps.* 40. 17.—2 *Pe.* 3. 12.

Faith is the substance of things hoped for, the evidence of things not seen.

If in this life only we have hope in Christ, we are of all men most miserable.

Eye hath not seen, nor ear heard, neither have entered into the heart of man, the things which God hath prepared for them that love him. But God hath revealed them unto us by his Spirit.— After that ye believed ye were sealed with that holy Spirit of promise, which is the earnest of our inheritance until the redemption of the purchased possession.

Jesus saith unto him, Thomas, because thou hast seen me, thou hast believed; blessed are they that have not seen, and yet have believed.—Whom having not seen, ye love; in whom, though now ye see him not, yet believing, ye rejoice with joy unspeakable and full of glory: receiving the end of your faith, even the salvation of your souls.

We walk by faith, not by sight.—Cast not away therefore your confidence, which hath great recompence of reward.

HEB. 11. 1. 1 *Co.* 15. 19. 1 *Co.* 2. 9, 10.—*Ep.* 1. 13, 14.—*Jno.* 20. 29.—
          1 *Pe.* 1. 8, 9. 2 *Co.* 5. 7.—*He.* 10. 35.

It is I; be not afraid.

When I saw him, I fell at his feet as dead. And he laid his right hand upon me, saying unto me, Fear not; I am the first and the last: I am he that liveth, and was dead; and, behold, I am alive for evermore, Amen; and have the keys of hell and of death.—I, even I, am he that blotteth out thy transgressions for mine own sake, and will not remember thy sins.

Woe is me! for I am undone; . . . mine eyes have seen the King, the LORD of hosts. Then flew one of the seraphims unto me, having a live coal in his hand, which he had taken with the tongs from off the altar: and he laid it upon my mouth, and said, Lo, this hath touched thy lips; and thine iniquity is taken away, and thy sin purged.—I have blotted out, as a thick cloud, thy transgressions, and, as a cloud, thy sins: return unto me; for I have redeemed thee.

If any man sin, we have an advocate with the Father, Jesus Christ the righteous.

JOHN 6. 20. *Re.* 1. 17, 18.—*Is.* 43. 25. *Is.* 6. 5-7.—*Is.* 44. 22. 1 *Jno.* 2. 1.

For this purpose the Son of God was manifested, that he might destroy the works of the devil.

We wrestle not against flesh and blood, but against principalities, against powers, against the rulers of the darkness of this world, against spiritual wickedness in high places.—Forasmuch . . . as the children are partakers of flesh and blood, he also himself likewise took part of the same; that through death he might destroy him that had the power of death, that is, the devil.—And having spoiled principalities and powers, he made a shew of them openly, triumphing over them.—I heard a loud voice saying in heaven, Now is come salvation, and strength, and the kingdom of our God, and the power of his Christ: for the accuser of our brethren is cast down, which accused them before our God day and night. And they overcame him by the blood of the Lamb, and by the word of their testimony; and they loved not their lives unto the death.

Thanks be to God, which giveth us the victory through our Lord Jesus Christ.

1 *JOHN* 3. 8. *Ep.* 6. 12.—*He.* 2. 14.—*Col.* 2. 15.—*Re.* 12. 10, 11.
1 *Co.* 15. 57.

MAY 10 EVENING

Vanity of vanities; all is vanity.

We spend our years as a tale that is told. The days of our years are threescore years and ten; and if by reason of strength they be fourscore years, yet is their strength labour and sorrow; for it is soon cut off, and we fly away.

If in this life only we have hope in Christ, we are of all men most miserable.—Here have we no continuing city, but we seek one to come.—I am the LORD, I change not.—Our conversation (citizenship) is in heaven; from whence also we look for the Saviour, the Lord Jesus Christ; who shall change our vile body, that it may be fashioned like unto his glorious body, according to the working whereby he is able even to subdue all things unto himself.—The creature was made subject to vanity, not willingly, but by reason of him who hath subjected the same in hope.

Jesus Christ the same yesterday, and to day, and for ever.— Holy, holy, holy, Lord God Almighty, which was, and is, and is to come.

ECCLES. 1. 2. *Ps.* 90. 9, 10. 1 *Co.* 15. 19.—*He.* 13. 14.—*Mal.* 3. 6.—
Phi. 3. 20, 21.—*Ro.* 8. 20. *He.* 13. 8.—*Re.* 4. 8.

Awake to righteousness, and sin not.

Ye are all the children of light, and the children of the day. Therefore let us not sleep, as do others; but let us watch and be sober.

It is high time to awake out of sleep: for now is our salvation nearer than when we believed. The night is far spent, the day is at hand: let us therefore cast off the works of darkness, and let us put on the armour of light.—Wherefore take unto you the whole armour of God, that ye may be able to withstand in the evil day, and having done all, to stand.—Cast away from you all your transgressions, whereby ye have transgressed: and make you a new heart and a new spirit.—Lay apart all filthiness and superfluity of naughtiness, and receive with meekness the engrafted word, which is able to save your souls.—Little children, abide in him; that, when he shall appear, we may have confidence, and not be ashamed before him at his coming. If ye know that he is righteous, ye know that every one that doeth righteousness is born of him.

1 *COR.* 15. 34. 1 *Th.* 5. 5, 6. *Ro.* 13. 11, 12.—*Ep.* 6. 13.—*Eze.* 18. 31.
Ja. 1. 21.—1 *Jno.* 2. 28, 29.

My sheep hear my voice.

Behold, I stand at the door, and knock: If any man hear my voice, and open the door, I will come in to him, and will sup with him, and he with me.

I sleep, but my heart waketh: it is the voice of my beloved that knocketh, saying, Open to me, my sister, my love, my dove, my undefiled. I opened to my beloved; but my beloved had withdrawn himself, and was gone: my soul failed when he spake: I sought him, but I could not find him; I called him, but he gave me no answer.

Speak; for thy servant heareth.—When Jesus came to the place, he looked up, and saw him, and said unto him, Zacchaeus, make haste and come down; for to day I must abide at thy house. And he made haste, and came down, and received him joyfully. —I will hear what God the LORD will speak: for he will speak peace unto his people, and to his saints: but let them not turn again to folly.

IOHN 10. 27. *Re.* 3. 20. *Ca.* 5. 2, 6. 1 *Sa.* 3. 10.—*Lu.* 19. 5, 6.—*Ps.* 85. 8.

Beloved, let us love one another: for love is of God; and every one that loveth is born of God, and knoweth God.

The love of God is shed abroad in our hearts by the Holy Ghost, which is given unto us.—Ye have not received the spirit of bondage again to fear; but ye have received the Spirit of adoption, whereby we cry, Abba, Father. The Spirit itself beareth witness with our spirit, that we are the children of God.—He that believeth on the Son of God hath the witness in himself.

In this was manifested the love of God toward us, because that God sent his only begotten Son into the world, that we might live through him.—In whom we have redemption through his blood, the forgiveness of sins, according to the riches of his grace.—That in the ages to come he might shew the exceeding riches of his grace in his kindness toward us through Christ Jesus.

Beloved, if God so loved us, we ought also to love one another.

1 *JOHN* 4. 7. *Ro.* 5. 5.—*Ro.* 8. 15, 16.—1 *Jno.* 5. 10. 1 *Jno.* 4. 9.—
Ep. 1. 7.—*Ep.* 2. 7. 1 *Jno.* 4. 11.

Reproach hath broken my heart.

Is not this the carpenter's son?—Can there any good thing come out of Nazareth?—Say we not well that thou are a Samaritan, and hast a devil?—He casteth out devils through the prince of the devils.—We know that this man is a sinner.—He deceiveth the people.—This man blasphemeth.—Behold a man gluttonous, and a winebibber, a friend of publicans and sinners.

It is enough for the disciple that he be as his master, and the servant as his lord.—This is thankworthy, if a man for conscience toward God endure grief, suffering wrongfully. For even hereunto were ye called: because Christ also suffered for us, leaving us an example, that we should follow his steps. Who did no sin, neither was guile found in his mouth: who when he was reviled, reviled not again; when he suffered, he threatened not; but committed himself to him that judgeth righteously.—If ye be reproached for the name of Christ, happy are ye.

PSA. 69. 20. *Mat.* 13. 55.—*Jno.* 1. 46.—*Jno.* 8. 48.—*Mat.* 9. 34.—*Jno.* 9. 24.
—*Jno.* 7. 12.—*Mat.* 9. 3.—*Mat.* 11. 19. *Mat.* 10. 25.—1 *Pe.* 2. 19-23.—
1 *Pe.* 4. 14.

Pray every where, lifting up holy hands, without wrath and doubting.

The true worshippers shall worship the Father in spirit and in truth: for the Father seeketh such to worship him. God is a Spirit: and they that worship him must worship him in spirit and in truth.—Then shalt thou call, and the LORD shall answer; thou shalt cry, and he shall say, Here I am.—When ye stand praying, forgive, if ye have ought against any.

Without faith it is impossible to please him: for he that cometh to God must believe that he is, and that he is a rewarder of them that diligently seek him.—Let him ask in faith, nothing wavering. For he that wavereth is like a wave of the sea, driven with the wind and tossed. For let not that man think that he shall receive anything of the LORD.

If I regard iniquity in my heart, the LORD will not hear me.— My little children, these things write I unto you, that ye sin not. And if any man sin, we have an advocate with the Father, Jesus Christ the righteous: and he is the propitiation for our sins.

1 *TIM.* 2. 8. *Jno.* 4. 23, 24.—*Is.* 58. 9.—*Mar.* 11. 25. *He.* 11. 6.—*Ja.* 1. 6, 7.
Ps. 66. 18.—1 *Jno.* 2. 1, 2.

My heart panteth, my strength faileth me.

Hear my cry, O God; attend unto my prayer. From the end of the earth will I cry unto thee, when my heart is overwhelmed: lead me to the rock that is higher than I.

He said unto me, My grace is sufficient for thee: for my strength is made perfect in weakness. Most gladly therefore will I rather glory in my infirmities, that the power of Christ may rest upon me. For when I am weak, then am I strong.

When (Peter) saw the wind boisterous, he was afraid; and beginning to sink, he cried, saying, Lord, save me. And immediately Jesus stretched forth his hand, and caught him, and said unto him, O thou of little faith, wherefore didst thou doubt?—If thou faint in the day of adversity, thy strength is small.—He giveth power to the faint; and to them that have no might he increaseth strength. —The eternal God is thy refuge, and underneath are the everlasting arms.—Strengthened with all might, according to his glorious power.

PSA. 38. 10. *Ps.* 61. 1, 2. 2 *Co.* 12. 9, 10. *Mat.* 14. 30, 31.—*Pr.* 24. 10.—
Is. 40. 29.—*De.* 33. 27.—*Col.* 1. 11.

The fellowship of His sufferings.

It is enough for the disciple that he be as his master, and the servant as his lord.

He is despised and rejected of men; a man of sorrows, and acquainted with grief; and we hid as it were our faces from him; he was despised, and we esteemed him not.—In the world ye shall have tribulation.—Because ye are not of the world, but I have chosen you out of the world, therefore the world hateth you.

I looked for some to take pity, but there was none.—At my first answer no man stood with me, but all men forsook me.

The foxes have holes, and the birds of the air have nests; but the Son of man hath not where to lay his head.—Here have we no continuing city, but we seek one to come.

Let us run with patience the race that is set before us, looking unto Jesus the author and finisher of our faith; who for the joy that was set before him endured the cross, despising the shame, and is set down at the right hand of the throne of God.

PHI. 3. 10. Mat. 10. 25. I.., 53. 3.—Jno. 16. 33.—Jno. 15. 19. Ps. 69. 20.—
2 Ti. 4. 16. Mat. 8. 20.—He. 13. 14. He. 12. 1, 2.

They overcame . . . by the blood of the Lamb.

Who shall lay anything to the charge of God's elect? It is God that justifieth. Who is he that condemneth? It is Christ that died. —It is the blood that maketh an atonement for the soul.—I am the LORD. The blood shall be to you for a token upon the houses where ye are: and when I see the blood, I will pass over you.

There is . . . no condemnation to them which are in Christ Jesus.

What are these which are arrayed in white robes? and whence came they? These are they which came out of great tribulation, and have washed their robes, and made them white in the blood of the Lamb.

Unto him that loved us, and washed us from our sins in his own blood, and hath made us kings and priests unto God and his Father; to him be glory and dominion for ever and ever. Amen.

REV. 12. 11. Ro. 8. 33, 34.—Le. 17. 11.—Ex. 12. 12, 13. Ro. 8. 1.
Re. 7. 13, 14. Re. 1. 5, 6.

God shall wipe away all tears: . . . there shall be no more death, neither sorrow, . . . for the former things are passed away.

He will swallow up death in victory; and the LORD GOD will wipe away tears from off all faces; and the rebuke of his people shall he take away from off all the earth: for the LORD hath spoken it.—Thy sun shall no more go down; neither shall thy moon withdraw itself: for the LORD shall be thine everlasting light, and the days of thy mourning shall be ended.—The inhabitant shall not say, I am sick: the people that dwell therein shall be forgiven their iniquity.—The voice of weeping shall be no more heard in her, nor the voice of crying.—Sorrow and sighing shall flee away.

I will ransom them from the power of the grave; I will redeem them from death: O death, I will be thy plagues; O grave, I will be thy destruction.—The last enemy that shall be destroyed is death. Then shall be brought to pass the saying that is written, Death is swallowed up in victory.

The things which are not seen are eternal.

REV. 21. 4. *Is.* 25. 8.—*Is.* 60. 20.—*Is.* 33. 24.—*Is.* 65. 19.—*Is.* 35. 10.
Ho. 13. 14.—1 *Co.* 15. 26, 54. 2 *Co.* 4. 18.

Raised up together in Christ Jesus.

Fear not; . . . I am he that liveth.—Father, I will that they also, whom thou hast given me, be with me where I am.

We are members of his body, of his flesh, and of his bones.—He is the head of the body, the church: who is the beginning, the firstborn from the dead.—Ye are complete in him, which is the head.

Forasmuch . . . as the children are partakers of flesh and blood, he also himself likewise took part of the same; that through death he might destroy him that had the power of death, that is, the devil: and deliver them who through fear of death were all their lifetime subject to bondage.

This corruptible must put on incorruption, and this mortal must put on immortality. So when this corruptible shall have put on incorruption, and this mortal shall have put on immortality, then shall be brought to pass the saying that is written, Death is swallowed up in victory.

EPH. 2. 6. *Re.* 1. 17, 18.—*Jno.* 17. 24. *Ep.* 5. 30.—*Col.* 1. 18.—*Col.* 2. 10.
He. 2. 14, 15. 1 *Co.* 15. 53, 54.

A servant of Jesus Christ.

Ye call me Master and Lord: and ye say well; for so I am.—
If any man serve me, let him follow me; and where I am, there
shall also my servant be: if any man serve me, him will my Father
honour.—Take my yoke upon you, and learn of me; for I am
meek and lowly in heart: and ye shall find rest unto your souls.
For my yoke is easy, and my burden is light.

What things were gain to me, those I counted loss for Christ.—
Being made free from sin, and become servants to God, ye have
your fruit unto holiness, and the end everlasting life.

Henceforth I call you not servants; for the servant knoweth not
what his lord doeth: but I have called you friends; for all things
that I have heard of my Father I have made known unto you.—
Thou art no more a servant, but a son.

Stand fast therefore in the liberty wherewith Christ hath made
us free, and be not entangled again with the yoke of bondage. For,
brethren, ye have been called unto liberty; only use not liberty
for an occasion to the flesh.

ROM. 1. 1. *Jno.* 13. 13.—*Jno.* 12. 26.—*Mat.* 11. 29, 30. *Phi.* 3. 7.—
Ro. 6. 22. *Jno.* 15. 15.—*Gal.* 4. 7. *Gal.* 5. 1, 13.

I will bless the Lord, who hath given me counsel.

His name shall be called Wonderful, Counsellor.—Counsel is
mine, and sound wisdom: I am understanding, I have strength.—
Thy word is a lamp unto my feet, and a light unto my path.—
Trust in the LORD with all thine heart; and lean not unto thine
own understanding. In all thy ways acknowledge him, and he
shall direct thy paths.

O LORD, I know that the way of man is not in himself: it is not
in man that walketh to direct his steps.—Thine ears shall hear a
word behind thee, saying, This is the way, walk ye in it, when ye
turn to the right hand, and when ye turn to the left.—Commit thy
works unto the LORD, and thy thoughts shall be established.—He
knoweth the way that I take.—Man's goings are of the LORD: how
can a man then understand his own way?

Thou shalt guide me with thy counsel, and afterward receive me
to glory.—This God is our God for ever and ever: he will be our
guide even unto death.

PSA. 16. 7. *Is.* 9. 6.—*Pr.* 8. 14.—*Ps.* 119. 105.—*Pr.* 3. 5, 6. *Je.* 10. 23.—
Is. 30. 21.—*Pr.* 16. 3.—*Job* 23. 10.—*Pr.* 20. 24. *Ps.* 73. 24.—*Ps.* 48. 14.

I am the Lord your God; walk in my statutes, and keep my judgments, and do them.

As he which hath called you is holy, so be ye holy in all manner of conversation.—He that saith he abideth in him ought himself also so to walk, even as he walked. If ye know that he is righteous, ye know that every one that doeth righteousness is born of him.—Circumcision is nothing, and uncircumcision is nothing, but the keeping of the commandments of God.—Whosoever shall keep the whole law, and yet offend in one point, he is guilty of all.

Not that we are sufficient of ourselves to think any thing, as of ourselves; but our sufficiency is of God.—Teach me, O LORD, the way of thy statutes.

Work out your own salvation with fear and trembling. For it is God which worketh in you both to will and to do of his good pleasure.—The God of peace, . . . make you perfect in every good work to do his will, working in you that which is well pleasing in his sight, through Jesus Christ.

EZE. 20. 19.   1 *Pe.* 1. 15.—1 *Jno.* 2. 6, 29.—1 *Co.* 7. 19.—*Ja.* 2. 10.
    2 *Co.* 3. 5.—*Ps.* 119. 33.   *Phi.* 2. 12, 13.—*He.* 13. 20, 21.

I have exalted one chosen out of the people.

Verily he took not on him the nature of angels; but he took on him the seed of Abraham. In all things it behoved him to be made like unto his brethren.—Upon the likeness of the throne was the likeness as the appearance of a man above upon it.—The Son of man . . . which is in heaven.—Behold my hands and my feet, that it is I myself: handle me, and see; for a spirit hath not flesh and bones, as ye see me have.

He made himself of no reputation, and took upon him the form of a servant, and was made in the likeness of men: and being found in fashion as a man, he humbled himself, and became obedient unto death, even the death of the cross. Wherefore God also hath highly exalted him, and given him a name which is above every name: that at the name of Jesus every knee should bow.—Be watchful, and strengthen the things which remain, that are ready to die: for I have not found thy works perfect before God.

PSA. 89. 19.   *He.* 2, 16, 17.—*Eze.* 1. 26.—*Jno.* 3. 13.—*Lu.* 24. 39.
        Phi. 2. 7-10.—*Re.* 3. 2.

As the Father hath life in himself; so hath he given to the Son to have life in himself.

Our Saviour Jesus Christ, . . . hath abolished death, and hath brought life and immortality to light through the gospel.—I am the resurrection, and the life.—Because I live, ye shall live also.— We are made partakers of Christ.—Partakers of the Holy Ghost.— Partakers of the divine nature.—The first man Adam was made a living soul; the last Adam was made a quickening spirit.—Behold, I shew you a mystery; We shall not all sleep, but we shall be changed, in a moment, in the twinkling of an eye, at the last trump: for the trumpet shall sound, and the dead shall be raised incorruptible, and we shall be changed.

Holy, holy, holy, Lord God Almighty, which was, and is, and is to come.—Who liveth for ever and ever.—The blessed and only Potentate, the King of kings, and Lord of lords; who only hath immortality.—Unto the King eternal, immortal, . . . be honour and glory for ever and ever. Amen.

JNO. 5. 26. 2 *Ti.* 1. 10.—*Jno.* 11. 25.—*Jno.* 14. 19.—*He.* 3. 14.— *He.* 6. 4.—2 *Pe.* 1. 4.—1 *Co.* 15. 45, 51, 52. *Re.* 4. 8, 9.— 1 *Ti.* 6. 15, 16.—1 *Ti.* 1. 17.

Let us not be desirous of vain glory.

Gideon said unto them, I would desire a request of you, that ye would give me every man the earrings of his prey. (For they had golden earrings, because they were Ishmaelites.) And they answered, We will willingly give them. And they spread a garment, and did cast therein every man the earrings of his prey. And Gideon made an ephod thereof, and put it in his city, even in Ophrah: and all Israel went thither a whoring after it: which thing became a snare unto Gideon, and to his house.

Seekest thou great things for thyself? seek them not.—Lest I should be exalted above measure through the abundance of the revelations, there was given to me a thorn in the flesh.

Let nothing be done, through strife or vain glory; but in lowliness of mind let each esteem other better than themselves.— Charity envieth not; charity vaunteth not itself, is not puffed up, doth not behave itself unseemly, seeketh not her own.

Take my yoke upon you, and learn of me.

GAL. 5. 26. *Ju.* 8. 24, 25, 27. *Je.* 45. 5.—2 *Co.* 12. 7. *Phi.* 2. 3.— 1 *Co.* 13. 4, 5. *Mat.* 11. 29.

Wash me thoroughly from mine iniquity.

I will cleanse them from all their iniquity, whereby they have sinned against me; and I will pardon all their iniquities, whereby they have sinned, and whereby they have transgressed against me.—Then will I sprinkle clean water upon you, and ye shall be clean: from all your filthiness, and from all your idols, will I cleanse you.

Except a man be born of water and of the Spirit, he cannot enter into the kingdom of God.—If the blood of bulls and of goats, and the ashes of a heifer sprinkling the unclean, sanctifieth to the purifying of the flesh: how much more shall the blood of Christ, who through the eternal Spirit offered himself without spot to God, purge your conscience from dead works to serve the living God?

He saved them for his name's sake, that he might make his mighty power to be known.—Not unto us, O LORD, not unto us, but unto thy name give glory, for thy mercy, and for thy truth's sake.

PSA. 51. 2. *Je.* 33. 8.—*Eze.* 36. 25.—*Jno.* 3. 5.—*He.* 9. 13, 14.
Ps. 106. 8.—*Ps.* 115. 1.

Fellowship in the gospel.

As the body is one, and hath many members, and all the members of that one body, being many, are one body: so also is Christ. For by one Spirit are we all baptized into one body, whether we be Jews or Gentiles, whether we be bond or free; and have been all made to drink into one Spirit.

God is faithful, by whom ye were called unto the fellowship of his Son Jesus Christ our Lord.—That which we have seen and heard declare we unto you, that ye also may have fellowship with us: and truly our fellowship is with the Father, and with his Son Jesus Christ.

If we walk in the light, as he is in the light, we have fellowship one with another, and the blood of Jesus Christ his Son cleanseth us from all sin.—These words spake Jesus. Neither pray I for these alone, but for them also which shall believe on me through their word: that they all may be one; as thou, Father, art in me, and I in thee, that they also may be one in us.

PHI. 1. 5. 1 *Co.* 12. 12, 13. 1 *Co.* 1. 9.—1 *Jno.* 1. 3. 1 *Jno.* 1. 7.—
Jno. 17. 1, 20, 21.

Take heed unto thyself.

Every man that striveth for the mastery is temperate in all things. Now they do it to obtain a corruptible crown; but we an incorruptible. I therefore so run, not as uncertainly; so fight I, not as one that beateth the air: but I keep under my body, and bring it into subjection: lest that by any means, when I have preached to others, I myself should be a castaway.—Put on the whole armour of God, that ye may be able to stand against the wiles of the devil. For we wrestle not against the flesh and blood, but against principalities, against powers, against the rulers of the darkness of this world, against spiritual wickedness in high places.

They that are Christ's have crucified the flesh with the affections and lusts. If we live in the Spirit, let us also walk in the Spirit.— For as many as are led by the Spirit of God, they are the sons of God.—Meditate upon these things; give thyself wholly to them; that thy profiting may appear to all.

1 *TIM.* 4. 16. 1 *Co.* 9. 25-27.—*Ep.* 6. 11, 12. *Ga.* 5. 24, 25.— *Ro.* 8. 14.—1 *Ti.* 4. 15.

Jesus saith unto her, Mary.

Fear not: for I have redeemed thee, I have called thee by thy name: thou art mine.—The sheep hear his voice: and he calleth his own sheep by name. And the sheep follow him: for they know his voice.

Behold, I have graven thee upon the palms of my hands; thy walls are continually before me.

The foundation of God standeth sure, having this seal, The Lord knoweth them that are his.—We have a great high priest, that is passed into the heavens, Jesus the Son of God.

Thou shalt take two onyx stones, and grave on them the names of the children of Israel. And Aaron shall bear their names before the LORD upon his two shoulders for a memorial. And thou shalt make the breastplate of judgment. And thou shalt set in it . . . four rows of stones. And the stones shall be with the names of the children of Israel, . . . and they shall be upon Aaron's heart, when he goeth in before the LORD.

JOHN 20. 16. *Is.* 43. 1.—*Jno.* 10. 3, 4. *Is.* 49. 16. 2 *Ti.* 2. 19.—*He.* 4. 14. *Ex.* 28. 9, 12, 15, 17, 21, 30.

My brethren, be strong in the Lord, and in the power of his might.

My grace is sufficient for thee: for my strength is made perfect in weakness. Most gladly therefore will I rather glory in my infirmities, that the power of Christ may rest upon me. Therefore I take pleasure in infirmities, in reproaches, in necessities, in persecutions, in distresses for Christ's sake: for when I am weak, then am I strong.—I will go in the strength of the Lord GOD: I will make mention of thy righteousness, even of thine only.—The gospel of Christ . . . is the power of God unto salvation.

I can do all things through Christ which strengtheneth me.—I also labour, striving according to his working, which worketh in me mightily.—We have this treasure in earthen vessels, that the excellency of the power may be of God, and not of us.

The joy of the LORD is your strength.—Strengthened with all might, according to his glorious power, unto all patience and long-suffering with joyfulness.

EPH. 6. 10. 2 *Co.* 12. 9, 10.—*Ps.* 71. 16.—*Ro.* 1. 16. *Phi.* 4. 13.—
Col. 1. 29.—2 *Co.* 4. 7. *Ne.* 8. 10.—*Col.* 1. 11.

Jesus Christ our Lord.

Jesus: for he shall save his people from their sins.—He humbled himself, and became obedient unto death, even the death of the cross. Wherefore God also hath highly exalted him, and given him a name which is above every name: that at the name of Jesus every knee should bow, of things in heaven, and things in earth, and things under the earth.

Messias . . . which is called Christ.—The LORD hath anointed me to preach good tidings unto the meek; he hath sent me to bind up the brokenhearted, to proclaim liberty to the captives.

The last Adam was made a quickening spirit. The second man is the Lord from heaven.—My LORD and my God.—Ye call me Master and Lord: and ye say well; for so I am. If I then, your Lord and Master have washed your feet; ye also ought to wash one another's feet. For I have given you an example, that ye should do as I have done to you.

1 *COR.* 1. 9. *Mat.* 1. 21.—*Phi.* 2. 8-10. *Jno.* 4. 25.—*Is.* 61. 1.
1 *Co.* 15. 45, 47. *Jno.* 20. 28.—*Jno.* 13. 13-15.

Peace I leave with you, my peace I give unto you: not as the world giveth, give I unto you.

The world passeth away, and the lust thereof.—Surely every man walketh in a vain shew: surely they are disquieted in vain: he heapeth up riches, and knoweth not who shall gather them.— What fruit had ye then in those things whereof ye are now ashamed? for the end of those things is death.

Martha, Martha, thou are careful and troubled about many things: but one thing is needful: and Mary hath chosen that good part, which shall not be taken away from her.—I would have you without carefulness.

These things I have spoken unto you that in me ye might have peace. In the world ye shall have tribulation: but be of good cheer: I have overcome the world.—The Lord of peace himself give you peace always by all means.—The LORD bless thee, and keep thee: the LORD make his face shine upon thee, and be gracious unto thee: the LORD lift up his countenance upon thee, and give thee peace.

JNO. 14. 27. 1 *Jno.* 2. 17.—*Ps.* 39. 6.—*Ro.* 6. 21. *Lu.* 10. 41, 42.—
    1 *Co.* 7. 32. *Jno.* 16. 33.—2 *Th.* 3. 16.—*Nu.* 6. 24-26.

The Spirit helpeth our infirmities.

The Comforter, which is the Holy Ghost.—What? know ye not that your body is the temple of the Holy Ghost which is in you, which ye have of God?—It is God which worketh in you.

We know not what we should pray for as we ought: but the Spirit itself maketh intercession for us with groanings which cannot be uttered. And he that searcheth the hearts knoweth what is the mind of the Spirit, because he maketh intercession for the saints according to the will of God.

He knoweth our frame; he remembereth that we are dust.— A bruised reed shall he not break, and the smoking flax shall he not quench.

The spirit indeed is willing, but the flesh is weak.

The LORD is my shepherd; I shall not want. He maketh me to lie down in green pastures: he leadeth me beside the still waters.

ROM. 8. 26. *Jno.* 14. 26.—1 *Co.* 6. 19.—*Phi.* 2. 13. *Ro.* 8. 26, 27.
    Ps. 103. 14.—*Is.* 42. 3. *Mat.* 26. 41. *Ps.* 23. 1, 2.

Thou shalt put the two stones upon the shoulders of the ephod for stones of memorial unto the children of Israel: and Aaron shall bear their names before the Lord.

Jesus . . . because he continueth ever, hath an unchangeable priesthood. Wherefore he is able also to save them to the uttermost that come unto God by him, seeing he ever liveth to make intercession for them.—Him that is able to keep you from falling, and to present you faultless before the presence of his glory.

Seeing . . . that we have a great high priest, that is passed into the heavens, Jesus the Son of God, let us hold fast our profession. For we have not a high priest which cannot be touched with the feeling of our infirmities; but was in all points tempted like as we are, yet without sin. Let us therefore come boldly unto the throne of grace.

The beloved of the LORD shall dwell in safety by him: and the LORD shall cover him all the day long, and he shall dwell between his shoulders.

EXOD. 28. 12. *He.* 7. 24, 25.—*Jude* 24. *He.* 4. 14-16. *De.* 33. 12.

On that night could not the king sleep.

Thou holdest mine eyes waking.—Who is like unto the LORD our God, . . . who humbleth himself to behold the things that are in heaven, and in the earth!

He doeth according to his will in the army of heaven, and among the inhabitants of the earth.—Thy way is in the sea, and thy path in the great waters, and thy footsteps are not known.—Surely the wrath of man shall praise thee: the remainder of wrath shalt thou restrain.

The eyes of the LORD run to and fro throughout the whole earth, to shew himself strong in the behalf of them whose heart is perfect toward him.—We know that all things work together for good to them that love God.

Are not two sparrows sold for a farthing? and one of them shall not fall on the ground without your Father. But the very hairs of your head are all numbered.

EST. 6. 1. *Ps.* 77. 4.—*Ps.* 113. 5, 6. *Da.* 4. 35.—*Ps.* 77. 19.—*Ps.* 76. 10. 2 *Ch.* 16. 9.—*Ro.* 8. 28. *Mat.* 10. 29, 30.

Grieve not the holy Spirit of God, whereby ye are sealed unto the day of redemption.

The love of the Spirit.—The Comforter, which is the Holy Ghost.—In all their affliction he was afflicted, and the angel of his presence saved them: in his love and in his pity he redeemed them; and he bare them, and carried them all the days of old. But they rebelled, and vexed his holy Spirit: therefore he was turned to be their enemy, and he fought against them.

Hereby know we that we dwell in him, and he in us, because he hath given us of his Spirit.—After that ye believed, ye were sealed with that holy Spirit of promise, which is the earnest of our inheritance until the redemption of the purchased possession.— This I say then, Walk in the Spirit, and ye shall not fulfil the lust of the flesh. For the flesh lusteth against the spirit, and the spirit against the flesh: and these are contrary the one to the other: so that ye cannot do the things that ye would.

The Spirit helpeth our infirmities.

EPH. 4. 30. *Ro.* 15. 30.—*Jno.* 14. 26.—*Is.* 63. 9, 10. 1 *Jno.* 4. 13.— *Ep.* 1. 13, 14.—*Gal.* 5. 16, 17. *Ro.* 8. 26.

I will go and return to my place, till they acknowledge their offence, and seek my face.

Your iniquities have separated between you and your God, and your sins have hid his face from you.—My beloved had withdrawn himself, and was gone: . . . I sought him, but I could not find him; I called him, but he gave me no answer.—I hid me, and was wroth, and he went on forwardly in the way of his heart. I have seen his ways, and will heal him.—Hast thou not procured this unto thyself, in that thou hast forsaken the LORD thy God, when he led thee by the way?

He arose, and came to his father. But when he was yet a great way off, his father saw him, and had compassion, and ran, and fell on his neck, and kissed him.—I will heal their backsliding, I will love them freely: for mine anger is turned away.

If we confess our sins, he is faithful and just to forgive us our sins, and to cleanse us from all unrighteousness.

HOSEA 5. 15. *Is.* 59. 2.—*Ca.* 5. 6.—*Is.* 57. 17, 18.—*Je.* 2. 17. *Lu.* 15. 20. —*Ho.* 14. 4. 1 *Jno.* 1. 9.

How great is thy goodness, which thou hast laid up for them that fear thee!

Since the beginning of the world men have not heard, nor perceived by the ear, neither hath the eye seen, O God, beside thee, what he hath prepared for him that waiteth for him.—Eye hath not seen, nor ear heard, neither have entered into the heart of man, the things which God hath prepared for them that love him. But God hath revealed them unto us by his Spirit.—Thou wilt shew me the path of life: in thy presence is fulness of joy; at thy right hand there are pleasures for evermore.

How excellent is thy loving kindness, O God! therefore the children of men put their trust under the shadow of thy wings. They shall be abundantly satisfied with the fatness of thy house; and thou shalt make them drink of the river of thy pleasures. For with thee is the fountain of life: in thy light shall we see light.

Godliness is profitable unto all things, having promise of the life that now is, and of that which is to come.

PSA. 31. 19. *Is.* 64. 4.—1 *Co.* 2. 9, 10.—*Ps.* 16. 11. *Ps.* 36. 7-9. 1 *Ti.* 4. 8.

The Son of God, . . . hath his eyes like unto a flame of fire.

The heart is deceitful above all things, and desperately wicked: who can know it? I the LORD search the heart, I try the reins, even to give every man according to his ways, and according to the fruit of his doings.—Thou hast set our iniquities before thee, our secret sins in the light of thy countenance.—The Lord turned, and looked upon Peter. And Peter went out, and wept bitterly.

Jesus did not commit himself unto them, because he knew all men, and needed not that any should testify of man: for he knew what was in man.—He knoweth our frame; he remembereth that we are dust.—A bruised reed shall he not break, and the smoking flax shall he not quench.

The Lord knoweth them that are his.—I am the good shepherd, and know my sheep. My sheep hear my voice, and I know them, and they follow me: and I give unto them eternal life; and they shall never perish, neither shall any man pluck them out of my hand.

REV. 2. 18. *Je.* 17. 9, 10.—*Ps.* 90. 8.—*Lu.* 22. 61, 62. *Jno.* 2. 24, 25.—*Ps.* 103. 14.—*Is.* 42. 3. 2 *Ti.* 2. 19.—*Jno.* 10. 14, 27, 28.

Our Lord Jesus, that great shepherd of the sheep.

The chief Shepherd.—I am the good shepherd, and know my sheep, and am known of mine. My sheep hear my voice, and I know them, and they follow me: and I give unto them eternal life; and they shall never perish, neither shall any man pluck them out of my hand.

The LORD is my shepherd; I shall not want. He maketh me to lie down in green pastures: he leadeth me beside the still waters. He restoreth my soul: he leadeth me in the paths of righteousness for his name's sake.

All we like sheep have gone astray; we have turned every one to his own way; and the LORD hath laid on him the iniquity of us all.—I am the good shepherd: the good shepherd giveth his life for the sheep.—I will seek that which was lost, and bring again that which was driven away, and will bind up that which was broken, and will strengthen that which was sick.—Ye were as sheep going astray; but are now returned unto the Shepherd and Bishop of your souls.

HEB. 13. 20. 1 Pe. 5. 4.—Jno. 10. 14, 27, 28. Ps. 23. 1-3. Is. 53. 6.— Jno. 10. 11.—Eze. 34. 16.—1 Pe. 2. 25.

MAY 26   EVENING

The city had no need of the sun, neither of the moon, to shine in it: for the glory of God did lighten it, and the Lamb is the light thereof.

I saw in the way a light from heaven, above the brightness of the sun, shining round about me. And I said, Who art thou, Lord? And he said, I am Jesus whom thou persecutest.—Jesus taketh Peter, James, and John his brother, and bringeth them up into an high mountain apart, and was transfigured before them: and his face did shine as the sun, and his raiment was white as the light.—The sun shall be no more thy light by day; neither for brightness shall the moon give light unto thee: but the LORD shall be unto thee an everlasting light, and thy God thy glory. Thy sun shall no more go down; neither shall thy moon withdraw itself: for the LORD shall be thine everlasting light, and the days of thy mourning shall be ended.

The God of all grace, . . . hath called us unto his eternal glory by Christ Jesus.

REV. 21. 23. Ac. 26. 13, 15.—Mat. 17. 1, 2.—Is. 60. 19, 20. 1 Pe. 5. 10.

The Lord is good, a strong hold in the day of trouble; and he knoweth them that trust in him.

Praise the LORD of hosts: for the Lord is good; for his mercy endureth for ever.—God is our refuge and strength, a very present help in trouble.—I will say of the LORD, He is my refuge and my fortress: my God; in him will I trust.—Who is like unto thee, O people saved by the LORD, the shield of thy help, and who is the sword of thy excellency!—As for God, his way is perfect; the word of the LORD is tried: he is a buckler to all them that trust in him. For who is God, save the LORD? and who is a rock, save our God?

If any man love God, the same is known of him.—The foundation of God standeth sure, having this seal, The Lord knoweth them that are his. And, Let every one that nameth the name of Christ depart from iniquity.—The LORD knoweth the way of the righteous: but the way of the ungodly shall perish.—Thou hast found grace in my sight, and I know thee by name.

NAHUM 1. 7. *Je.* 33. 11.—*Ps.* 46. 1.—*Ps.* 91. 2.—*De.* 33. 29.—
2 *Sa.* 22. 31, 32. 1 *Co.* 8. 3.—2 *Ti.* 2. 19.—*Ps.* 1. 6.—*Ex.* 33. 17.

I would have you without carefulness.

He careth for you.—The eyes of the LORD run to and fro throughout the whole earth, to shew himself strong in the behalf of them whose heart is perfect toward him.

O taste and see that the LORD is good: blessed is the man that trusteth in him. The young lions do lack, and suffer hunger: but they that seek the LORD shall not want any good thing.—Therefore I say unto you, Take no thought for your life, what ye shall eat, or what ye shall drink; nor yet for your body, what ye shall put on. Is not the life more than meat, and the body than raiment? Behold the fowls of the air: for they sow not, neither do they reap, nor gather into barns; yet your heavenly Father feedeth them Are ye not much better than they?—Be careful for nothing; but in every thing by prayer and supplication with thanksgiving let your requests be made known unto God. And the peace of God, which passeth all understanding, shall keep your hearts and minds through Christ Jesus.

1 *COR.* 7. 32. 1 *Pe.* 5. 7.—2 *Ch.* 16. 9. *Ps.* 34. 8, 10.—*Mat.* 6. 25, 26.—
Phi. 4. 6, 7.

We look for the Saviour.

The grace of God that bringeth salvation hath appeared to all men, teaching us that, denying ungodliness and worldly lusts, we should live soberly, righteously, and godly, in this present world; looking for that blessed hope, and the glorious appearing of the great God and our Saviour Jesus Christ; who gave himself for us, that he might redeem us from all iniquity, and purify unto himself a peculiar people, zealous of good works.—We, according to his promise, look for new heavens and a new earth, wherein dwelleth righteousness. Wherefore, beloved, seeing that ye look for such things, be diligent that ye may be found of him in peace, without spot, and blameless.

Christ was once offered to bear the sins of many; and unto them that look for him shall he appear the second time without sin unto salvation.—And it shall be said in that day, Lo, this is our God; we have waited for him, and he will save us: this is the LORD; we have waited for him, we will be glad and rejoice in his salvation.

PHI. 3. 20. *Tit.* 2. 11-14.—2 *Pe.* 3. 13, 14. *He.* 9. 28.—*Is.* 25. 9.

So run, that ye may obtain.

The slothful man saith, There is a lion without.—Let us lay aside every weight, and the sin which doth so easily beset us, and let us run with patience the race that is set before us, looking unto Jesus the author and finisher of our faith.

Let us cleanse ourselves from all filthiness of the flesh and spirit, perfecting holiness in the fear of God.

I press toward the mark.—I . . . so run, not as uncertainly; . . . I keep under my body, and bring it into subjection: lest that by any means, . . . I myself should be a castaway.

The fashion of this world passeth away.

Nevertheless we, according to his promise, look for new heavens and a new earth, wherein dwelleth righteousness. Wherefore, beloved, seeing that ye look for such things, be diligent.—Gird up the loins of your mind, be sober, and hope to the end for the grace that is to be brought unto you at the revelation of Jesus Christ.

1 *COR.* 9. 24. *Pr.* 22. 13.—*He.* 12. 1, 2. 2 *Co.* 7 .1. *Phi.* 3. 14.—
1 *Co.* 9. 26, 27. 1 *Co.* 7. 31. 2 *Pe.* 3. 13, 14.—1 *Pe.* 1. 13.

**The life of the flesh is in the blood: and I have given it to you upon
the altar to make an atonement for your souls: for it is the
blood that maketh an atonement for the soul.**

Behold the Lamb of God, which taketh away the sin of the
world.—The blood of the Lamb.—The precious blood of Christ,
as of a lamb without blemish and without spot.—Without shedding of blood is no remission.—The Blood of Jesus Christ his
Son cleanseth us from all sin.

By his own blood he entered in once into the holy place, having
obtained eternal redemption for us.—Having therefore, brethren,
boldness to enter into the holiest by the blood of Jesus, by a new
and living way, which he hath consecrated for us, through the veil,
that is to say, his flesh; let us draw near with a true heart in full
assurance of faith.

Ye are bought with a price: therefore glorify God in your body,
and in your spirit, which are God's.

LEV. 17. 11. *Jno.* 1. 29.—*Re.* 7. 14.—1 *Pe.* 1. 19.—*He.* 9. 22.—1 *Jno.* 1. 7.
He. 9. 12.—*He.* 10. 19, 20, 22. 1 *Co.* 6. 20.

**Oh that I had wings like a dove! for then would I fly away, and
be at rest.**

It came to pass, when the sun did arise, that God prepared a
vehement east wind; and the sun beat upon the head of Jonah,
that he fainted, and wished in himself to die, and said, It is better
for me to die than to live.

Job spake, and said, Wherefore is light given to him that is in
misery, and life unto the bitter in soul; which long for death, but
it cometh not; and dig for it more than for hid treasures?—Many
are the afflictions of the righteous: but the LORD delivereth him
out of them all.

Now is my soul troubled; and what shall I say? Father, save
me from this hour.—In all things it behoved him to be made like
unto his brethren, that he might be a merciful and faithful high
priest in things pertaining to God, to make reconciliation for the
sins of the people. For in that he himself hath suffered being tempted, he is able to succour them that are tempted.

PSA. 55. 6. *Jon.* 4. 8. *Job* 3. 2, 20, 21.—*Ps.* 34. 19. *Jno.* 12. 27.—
He. 2. 17, 18.

Let us labour to enter into that rest.

Enter ye in at the strait gate: for wide is the gate, and broad is the way, that leadeth to destruction: . . . strait is the gate, and narrow is the way, which leadeth unto life, and few there be that find it.—The kingdom of heaven suffereth violence, and the violent take it by force.—Labour not for the meat which perisheth, but for that meat which endureth unto everlasting life, which the Son of man shall give unto you.—Give diligence to make your calling and election sure: . . . for so an entrance shall be ministered unto you abundantly into the everlasting kingdom of our Lord and Saviour Jesus Christ.—So run, that ye may obtain. And every man that striveth for the mastery is temperate in all things. Now they do it to obtain a corruptible crown; but we an incorruptible.

For he that is entered into his rest, he also hath ceased from his own works, as God did from his.—The LORD shall be unto thee an everlasting light, and thy God thy glory.

HEB. 4. 11. *Mat.* 7. 13, 14.—*Mat.* 11. 12.—*Jno.* 6. 27.—2 *Pe.* 1. 10, 11.—
1 *Co.* 9. 24, 25. *He.* 4. 10.—*Is.* 60. 19.

Thou hearest me always.

Jesus lifted up his eyes, and said, Father, I thank thee that thou hast heard me.—Father, glorify thy name. Then came there a voice from heaven, saying, I have both glorified it, and will glorify it again.—Lo, I come to do thy will, O God.—Not my will, but thine, be done.

As he is, so are we in this world.—This is the confidence that we have in him, that, if we ask any thing according to his will, he heareth us.

Whatsoever we ask, we receive of him, because we keep his commandments, and do those things that are pleasing in his sight.

Without faith it is impossible to please him: for he that cometh to God must believe that he is, and that he is a rewarder of them that diligently seek him.

He ever liveth to make intercession for them. We have an advocate with the Father, Jesus Christ the righteous.

JOHN 11. 42. *Jno.* 11. 41.—*Jno.* 12. 28.—*He.* 10. 7.—*Lu.* 22. 42.—
1 *Jno.* 4. 17.—1 *Jno.* 5. 14. 1 *Jno.* 3. 22. *He.* 11. 6. *He.* 7. 25.—1 *Jno.* 2. 1.

Thy name shall be called Israel: for as a prince hast thou power with God and with men, and hast prevailed.

By his strength he had power with God: yea, he had power over the angel, and prevailed: he wept, and made supplication unto him.—[Abraham] staggered not at the promise of God through unbelief; but was strong in faith, giving glory to God.

Have faith in God. For verily I say unto you, That whosoever shall say unto this mountain, Be thou removed, and be thou cast into the sea; and shall not doubt in his heart, but shall believe that those things which he saith shall come to pass; he shall have whatsoever he saith. Therefore I say unto you, What things soever ye desire, when ye pray, believe that ye receive them, and ye shall have them.—If thou canst believe, all things are possible to him that believeth.—Blessed is she that believed: for there shall be a performance of those things which were told her from the Lord.

Lord, increase our faith.

GEN. 32. 28. *Ho.* 12. 3, 4.—*Ro.* 4. 20. *Mar.* 11. 22-24.—*Mar.* 9. 23.—
Lu. 1. 45.—*Lu.* 17. 5.

Little children, abide in him.

He that wavereth is like a wave of the sea driven with the wind and tossed. Let not that man think that he shall receive any thing of the Lord. A double minded man is unstable in all his ways.

I marvel that ye are so soon removed from him that called you into the grace of Christ unto another gospel: which is not another. Though we, or an angel from heaven, preach any other gospel unto you than that which we have preached unto you, let him be accursed.

Christ is become of no effect unto you, whosoever of you are justified by the law; ye are fallen from grace. Ye did run well; who did hinder you?

As the branch cannot bear fruit of itself, except it abide in the vine; no more can ye, except ye abide in me. If ye abide in me, and my words abide in you, ye shall ask what ye will, and it shall be done unto you.—For all the promises of God in him are yea, and in him, Amen, unto the glory of God by us.

1 *JOHN* 2. 28. *Ja.* 1. 6-8. *Ga.* 1. 6-8. *Ga.* 5. 4, 7. *Jno.* 15. 4, 7.—
2 *Co.* 1. 20.

The fruit of the Spirit is longsuffering, gentleness.

The LORD, the LORD God, merciful and gracious, longsuffering, and abundant in goodness and truth.

Walk worthy of the vocation wherewith ye are called, with all lowliness and meekness, with longsuffering, forbearing one another in love.—Be ye kind one to another, tenderhearted, forgiving one another, even as God for Christ's sake hath forgiven you.—The wisdom that is from above is first pure, then peaceable, gentle, and easy to be intreated, full of mercy and good fruits, without partiality, and without hypocrisy.—Charity suffereth long, and is kind.

In due season we shall reap, if we faint not.—Be patient therefore, brethren, unto the coming of the Lord. Behold, the husbandman waiteth for the precious fruit of the earth, and hath long patience for it, until he receive the early and latter rain. Be ye also patient; stablish your hearts: for the coming of the Lord draweth nigh.

GAL. 5. 22. Ex. 34. 6. Ep. 4. 1, 2.—Ep. 4. 32.—Ja. 3. 17.—1 Co. 13. 4.
Gal. 6. 9.—Ja. 5. 7, 8.

Emmanuel, . . . God with us.

Will God in very deed dwell with men on the earth? behold, heaven and the heaven of heavens cannot contain thee.—The Word was made flesh, and dwelt among us, (and we beheld his glory, the glory as of the only begotten of the Father,) full of grace and truth.—Great is the mystery of godliness: God was manifest in the flesh.

God hath in these last days spoken unto us by his Son, whom he hath appointed heir of all things, by whom also he made the worlds.

The first day of the week, when the doors were shut where the disciples were assembled, . . . came Jesus and stood in the midst. Then were the disciples glad, when they saw the Lord. After eight days again his disciples were within, and Thomas with them. Then saith [Jesus] to Thomas, Reach hither thy finger, and behold my hands; and reach hither thy hand, and thrust it into my side: and be not faithless, but believing. Thomas . . . said, . . . My Lord and my God.—Unto us a Son is given: the mighty God.

MAT. 1. 23. 2 Ch. 6. 18.—Jno. 1. 14.—1 Ti. 3. 16. He. 1. 2.
Jno. 20. 19, 20, 26-28.—Is. 9. 6.

Thus shall ye eat it; with your loins girded, and ye shall eat it in haste: it is the Lord's passover.

Arise ye, and depart; for this is not your rest.—Here have we no continuing city, but we seek one to come.—There remaineth therefore a rest to the people of God.

Let your loins be girded about, and your lights burning; and ye yourselves like unto men that wait for their lord, when he will return from the wedding; that when he cometh and knocketh, they may open unto him immediately. Blessed are those servants, whom the lord when he cometh shall find watching.—Gird up the loins of your mind, be sober, and hope to the end for the grace that is to be brought unto you at the revelation of Jesus Christ.— This one thing I do, forgetting those things which are behind, . . . I press toward the mark for the prize of the high calling of God in Christ Jesus. Let us therefore, as many as be perfect, be thus minded.

EXOD. 12. 11. *Mi.* 2. 10.—*He.* 13. 14.—*He.* 4. 9. *Lu.* 12. 35-37.— 1 *Pe.* 1. 13. *Phi.* 3. 13-15.

The Lord is the portion of mine inheritance and of my cup.

Heirs of God, and joint-heirs with Christ.—All things are your's.—My beloved is mine.—The Son of God . . . loved me, and gave himself for me.

The LORD spake unto Aaron, Thou shalt have no inheritance in their land, neither shalt thou have any part among them: I am thy part and thine inheritance among the children of Israel.

Whom have I in heaven but thee? and there is none upon earth that I desire beside thee. My flesh and my heart faileth: but God is the strength of my heart, and my portion for ever.

Though I walk through the valley of the shadow of death, I will fear no evil: for thou art with me; thy rod and thy staff they comfort me.—I know whom I have believed, and am persuaded that he is able to keep that which I have committed unto him against that day.

O God, thou art my God; early will I seek thee: my soul thirsteth for thee, my flesh longeth for thee in a dry and thirsty land.

PSA. 16. 5. *Ro.* 8. 17.—1 *Co.* 3. 21.—*Ca.* 2. 16.—*Ga.* 2. 20. *Nu.* 18. 20. *Ps.* 73. 25, 26. *Ps.* 23. 4.—2 *Ti.* 1. 12. *Ps.* 63. 1.

Watch, for ye know neither the day nor the hour wherein the Son of man cometh.

Take heed to yourselves, lest at any time your hearts be over-charged with surfeiting, and drunkenness, and cares of this life, and so that day come upon you unawares. For as a snare shall it come on all them that dwell on the face of the whole earth. Watch ye therefore, and pray always, that ye may be accounted worthy to escape all these things that shall come to pass, and to stand before the Son of man.

The day of the Lord so cometh as a thief in the night. For when they shall say, Peace and safety; then sudden destruction cometh upon them, as travail upon a woman with child; and they shall not escape. But ye, brethren, are not in darkness, that that day should overtake you as a thief. Ye are all the children of light, and the children of the day; we are not of the night, nor of darkness. Therefore let us not sleep, as do others; but let us watch and be sober.

MAT. 25. 13. *Lu.* 21. 34-36. 1 *Thes.* 5. 2-6.

I am the Almighty God; walk before me, and be thou perfect.

Not as though I had already attained, either were already perfect. I count not myself to have apprehended: but this one thing I do, forgetting those things which are behind, and reaching forth unto those things which are before, I press toward the mark for the prize of the high calling of God in Christ Jesus.

Enoch walked with God: and he was not; for God took him.

Grow in grace, and in the knowledge of our Lord and Saviour Jesus Christ.—We all, with open face beholding as in a glass the glory of the Lord, are changed into the same image from glory to glory, even as by the Spirit of the Lord.

These words spake Jesus, I pray not that thou shouldest take them out of the world, but that thou shouldest keep them from the evil. I in them, and thou in me, that they may be made perfect in one.

GEN. 17. 1. *Phi.* 3. 12-14. *Ge.* 5. 24. 2 *Pe.* 3. 18.—2 *Co.* 3. 18.
Jno. 17. 1, 15, 23.

The glory of this latter house shall be greater than of the former, and in this place will I give peace.

The house that is to be builded for the LORD must be exceeding magnifical, of fame and of glory throughout all countries.—The glory of the LORD . . . filled the LORD's house.

Destroy this temple, and in three days I will raise it up. He spake of the temple of his body.—That which was made glorious had no glory in this respect, by reason of the glory that excelleth. —The Word was made flesh, and dwelt among us, (and we beheld his glory, the glory as of the only begotten of the Father,) full of grace and truth.—God . . . hath in these last days spoken unto us by his Son, whom he hath appointed heir of all things, by whom also he made the worlds.

Glory to God in the highest, and on earth peace, good will toward men.—The Prince of Peace.—He is our peace.—The peace of God, which passeth all understanding, shall keep your hearts and minds through Christ Jesus.

HAG. 2. 9. *1 Ch.* 22. 5.—*2 Ch.* 7. 2. *Jno.* 2. 19, 21—*2 Co.* 3. 10.— *Jno.* 1. 14. *He.* 1. 1, 2. *Lu.* 2. 14.—*Is.* 9. 6.—*Ep.* 2. 14.—*Phi.* 4. 7.

Let us put on the armour of light.

Put . . . on the Lord Jesus Christ. That I may win Christ, and be found in him, not having mine own righteousness, which is of the law, but that which is through the faith of Christ, the righteousness which is of God by faith.—The righteousness of God which is by faith of Jesus Christ unto all and upon all them that believe.

He hath covered me with the robe of righteousness.—I will go in the strength of the LORD GOD: I will make mention of thy righteousness, even of thine only.

Ye were sometime darkness, but now are ye light in the Lord: walk as children of light. Have no fellowship with the unfruitful works of darkness, but rather reprove them. All things that are reproved are made manifest by the light: for whatsoever doth make manifest is light. Awake thou that sleepest, and rise from the dead, and Christ shall give thee light. See then that ye walk circumspectly.

ROM. 13. 12. *Ro.* 13. 14.—*Phi.* 3. 8, 9.—*Ro.* 3. 22. *Is.* 61. 10.—*Ps.* 71. 16. *Ep.* 5. 8, 11, 13-15.

When ye shall have done all those things which are commanded you, say, We are unprofitable servants.

Where is boasting then? It is excluded. By what law? of works? Nay: but by the law of faith.—What hast thou that thou didst not receive? now if thou didst receive it, why dost thou glory, as if thou hadst not received it?—By grace are ye saved through faith; and that not of yourselves: it is the gift of God: not of works, lest any man should boast. For we are his workmanship, created in Christ Jesus unto good works, which God hath before ordained that we should walk in them.

By the grace of God I am what I am: and his grace which was bestowed upon me was not in vain; but I laboured more abundantly than they all: yet not I, but the grace of God which was with me.—For of him, and through him, and to him, are all things.—All things come of thee, and of thine own have we given thee.

Enter not into judgment with thy servant: for in thy sight shall no man living be justified.

LUKE 17. 10. *Ro.* 3. 27.—1 *Co.* 4. 7.—*Ep.* 2. 8-10. 1 *Co.* 15. 10.—
Ro. 11. 36.—1 *Ch.* 29. 14. *Ps.* 143. 2.

He knoweth our frame; he remembereth that we are dust.

The LORD God formed man of the dust of the ground, and breathed into his nostrils the breath of life; and man became a living soul.

I will praise thee; for I am fearfully and wonderfully made: marvellous are thy works; and that my soul knoweth right well. My substance was not hid from thee, when I was made in secret. Thine eyes did see my substance, yet being unperfect; and in thy book all my members were written, which in continuance were fashioned, when as yet there was none of them.

Have we not all one father? hath not one God created us?—In him we live, and move, and have our being.—Like as a father pitieth his children, so the LORD pitieth them that fear him.

He, being full of compassion, forgave their iniquity, and destroyed them not: yea, many a time turned he his anger away, and did not stir up all his wrath. For he remembered that they were but flesh; a wind that passeth away, and cometh not again.

PSA. 103. 14. *Ge.* 2. 7. *Ps.* 139. 14-16. *Mal.* 2. 10.—*Ac.* 17. 28.
—*Ps.* 103. 13. *Ps.* 78. 38, 39.

He will rest in his love.

The LORD did not set his love upon you, nor choose you, because ye were more in number than any people; for ye were the fewest of all people: but because the LORD loved you.—We love him, because he first loved us.—You . . . hath he reconciled in the body of his flesh through death, to present you holy and unblameable and unreproveable in his sight.

Herein is love, not that we loved God, but that he loved us, and sent his Son to be the propitiation for our sins.—God commendeth his love toward us, in that while we were yet sinners, Christ died for us.

Lo, a voice from heaven, saying, This is my beloved Son, in whom I am well pleased.—Therefore doth my Father love me, because I lay down my life, that I might take it again.—His son . . . who being the brightness of his glory, and the express image of his person, and upholding all things by the word of his power, when he had by himself purged our sins, sat down on the right hand of the Majesty on high.

ZEP. 3. 17. De. 7. 7, 8.—1 Jno. 4. 19.—Col. 1. 21, 22. 1 Jno. 4. 10.—
Ro. 5. 8. Mat. 3. 17.—Jno. 10. 17.—He. 1. 2, 3.

A new and living way.

Cain went out from the presence of the LORD.—Your iniquities have separated between you and your God, and your sins have hid his face from you.—Without holiness, no man shall see the Lord.

I am the way, and the truth, and the life: no man cometh unto the Father, but by me.—Our Saviour Jesus Christ . . . hath abolished death, and hath brought life and immortality to light through the gospel.

The way into the holiest of all was not yet made manifest, while as the first tabernacle was yet standing.—He is our peace, who hath made both one, and hath broken down the middle wall of partition between us.—The veil of the temple was rent in twain from the top to the bottom.

Strait is the gate, and narrow is the way, which leadeth unto life, and few there be that find it.—Thou wilt shew me the path of life: in thy presence is fulness of joy; at thy right hand there are pleasures for evermore.

HEB. 10. 20. Ge. 4. 16.—Is. 59. 2.—He. 12. 14. Jno. 14. 6.—2 Ti. 1. 10.
He. 9. 8.—Ep. 2. 14.—Mat. 27. 51. Mat. 7. 14.—Ps. 16. 11.

Men ought always to pray, and not to faint.

Which of you shall have a friend, and shall go unto him at midnight, and say unto him, Friend, lend me three loaves; for a friend of mine in his journey is come to me, and I have nothing to set before him? And he from within shall answer and say, Trouble me not: the door is now shut, and my children are with me in bed; I cannot rise and give thee. I say unto you, Though he will not rise and give him, because he is his friend, yet because of his importunity he will rise and give him as many as he needeth.
—Praying always with all prayer and supplication in the Spirit and watching thereunto with all perseverance and supplication for all saints.

I will not let thee go, except thou bless me,—As a prince hast thou power with God and with men.—Continue in prayer, and watch in the same with thanksgiving.

[Jesus] went out into a mountain to pray, and continued all night in prayer to God.

LUKE 18. 1. *Lu.* 11. 5-8.—*Ep.* 6. 18. *Ge.* 32. 26, 28.—*Col.* 4. 2. *Lu.* 6. 12.

Forgive all my sins.

Come now, and let us reason together, saith the LORD: though your sins be as scarlet, they shall be as white as snow; though they be red like crimson, they shall be as wool.

Be of good cheer; thy sins be forgiven thee.—I, even I, am he that blotteth out thy transgressions for mine own sake, and will not remember thy sins.

The Son of man hath power on earth to forgive sins.—In whom we have redemption through his blood, the forgiveness of sins, according to the riches of his grace.—Not by works of righteousness which we have done, but according to his mercy he saved us, by the washing of regeneration, and renewing of the Holy Ghost; which he shed on us abundantly through Jesus Christ our Saviour. —Having forgiven you all trespasses; blotting out the handwriting of ordinances that was against us, which was contrary to us, and took it out of the way, nailing it to his cross.

Bless the LORD, O my soul, . . . who forgiveth all thine iniquities.

PSA. 25. 18. *Is.* 1. 18. *Mat.* 9. 2.—*Is.* 43. 25. *Mat.* 9. 6.—*Ep.* 1. 7.— *Tit.* 3. 5, 6.—*Col.* 2. 13, 14. *Ps.* 103. 2, 3.

The Lord made all that he did to prosper in his hand.

Blessed is every one that feareth the LORD; that walketh in his ways. For thou shalt eat the labour of thine hands: happy shalt thou be, and it shall be well with thee.—Trust in the LORD, and do good; so shalt thou dwell in the land, and verily thou shalt be fed. Delight thyself also in the LORD; and he shall give thee the desires of thine heart.—Be not afraid, neither be thou dismayed: for the LORD thy God is with thee whithersoever thou goest.

Seek ye first the kingdom of God, and his righteousness; and all these things shall be added unto you.

As long as he sought the LORD, God made him to prosper.— Beware that thou forget not the LORD thy God, in not keeping his commandments, and his judgments, and his statutes, which I command thee this day: and thou say in thine heart, My power and the might of mine hand hath gotten me this wealth.

Is not the LORD your God with you? and hath he not given you rest on every side?

GEN. 39. 3. *Ps.* 128. 1, 2.—*Ps.* 37. 3, 4.—*Jos.* 1. 9. *Mat.* 6. 33. 2 *Ch.* 26. *5.*
—*De.* 8. 11, 17. 1 *Ch.* 22. 18.

Why reason ye these things in your hearts?

Being not weak in faith, [Abraham] considered not his own body now dead, when he was about an hundred years old, neither yet the deadness of Sarah's womb; he staggered not at the promise of God through unbelief; but was strong in faith, giving glory to God.

Is it easier to say to the sick of the palsy, Thy sins be forgiven thee; or to say, Arise, and take up thy bed, and walk?—If thou canst believe, all things are possible to him that believeth.

All power is given unto me in heaven and in earth.—Why are ye so fearful? how is it that ye have no faith?—Behold the fowls of the air; . . . your heavenly Father feedeth them. Are ye not much better than they?—Why reason ye among yourselves, because ye have brought no bread? Do ye not . . . remember the five loaves of the five thousand?

My God shall supply all your need according to his riches in glory by Christ Jesus.

MARK 2. 8. *Ro.* 4. 19, 20. *Mar.* 2. 9.—*Mar.* 9. 23. *Mat.* 28. 18.—
Mar. 4. 40.—*Mat.* 6. 26.—*Mat.* 16. 8, 9. *Phi.* 4. 19.

Never man spake like this man.

Thou art fairer than the children of men: grace is poured into thy lips: therefore God hath blessed thee for ever.—The Lord God hath given me the tongue of the learned, that I should know how to speak a word in season to him that is weary.—His mouth is most sweet: yea, he is altogether lovely. This is my beloved, and this is my friend.

All bare him witness, and wondered at the gracious words which proceeded out of his mouth.—He taught them as one having authority, and not as the scribes.

Let the word of Christ dwell in you richly in all wisdom.—The sword of the Spirit . . . is the word of God.—The word of God is quick, and powerful, and sharper than any two-edged sword.— The weapons of our warfare are not carnal, but mighty through God to the pulling down of strong holds; casting down imaginations, and every high thing that exalteth itself against the knowledge of God, and bringing into captivity every thought to the obedience of Christ.

JOHN 7. 46. *Ps.* 45. 2.—*Is.* 50. 4.—*Ca.* 5. 16. *Lu.* 4. 22.—*Mat.* 7. 29. *Col.* 3. 16.—*Ep.* 6. 17.—*He.* 4. 12.—*2 Co.* 10. 4, 5.

The triumphing of the wicked is short.

Thou shalt bruise his heel.—This is your hour, and the power of darkness.—As the children are partakers of flesh and blood, he also himself likewise took part of the same; that through death he might destroy him that had the power of death, that is, the devil.—Having spoiled principalities and powers, he made a shew of them openly, triumphing over them in it.

Be sober, be vigilant; because your adversary the devil, as a roaring lion, walketh about, seeking whom he may devour: whom resist stedfast in the faith.—Resist the devil, and he will flee from you.

The wicked plotteth against the just, and gnasheth upon him with his teeth. The Lord shall laugh at him: for he seeth that his day is coming.—The God of peace shall bruise Satan under your feet shortly.—The devil . . . was cast into the lake of fire and brimstone, . . . and shall be tormented day and night for ever and ever.

JOB 20. 5. *Ge.* 3. 15.—*Lu.* 22. 53.—*He.* 2. 14.—*Col.* 2. 15. *1 Pe.* 5. 8, 9.—*Ja.* 4. 7. *Ps.* 37. 12, 13.—*Ro.* 16. 20.—*Re.* 20. 10.

The younger son took his journey into a far country, and there wasted his substance with riotous living.

Such were some of you: but ye are washed, but ye are sanctified, but ye are justified in the name of the Lord Jesus, and by the Spirit of our God.—We . . . were by nature the children of wrath, even as others. But God, who is rich in mercy, for his great love wherewith he loved us, even when we were dead in sins, hath quickened us together with Christ, (by grace ye are saved;) and hath raised us up together, and made us sit together in heavenly places in Christ Jesus.

Herein is love, not that we loved God, but that he loved us, and sent his Son to be the propitiation for our sins.

God commendeth his love toward us, in that, while we were yet sinners, Christ died for us. If, when we were enemies, we were reconciled to God by the death of his Son, much more, being reconciled, we shall be saved by his life.

LUKE 15. 13. 1 *Co.* 6. 11.—*Ep.* 2. 3-6. 1 *Jno.* 4. 10. *Ro.* 5. 8, 10.

As Christ forgave you, so also do ye.

There was a certain creditor which had two debtors: the one owed five hundred pence, and the other fifty. And when they had nothing to pay, he frankly forgave them both.—I forgave thee all that debt; shouldest not thou also have had compassion on thy fellow-servant, even as I had pity on thee?

When ye stand praying, forgive, if ye have ought against any: that your Father also which is in heaven may forgive you your trespasses. But if ye do not forgive, neither will your Father which is in heaven forgive your trespasses.—Put on, . . . as the elect of God, holy and beloved, bowels of mercies, kindness, humbleness of mind, meekness, longsuffering; forbearing one another, and forgiving one another, if any man have a quarrel against any.

How oft shall my brother sin against me, and I forgive him? till seven times? Jesus saith unto him, I say not unto thee, Until seven times: but, Until seventy times seven.

Charity . . . is the bond of perfectness.

COL. 3. 13. *Lu.* 7. 41, 42.—*Mat.* 18. 32, 33. *Mar.* 11. 25, 26.—
Col. 3. 12, 13. *Mat.* 18. 21, 22. *Col.* 3. 14.

He arose, and came to his father. But when he was yet a great way off, his father saw him, and ran, and fell on his neck, and kissed him.

The LORD is merciful and gracious, slow to anger, and plenteous in mercy. He will not always chide: neither will he keep his anger for ever. He hath not dealt with us after our sins; nor rewarded us according to our iniquities. For as the heaven is high above the earth, so great is his mercy toward them that fear him. As far as the east is from the west, so far hath he removed our transgressions from us. Like as a father pitieth his children, so the LORD pitieth them that fear him.

Ye have received the Spirit of adoption, whereby we cry, Abba, Father. The Spirit itself beareth witness with our spirit, that we are the children of God.—Ye who sometime were far off are made nigh by the blood of Christ.—Now therefore ye are no more strangers and foreigners, but fellow-citizens with the saints, and of the household of God.

LUKE 15. 20. *Ps.* 103. 8-13. *Ro.* 8. 15, 16.—*Ep.* 2. 13, 19.

Behold, I make all things new.

Except a man be born again, he cannot see the kingdom of God.—If any man be in Christ, he is a new creature; old things are passed away; behold, all things are become new.

A new heart also will I give you, and a new spirit will I put within you: and I will take away the stony heart out of your flesh, and I will give you an heart of flesh.—Purge out therefore the old leaven, that ye may be a new lump.—The new man, which after God is created in righteousness and true holiness.

Thou shalt be called by a new name, which the mouth of the LORD shall name.

Behold, I create new heavens and a new earth: and the former shall not be remembered, nor come into mind.—Seeing . . . that all these things shall be dissolved, what manner of persons ought ye to be in all holy conversation and godliness?

REV. 21. 5. *Jno.* 3. 3.—2 *Co.* 5. 17. *Eze.* 36. 26.—1 *Co.* 5. 7.— *Ep.* 4. 24. *Is.* 62. 2. *Is.* 65. 17.—2 *Pe.* 3. 11.

Every thing that may abide the fire, ye shall make it go through the fire, and it shall be clean.

The LORD your God proveth you, to know whether ye love the LORD your God with all your heart, and with all your soul.—He shall sit as a refiner and purifier of silver: and he shall purify the sons of Levi, and purge them as gold and silver, that they may offer unto the LORD an offering in righteousness.—Every man's work shall be made manifest: for the day shall declare it, because it shall be revealed by fire; and the fire shall try every man's work of what sort it is.

I will turn my hand upon thee, and purely purge away thy dross, and take away all thy tin.—I will melt them, and try them.

Thou, O God, hast proved us; thou hast tried us, as silver is tried. We went through fire and through water: but thou broughtest us out into a wealthy place.

When thou walkest through the fire, thou shalt not be burned; neither shall the flame kindle upon thee.

NUM. 31. 23. *De.* 13. 3.—*Mal.* 3. 3.—1 *Co.* 3. 13. *Is.* 1. 25.—*Je.* 9. 7. *Ps.* 66. 10, 12. *Is.* 43. 2.

We, being dead to sins, should live unto righteousness.

Put off, concerning the former conversation, the old man, which is corrupt according to the deceitful lusts; and be renewed in the spirit of your mind; and . . . put on the new man, which after God is created in righteousness and true holiness.

Ye are dead, and your life is hid with Christ in God.—As Christ was raised up from the dead by the glory of the Father, even so we also should walk in newness of life. Knowing this, that our old man is crucified with him, that the body of sin might be destroyed, that henceforth we should not serve sin. For he that is dead is freed from sin. Likewise reckon ye also yourselves to be dead indeed unto sin, but alive unto God through Jesus Christ our LORD. Let not sin therefore reign in your mortal body, that ye should obey it in the lusts thereof; but yield yourselves unto God, as those that are alive from the dead, and your members as instruments of righteousness unto God.

1 *PETER* 2. 24. *Ep.* 4. 22-24. *Col.* 3. 3.—*Ro.* 6. 4, 6, 7, 11-13.

Abide in me, and I in you.

I am crucified with Christ: nevertheless I live; yet not I, but Christ liveth in me: and the life which I now live in the flesh I live by the faith of the Son of God, who loved me, and gave himself for me.

I know that in me (that is, in my flesh,) dwelleth no good thing: for to will is present with me; but how to perform that which is good I find not. O wretched man that I am! who shall deliver me from the body of this death? I thank God through Jesus Christ our Lord.—If Christ be in you, the body is dead because of sin; but the Spirit is life because of righteousness.—If ye continue in the faith grounded and settled, and be not moved away from the hope of the gospel, which ye have heard.

Little children, abide in him; that, when he shall appear, we may have confidence, and not be ashamed before him at his coming.—He that saith he abideth in him ought himself also so to walk, even as he walked.

JOHN 15. 4. *Gal.* 2. 20. *Ro.* 7. 18, 24, 25.—*Ro.* 8. 10.—*Col.* 1. 23.
1 *Jno.* 2. 28.—1 *Jno.* 2. 6.

Dost thou believe on the Son of God?

Who is he, Lord, that I might believe on him?

The brightness of his glory, and the express image of his person.—The blessed and only Potentate, the King of kings, and Lord of lords; who only hath immortality, dwelling in the light which no man can approach unto; whom no man hath seen, nor can see: to whom be honour and power everlasting. Amen.—I am Alpha and Omega, the beginning and the ending, saith the Lord, which is, and which was, and which is to come, the Almighty.

Lord, I believe.—I know whom I have believed, and am persuaded that he is able to keep that which I have committed unto him against that day.

Behold, I lay in Sion a chief corner stone, elect, precious: and he that believeth on him shall not be confounded. Unto you therefore which believe he is precious.

JOHN 9. 35. *Jno.* 9. 36. *He.* 1. 3.—1 *Ti.* 6. 15, 16.—*Re.* 1. 8. *Jno.* 9. 38.—
2 *Ti.* 1. 12. 1 *Pe.* 2. 6, 7.

As the sufferings of Christ abound in us, so our consolation also aboundeth by Christ.

The fellowship of his sufferings.—Rejoice, inasmuch as ye are partakers of Christ's sufferings; that, when his glory shall be revealed, ye may be glad also with exceeding joy.—For if we be dead with him, we shall also live with him.—If children, then heirs; heirs of God, and joint-heirs with Christ; if so be that we suffer with him, that we may be also glorified together.

God, willing more abundantly to shew unto the heirs of promise the immutability of his counsel, confirmed it by an oath: that by two immutable things, in which it was impossible for God to lie, we might have a strong consolation, who have fled for refuge to lay hold upon the hope set before us.—Our Lord Jesus Christ himself, and God, even our Father, which hath loved us, and hath given us everlasting consolation and good hope through grace, comfort your hearts, and stablish you in every good word and work.

2 COR. 1. 5. Phi. 3. 10.—1 Pe. 4. 13.—2 Ti. 2. 11.—Ro. 8. 17. He. 6. 17, 18.—2 Thes. 2. 16, 17.

Martha, Martha, thou art careful and troubled about many things.

Consider the ravens: for they neither sow nor reap. Consider the lilies how they grow: they toil not, they spin not. Seek not ye what ye shall eat, or what ye shall drink, neither be ye of doubtful mind. Your Father knoweth that ye have need of these things.

Having food and raiment let us be therewith content. . . . They that will be rich fall into temptation and a snare, and into many foolish and hurtful lusts, which drown men in destruction and perdition. For the love of money is the root of all evil: which while some coveted after, they have erred from the faith, and pierced themselves through with many sorrows.

The cares of this world, and the deceitfulness of riches, and the lust of other things entering in, choke the word, and it becometh unfruitful.

Let us lay aside every weight, and the sin which doth so easily beset us, and let us run with patience the race that is set before us.

LUKE 10. 41. Lu. 12. 24, 27, 29, 30. 1 Ti. 6. 8-10.—Mar. 4. 19. He. 12. 1.

The secret things belong unto the Lord our God: but those which are revealed belong unto us.

LORD, my heart is not haughty, nor mine eyes lofty: neither do I exercise myself in great matters, or in things too high for me. Surely I have behaved and quieted myself, as a child that is weaned of his mother: my soul is even as a weaned child.

The secret of the LORD is with them that fear him: and he will shew them his covenant.—There is a God in heaven that revealeth secrets.—Lo, these are parts of his ways: but how little a portion is heard of him?

Henceforth I call you not servants; for the servant knoweth not what his lord doeth: but I have called you friends; for all things that I have heard of my Father I have made known unto you.—If ye love me, keep my commandments. And I will pray the Father, and he shall give you another Comforter, that he may abide with you for ever; even the Spirit of truth.

DEUT. 29. 29. *Ps*. 131. 1, 2. *Ps*. 25. 14.—*Da*. 2. 28.—*Job*. 26. 14
Jno. 15. 15.—*Jno*. 14. 15-17.

The Spirit . . . maketh intercession for the saints according to the will of God.

Verily, verily, I say unto you, Whatsoever ye shall ask the Father in my name, he will give it you. Hitherto have ye asked nothing in my name: ask, and ye shall receive, that your joy may be full.—Praying always with all prayer and supplication in the Spirit.

This is the confidence that we have in him, that, if we ask any thing according to his will, he heareth us: and if we know that he hear us, whatsoever we ask, we know that we have the petitions that we desired of him.—This is the will of God, even your sanctification.

God hath . . . called us . . . unto holiness: . . . who hath also given unto us his Holy Spirit.

Rejoice evermore. Pray without ceasing. In every thing give thanks: for this is the will of God in Christ Jesus concerning you. Quench not the Spirit.

ROM. 8. 27. *Jno*. 16. 23, 24.—*Ep*. 6. 18. 1 *Jno*. 5. 14, 15.—1 *Th*. 4. 3.
1 *Th*. 4. 7, 8. 1 *Th*. 5. 16-19.

See that ye walk circumspectly, not as fools, but as wise, redeeming the time, because the days are evil.

Take diligent heed to do the commandment and the law, . . . to love the LORD your God, and to walk in all his ways, and to keep his commandments, and to cleave unto him, and to serve him with all your heart and with all your soul.—Walk in wisdom toward them that are without, redeeming the time. Let your speech be always with grace, seasoned with salt, that ye may know how ye ought to answer every man.—Abstain from all appearance of evil.

While the bridegroom tarried, they all slumbered and slept. And at midnight there was a cry made, Behold, the bridegroom cometh; go ye out to meet him.—Watch therefore, for ye know neither the day nor the hour wherein the Son of man cometh.

Brethren, give diligence to make your calling and election sure; for if ye do these things, ye shall never fall.—Blessed are those servants, whom the lord when he cometh shall find watching.

EPH. 5. 15, 16. Jos. 22. 5.—Col. 4. 5, 6.—1 Thes. 5. 22. Mat. 25. 5, 6, 13. 2 Pe. 1. 10.—Lu. 12. 37.

Hold that fast which thou hast, that no man take thy crown.

If I may but touch his garment, I shall be whole.—Lord, if thou wilt, thou canst make me clean. I will; be thou clean.—Faith as a grain of mustard seed.

Cast not away . . . your confidence, which hath great recompence of reward.—Work out your own salvation with fear and trembling. It is God which worketh in you both to will and to do of his good pleasure.

First the blade, then the ear, after that the full corn in the ear.— Then shall we know, if we follow on to know the LORD.—The kingdom of heaven suffereth violence, and the violent take it by force.—So run, that ye may obtain.

I have fought a good fight, I have finished my course, I have kept the faith: henceforth there is laid up for me a crown of righteousness, which the Lord, the righteous judge, shall give me at that day.

REV. 3. 11. Mat. 9. 21—Mat. 8. 2, 3.—Mat. 17. 20. He. 10. 35. —Phi. 2. 12, 13. Mar. 4. 28.—Ho. 6. 3.—Mat. 11. 12.—1 Co. 9. 24. 2 Ti. 4. 7, 8.

In every thing by prayer and supplication with thanksgiving let your requests be made known unto God.

I love the LORD, because he hath heard my voice and my supplications. Because he hath inclined his ear unto me, therefore will I call upon him as long as I live.

When ye pray, use not vain repetitions, as the heathen do: for they think that they shall be heard for their much speaking.—The Spirit . . . helpeth our infirmities: for we know not what we should pray for as we ought: but the Spirit itself maketh intercession for us with groanings which cannot be uttered.

I will therefore that men pray every where, lifting up holy hands, without wrath and doubting.—Praying always with all prayer and supplication in the Spirit, and watching thereunto with all perseverance and supplication for all saints.

If two of you shall agree on earth as touching any thing that they shall ask, it shall be done for them of my Father which is in heaven.

PHI. 4. 6. *Ps.* 116. 1, 2. *Mat.* 6. 7.—*Ro.* 8. 26. 1 *Ti.* 2. 8.—*Ep.* 6. 18. *Mat.* 18. 19.

All thy works shall praise thee, O Lord ; and thy saints shall bless thee.

Bless the LORD, O my soul: and all that is within me, bless his holy name. Bless the LORD, O my soul, and forget not all his benefits.—I will bless the LORD at all times : his praise shall continually be in my mouth.—Every day will I bless thee ; and I will praise thy name for ever and ever.

Because thy lovingkindness is better than life, my lips shall praise thee. Thus will I bless thee while I live: I will lift up my hands in thy name. My soul shall be satisfied as with marrow and fatness; and my mouth shall praise thee with joyful lips.

My soul doth magnify the Lord, and my spirit hath rejoiced in God my Saviour.

Thou art worthy, O Lord, to receive glory and honour and power: for thou hast created all things, and for thy pleasure they are and were created.

PSA. 145. 10. *Ps.* 103. 1, 2.—*Ps.* 34. 1.—*Ps.* 145. 2. *Ps.* 63. 3-5. *Lu.* 1. 46, 47. *Re.* 4. 11.

Thou shalt put the mercy seat above upon the ark, and there I will meet with thee.

The way into the holiest of all was not yet made manifest.—Jesus, when he had cried again with a loud voice, yielded up the ghost. And, behold, the veil of the temple was rent in twain from the top to the bottom.

Having . . . brethren, boldness to enter into the holiest by the blood of Jesus, by a new and living way, which he hath consecrated for us, through the veil, that is to say, his flesh; . . . let us draw near with a true heart in full assurance of faith, having our hearts sprinkled from an evil conscience, and our bodies washed with pure water.—Let us therefore come boldly unto the throne of grace, that we may obtain mercy, and find grace to help in time of need.

Christ Jesus: whom God hath set forth to be a propitiation [mercy seat] through faith in his blood, to declare his righteousness for the remission of sins that are past, through the forbearance of God.—Through him we . . . have access by one Spirit unto the Father.

EXOD. 25. 21, 22. *He.* 9. 8.—*Mat.* 27. 50, 51. *He.* 10. 19, 20, 22.—
He. 4. 16. *Ro.* 3. 24, 25.—*Ep.* 2. 18.

Faith as a grain of mustard seed.

Barak said unto [Deborah], if thou wilt go with me, then I will go: but if thou wilt not go with me, then I will not go. God subdued on that day Jabin the king of Canaan.—Gideon . . . feared his father's household, and the men of the city, that he could not do it by day, . . . did it by night. And Gideon said unto God, If thou wilt save Israel by mine hand as thou hast said, . . . let me prove, I pray thee. And God did so.

Thou hast a little strength, and hast kept my word, and hast not denied my name.—Who hath despised the day of small things?

We are bound to thank God always for you, brethren, as it is meet, because that your faith groweth exceedingly.—Lord, increase our faith.—I will be as the dew unto Israel: he shall grow as the lily, cast forth his roots as Lebanon. His branches shall spread, and his beauty shall be as the olive tree, and his smell as Lebanon.

MAT. 17. 20. *Ju.* 4. 8, 23.—*Ju.* 6. 27, 36, 39, 40. *Re.* 3. 8.—*Zec.* 4. 10.
2 Th. 1. 3.—*Lu.* 17. 5.—*Ho.* 14. 5, 6.

Holiness, without which no man shall see the Lord.

Except a man be born again, he cannot see the kingdom of God.—There shall in no wise enter into it any thing that defileth.—There is no spot in thee.

Ye shall be holy: for I the LORD your God am holy.—As obedient children, not fashioning yourselves according to the former lusts in your ignorance: but as he which hath called you is holy, so be ye holy in all manner of conversation; because it is written, Be ye holy; for I am holy. And if ye call on the Father, who without respect of persons judgeth according to every man's work, pass the time of your sojourning here in fear.—Put off concerning the former conversation the old man, which is corrupt according to the deceitful lusts; and be renewed in the spirit of your mind; and . . . put on the new man, which after God is created in righteousness and true holiness.—He hath chosen us in him before the foundation of the world, that we should be holy and without blame before him in love.

HEB. 12. 14. *Jno.* 3. 3.—*Re.* 21. 27.—*Ca.* 4. 7. *Le.* 19. 2.—*1 Pe.* 1. 14-17.—*Ep.* 4. 22-24.—*Ep.* 1. 4.

Gold tried in the fire.

There is no man that hath left house, or brethren, or sisters, or father, or mother, or wife, or children, or lands, for my sake, and the gospel's, but he shall receive an hundredfold now in this time, houses, and brethren, and sisters, and mothers, and children, and lands, with persecutions; and in the world to come eternal life.

Beloved, think it not strange concerning the fiery trial which is to try you, as though some strange thing happened unto you.—Now for a season, if need be, ye are in heaviness through manifold temptations: that the trial of your faith, being much more precious than of gold that perisheth, though it be tried with fire, might be found unto praise and honour and glory at the appearing of Jesus Christ.

The God of all grace, who hath called us unto his eternal glory by Christ Jesus, after that ye have suffered a while, make you perfect, stablish, strengthen, settle you.—In the world ye shall have tribulation: but be of good cheer; I have overcome the world.

REV. 3. 18. *Mar.* 10. 29, 30. 1 *Pe.* 4. 12.—1 *Pe.* 1. 6, 7. 1 *Pe.* 5. 10.—*Jno.* 16. 33.

Take this child away, and nurse it for me, and I will give thee thy wages.

Go ye . . . into the vineyard, and whatsoever is right I will give you.—Whosoever shall give you a cup of water to drink in my name, because ye belong to Christ, verily I say unto you, he shall not lose his reward.—The liberal soul shall be made fat: and he that watereth shall be watered also himself.—God is not unrighteous to forget your work and labour of love, . . . in that ye have ministered to the saints, and do minister.

Every man shall receive his own reward according to his own labour.

Lord, when saw we thee an hungered, and fed thee? or thirsty, and gave thee drink? When saw we thee a stranger, and took thee in? or naked, and clothed thee? And the King shall answer and say unto them, . . . Inasmuch as ye have done it unto one of the least of these my brethren, ye have done it unto me. Come, ye blessed of my Father, inherit the kingdom prepared for you from the foundation of the world.

EXOD. 2. 9. *Mat.* 20. 4.—*Mar.* 9. 41.—*Pr.* 11. 25.—*He.* 6. 10.
1 *Co.* 3. 8. *Mat.* 25. 37, 38, 40, 34.

Thou compassest my path and my lying down.

Jacob awaked out of his sleep, and he said, Surely the LORD is in this place; and I knew it not. And he was afraid, and said, How dreadful is this place! this is none other but the house of God, and this is the gate of heaven.

The eyes of the LORD run to and fro throughout the whole earth, to shew himself strong in the behalf of them whose heart is perfect toward him.

I will both lay me down in peace, and sleep: for thou, LORD, only, makest me dwell in safety.

Because thou hast made the LORD, which is my refuge, even the most High, thy habitation, there shall no evil befall thee, neither shall any plague come nigh thy dwelling. For he shall give his angels charge over thee, to keep thee in all thy ways.—When thou liest down, thou shalt not be afraid: yea, thou shalt lie down, and thy sleep shall be sweet.—So he giveth his beloved sleep.

PSA. 139. 3. *Ge.* 28. 16, 17. 2 *Ch.* 16. 9. *Ps.* 4. 8. *Ps.* 91. 9-11.
—*Pr.* 3. 24. *Ps.* 127. 2.

Christ suffered for us, leaving us an example that ye should follow his steps.

Even the Son of man came not to be ministered unto, but to minister.—Whosoever of you will be the chiefest, shall be servant of all.

Jesus of Nazareth . . . went about doing good.—Bear ye one another's burdens, and so fulfill the law of Christ.

The meekness and gentleness of Christ.—In lowliness of mind let each esteem other better than themselves.

Father, forgive them: for they know not what they do.—Be ye kind one to another, tender-hearted, forgiving one another, even as God for Christ's sake hath forgiven you.

He that saith he abideth in him, ought himself also so to walk, even as he walked.—Looking unto Jesus the author and finisher of our faith; who for the joy that was set before him endured the cross, despising the shame, and is set down at the right hand of the throne of God.

1 *PETER* 2. 21. *Mar.* 10. 45.—*Mar.* 10. 44. *Ac.* 10. 38.—*Gal.* 6.2.
2 *Co.* 10. 1.—*Phi.* 2. 3. *Lu.* 23. 34.—*Ep.* 4. 32. 1 *Jno.* 2. 6.—*He.* 12. 2.

I sought him, but I could not find him : I called him, but he gave me no answer.

O Lord, what shall I say, when Israel turneth their backs before their enemies! and the LORD said unto Joshua, Get thee up; wherefore liest thou thus upon thy face? Israel hath sinned, . . . for they have even taken of the accursed thing, . . . and they have put it even among their own stuff.

Behold, the LORD's hand is not shortened, that it cannot save; neither his ear heavy, that it cannot hear: but your iniquities have separated between you and your God, and your sins have hid his face from you, that he will not hear.

If I regard iniquity in my heart, the Lord will not hear me.

Beloved, if our heart condemn us not, then have we confidence toward God. And whatsoever we ask, we receive of him, because we keep his commandments, and do those things that are pleasing in his sight.

CANT. 5. 6. *Jos.* 7. 8, 10, 11. *Is.* 59. 1, 2. *Ps.* 66. 18. 1 *Jno.* 3. 21, 22.

Ye are dead, and your life is hid with Christ in God.

How shall we, that are dead to sin, live any longer therein?—I am crucified with Christ, nevertheless I live; yet not I, but Christ liveth in me: and the life which I now live in the flesh, I live by the faith of the Son of God, who loved me, and gave himself for me.—He died for all, that they which live should not henceforth live unto themselves, but unto him which died for them, and rose again.—If any man be in Christ, he is a new creature; old things are passed away; behold, all things are become new.

We are in him that is true, even in his Son Jesus Christ.—As thou, Father, art in me, and I in thee, that they also may be one in us.—Ye are the body of Christ, and members in particular.—Because I live, ye shall live also.

To him that overcometh will I give to eat of the hidden manna, and will give him a white stone, and in the stone a new name written, which no man knoweth saving he that receiveth it.

COL. 3. 3. *Ro.* 6. 2.—*Gal.* 2. 20.—2 *Co.* 5. 15.—2 *Co.* 5. 17. 1 *Jno.* 5. 20.— *Jno.* 17. 21.—1 *Co.* 12. 27.—*Jno.* 14. 19. *Re.* 2. 17.

Behold how he loved.

He died for all.—Greater love hath no man than this, that a man lay down his life for his friends.

He . . . liveth to make intercession for them.—I go to prepare a place for you.

I will come again, and receive you unto myself; that where I am, there ye may be also.—Father, I will that they also, whom thou hast given me, be with me where I am.—Having loved his own which were in the world, he loved them unto the end.

We love him, because he first loved us.—The love of Christ constraineth us; because we thus judge, that if one died for all, then were all dead: and that he died for all, that they which live should not henceforth live unto themselves, but unto him which died for them, and rose again.

If ye keep my commandments, ye shall abide in my love; even as I have kept my Father's commandments, and abide in his love.

JOHN 11. 36. 2 *Co.* 5. 15.—*Jno.* 15. 13. *He.* 7, 25.—*Jno.* 14. 2. *Jno.* 14. 3.—*Jno.* 17. 24.—*Jno.* 13. 1. 1 *Jno.* 4. 19.—2 *Co.* 5. 14, 15. *Jno.* 15. 10.

I will pray the Father, and he shall give you another Comforter, even the Spirit of truth.

It is expedient for you that I go away: for if I go not away, the Comforter will not come unto you; but if I depart, I will send him unto you.

The Spirit itself beareth witness with our spirit, that we are the children of God.—Ye have not received the spirit of bondage again to fear; but ye have received the Spirit of adoption, whereby we cry, Abba, Father.—The Spirit . . . helpeth our infirmities: for we know not what we should pray for as we ought: but the Spirit itself maketh intercession for us with groanings which cannot be uttered.

The God of hope fill you with all joy and peace in believing, that ye may abound in hope, through the power of the Holy Ghost. —Hope maketh not ashamed; because the love of God is shed abroad in our hearts by the Holy Ghost which is given unto us.

Hereby know we that we dwell in him, and he in us, because he hath given us of his Spirit.

JOHN 14. 16, 17. *Jno.* 16. 7. *Ro.* 8. 16.—*Ro.* 8. 15.—*Ro.* 8. 26. *Ro.* 15. 13.—*Ro.* 5. 5. 1 *Jno.* 4. 13.

Shall I not seek rest for thee, that it may be well with thee?

There remaineth . . . a rest to the people of God.—My people shall dwell in a peaceable habitation, and in sure dwellings, and in quiet resting places.—There the wicked cease from troubling; and there the weary be at rest.—They . . . rest from their labours.

The forerunner is for us entered, even Jesus, made an high priest for ever after the order of Melchisedec.

Come unto me, all ye that labour and are heavy laden, and I will give you rest. Take my yoke upon you, and learn of me; for I am meek and lowly in heart: and ye shall find rest unto your souls. For my yoke is easy, and my burden is light.—In returning and rest shall ye be saved; in quietness and in confidence shall be your strength.

The LORD is my shepherd; I shall not want. He maketh me to lie down in green pastures: he leadeth me beside the still waters.

RUTH 3. 1. *He.* 4. 9.—*Is.* 32. 18.—*Job* 3. 17.—*Re.* 14. 13. *Heb.* 6. 20. *Mat.* 11. 28-30.—*Is.* 30. 15. *Ps.* 23. 1, 2.

The ark of the covenant of the Lord went before them to search out a resting place for them.

My times are in thy hand.—He shall choose our inheritance for us.—Lead me, O LORD, in thy righteousness; . . . make thy way straight before my face.

Commit thy way unto the LORD; trust also in him; and he shall bring it to pass.—In all thy ways acknowledge him, and he shall direct thy paths.—Thine ears shall hear a word behind thee, saying, This is the way, walk ye in it, when ye turn to the right hand, and when ye turn to the left.

The LORD is my shepherd; I shall not want. He maketh me to lie down in green pastures; he leadeth me beside the still waters.— Like as a father pitieth his children, so the LORD pitieth them that fear him. For he knoweth our frame; he remembereth that we are dust.—Your heavenly Father knoweth that ye have need of all these things.—Casting all your care upon him; for he careth for you.

NUM. 10. 33. *Ps.* 31. 15.—*Ps.* 47. 4.—*Ps.* 5. 8.—*Ps.* 37. 5.—*Pro.* 3. 6.— *Is.* 30. 21. *Ps.* 23. 1, 2.—*Ps.* 103. 13. 14.—*Mat.* 6. 32.—1 *Pe.* 5. 7.

Master, where dwellest thou? He saith unto them, Come and see.

In my Father's house are many mansions: if it were not so, I would have told you. I go to prepare a place for you. And if I go and prepare a place for you, I will come again, and receive you unto myself; that where I am, there ye may be also.—To him that overcometh will I grant to sit with me in my throne.

Thus saith the high and lofty One that inhabiteth eternity, whose name is Holy; I dwell in the high and holy place, with him also that is of a contrite and humble spirit, to revive the spirit of the humble, and to revive the heart of the contrite ones.

Behold, I stand at the door, and knock: if any man hear my voice, and open the door, I will come in to him, and will sup with him, and he with me.

Lo, I am with you alway, even unto the end of the world.— How excellent is thy lovingkindness, O God! therefore the children of men put their trust under the shadow of thy wings.

JOHN 1. 38, 39. *Jno.* 14. 2, 3.—*Re.* 3. 21. *Is.* 57. 15. *Re.* 3. 20. *Mat.* 28. 20.—*Ps.* 36. 7.

When he shall appear, we shall be like him; for we shall see him as he is.

As many as received him, to them gave he power to become the sons of God, even to them that believe on his name.—Whereby are given unto us exceeding great and precious promises; that by these ye might be partakers of the divine nature, having escaped the corruption that is in the world through lust.

Since the beginning of the world men have not heard, nor perceived by the ear, neither hath the eye seen, O God, beside thee, what he hath prepared for him that waiteth for him.

Now we see through a glass, darkly; but then face to face: now I know in part; but then shall I know even as also I am known.—Christ . . . shall change our vile body, that it may be fashioned like unto his glorious body, according to the working whereby he is able even to subdue all things unto himself.—As for me, I will behold thy face in righteousness: I shall be satisfied, when I awake, with thy likeness.

1 *JOHN* 3. 2. *Jno.* 1. 12.—2 *Pe.* 1. 4. *Is.* 64. 4. 1 *Co.* 13. 12.—
Phi. 3, 20, 21.—*Ps.* 17. 15.

The man that is my fellow, saith the Lord of hosts.

In him dwelleth all the fulness of the Godhead bodily.—I have laid help upon one that is mighty; I have exalted one chosen out of the people.—I have trodden the winepress alone; and of the people there was none with me.

Great is the mystery of godliness: God was manifest in the flesh.—Unto us a child is born, unto us a son is given, and the government shall be upon his shoulder; and his name shall be called Wonderful, Counsellor, The mighty God, The everlasting Father, The Prince of Peace.

The brightness of his glory, and the express image of his person, and upholding all things by the word of his power, when he had by himself purged our sins, sat down on the right hand of the Majesty on high.—Unto the Son he saith, Thy throne, O God, is for ever and ever.

Let all the angels of God worship him.

King of kings, and Lord of lords.

ZEC. 13. 7. *Col.* 2. 9.—*Ps.* 89. 19.—*Is.* 63. 3. 1 *Ti.* 3. 16.—*Is.* 9. 6.
He. 1. 3, 8, 6. *Re.* 19. 16.

Oh that thou wouldest bless me indeed, and that thou wouldest keep me from evil! And God granted him that which he requested.

The blessing of the LORD, it maketh rich, and he addeth no sorrow with it.—When he giveth quietness, who then can make trouble? and when he hideth his face, who then can behold him?

Salvation belongeth unto the LORD: thy blessing is upon thy people.—How great is thy goodness, which thou hast laid up for them that fear thee; which thou hast wrought for them that trust in thee before the sons of men!—I pray not that thou shouldest take them out of the world, but that thou shouldest keep them from the evil.

Ask, and it shall be given you; seek, and ye shall find; knock, and it shall be opened unto you: for every one that asketh receiveth; and he that seeketh findeth; and to him that knocketh it shall be opened.—The LORD redeemeth the soul of his servants: and none of them that trust in him shall be desolate.

1 *CHRON.* 4. 10. *Pr.* 10. 22.—*Job* 34. 29. *Ps.* 3. 8.—*Ps.* 31. 19—
Jno. 17. 15. *Mat.* 7. 7, 8.—*Ps.* 34. 22.

It is a night to be much observed unto the Lord for bringing them out from the land of Egypt.

The Lord Jesus the same night in which he was betrayed took bread: and when he had given thanks, he brake it, and said, Take, eat: this is my body, which is broken for you: this do in remembrance of me. After the same manner also he took the cup, when he had supped, saying, This cup is the new testament in my blood: this do ye, as oft as ye drink it, in remembrance of me.

He . . . kneeled down, and prayed. And being in an agony he prayed more earnestly: and his sweat was as it were great drops of blood falling down to the ground.

It was the preparation of the passover, and about the sixth hour: . . . they took Jesus, and led him away; . . . into a place called . . . Golgotha: where they crucified him.

Christ our passover is sacrificed for us: therefore let us keep the feast.

EXOD. 12. 42. 1 *Co.* 11. 23-25. *Lu.* 22. 41, 44. *Jno.* 19. 14, 16-18.
1 *Co.* 5. 7, 8.

Who shall be able to stand?

Who may abide the day of his coming? and who shall stand when he appeareth? for he is like a refiner's fire, and like fullers' soap.

I beheld, and, lo, a great multitude, which no man could number, of all nations, and kindreds, and people, and tongues, stood before the throne, and before the Lamb, clothed with white robes, and palms in their hands. These are they which came out of great tribulation, and have washed their robes, and made them white in the blood of the Lamb. They shall hunger no more, neither thirst any more; neither shall the sun light on them, nor any heat. For the Lamb, which is in the midst of the throne, shall feed them, and shall lead them unto living fountains of waters: and God shall wipe away ll tears from their eyes.

There is no conden nation to them which are in Christ Jesus, who walk not after the flesh, but after the Spirit.—Stand fast therefore in the liberty wherewith Christ hath made us free.

REV. 6. 17. *Is.* 3. 2. *Re.* 7. 9, 14-17. *Ro.* 8. 1.—*Gal.* 5. 1.

Enter not into judgment with thy servant: for in thy sight shall no man living be justified.

Come now, and let us reason together, saith the LORD: though your sins be as scarlet, they shall be as white as snow; though they be red like crimson, they shall be as wool.

Let him take hold of my strength, that he may make peace with me; and he shall make peace with me.—Acquaint now thyself with him, and be at peace.

Being justified by faith, we have peace with God through our Lord Jesus Christ.—A man is not justified by the works of the law, but by the faith of Jesus Christ.—By the deeds of the law there shall no flesh be justified in his sight.

By him all that believe are justified from all things, from which ye could not be justified by the law of Moses.

Thanks be to God, which giveth us the victory through our Lord Jesus Christ.

PSA. 143. 2. *Is.* 1. 18. *Is.* 27. 5.—*Job* 22. 21. *Ro.* 5. 1.—*Ga.* 2. 16.— *Ro.* 3. 20. *Ac.* 13. 39. 1 *Co.* 15. 57.

I know that my Redeemer liveth.

If, when we were enemies, we were reconciled to God by the death of his Son, much more, being reconciled, we shall be saved by his life.—This man, because he continueth ever, hath an unchangeable priesthood. Wherefore he is able also to save them to the uttermost that come unto God by him, seeing he ever liveth to make intercession for them.

Because I live, ye shall live also.—If in this life only we have hope in Christ, we are of all men most miserable. But now is Christ risen from the dead, and become the firstfruits of them that slept.

The Redeemer shall come to Zion, and unto them that turn from transgression in Jacob, saith the LORD.—We have redemption through his blood, the forgiveness of sins, according to the riches of his grace.—Ye were not redeemed with corruptible things, as silver and gold, from your vain conversation received by tradition from your fathers; but with the precious blood of Christ, as of a lamb without blemish and without spot.

JOB 19. 25. *Ro.* 5. 10.—*He.* 7. 24, 25. *Jno.* 14. 19.—1 *Co.* 15. 19, 20.
—*Is.* 59. 20.—*Ep.* 1. 7.—1 *Pe.* 1. 18, 19.

The Spirit speaketh expressly, that in the latter times some shall depart from the faith, giving heed to seducing spirits.

Take heed therefore how ye hear.—Let the word of Christ dwell in you richly in all wisdom.—Above all, taking the shield of faith, wherewith ye shall be able to quench all the fiery darts of the wicked.

Great peace have they which love thy law: and nothing shall offend them. How sweet are thy words unto my taste! yea, sweeter than honey to my mouth! Through thy precepts I get understanding: therefore I hate every false way.

Thy word is a lamp unto my feet, and a light unto my path.— I have more understanding than all my teachers: for thy testimonies are my meditation.

Satan himself is transformed into an angel of light.—But though we, or an angel from heaven, preach any other gospel unto you than that which we have preached unto you, let him be accursed.

1 *TIM.* 4. 1. *Lu.* 8. 18.—*Col.* 3. 16.—*Ep.* 6. 16. *Ps.* 119. 165, 103, 104.
Ps. 119. 105, 99. 2 *Co.* 11. 14.—*Gal.* 1. 8.

His commandments are not grievous.

This is the will of him that sent me, that every one which seeth the Son, and believeth on him, may have everlasting life.—Whatsoever we ask, we receive of him, because we keep his commandments, and do those things that are pleasing in his sight.

My yoke is easy, and my burden is light.—If ye love me, keep my commandments.—He that hath my commandments, and keepeth them, he it is that loveth me: and he that loveth me shall be loved of my Father, and I will love him, and will manifest myself to him.

Happy is the man that findeth wisdom, and the man that getteth understanding.—Her ways are ways of pleasantness, and all her paths are peace.—Great peace have they which love thy law: and nothing shall offend them.—I delight in the law of God after the inward man.

This is his commandment, That we should believe on the name of his Son Jesus Christ, and love one another.—Love worketh no ill to his neighbour: therefore love is the fulfilling of the law.

1 *JOHN* 5. 3. *Jno.* 6. 40.—1 *Jno.* 3. 22. *Mat.* 11. 30.—*Jno.* 14. 15, 21.
Pr. 3. 13, 17.—*Ps.* 119. 165.—*Ro.* 7. 22. 1 *Jno.* 3. 23.—*Ro.* 13. 10.

Remember not the sins of my youth, nor my transgressions.

I have blotted out, as a thick cloud, thy transgressions, and, as a cloud, thy sins.—I, even I, am he that blotteth out thy transgressions for mine own sake, and will not remember thy sins.—Come now, and let us reason together, saith the LORD: though your sins be as scarlet, they shall be as white as snow; though they be red like crimson, they shall be as wool.—I will forgive their iniquity, and I will remember their sin no more.—Thou wilt cast all their sins into the depths of the sea.

Thou hast in love to my soul delivered it from the pit of corruption: for thou hast cast all my sins behind thy back.—Who is a God like unto thee, that pardoneth iniquity? . . . he retaineth not his anger for ever, because he delighteth in mercy.—Unto him that loved us, and washed us from our sins in his own blood, . . . to him be glory and dominion for ever and ever. Amen.

PSA. 25. 7. *Is.* 44. 22.—*Is.* 43. 25.—*Is.* 1. 18.—*Je.* 31. 34.—*Mi.* 7. 19.
Is. 38. 17.—*Mi.* 7. 18.—*Re.* 1. 5.

As many as I love, I rebuke and chasten.

My son, despise not thou the chastening of the Lord, nor faint when thou art rebuked of him: for whom the Lord loveth he chasteneth, and scourgeth every son whom he receiveth.—Even as a father the son in whom he delighteth.—He maketh sore, and bindeth up: he woundeth, and his hands make whole.—Humble yourselves therefore under the mighty hand of God, that he may exalt you in due time.—I have chosen thee in the furnace of affliction.

He doth not afflict willingly nor grieve the children of men.— He hath not dealt with us after our sins; nor rewarded us according to our iniquities. For as the heaven is high above the earth, so great is his mercy toward them that fear him. As far as the east is from the west, so far hath he removed our transgressions from us. Like as a father pitieth his children, so the LORD pitieth them that fear him. For he knoweth our frame; he remembereth that we are dust.

REV. 3. 19. *He.* 12. 5, 6.—*Pr.* 3. 12.—*Job* 5. 18.—1 *Pe.* 5. 6.—*Is.* 48. 10. *La.* 3. 33.—*Ps.* 103. 10-14.

God is in heaven, and thou upon earth: therefore let thy words be few.

When ye pray, use not vain repetitions, as the heathen do: for they think that they shall be heard for their much speaking. Be not ye therefore like unto them: for your Father knoweth what things ye have need of, before ye ask him.

They . . . called on the name of Baal from morning even until noon, saying, O Baal, hear us.

Two men went up into the temple to pray; the one a Pharisee, and the other a publican. The Pharisee stood and prayed thus with himself, God, I thank thee, that I am not as other men are, extortioners, unjust, adulterers, or even as this publican. And the publican, standing afar off, would not lift up so much as his eyes unto heaven, but smote upon his breast, saying, God be merciful to me a sinner. I tell you, this man went down to his house justified rather than the other.

Lord, teach us to pray.

ECCLES. 5. 2. *Mat.* 6. 7, 8. 1 *Ki.* 18. 26. *Lu.* 18. 10, 11, 13, 14. *Lu.* 11. 1.

The fruit of the Spirit is goodness.

Be ye . . . followers of God, as dear children.—Love your enemies, bless them that curse you, do good to them that hate you,
and pray for them which despitefully use you, and persecute you;
that ye may be the children of your Father which is in heaven:
for he maketh his sun to rise on the evil and on the good, and
sendeth rain on the just and on the unjust.—Be ye therefore merciful, as your Father also is merciful.

The fruit of the Spirit is in all goodness and righteousness and
truth.

After that the kindness and love of God our Saviour toward
man appeared, not by works of righteousness which we have done,
but according to his mercy he saved us, by the washing of regeneration, and renewing of the Holy Ghost; which he shed on us
abundantly through Jesus Christ our Saviour.—The LORD is good
to all: and his tender mercies are over all his works.—He that
spared not his own Son, but delivered him up for us all, how shall
he not with him also freely give us all things?

*GAL. 5. 22. Ep. 5. 1.—Mat. 5. 44, 45.—Lu. 6. 36. Ep. 5. 9. Tit. 3. 4-6.—
Ps. 145. 9.—Ro. 8. 32.*

Eben-ezer . . . Hitherto hath the Lord helped us.

I was brought low, and he helped me.—Blessed be the LORD,
because he hath heard the voice of my supplications. The LORD is
my strength and my shield; my heart trusted in him, and I am
helped: therefore my heart greatly rejoiceth; and with my song
will I praise him.

It is better to trust in the LORD than to put confidence in man.
It is better to trust in the LORD than to put confidence in princes.—
Happy is he that hath the God of Jacob for his help, whose hope
is in the LORD his God.—He led them forth by the right way, that
they might go to a city of habitation.—There failed not ought of
any good thing which the LORD hath spoken unto the house of
Israel; all came to pass.

When I sent you without purse, and scrip, and shoes, lacked ye
any thing? And they said, Nothing.—Because thou hast been my
help, therefore in the shadow of thy wings will I rejoice.

*2 SAM. 7. 12. Ps. 116. 6.—Ps. 28. 6, 7. Ps. 118. 8, 9.—Ps. 146. 5.—
Ps. 107. 7.—Jos. 21. 45. Lu. 22. 35.—Ps. 63. 7.*

This is the ordinance of the passover: There shall no stranger eat thereof.

We have an altar, whereof they have no right to eat which serve the tabernacle.—Except a man be born again, he cannot see the kingdom of God.—At that time ye were without Christ, being aliens from the commonwealth of Israel, and strangers from the covenants of promise. But now, in Christ Jesus, ye who sometime were far off, are made nigh by the blood of Christ.

For he is our peace, who hath made both one, . . . having abolished in his flesh the enmity, even the law of commandments contained in ordinances; for to make in himself of twain one new man, so making peace.

Now therefore ye are no more strangers and foreigners, but fellow-citizens with the saints, and of the household of God.

If any man hear my voice, and open the door, I will come in to him, and will sup with him, and he with me.

EXOD. 12. 43. *He.* 13. 10.—*Jno.* 3. 3.—*Ep.* 2. 12, 13. *Ep.* 2. 14, 15. *Ep.* 2. 19. *Re.* 3. 20.

[Jesus] prayed the third time, saying the same words.

Who in the days of his flesh . . . offered up prayers and supplications with strong crying and tears unto him that was able to save him from death.

Then shall we know, if we follow on to know the LORD.—Continuing instant in prayer.—Praying always with all prayer and supplication in the Spirit, and watching thereunto with all perseverance and supplication.—By prayer and supplication with thanksgiving let your requests be made known unto God. And the peace of God, which passeth all understanding, shall keep your hearts and minds through Christ Jesus.

Nevertheless not as I will, but as thou wilt.—This is the confidence that we have in him, that, if we ask any thing according to his will, he heareth us.

Delight thyself . . . in the LORD; and he shall give thee the desires of thine heart. Commit thy way unto the LORD; trust also in him; and he shall bring it to pass.

MAT. 26. 44. *He.* 5. 7. *Hos.* 6. 3.—*Ro.* 12. 12.—*Ep.* 6. 18.—*Phi.* 4. 6, 7. *Mat.* 26. 39.—1 *Jno.* 5. 14. *Ps.* 37. 4, 5.

If children, then heirs; heirs of God, and joint-heirs with Christ.

If ye be Christ's, then are ye Abraham's seed, and heirs according to the promise.

Behold, what manner of love the Father hath bestowed upon us, that we should be called the sons of God.—Thou art no more a servant, but a son; and if a son, then an heir of God through Christ.—Having predestinated us unto the adoption of children by Jesus Christ to himself, according to the good pleasure of his will.

Father, I will that they also, whom thou hast given me, be with me where I am; that they may behold my glory, which thou hast given me.

He that overcometh, and keepeth my works unto the end, to him I will give power over the nations.—To him that overcometh will I grant to sit with me in my throne, even as I also overcame, and am set down with my Father in his throne.

ROM. 8. 17. *Gal.* 3. 29. 1 *Jno.* 3. 1.—*Gal.* 4. 7.—*Ep.* 1. 5. *Jno.* 17. 24. *Re.* 2. 26.—*Re.* 3. 21.

Things which are despised, hath God chosen.

Behold, are not all these which speak Galilæans ?

Jesus, . . . saw two brethren, . . . casting a net into the sea: for they were fishers. And he saith unto them, Follow me.—Now when they saw the boldness of Peter and John, and perceived that they were unlearned and ignorant men, they marvelled; and they took knowledge of them, that they had been with Jesus.

My speech and my preaching was not with enticing words of man's wisdom, but in demonstration of the Spirit and of power: that your faith should not stand in the wisdom of men, but in the power of God.

Ye have not chosen me, but I have chosen you, and ordained you, that ye should go and bring forth fruit. He that abideth in me, and I in him, the same bringeth forth much fruit: for without me ye can do nothing.—We have this treasure in earthen vessels, that the excellency of the power may be of God.

1 *COR* 1. 28. *Ac.* 2. 7. *Mat.* 4. 18, 19.—*Ac.* 4. 13. 1 *Co.* 2. 4, 5. *Jno.* 15. 16, 5.—2 *Co.* 4. 7.

Leaning on Jesus' bosom.

As one whom his mother comforteth, so will I comfort you.—They brought young children to him, that he should touch them. And he took them up in his arms, put his hands upon them, and blessed them.—Jesus called his disciples unto him, and said, I have compassion on the multitude, because they continue with me now three days, and have nothing to eat; and I will not send them away fasting, lest they faint in the way.—A high Priest . . . touched with the feeling of our infirmities.—In his love and in his pity he redeemed them.

I will not leave you comfortless (marg. orphans): I will come to you.—Can a woman forget her sucking child, that she should not have compassion on the son of her womb? yea, they may forget, yet will I not forget thee.

The Lamb which is in the midst of the throne shall feed them, and shall lead them unto living fountains of waters: and God shall wipe away all tears from their eyes.

JOHN 13. 23. *Is.* 66. 13.—*Mar.* 10. 13, 16.—*Mat.* 15. 32.—*He.* 4. 15.—
Is. 63. 9. *Jno.* 14. 18.—*Is.* 49. 15. *Re.* 7. 17.

Jesus Christ the righteous: the propitiation for our sins.

Toward the mercy seat shall the faces of the cherubims be. And thou shalt put the mercy seat above upon the ark; and in the ark thou shalt put the testimony that I shall give thee. I will meet with thee, and I will commune with thee from above the mercy seat.

Surely his salvation is nigh them that fear him; mercy and truth are met together; righteousness and peace have kissed each other.

If thou, LORD, shouldest mark iniquities, O Lord, who shall stand? But there is forgiveness with thee, that thou mayest be feared. Let Israel hope in the LORD: for with the LORD there is mercy, and with him is plenteous redemption. And he shall redeem Israel from all his iniquities.—All have sinned, and come short of the glory of God; being justified freely by his grace through the redemption that is in Christ Jesus: whom God hath set forth to be a propitiation through faith in his blood, to declare his righteousness for the remission of sins.

1 *JOHN* 2. 1, 2. *Ex.* 25. 20-22. *Ps.* 85. 9, 10. *Ps.* 130. 3, 4, 7, 8.—
Ro. 3. 23-25.

We have known and believed the love that God hath to us.

God, who is rich in mercy, for his great love wherewith he loved us, even when we were dead in sins, hath quickened us together with Christ, (by grace ye are saved;) and hath raised us up together, and made us sit together in heavenly places in Christ Jesus: that in the ages to come he might shew the exceeding riches of his grace in his kindness toward us through Christ Jesus.

God so loved the world, that he gave his only begotten Son, that whosoever believeth in him should not perish, but have everlasting life.——He that spared not his own Son, but delivered him up for us all, how shall he not with him also freely give us all things?——The LORD is good to all: and his tender mercies are over all his works.

We love him, because he first loved us.

Blessed is she that believed: for there shall be a performance of those things which were told her from the Lord.

1 *JOHN* 4. 16. *Ep.* 2. 4-7. *Jno.* 3. 16.—*Ro.* 8. 32.—*Ps.* 145. 9. 1 *Jno.* 4. 19. *Lu.* 1. 45.

Mind not high things, but condescend to men of low estate.

My brethren, have not the faith of our Lord Jesus Christ, the Lord of glory, with respect of persons. Hath not God chosen the poor of this world rich in faith, and heirs of the kingdom which he hath promised to them that love him?

Let no man seek his own, but every man another's wealth.—— Having food and raiment let us be therewith content. But they that will be rich fall into temptation and a snare, and into many foolish and hurtful lusts, which drown men in destruction and perdition.

God hath chosen the foolish things of the world to confound the wise: and God hath chosen the weak things of the world to confound the things which are mighty; and base things of the world, and things which are despised, hath God chosen, yea, and things which are not, to bring to nought things that are: that no flesh should glory in his presence.

LORD, my heart is not haughty, nor mine eyes lofty.

ROM. 12. 16. *Ja.* 2. 1, 5. 1 *Co.* 10. 24.—1 *Ti.* 6. 8, 9. 1 *Co.* 1. 27-29. *Ps.* 131. 1.

Let your speech be always with grace.

A word fitly spoken is like apples of gold in pictures of silver. As an earring of gold, and an ornament of fine gold, so is a wise reprover upon an obedient ear.—Let no corrupt communication proceed out of your mouth, but that which is good to the use of edifying, that it may minister grace unto the hearers.—A good man out of the good treasure of the heart bringeth forth good things: and an evil man out of the evil treasure bringeth forth evil things.—By thy words thou shalt be justified.—The tongue of the wise is health.

They that feared the LORD spake often one to another: and the LORD hearkened, and heard it, and a book of remembrance was written before him for them that feared the LORD, and that thought upon his name.

If thou take forth the precious from the vile, thou shalt be as my mouth.—Therefore, as ye abound in every thing, in faith, and utterance, and knowledge, and in all diligence, . . . see that ye abound in this grace also.

COL. 4. 6. *Pr.* 25. 11, 12.—*Ep.* 4. 29.—*Mat.* 12. 35, 37.—*Pr.* 12. 18. *Mal.* 3. 16. *Je.* 15. 19.—2 *Co.* 8. 7.

Thy lovingkindness is before mine eyes.

The LORD is gracious, and full of compassion; slow to anger, and of great mercy.—Your Father which is in heaven: . . . maketh his sun to rise on the evil and on the good, and sendeth rain on the just and on the unjust.

Be ye . . . followers of God, as dear children; and walk in love, as Christ also hath loved us, and hath given himself for us an offering and a sacrifice to God for a sweet-smelling savour.— Be ye kind to one another, tenderhearted, forgiving one another, even as God for Christ's sake hath forgiven you.—Seeing ye have purified your souls in obeying the truth through the Spirit unto unfeigned love of the brethren, see that ye love one another with a pure heart fervently.—The love of Christ constraineth us.

Love ye your enemies, and do good, and lend, hoping for nothing again; and your reward shall be great, and ye shall be the children of the Highest: for he is kind unto the unthankful and to the evil. Be ye therefore merciful, as your Father also is merciful.

PSA. 26. 3. *Ps.* 145. 8.—*Mat.* 5. 45. *Ep.* 5. 1, 2.—*Ep.* 4. 32.—1 *Pe.* 1. 22.— 2 *Co.* 5. 14. *Lu.* 6. 35, 36.

Then was Jesus led up of the spirit into the wilderness to be tempted of the devil.

In the days of his flesh, when he had offered up prayers and supplications with strong crying and tears unto him that was able to save him from death, and was heard in that he feared; though he were a Son, yet learned he obedience by the things which he suffered; and being made perfect, he became the author of eternal salvation unto all them that obey him.—We have not an high priest which cannot be touched with the feeling of our infirmities; but was in all points tempted like as we are, yet without sin.

There hath no temptation taken you but such as is common to man: but God is faithful, who will not suffer you to be tempted above that ye are able; but will with the temptation also make a way to escape, that ye may be able to bear it.—My grace is sufficient for thee: for my strength is made perfect in weakness.

MAT. 4. 1. *He.* 5. 7-9.—*He.* 4. 15. 1 *Co.* 10. 13.—2 *Co.* 12. 9.

The Son of man came to give his life a ransom for many.

If the blood of bulls and of goats, and the ashes of an heifer sprinkling the unclean, sanctifieth to the purifying of the flesh: how much more shall the blood of Christ, who through the eternal Spirit offered himself without spot to God, purge your conscience from dead works to serve the living God?

He is brought as a lamb to the slaughter.—I lay down my life for the sheep. No man taketh it from me, but I lay it down of myself. I have power to lay it down, and I have power to take it again.

The life of the flesh is in the blood: and I have given it to you upon the altar, to make an atonement for your souls: for it is the blood that maketh an atonement for the soul.—Without shedding of blood is no remission.

While we were yet sinners, Christ died for us. Much more then, being now justified by his blood, we shall be saved from wrath through him.

MAT. 20. 28. *He.* 9. 13, 14. *Is.* 53. 7.—*Jno.* 10. 15, 18. *Le.* 17. 11.— *He.* 9. 22. *Ro.* 5. 8, 9.

If we confess our sins, he is faithful and just to forgive us our sins, and to cleanse us from all unrighteousness.

I acknowledge my transgressions: and my sin is ever before me. Against thee, thee only, have I sinned, and done this evil in thy sight.

And he arose, and came to his father. But when he was yet a great way off, his father saw him, and had compassion, and ran, and fell on his neck, and kissed him.—I have blotted out as a thick cloud, thy transgressions, and, as a cloud, thy sins: return unto me; for I have redeemed thee.—Your sins are forgiven you for his name's sake.—God for Christ's sake hath forgiven you.—That he might be just, and the justifier of him which believeth in Jesus.

Then will I sprinkle clean water upon you, and ye shall be clean. —They shall walk with me in white: for they are worthy.

This is he that came by water and blood, even Jesus Christ: not by water only, but by water and blood.

1 *JOHN* 1. 9. *Ps.* 51. 3, 4. *Lu.* 15. 20.—*Is.* 44. 22.—1 *Jno.* 2. 12.—
Ep. 4. 32.—*Ro.* 3. 26. *Eze.* 36. 25.—*Re.* 3. 4. 1 *Jno.* 5. 6.

Shall the throne of iniquity have fellowship with thee?

Truly our fellowship is with the Father, and with his Son Jesus Christ.—Beloved, now are we the sons of God, and it doth not yet appear what we shall be: but we know that, when he shall appear, we shall be like him; for we shall see him as he is. And every man that hath this hope in him purifieth himself, even as he is pure.

The prince of this world cometh, and hath nothing in me.— An high priest . . . holy, harmless, undefiled.

We wrestle not against flesh and blood, but against principalities, against powers, against the rulers of the darkness of this world, against spiritual wickedness in high places.—The prince of the power of the air, the spirit that now worketh in the children of disobedience.

Whosoever is born of God sinneth not; but he that is begotten of God keepeth himself, and that wicked one toucheth him not. And we know that we are of God, and the whole world lieth in wickedness.

PSA. 94. 20. 1 *Jno.* 1. 3.—1. *Jno.* 3. 2, 3. *Jno.* 14. 30.—*He.* 7. 26.
Ep. 6. 12.—*Ep.* 2. 2. 1 *Jno.* 5. 18, 19.

I have caused thine iniquity to pass from thee, and I will clothe thee with change of raiment.

Blessed is he whose transgression is forgiven, whose sin is covered.—We are all as an unclean thing.—I know that in me (that is, in my flesh,) dwelleth no good thing: for to will is present with me; but how to perform that which is good I find not.

As many of you as have been baptized into Christ have put on Christ.—Ye have put off the old man with his deeds; and have put on the new man, which is renewed in knowledge after the image of him that created him.—Not having mine own righteousness which is of the law, but . . . the righteousness which is of God by faith.

Bring forth the best robe, and put it on him.—The fine linen is the righteousness of saints.—I will greatly rejoice in the LORD, my soul shall be joyful in my God; for he hath clothed me with the garments of salvation, he hath covered me with the robe of righteousness.

ZEC. 3. 4. *Ps.* 32. 1.—*Is.* 64. 6.—*Ro.* 7. 18. *Gal.* 3. 27.—*Col.* 3. 9, 10.—
Phi. 3. 9. *Lu.* 15. 22.—*Re.* 19. 8.—*Is.* 61. 10.

The day shall declare it.

Judge nothing before the time, until the Lord come, who both will bring to light the hidden things of darkness, and will make manifest the counsels of the hearts: and then shall every man have praise of God.

Why dost thou judge thy brother? or why dost thou set at nought thy brother? for we shall all stand before the judgment seat of Christ. So then every one of us shall give account of himself to God. Let us not therefore judge one another any more.

God shall judge the secrets of men by Jesus Christ.—The Father judgeth no man, but hath committed all judgment unto the Son: and hath given him authority to execute judgment also, because he is the Son of man.

The Great, the Mighty God, the LORD of hosts, is his name, great in counsel, and mighty in work: for thine eyes are open upon all the ways of the sons of men: to give every one according to his ways, and according to the fruit of his doings.

1 COR. 3. 13. *1 Co.* 4. 5. *Ro.* 14. 10, 12, 13. *Ro.* 2. 16.—*Jno.* 5. 22, 27.
Je. 32. 18, 19.

The disciple is not above his master.

Ye call me Master and Lord: and ye say well; for so I am.

It is enough for the disciple that he be as his master, and the servant as his lord.——If they have persecuted me, they will also persecute you; if they have kept my saying, they will keep your's also.——I have given them thy word; and the world hath hated them, because they are not of the world, even as I am not of the world.

Consider him that endured such contradiction of sinners against himself, lest ye be wearied and faint in your minds. Ye have not yet resisted unto blood, striving against sin.

Let us run with patience the race that is set before us, looking unto Jesus the author and finisher of our faith; who for the joy that was set before him endured the cross, despising the shame, and is set down at the right hand of the throne of God.——Forasmuch . . . as Christ hath suffered for us in the flesh, arm yourselves likewise with the same mind.

MAT. 10 24. *Jno.* 13. 13. *Mat.* 10. 25.——*Jno.* 15. 20.——*Jno.* 17. 14.
He. 12. 3, 4. *He.* 12. 1, 2.——1 *Pe.* 4. 1.

My son, give me thine heart.

O that there were such an heart in them, that they would fear me, and keep all my commandments always, that it might be well with them, and with their children for ever!

Thy heart is not right in the sight of God.——Because the carnal mind is enmity against God: for it is not subject to the law of God, neither indeed can be. So then they that are in the flesh cannot please God.

They . . . first gave their own selves to the Lord.——In every work that [Hezekiah] began . . . to seek his God, he did it with all his heart, and prospered.

Keep thy heart with all diligence; for out of it are the issues of life.

Whatsoever ye do, do it heartily, as to the Lord.——As the servants of Christ, doing the will of God from the heart; with good will doing service, as to the Lord, and not to men.

I will run the way of thy commandments, when thou shalt enlarge my heart.

PROV. 23. 26. *De.* 5. 29. *Ac.* 8. 21.——*Ro.* 8. 7, 8. 2 *Co.* 8. 5.——
2 *Ch.* 31. 21. *Pr.* 4. 23. *Col.* 3. 23.——*Ep.* 6. 6, 7. *Ps.* 119. 32.

I am with thee to save thee.

Shall the prey be taken from the mighty, or the lawful captive delivered? But thus saith the LORD, Even the captives of the mighty shall be taken away, and the prey of the terrible shall be delivered: for I will contend with him that contendeth with thee. And all flesh shall know that I the LORD am thy Saviour and thy Redeemer, the mighty One of Jacob.—Fear thou not; for I am with thee: be not dismayed; for I am thy God: I will strengthen thee; yea, I will help thee; yea, I will uphold thee with the right hand of my righteousness.

We have not an high priest which cannot be touched with the feeling of our infirmities; but was in all points tempted like as we are, yet without sin.—In that he himself hath suffered being tempted, he is able to succour them that are tempted.—The steps of a good man are ordered by the LORD: and he delighteth in his way. Though he fall, he shall not be utterly cast down: for the LORD upholdeth him with his hand.

JER. 15. 20. *Is.* 49. 24-26.—*Is.* 41. 10. *He.* 4. 15.—*He.* 2. 18.—
Ps. 37. 23, 24.

He satisfieth the longing soul, and filleth the hungry soul with goodness.

Ye have tasted that the Lord is gracious.

O God, thou art my God; early will I seek thee: my soul thirsteth for thee, my flesh longeth for thee in a dry and thirsty land, where no water is; to see thy power and thy glory.—My soul longeth, yea, even fainteth for the courts of the LORD: my heart and my flesh crieth out for the living God.—Having a desire to depart, and to be with Christ; which is far better.

I shall be satisfied, when I awake, with thy likeness.—They shall hunger no more, neither thirst any more; neither shall the sun light on them, nor any heat. For the Lamb which is in the midst of the throne shall feed them, and shall lead them unto living fountains of waters: and God shall wipe away all tears from their eyes.—They shall be abundantly satisfied with the fatness of thy house; and thou shalt make them drink of the river of thy pleasures.—My people shall be satisfied with my goodness, saith the LORD.

PSA. 107. 9. *1 Pe.* 2. 3. *Ps.* 63. 1, 2.—*Ps.* 84. 2.—*Phi.* 1. 23. *Ps.* 17. 15.—
Re. 7. 16, 17.—*Ps.* 36. 8.—*Je.* 31. 14.

My presence shall go with thee, and I will give thee rest.

Be strong and of a good courage, fear not, nor be afraid of them: for the LORD thy God, he it is that doth go with thee; he will not fail thee, nor forsake thee. The LORD, he it is that doth go before thee; he will be with thee, he will not fail thee, neither forsake thee: fear not, neither be dismayed.—Have not I commanded thee? Be strong and of a good courage; be not afraid, neither be thou dismayed: for the LORD thy God is with thee whithersoever thou goest.—In all thy ways acknowledge him, and he shall direct thy paths.

He hath said, I will never leave thee, nor forsake thee. So that we may boldly say, The Lord is my helper, and I will not fear what man shall do unto me.—Our sufficiency is of God.

Lead us not into temptation.—O LORD, I know that the way of man is not in himself: it is not in man that walketh to direct his steps.—My times are in thy hand.

EXOD. 33. 14. *De.* 31. 6, 8.—*Jos.* 1. 9.—*Pr.* 3. 6 *Heb.* 13. 5, 6.—2 *Cor.* 3. 5.
Mat. 6. 13.—*Je.* 10. 23.—*Ps.* 31. 15.

Let us consider one another to provoke unto love and to good works.

How forcible are right words!—I stir up your pure minds by way of remembrance.

They that feared the LORD spake often one to another: and the LORD hearkened, and heard it, and a book of remembrance was written before him for them that feared the LORD, and that thought upon his name.—If two of you shall agree on earth as touching any thing that they shall ask, it shall be done for them of my Father which is in heaven.

The LORD God said, It is not good that the man should be alone. —Two are better than one; because they have a good reward for their labour. For if they fall, the one will lift up his fellow: but woe to him that is alone when he falleth; for he hath not another to help him up.

Let . . . no man put a stumblingblock or an occasion to fall in his brother's way.—Bear ye one another's burdens, and so fulfil the law of Christ. Considering thyself, lest thou also be tempted.

HEB. 10. 24. *Job* 6. 25.—2 *Pe.* 3. 1. *Mal.* 3. 16.—*Mat.* 18. 19.
Ge. 2. 18.—*Ec.* 4. 9, 10. *Ro.* 14. 13.—*Ga.* 6. 2, 1.

I am my Beloved's, and His desire is toward me.

I know whom I have believed, and am persuaded that he is able to keep that which I have committed unto him against that day.—I am persuaded, that neither death, nor life, nor angels, nor principalities, nor powers, nor things present, nor things to come, nor height, nor depth, nor any other creature, shall be able to separate us from the love of God, which is in Christ Jesus our Lord.—Those that thou gavest me I have kept, and none of them is lost.

The LORD taketh pleasure in his people.—My delights were with the sons of men.—His great love wherewith he loved us.—Greater love hath no man than this, that a man lay down his life for his friends.

Ye are bought with a price: therefore glorify God in your body, and in your spirit, which are God's.—Whether we live, we live unto the Lord; and whether we die, we die unto the Lord: whether we live therefore, or die, we are the Lord's.

CANT. 7. 10. 2. *Ti.* 1. 12.—*Ro.* 8. 38, 39.—*Jno.* 17. 12. *Ps.* 149. 4.—
Pr. 8. 31.—*Ep.* 2. 4.—*Jno.* 15. 13. 1 *Co.* 6. 20.—*Ro.* 14. 8.

Seek ye out of the book of the Lord.

Ye shall lay up these my words in your heart and in your soul, and bind them for a sign upon your hand, that they may be as frontlets between your eyes.—This book of the law shall not depart out of thy mouth; but thou shalt meditate therein day and night, that thou mayest observe to do according to all that is written therein: for then thou shalt make thy way prosperous, and then thou shalt have good success.

The law of his God is in his heart; none of his steps shall slide.—By the word of thy lips I have kept me from the paths of the destroyer.—Thy word have I hid in mine heart, that I might not sin against thee.

We have . . . a more sure word of prophecy; whereunto ye do well that ye take heed, as unto a light that shineth in a dark place, until the day dawn, and the day star arise in your hearts.—That we through patience and comfort of the scriptures might have hope.

ISA. 34. 16. *De.* 11. 18.—*Jos* 1. 8. *Ps.* 37. 31.—*Ps.* 17. 4.—*Ps.* 119. 11.
2 *Pe.* 1. 19.—*Ro.* 15. 4.

Out of the abundance of the heart the mouth speaketh.

Let the word of Christ dwell in you richly in all wisdom.

Keep thy heart with all diligence; for out of it are the issues of life.—Death and life are in the power of the tongue.—The mouth of the righteous speaketh wisdom, and his tongue talketh of judgment. The law of his God is in his heart: none of his steps shall slide.—Let no corrupt communication proceed out of your mouth, but that which is good to the use of edifying, that it may minister grace unto the hearers.

We cannot but speak the things which we have seen and heard. —I believed, therefore have I spoken.

Whosoever . . . shall confess me before men, him will I confess also before my Father which is in heaven.—With the heart man believeth unto righteousness; and with the mouth confession is made unto salvation.

MAT. 12. 34. *Col.* 3. 16. *Pr.* 4. 23.—*Pr.* 18. 21.—*Ps.* 37. 30, 31.—*Ep.* 4. 29. *Ac.* 4. 20.—*Ps.* 116. 10. *Mat.* 10. 32.—*Ro.* 10. 10.

I trust I shall shortly see thee, and we shall speak face to face.

Oh that thou wouldest rend the heavens, that thou wouldest come down!—As the hart panteth after the water brooks, so panteth my soul after thee, O God. My soul thirsteth for God, for the living God: when shall I come and appear before God?— Make haste, my beloved, and be thou like to a roe or to a young hart upon the mountains of spices.

Our conversation is in heaven; from whence also we look for the Saviour, the Lord Jesus Christ.—Looking for that blessed hope, and the glorious appearing of the great God and our Saviour Jesus Christ.—God our Saviour, and Lord Jesus Christ, which is our hope.—Whom having not seen, ye love.

He which testifieth these things saith, Surely I come quickly; Amen. Even so, come, Lord Jesus.—It shall be said in that day, Lo, this is our God; we have waited for him, and he will save us: this is the LORD; we have waited for him, we will be glad and rejoice in his salvation.

3 *JOHN* 14. *Is.* 64. 1.—*Ps.* 42. 1, 2.—*Ca.* 8. 14. *Phi.* 3. 20.—*Tit.* 2. 13.— 1 *Ti.* 1. 1.—1 *Pe.* 1. 8. *Re.* 22. 20.—*Is.* 25. 9.

Thy will be done in earth, as it is in heaven.

Bless the LORD, ye his angels, that excel in strength, that do his commandments, hearkening unto the voice of his word. Bless ye the LORD, all ye his hosts; ye ministers of his, that do his pleasure.

I came down from heaven not to do mine own will, but the will of him that sent me.—I delight to do thy will, O my God: yea, thy law is within my heart.—O my Father, if this cup may not pass away from me, except I drink it, thy will be done.

Not every one that saith unto me, Lord, Lord, shall enter into the kingdom of heaven; but he that doeth the will of my Father which is in heaven.—Not the hearers of the law are just before God, but the doers of the law shall be justified.—If ye know these things, happy are ye if ye do them.—To him that knoweth to do good, and doeth it not, to him it is sin.

Be not conformed to this world: but ye be transformed by the renewing of your mind.

MAT. 6. 10. *Ps.* 103. 20, 21. *Jno.* 6. 38.—*Ps.* 40. 8.—*Mat.* 26. 42. *Mat.* 7. 21.—*Ro.* 2. 13.—*Jno.* 13. 17.—*Jas.* 4. 17. *Ro.* 12. 2.

The ear trieth words, as the mouth tasteth meat.

Beloved, believe not every spirit, but try the spirits whether they are of God: because many false prophets are gone out into the world.—Judge not according to the appearance, but judge righteous judgment.—I speak as to wise men; judge ye what I say. —Let the word of Christ dwell in you richly in all wisdom.

He that hath an ear, let him hear what the Spirit saith.—He that is spiritual judgeth all things.

Take heed what ye hear.—I know thy works, . . . and how . . . thou hast tried them which say they are apostles, and are not, and hast found them liars.—Prove all things; hold fast that which is good.

He calleth his own sheep by name, and leadeth them out. And when he putteth forth his own sheep, he goeth before them, and the sheep follow him: for they know his voice. And a stranger will they not follow, but will flee from him: for they know not the voice of strangers.

JOB 34. 3. 1 *Jno.* 4. 1.—*Jno.* 7. 24.—1 *Co.* 10. 15.—*Col.* 3. 16. *Re.* 2. 29.— 1 *Co.* 2. 15. *Mar.* 4. 24.—*Re.* 2. 2.—1 *Th.* 5. 21. *Jno.* 10. 3-5.

Ye shall be unto me a kingdom of priests, and a holy nation.

Thou wast slain, and hast redeemed us to God by thy blood out of every kindred, and tongue, and people, and nation; and hast made us unto our God kings and priests.—Ye are a chosen generation, a royal priesthood, a holy nation, a peculiar people; that ye should shew forth the praises of him who hath called you out of darkness into his marvellous light.

Ye shall be named the Priests of the LORD: men shall call you the Ministers of our God.—Priests of God and of Christ.

Wherefore, holy brethren, partakers of the heavenly calling, consider the Apostle and High Priest of our profession, Christ Jesus.—By him therefore let us offer the sacrifice of praise to God continually, that is, the fruit of our lips giving thanks to his name.

For we are his workmanship, created in Christ Jesus unto good works, which God hath before ordained that we should walk in them.—The temple of God is holy, which temple ye are.

EXOD. 19. 6. *Re.* 5. 9, 10.—1 *Pe.* 2. 9. *Is.* 61. 6.—*Re.* 20. 6. *He.* 3. 1.—
He. 13. 15. *Ep.* 2. 10.—1 *Cor.* 3. 17.

We made our prayer unto our God, and set a watch against them.

Watch and pray, that ye enter not into temptation.—Continue in prayer, and watch in the same with thanksgiving.—Casting all your care upon him; for he careth for you. Be sober, be vigilant; because your adversary the devil, as a roaring lion, walketh about, seeking whom he may devour: whom resist stedfast in the faith.

Why call ye me, Lord, Lord, and do not the things which I say?—Be ye doers of the word, and not hearers only, deceiving your own selves.

Wherefore criest thou unto me? speak unto the children of Israel, that they go forward.

Be careful for nothing; but in every thing by prayer and supplication with thanksgiving let your requests be made known unto God. And the peace of God, which passeth all understanding, shall keep your hearts and minds through Christ Jesus.

NEH. 4. 9. *Mat.* 26. 41.—*Col.* 4. 2.—1 *Pe.* 5. 7-9. *Lu.* 6. 46.—*Ja.* 1. 22.
Ex. 14. 15. *Phi* 4. 6, 7.

Thou art a gracious God, and merciful, slow to anger, and of great kindness, and repentest thee of the evil.

I beseech thee, let the power of my Lord be great, according as thou hast spoken, saying, The LORD is longsuffering, and of great mercy, forgiving iniquity and transgression, and by no means clearing the guilty; visiting the iniquity of the fathers upon the children unto the third and fourth generation.

O remember not against us former iniquities: let thy tender mercies speedily prevent us. Help us, O God of our salvation, for the glory of thy name: and deliver us, and purge away our sins, for thy name's sake.—O LORD, though our iniquities testify against us, do thou it for thy name's sake: for our backslidings are many; we have sinned against thee.—We acknowledge, O LORD, our wickedness, and the iniquity of our fathers: for we have sinned against thee.

If thou, LORD, shouldest mark iniquities, O LORD, who shall stand? But there is forgiveness with thee, that thou mayest be feared.

JONAH 4. 2. *Nu.* 14. 17, 18. *Ps.* 79. 8, 9.—*Je.* 14. 7, 20. *Ps.* 130. 3. 4.

Sanctification of the Spirit.

Awake, O north wind; and come, thou south; blow upon my garden, that the spices thereof may flow out.

Behold this selfsame thing, that ye sorrowed after a godly sort, what carefulness it wrought in you, yea, what clearing of yourselves, yea, what indignation, yea, what fear, yea, what vehement desire, yea, what zeal, yea, what revenge!—Fruit of the Spirit is in all goodness and righteousness and truth: proving what is acceptable unto the Lord.

The Comforter is the Holy Ghost.—The love of God is shed abroad in our hearts by the Holy Ghost which is given unto us.

The fruit of the Spirit is love, joy, peace.

In a great trial of affliction the abundance of their joy and their deep poverty abounded unto the riches of their liberality.

All these worketh that one and the selfsame Spirit, dividing to every man severally as he will.

2 THES. 2. 13. *Ca.* 4. 16. 2. *Co.* 7. 11.—*Ep.* 5. 9, 10. *Jno.* 14. 16.—*Ro.* 5. 5. *Ga.* 5. 22. 2 *Co.* 8. 2. 1 *Co.* 12. 11.

He calleth his own sheep by name, and leadeth them out.

The foundation of God standeth sure, having this seal, The Lord knoweth them that are his; and, Let every one that nameth the name of Christ, depart from iniquity.—Many will say to me in that day, Lord, Lord, have we not prophesied in thy name? and in thy name have cast out devils? and in thy name done many wonderful works? And then will I profess unto them, I never knew you: depart from me, ye that work iniquity.—The LORD knoweth the way of the righteous; but the way of the ungodly shall perish.

Behold, I have graven thee upon the palms of my hands; thy walls are continually before me.—Set me as a seal upon thine heart, as a seal upon thine arm.—The LORD is good, a strong hold in the day of trouble; and he knoweth them that trust in him.

I go to prepare a place for you. And if I go and prepare a place for you, I will come again, and receive you unto myself; that where I am, there ye may be also.

JOHN 10.3 *2 Ti.* 2. 19.—*Mat.* 7. 22, 23.—*Ps.* 1. 6. *Is.* 49. 16.—*Ca.* 8. 6.— *Na.* 1. 7. *Jno.* 14. 2, 3.

She hath done what she could.

This poor widow hath cast in more than they all.—Whosoever shall give you a cup of water to drink in my name, because ye belong to Christ, verily I say unto you, he shall not lose his reward.—If there be first a willing mind, it is accepted according to that a man hath, and not according to that he hath not.

Let us not love in word, neither in tongue; but in deed and in truth.—If a brother or sister be naked, and destitute of daily food, and one of you say unto them, Depart in peace, be ye warmed and filled; notwithstanding ye give them not those things which are needful to the body; what doth it profit?—He which soweth bountifully, shall reap also bountifully. Every man according as he purposeth in his heart, so let him give; not grudgingly, or of necessity: for God loveth a cheerful giver.

When ye shall have done all those things which are commanded you, say, We are unprofitable servants: we have done that which was our duty to do.

MARK 14. 8. *Lu.* 21. 3.—*Mar.* 9. 41.—*2 Co.* 8. 12. *1 Jno.* 3. 18. —*Ja.* 2. 15, 16.—*2 Cor.* 9. 6, 7. *Lu.* 17. 10.

He that is mighty hath done to me great things; and holy is his name.

Who is like unto thee, O LORD, among the gods? who is like thee, glorious in holiness, fearful in praises, doing wonders?—Among the gods there is none like unto thee, O LORD; neither are there any works like unto thy works.—Who shall not fear thee, O Lord, and glorify thy name? for thou only art holy.—Hallowed be thy name.

Blessed be the Lord God of Israel; for he hath visited and redeemed his people.

Who is this that cometh from Edom, with dyed garments from Bozrah? this that is glorious in his apparel, travelling in the greatness of his strength? I that speak in righteousness, mighty to save.—I have laid help upon one that is mighty; I have exalted one chosen out of the people.

Now unto him that is able to do exceeding abundantly above all that we ask or think, according to the power that worketh in us, . . . be glory.

LUKE 1. 49. *Ex.* 15. 11.—*Ps.* 86. 8.—*Re.* 15. 4.—*Mat.* 6. 9. *Lu.* 1. 68. *Is.* 63. 1.—*Ps.* 89. 19. *Ep.* 3. 20, 21.

The dew of Hermon.

Mount Sion, which is Hermon.—There the LORD commanded the blessing, even life for evermore.—I will be as the dew unto Israel: he shall grow as the lily, and cast forth his roots as Lebanon.

My doctrine shall drop as the rain, my speech shall distil as the dew, as the small rain upon the tender herb, and as the showers upon the grass.—As the rain cometh down, and the snow from heaven, and returneth not thither, but watereth the earth, and maketh it bring forth and bud, that it may give seed to the sower, and bread to the eater: so shall my word be that goeth forth out of my mouth: it shall not return unto me void, but it shall accomplish that which I please, and it shall prosper in the thing whereto I sent it.

God giveth not the Spirit by measure unto him.—And of his fulness have all we received, and grace for grace.—It is like the precious ointment upon the head . . . even Aaron's . . . that went down to the skirts of his garments.

PSA. 133. 3. *De.* 4. 48.—*Ps.* 133. 3.—*Ho.* 14. 5. *De.* 32. 2.—*Is.* 55. 10, 11. *Jno.* 3. 34.—*Jno.* 1. 16.—*Ps.* 133. 2.

They are not of the world, even as I am not of the world.

He is despised and rejected of men; a man of sorrows, and acquainted with grief.—In the world ye shall have tribulation: but be of good cheer; I have overcome the world.

Such an high priest became us, who is holy, harmless, undefiled, separate from sinners.—That ye may be blameless and harmless, the sons of God, without rebuke, in the midst of a crooked and perverse nation.

Jesus of Nazareth . . . went about doing good, and healing all that were oppressed of the devil; for God was with him.—As we have therefore opportunity, let us do good unto all men, especially unto them who are of the household of faith.

That was the true Light, which lighteth every man that cometh into the world.—Ye are the light of the world. A city that is set on a hill cannot be hid. Let your light so shine before men, that they may see your good works, and glorify your Father which is in heaven.

JOHN 17. 16. *Is.* 53. 3.—*Jno.* 16. 33. *He.* 7. 26.—*Phi.* 2. 15. *Ac.* 10. 38.—
Gal. 6. 10. *Jno.* 1. 9.—*Mat.* 5. 14, 16.

He that is of a merry heart hath a continual feast.

The joy of the LORD is your strength.—The kingdom of God is not meat and drink; but righteousness, and peace, and joy in the Holy Ghost.—Be filled with the Spirit; speaking to yourselves in psalms and hymns and spiritual songs, singing and making melody in your heart to the Lord; giving thanks always for all things unto God and the Father in the name of our Lord Jesus Christ.

By him . . . let us offer the sacrifice of praise to God continually, that is, the fruit of our lips giving thanks to his name.

Although the fig tree shall not blossom, neither shall fruit be in the vines; the labour of the olive shall fail, and the fields shall yield no meat; the flock shall be cut off from the fold, and there shall be no herd in the stalls: yet I will rejoice in the LORD, I will joy in the God of my salvation.—Sorrowful, yet alway rejoicing. —We glory in tribulations also.

PRO. 15. 15. *Ne.* 8. 10.—*Ro.* 14. 17.—*Ep.* 5. 18-20. *He.* 13. 15.
Hab. 3. 17, 18.—2 *Co.* 6. 10.—*Ro.* 5. 3.

What profit is there of circumcision?

Much every way.—Circumcise yourselves to the LORD, and take away the foreskins of your heart.—If . . . their uncircumcised hearts be humbled, and they then accept of the punishment of their iniquity: then will I remember my covenant with Jacob, and also my covenant with Isaac, and also my covenant with Abraham will I remember.

Jesus Christ was a minister of the circumcision for the truth of God, to confirm the promises made unto the fathers.—In whom also ye are circumcised with the circumcision made without hands, in putting off the body of the sins of the flesh by the circumcision of Christ.—You, being dead in your sins and the uncircumcision of your flesh, hath he quickened together with him, having forgiven you all trespasses.

Put off concerning the former conversation the old man, which is corrupt according to the deceitful lusts; and be renewed in the spirit of your mind; and . . . put on the new man, which after God is created in righteousness.

ROM. 3. 1. Ro. 3. 2.—Je. 4. 4.—Le. 26. 41, 42. Ro. 15. 8.—Col. 2. 11.— Col. 2. 13. Ep. 4. 22-24.

The veil of the temple was rent in twain from the top to the bottom.

The Lord Jesus the same night in which he was betrayed took bread: and when he had given thanks, he brake it, and said, Take, eat: this is my body, which is broken for you: this do in remembrance of me.—The bread that I will give is my flesh, which I will give for the life of the world.

Except ye eat the flesh of the Son of man, and drink his blood, ye have no life in you. Whoso eateth my flesh, and drinketh my blood, hath eternal life. He that eateth my flesh, and drinketh my blood, dwelleth in me, and I in him. As the living Father hath sent me, and I live by the Father: so he that eateth me, even he shall live by me. Doth this offend you? What and if ye shall see the Son of man ascend up where he was before? It is the spirit that quickeneth; the flesh profiteth nothing.

A new and living way, which he hath consecrated for us, through the veil, that is to say, his flesh; let us draw near.

MAT. 27. 51. 1 Co. 11. 23, 24.—Jno. 6. 51, 53, 54, 56, 57, 61-63. He. 10. 20, 22.

In that he died, he died unto sin once: but in that he liveth, he liveth unto God.

He was numbered with the transgressors.—Christ was once offered to bear the sins of many.—Who his own self bare our sins in his own body on the tree, that we, being dead to sins, should live unto righteousness: by whose stripes ye were healed.—By one offering he hath perfected for ever them that are sanctified.

This man, because he continueth ever, hath an unchangeable priesthood. Wherefore he is able also to save them to the uttermost that come unto God by him, seeing he ever liveth to make intercession for them.—While we were yet sinners Christ died for us. Much more then, being now justified by his blood, we shall be saved from wrath through him.

Forasmuch . . . as Christ hath suffered for us in the flesh, arm yourselves likewise with the same mind: for he that hath suffered in the flesh hath ceased from sin; that he no longer should live the rest of his time in the flesh to the lusts of men, but to the will of God.

ROM. 6. 10. *Is.* 53. 12.—*He.* 9. 28.—1 *Pe.* 2. 24.—*He.* 10. 14. *He.* 7. 24, 25. *Ro.* 5. 8, 9. 1 *Pe.* 4. 1, 2.

Keep yourselves in the love of God.

Abide in me, and I in you. As the branch cannot bear fruit of itself, except it abide in the vine; no more can ye, except ye abide in me. I am the vine, ye are the branches: He that abideth in me, and I in him, the same bringeth forth much fruit: for without me ye can do nothing.

The fruit of the Spirit is love.

Herein is my Father glorified, that ye bear much fruit; so shall ye be my disciples. As the Father hath loved me, so have I loved you: continue ye in my love. If ye keep my commandments, ye shall abide in my love; even as I have kept my Father's commandments, and abide in his love.—Whoso keepeth his word, in him verily is the love of God perfected.

This is my commandment, That ye love one another, as I have loved you.—God commendeth his love toward us, in that, while we were yet sinners, Christ died for us.—God is love; and he that dwelleth in love dwelleth in God, and God in him.

JUDE 21. *Jno.* 15. 4, 5. *Ga.* 5. 22. *Jno.* 15. 8-10.—1 *Jno.* 2. 5. *Jno.* 15. 12.—*Ro.* 5. 8.—1 *Jno.* 4. 16.

Then cometh the end.

Of that day and that hour knoweth no man, no, not the angels which are in heaven, neither the Son, but the Father. Take ye heed, watch and pray: for ye know not when the time is. And what I say unto you I say unto all, Watch.—The Lord is not slack concerning his promise, as some men count slackness; but is longsuffering to us-ward, not willing that any should perish, but that all should come to repentance.—The coming of the Lord draweth nigh. The judge standeth before the door.—Surely I come quickly.

Seeing . . . that all these things shall be dissolved, what manner of persons ought ye to be in all holy conversation and godliness?

The end of all things is at hand: be ye therefore sober, and watch unto prayer.—Let your loins be girded about, and your lights burning; and ye yourselves like unto men that wait for their lord, when he will return from the wedding; that when he cometh and knocketh, they may open unto him immediately.

1 *COR.* 15. 24. *Mar.* 13. 32, 33, 37.—*2 Pe.* 3. 9.—*Jas.* 5. 8, 9.—*Re.* 22. 20.
2 *Pe.* 3. 11. 1 *Pe.* 4. 7.—*Lu.* 12. 35, 36.

Brethren, pray for us.

Is any sick among you? let him call for the elders of the church; and let them pray over him. And the prayer of faith shall save the sick, and the Lord shall raise him up. Pray one for another, that ye may be healed. The effectual fervent prayer of a righteous man availeth much. Elias was a man subject to like passions as we are, and he prayed earnestly that it might not rain: and it rained not on the earth by the space of three years and six months. And he prayed again, and the heaven gave rain, and the earth brought forth her fruit.

Praying always with all prayer and supplication in the Spirit, and watching thereunto with all perseverance and supplication for all saints.

Without ceasing I make mention of you always in my prayers.— Always labouring fervently for you in prayers, that ye may stand perfect and complete in all the will of God.

1 *THES.* 5. 25. *Ja.* 5. 14-18. *Ep.* 6. 18. *Ro.* 1. 9.—*Col.* 4. 12.

Patient in tribulation.

It is the LORD: let him do what seemeth him good.—Whom, though I were righteous, yet would I not answer, but I would make supplication to my judge.—The LORD gave, and the LORD hath taken away; blessed be the name of the LORD.—What? shall we receive good at the hand of God, and shall we not receive evil?

Jesus wept.—A man of sorrows, and acquainted with grief.—Surely he hath borne our griefs, and carried our sorrows.

Whom the Lord loveth he chasteneth, and scourgeth every son whom he receiveth. Now no chastening for the present seemeth to be joyous, but grievous: nevertheless afterward it yieldeth the peaceable fruit of righteousness unto them which are exercised thereby.—Strengthened with all might, according to his glorious power, unto all patience and longsuffering with joyfulness.—In the world ye shall have tribulation: but be of good cheer; I have overcome the world.

ROM. 12. 12. 1 *Sa.* 3. 18.—*Job* 9. 15.—*Job* 1. 21.—*Job* 2. 10. *Jno.* 11. 35.—   *Is.* 53. 3, 4. *He.* 12. 6, 11.—*Col.* 1. 11.—*Jno.* 16. 33.

He staggered not at the promise of God through unbelief.

Have faith in God. Whosoever shall say unto this mountain, Be thou removed, and be thou cast into the sea; and shall not doubt in his heart, but shall believe that those things which he saith shall come to pass; he shall have whatsoever he saith. Therefore I say unto you, What things soever ye desire, when ye pray, believe that ye receive them, and ye shall have them.—Without faith it is impossible to please him: for he that cometh to God, must believe that he is, and that he is a rewarder of them that diligently seek him.

He that had received the promises offered up his only begotten son, of whom it was said, That in Isaac shall thy seed be called: accounting that God was able to raise him up, even from the dead.—Being fully persuaded that, what he had promised, he was able also to perform.

Is any thing too hard for the LORD?—With God all things are possible.—Lord, increase our faith.

ROM. 4. 20. *Mar.* 11. 22-24.—*He.* 11. 16. *He.* 11. 17-19.—*Ro.* 4. 21.   *Ge.* 18. 14.—*Mat.* 19. 26.—*Lu.* 17. 5.

We know that we have passed from death unto life.

He that heareth my word, and believeth on him that sent me, hath everlasting life, and shall not come into condemnation; but is passed from death unto life.—He that hath the Son hath life; and he that hath not the Son of God hath not life.

He which stablisheth us with you in Christ, and hath anointed us, is God; who hath also sealed us, and given the earnest of the Spirit in our hearts.—Hereby we know that we are of the truth, and shall assure our hearts before him. Beloved, if our heart condemn us not, then have we confidence toward God.—We know that we are of God, and the whole world lieth in wickedness.

You hath he quickened, who were dead in trespasses and sins.— Quickened . . . together with Christ.—Who hath delivered us from the power of darkness, and hath translated us into the kingdom of his dear Son.

1 *JOHN* 3. 14. *Jno.* 5. 24.—1 *Jno.* 5. 12. 2 *Co.* 1. 21, 22.—1 *Jno.* 3. 19, 21. —1 *Jno.* 5. 19. *Ep.* 2. 1, 5.—*Col.* 1. 13.

Thou wilt shew me the path of life.

Thus saith the LORD; Behold, I set before you the way of life, and the way of death.—I will teach you the good and the right way.—I am the way, the truth, and the life: no man cometh unto the Father, but by me.—Follow me.

There is a way which seemeth right unto a man, but the end thereof are the ways of death.—Wide is the gate, and broad is the way, that leadeth to destruction, and many there be which go in thereat: because strait is the gate, and narrow is the way, which leadeth unto life, and few there be that find it.

An highway shall be there, and a way, and it shall be called The way of holiness; the unclean shall not pass over it; but it shall be for those: the wayfaring men, though fools, shall not err therein.—Then shall we know, if we follow on to know the LORD.

In my Father's house are many mansions: if it were not so, I would have told you. I go to prepare a place for you.

PSA. 16. 11. *Je.* 21. 8—1 *Sa.* 12. 23.—*Jno.* 14. 6.—*Mat.* 4. 19. *Pr.* 14. 12.— *Mat.* 7. 13, 14. *Is.* 35. 8.—*Ho.* 6. 3. *Jno.* 14. 2.

By faith Abraham, . . . called to go out into a place which he should after receive for an inheritance, obeyed.

He shall choose our inheritance for us.—He led him about, he instructed him, he kept him as the apple of his eye. As an eagle stirreth up her nest, fluttereth over her young, spreadeth abroad her wings, taketh them, beareth them on her wings: so the LORD alone did lead him, and there was no strange god with him.

I am the LORD thy God which teacheth thee to profit, which leadeth thee by the way that thou shouldest go.—Who teacheth like Him?

We walk by faith, not by sight.—Here have we no continuing city, but we seek one to come.—Dearly beloved, I beseech you as strangers and pilgrims, abstain from fleshly lusts, which war against the soul.—Arise ye and depart; for this is not your rest: because it is polluted, it shall destroy you, even with a sore destruction.

HEB. 11. 8. *Ps.* 47. 4.—*De.* 32. 10-12. *Is.* 48. 17.—*Job* 36. 22. *2 Co.* 5. 7.—
He. 13. 14.—*1 Pe.* 2. 11.—*Mi.* 2. 10.

Give thanks at the remembrance of his holiness.

The heavens are not clean in his sight. How much more abominable and filthy is man, which drinketh iniquity like water?—Yea, the stars are not pure in his sight. How much less man, that is a worm?

Who is like unto thee, O LORD, among the gods? who is like thee, glorious in holiness?—Holy, holy, holy, is the LORD of hosts.

As he which hath called you is holy, so be ye holy in all manner of conversation; because it is written, Be ye holy; for I am holy.—Partakers of his holiness.

The temple of God is holy, which temple ye are.—What manner of persons ought ye to be in all holy conversation and godliness, . . . without spot, and blameless?

Let no corrupt communication proceed out of your mouth, but that which is good to the use of edifying. And grieve not the holy Spirit of God, whereby ye are sealed unto the day of redemption.

PSA. 97. 12. *Job* 15. 15, 16.—*Job* 25. 5, 6. *Ex.* 15. 11.—*Is.* 6. 3.
1 Pe. 1. 15, 16.—*He.* 12. 10. *1 Co.* 3. 17.—*2 Pe.* 3. 11, 14. *Ep.* 4. 29, 30.

Christ, who is the image of God.

The glory of the LORD shall be revealed, and all flesh shall see it together.—No man hath seen God at any time; the only begotten Son, which is in the bosom of the Father, he hath declared him. And the Word was made flesh, and dwelt among us, (and we beheld his glory, the glory as of the only begotten of the Father,) full of grace and truth.—He that hath seen me hath seen the Father.—The brightness of his glory, and the express image of his person.—God was manifest in the flesh.

In whom we have redemption through his blood, even the forgiveness of sins: who is the image of the invisible God, the first-born of every creature.—Whom he did foreknow, he also did predestinate to be conformed to the image of his Son, that he might be the firstborn among many brethren.

As we have borne the image of the earthy, we shall also bear the image of the heavenly.

2 COR. 4. 4. *Is.* 40. 5.—*Jno.* 1. 18, 14.—*Jno.* 14. 9.—*He.* 1. 3.—1 *Ti.* 3. 16. *Col.* 1. 14, 15.—*Ro.* 8. 29. 1 *Co.* 15. 49.

Thou hast girded me with strength unto the battle.

When I am weak, then am I strong.

Asa cried unto the LORD his God, and said, LORD, it is nothing with thee to help, whether with many, or with them that have no power: help us, O LORD our God; for we rest on thee, and in thy name we go against this multitude. O LORD, thou art our God; let not man prevail against thee.—Jehoshaphat cried out, and the LORD helped him.

It is better to trust in the LORD than to put confidence in man. It is better to trust in the LORD than to put confidence in princes. —There is no king saved by the multitude of an host: a mighty man is not delivered by much strength. An horse is a vain thing for safety: neither shall he deliver any by his great strength.

We wrestle not against flesh and blood, but against principalities, against powers, against the rulers of the darkness of this world, against spiritual wickedness in high places. Wherefore take unto you the whole armour of God.

PSA. 18. 39. 2 *Co.* 12. 10. 2 *Ch.* 14. 11.—2 *Ch.* 18. 31. *Ps.* 118. 8, 9.— *Ps.* 33. 16, 17. *Ep.* 6. 12, 13.

Walk in love.

A new commandment I give unto you, That ye love one another; as I have loved you, that ye also love one another.—Above all things have fervent charity among yourselves: for charity shall cover the multitude of sins.—Love covereth all sins.

When ye stand praying, forgive, if ye have ought against any: that your Father also which is in heaven may forgive you your trespasses.—Love ye your enemies, and do good, and lend, hoping for nothing again.—Rejoice not when thine enemy falleth, and let not thine heart be glad when he stumbleth.—Not rendering evil for evil, or railing for railing: but contrariwise blessing; knowing that ye are thereunto called, that ye should inherit a blessing.— If it be possible, as much as lieth in you, live peaceably with all men.—Be ye kind one to another, tender-hearted, forgiving one another, even as God for Christ's sake hath forgiven you.

My little children, let us not love in word, neither in tongue; but in deed and in truth.

EPH 5. 2. Jno. 13. 34.—1 Pe. 4. 8.—Pr. 10. 12. Mar. 11. 25.—Lu. 6. 35.— Pr. 24. 17.—1 Pe. 3. 9.—Ro. 12. 18.—Ep. 4. 32. 1 Jno. 3. 18.

Let your requests be made known unto God.

Abba, **Father**, all things are possible unto thee; take away this cup from me: nevertheless not what I will, but what thou wilt.— There was given to me a thorn in the flesh. For this thing I besought the Lord thrice, that it might depart from me. And he said unto me, My grace is sufficient for thee: for my strength is made perfect in weakness. Most gladly therefore will I rather glory in my infirmities.

I poured out my complaint before him; I shewed before him my trouble.—Hannah . . . was in bitterness of soul, and prayed unto the LORD, and wept sore. And she vowed a vow, and said, O LORD of hosts, if thou wilt indeed look on the affliction of thine handmaid, and . . . wilt give unto thine handmaid a man child, then I will give him unto the LORD all the days of his life. The LORD remembered her.

We know not what we should pray for as we ought.—He shall choose our inheritance for us.

PHIL. 4. 6. Mar. 14. 36.—2 Cor. 12. 7-9. Ps. 142. 2.—1 Sa. 1. 9-11, 20. Ro. 8. 26.—Ps. 47. 4.

Oh that thou wouldest rend the heavens, that thou wouldest come down.

Make haste, my beloved, and be thou like to a roe or to a young hart upon the mountains of spices.—We ourselves groan within ourselves, waiting for the adoption, to wit, the redemption of our body.—Bow thy heavens, O LORD, and come down: touch the mountains, and they shall smoke.

This same Jesus, which is taken up from you into heaven, shall so come in like manner as ye have seen him go into heaven.— Unto them that look for him shall he appear the second time without sin unto salvation.—It shall be said in that day, Lo, this is our God; we have waited for him, and he will save us: this is the LORD; we have waited for him, we will be glad and rejoice in his salvation.

He which testifieth these things saith, Surely I come quickly. Amen. Even so, come, Lord Jesus.—That blessed hope, . . . the glorious appearing of the great God and our Saviour Jesus Christ.—Our conversation is in heaven.

ISA. 64. 1. *Ca.* 8. 14.—*Ro.* 8. 23.—*Ps.* 144. 5. *Ac.* 1. 11.—*He.* 9. 28.— *Is.* 25. 9. *Re.* 22. 20.—*Tit.* 2. 13.—*Phil.* 3. 20.

Thou hast given me the heritage of those that fear thy name.

No weapon that is formed against thee shall prosper; and every tongue that shall rise against thee in judgment thou shalt condemn. This is the heritage of the servants of the LORD, and their righteousness is of me, saith the LORD.—The angel of the LORD encampeth round about them that fear him, and delivereth them. O taste and see that the LORD is good: blessed is the man that trusteth in him. O fear the LORD, ye his saints: for there is no want to them that fear him. The young lions do lack, and suffer hunger: but they that seek the LORD shall not want any good thing.—The lines are fallen unto me in pleasant places; yea, I have a goodly heritage.

Unto you that fear my name shall the Sun of righteousness arise with healing in his wings; and ye shall go forth, and grow up as calves of the stall.—He that spared not his own Son, but delivered him up for us all, how shall he not with him also freely give us all things?

PSA. 61. 5. *Is.* 54. 17.—*Ps.* 34. 7-10.—*Ps.* 16. 6. *Mal.* 4. 2.—*Ro.* 8. 32.

Seek those things which are above, where Christ sitteth on the right hand of God.

Get wisdom, get understanding.—The wisdom that is from above.—The depth saith, It is not in me: and the sea saith, It is not with me.—We are buried with him by baptism into death: that like as Christ was raised up from the dead by the glory of the Father, even so we also should walk in newness of life. For if we have been planted together in the likeness of his death, we shall be also in the likeness of his resurrection.

Let us lay aside every weight, and the sin which doth so easily beset us, and let us run with patience the race that is set before us.—God . . . hath quickened us together with Christ, . . . and hath raised us up together, and made us sit together in heavenly places in Christ Jesus.

They that say such things declare plainly that they seek a country.—Seek ye the LORD, all ye meek of the earth, which have wrought his judgment; seek righteousness, seek meekness.

COL. 3. 1. *Pr.* 4. 5.—*Ja.* 3. 17.—*Job* 28. 14.—*Ro.* 6. 4, 5. *He.* 12. 1.—
Ep. 2. 4-6. *He.* 11. 14.—*Zep.* 2. 3.

Nicodemus . . . he that came to Jesus by night.

Peter followed him afar off.—Among the chief rulers also many believed on him; but because of the Pharisees they did not confess him, lest they should be put out of the synagogue: for they loved the praise of men more than the praise of God.—The fear of man bringeth a snare: but whoso putteth his trust in the LORD shall be safe.

Him that cometh to me I will in no wise cast out.—A bruised reed shall he not break, and the smoking flax shall he not quench. —Faith as a grain of mustard seed.

God hath not given us the spirit of fear; but of power, and of love, and of a sound mind. Be not thou therefore ashamed of the testimony of our Lord.—Little children, abide in him; that, when he shall appear, we may have confidence, and not be ashamed before him at his coming.—Whosoever . . . shall confess me before men, him will I confess also before my Father which is in heaven.

JOHN 7. 50. *Mat.* 26. 58.—*Jno.* 12. 42, 43.—*Pr.* 29. 25. *Jno.* 6. 37.—
Is. 42. 3.—*Mat.* 17. 20. 2 *Ti.* 1. 7, 8.—1 *Jno.* 2. 28.—*Mat.* 10. 32.

Endure hardness, as a good soldier of Jesus Christ.

I have given him for a witness to the people, a leader and commander to the people.—It became him, for whom are all things, and by whom are all things, in bringing many sons unto glory, to make the captain of their salvation perfect through sufferings.— We must through much tribulation enter into the kingdom of God.

We wrestle not against flesh and blood, but against principalities, against powers, against the rulers of the darkness of this world, against spiritual wickedness in high places. Wherefore take unto you the whole armour of God.—We do not war after the flesh: (for the weapons of our warfare are not carnal, but mighty through God to the pulling down of strong holds.)

The God of all grace, who hath called us unto his eternal glory by Christ Jesus, after that ye have suffered a while, make you perfect, stablish, strengthen, settle you.

2 TIM. 2. 3. *Is.* 55. 4.—*He.* 2. 10.—*Ac.* 14. 22. *Ep.* 6. 12, 13.—
2 Co. 10. 3, 4. 1 *Pe.* 5. 10.

The unity of the Spirit.

There is one body, and one Spirit.—Through him we both have access by one Spirit unto the Father. Now therefore ye are no more strangers and foreigners, but fellow-citizens with the saints, and of the household of God; and are built upon the foundation of the apostles and prophets, Jesus Christ himself being the chief corner stone; in whom all the building fitly framed together growth unto an holy temple in the Lord: in whom ye also are builded together for an habitation of God through the Spirit.

Behold, how good and how pleasant it is for brethren to dwell together in unity! It is like the precious ointment upon the head, that ran down upon the beard, even Aaron's beard; that went down to the skirts of his garments.

Seeing ye have purified your souls in obeying the truth through the Spirit unto unfeigned love of the brethren, see that ye love one another with a pure heart fervently.

EPH. 4. 3. *Ep.* 4. 4.—*Ep.* 2. 18-22. *Ps.* 133. 1, 2. 1 *Pe.* 1. 22.

The fruit of the Spirit is . . . faith.

By grace are ye saved through faith; and that not of yourselves: it is the gift of God.—Without faith it is impossible to please him.—He that believeth on him is not condemned: but he that believeth not is condemned already, because he hath not believed in the name of the only begotten Son of God.—Lord, I believe; help thou mine unbelief.

Whoso keepeth his word, in him verily is the love of God perfected: hereby know we that we are in him.—Faith worketh by love.—Faith without works is dead.

We walk by faith, not by sight.—I am crucified with Christ: nevertheless I live; yet not I, but Christ liveth in me: and the life which I now live in the flesh I live by the faith of the Son of God, who loved me, and gave himself for me.—Whom having not seen, ye love; in whom, though now ye see him not, yet believing, ye rejoice with joy unspeakable and full of glory; receiving the end of your faith, even the salvation of your souls.

GAL. 5. 22.   *Ep.* 2. 8.—*He.* 11. 6.—*Jno.* 3. 18.—*Mar.* 9. 24.   1 *Jno.* 2, 5.— *Gal.* 5. 6.—*Ja.* 2. 20.   2 *Co.* 5. 7.—*Gal.* 2. 20.—1 *Pe.* 1. 8, 9.

The Lord is very pitiful, and of tender mercy.

Like as a father pitieth his children, so the LORD pitieth them that fear him.—The LORD is gracious and full of compassion. He will ever be mindful of his covenant.

He that keepeth thee will not slumber. Behold, he that keepeth Israel shall neither slumber nor sleep.—As an eagle stirreth up her nest, fluttereth over her young, spreadeth abroad her wings, taketh them, beareth them on her wings: so the LORD alone did lead him, and there was no strange god with him.

His compassions fail not. They are new every morning: great is thy faithfulness.

Jesus went forth, and saw a great multitude, and was moved with compassion toward them, and he healed their sick.—The same yesterday, and to day, and for ever.

The very hairs of your head are all numbered. Are not two sparrows sold for a farthing? and one of them shall not fall on the ground without your Father. Fear ye not therefore.

JAMES 5. 11. *Ps.* 103. 13.—*Ps.* 111. 4, 5.   *Ps.* 121. 3, 4.—*De.* 32. 11, 12. *La.* 3. 22, 23. *Mat.* 14. 14.—*He.* 13. 8. *Mat.* 10. 30, 29, 31.

The Lamb slain from the foundation of the world.

Your lamb shall be without blemish, . . . and the whole assembly of the congregation of Israel shall kill it in the evening. And they shall take of the blood, and strike it on the two side posts and on the upper door post of the houses, wherein they shall eat it, . . . and when I see the blood, I will pass over you.— The blood of sprinkling.—Christ our passover is sacrificed for us.—Being delivered by the determinate counsel and foreknowledge of God.—According to his own purpose and grace, which was given us in Christ Jesus before the world began.

We have redemption through his blood, the forgiveness of sins.

Forasmuch then as Christ hath suffered for us in the flesh, arm yourselves likewise with the same mind: for he that hath suffered in the flesh hath ceased from sin; that he no longer should live the rest of his time in the flesh to the lusts of men, but to the will of God.

REV. 13. 8. *Ex.* 12. 5-7, 13—*He.* 12. 24.—1 *Co.* 5. 7.—*Ac.* 2. 23.—2 *Ti.* 1. 9. *Ep.* 1. 7. 1 *Pe.* 4. 1, 2.

I have trodden the winepress alone.

Who is like unto thee, O LORD, among the gods? who is like thee, glorious in holiness, fearful in praises, doing wonders?—He saw that there was no man, and wondered that there was no intercessor: therefore his arm brought salvation unto him; and his righteousness, it sustained him.—Who his own self bare our sins in his own body on the tree.—Being made a curse for us.

O sing unto the LORD a new song; for he hath done marvellous things: his right hand, and his holy arm, hath gotten him the victory.—Having spoiled principalities and powers, he made a shew of them openly, triumphing over them in it.—He shall see of the travail of his soul, and shall be satisfied: by his knowledge shall my righteous servant justify many; for he shall bear their iniquities.

O my soul, thou hast trodden down strength.—We are more than conquerors through him that loved us.—They overcame . . . by the blood of the Lamb, and by the word of their testimony.

ISA. 63. 3. *Ex.* 15. 11.—*Is.* 59. 16.—1 *Pe.* 2. 24.—*Ga.* 3. 13. *Ps.* 98. 1.— *Col.* 2. 15.—*Is.* 53. 11. *Ju.* 5. 21.—*Ro.* 8. 37. *Re.* 12. 11.

His mercy is on them that fear Him.

Oh how great is thy goodness, which thou hast laid up for them that fear thee; which thou hast wrought for them that trust in thee before the sons of men! Thou shalt hide them in the secret of thy presence from the pride of man: thou shalt keep them secretly in a pavilion from the strife of tongues.

If ye call on the Father, who without respect of persons judgeth according to every man's work, pass the time of your sojourning here in fear.—The LORD is nigh unto all them that call upon him . . . in truth. He will fulfil the desire of them that fear him: he also will hear their cry, and will save them.

Because thine heart was tender, and thou hast humbled thyself before the LORD, . . . and hast rent thy clothes, and wept before me; I also have heard thee, saith the LORD.—To this man will I look, even to him that is poor and of a contrite spirit, and trembleth at my word.—The LORD is nigh unto them that are of a broken heart; and saveth such as be of a contrite spirit.

LUKE 1. 50. *Ps.* 31. 19, 20. 1 *Pe.* 1. 17.—*Ps.* 145. 18, 19. 2 *Ki.* 22. 19.—
Is. 66. 2.—*Ps.* 34. 18.

Them that honour me I will honour.

Whosoever . . . shall confess me before men. him will I confess also before my Father which is in heaven.—He that loveth father or mother more than me is not worthy of me: and he that loveth son or daughter more than me is not worthy of me. And he that taketh not his cross, and followeth after me, is not worthy of me. He that findeth his life shall lose it: and he that loseth his life for my sake shall find it.

Blessed is the man that endureth temptation: for when he is tried, he shall receive the crown of life, which the Lord hath promised to them that love him.

Fear none of these things which thou shalt suffer. Be thou faithful unto death, and I will give thee a crown of life.

Our light affliction, which is but for a moment, worketh for us a far more exceeding and eternal weight of glory.—Praise and honour and glory at the appearing of Jesus Christ.

1 SAM. 2. 30. *Mat.* 10. 32.—*Mat.* 10. 37-39. *Ja.* 1. 12. *Re.* 2. 10.
2 *Co.* 4. 17.—1 *Pe.* 1. 7.

It is finished: and he bowed his head, and gave up the ghost.

Jesus the author and finisher of our faith.—I have glorified thee on the earth: I have finished the work which thou gavest me to do.—We are sanctified through the offering of the body of Jesus Christ once for all. And every priest standeth daily ministering and offering oftentimes the same sacrifices, which can never take away sins: but this man, after he had offered one sacrifice for sins for ever, sat down on the right hand of God; from henceforth expecting till his enemies be made his footstool. For by one offering he hath perfected for ever them that are sanctified.—Blotting out the handwriting of ordinances that was against us, which was contrary to us, and took it out of the way, nailing it to his cross.

I lay down my life, that I might take it again. No man taketh it from me, but I lay it down of myself. I have power to lay it down, and I have power to take it again.—Greater love hath no man than this, that a man lay down his life for his friends.

JOHN 19. 30. *He.* 12. 2.—*Jno.* 17. 4.—*He.* 10. 10-14.—*Col.* 2. 14.
Jno. 10. 17, 18.—*Jno.* 15. 13.

He sent from above, he took me, he drew me out of many waters.

He brought me up . . . out of an horrible pit, out of the miry clay, and set my feet upon a rock, and established my goings.—You hath he quickened, who were dead in trespasses and sins; wherein in time past ye walked according to the course of this world. We all had our conversation in times past in the lusts of our flesh.

Hear my cry, O God; attend unto my prayer. From the end of the earth will I cry unto thee, when my heart is overwhelmed.—Out of the belly of hell cried I, and thou heardest my voice. For thou hadst cast me into the deep, in the midst of the seas; and the floods compassed me about: all thy billows and thy waves passed over me.—We went through fire and through water: but thou broughtest us out into a wealthy place.

When thou passest through the waters, I will be with thee; and through the rivers, they shall not overflow thee.

PSA. 18. 16. *Ps.* 40. 2.—*Ep.* 2. 1-3. *Ps.* 61. 1, 2.—*Jon.* 2. 2, 3.—*Ps.* 66. 12.
Is. 43. 2.

Walk in newness of life.

As ye have yielded your members servants to uncleanness and to iniquity unto iniquity; even so now yield your members servants to righteousness unto holiness.—I beseech you, . . . brethren, by the mercies of God, that ye present your bodies a living sacrifice, holy, acceptable unto God, which is your reasonable service. And be not conformed to this world: but be ye transformed by the renewing of your mind.

If any man be in Christ, he is a new creature: old things are passed away; behold, all things are become new.—In Christ Jesus neither circumcision availeth any thing, nor uncircumcision, but a new creature. And as many as walk according to this rule, peace be on them, and mercy.—This I say therefore, and testify in the Lord, that ye henceforth walk not as other Gentiles walk, in the vanity of their mind.—Ye have not so learned Christ; if so be that ye have heard him, and have been taught by him, as the truth is in Jesus. Put on the new man, which after God is created in righteousness and true holiness.

ROM. 6. 4. *Ro.* 6. 19.—*Ro.* 12. 1, 2. 2 *Co.* 5. 17.—*Gal.* 6. 15, 16.
—*Ep.* 4. 17, 20, 21, 24.

Thy will be done.

O Lord, I know that the way of man is not in himself: it is not in man that walketh to direct his steps.—Not as I will, but as thou wilt.—Surely I have behaved and quieted myself, as a child that is weaned of his mother: my soul is even as a weaned child.

We know not what we should pray for as we ought: but the Spirit itself maketh intercession for us with groanings which cannot be uttered. And he that searcheth the hearts knoweth what is the mind of the Spirit, because he maketh intercession for the saints according to the will of God.

Ye know not what ye ask.—He gave them their request; but sent leanness into their soul.—These things were our examples, to the intent we should not lust after evil things, as they also lusted.

I would have you without carefulness.—Thou wilt keep him in perfect peace, whose mind is stayed on thee: because he trusteth in thee.

MAT. 26. 42. *Je.* 10. 23.—*Mat.* 26. 39.—*Ps.* 131. 2. *Ro.* 8. 26, 27.
Mat. 20. 22—*Ps.* 106. 15.—1 *Co.* 10. 6. 1 *Co.* 7. 32.—*Is.* 26. 3.

Whom the Lord loveth he correcteth.

See now that I, even I, am he, and there is no god with me: I kill, and I make alive; I wound, and I heal: neither is there any that can deliver out of my hand.—I know the thoughts that I think toward you, saith the LORD, thoughts of peace, and not of evil, to give you an expected end.—My thoughts are not your thoughts, neither are your ways my ways, saith the LORD.

I will allure her, and bring her into the wilderness, and speak comfortably unto her.—As a man chasteneth his son, so the LORD thy God chasteneth thee.—Now no chastening for the present seemeth to be joyous, but grievous: nevertheless afterward it yieldeth the peaceable fruit of righteousness unto them which are exercised thereby.—Humble yourselves therefore under the mighty hand of God, that he may exalt you in due time.

I know, O LORD, that thy judgments are right, and that thou in faithfulness hast afflicted me.

PROV. 3. 12. *De.* 32. 39.—*Je.* 29. 11.—*Is.* 55. 8. *Ho.* 2. 14.—*De.* 8. 5.—*He.* 12. 11.—1 *Pe.* 5. 6. *Ps.* 119. 75.

The earth is the Lord's, and the fulness thereof.

She did not know that I gave her corn, and wine, and oil, and multiplied her silver and gold. Therefore will I return, and take away my corn in the time thereof, and my wine in the season thereof, and I will recover my wool and my flax.

All things come of thee, and of thine own have we given thee. For we are strangers before thee, and sojourners, as were all our fathers: our days on the earth are as a shadow, and there is none abiding. O LORD our God, all this store . . . cometh of thine hand, and is all thine own.—Of him, and through him, and to him, are all things: to whom be glory for ever. Amen.

The living God . . . giveth us richly all things to enjoy.—Every creature of God is good, and nothing to be refused, if it be received with thanksgiving: for it is sanctified by the word of God and prayer.

My God shall supply all your need according to his riches in glory by Christ Jesus.

PSA. 24. 1. *Ho.* 2. 8, 9. 1 *Ch.* 29. 14-16.—*Ro.* 11. 36. 1 *Ti.* 6. 17.—1 *Ti.* 4. 4, 5. *Phi.* 4. 19.

The Comforter, which is the Holy Ghost, whom the Father will send in my name.

If thou knewest the gift of God, and who it is that saith to thee, Give me to drink; thou wouldest have asked of him, and he would have given thee living water.—If ye . . . being evil, know how to give good gifts unto your children: how much more shall your heavenly Father give the Holy Spirit to them that ask him?— Verily, verily, I say unto you, Whatsoever ye shall ask the Father in my name, he will give it you. Hitherto have ye asked nothing in my name: ask, and ye shall receive, that your joy may be full.— Ye have not, because ye ask not.

When . . . the Spirit of truth is come, he will guide you into all truth: for he shall not speak of himself; but whatsoever he shall hear, that shall he speak: and he will shew you things to come. He shall glorify me: for he shall receive of mine, and shall shew it unto you.

They rebelled, and vexed his Holy Spirit: therefore he was turned to be their enemy, and he fought against them.

JOHN 14. 26. *Jno.* 4. 10.—*Lu.* 11. 13.—*Jno.* 16. 23, 24.—*Jas.* 4. 2. *Jno.* 16. 13, 14. *Is.* 63. 10.

What think ye of Christ?

Lift up your heads, O ye gates; even lift them up, ye everlasting doors; and the King of glory shall come in. Who is this King of glory? The LORD of hosts, he is the King of glory.—He hath on his vesture and on his thigh a name written, KING OF KINGS, AND LORD OF LORDS.

Unto you . . . which believe he is precious: but unto them which be disobedient, the stone which the builders disallowed, the same is made the head of the corner.—Christ crucified, unto the Jews a stumblingblock, and unto the Greeks foolishness; but unto them which are called, both Jews and Greeks, Christ the power of God, and the wisdom of God.

I count all things but loss for the excellency of the knowledge of Christ Jesus my Lord: for whom I have suffered the loss of all things, and do count them but dung, that I may win Christ.—Lord, thou knowest all things: thou knowest that I love thee.

MAT. 22. 42. *Ps.* 24. 9, 10.—*Re.* 19. 16. 1 *Pe.* 2. 7.—1 *Co.* 1. 23, 24. *Phi.* 3. 8.—*Jno.* 21. 17.

The path of the just is as the shining light, that shineth more and more unto the perfect day.

Not as though I had already attained, either were already perfect: but I follow after, if that I may apprehend that for which also I am apprehended of Christ Jesus.—Then shall we know, if we follow on to know the LORD.

Then shall the righteous shine forth as the sun in the kingdom of their Father.—We all, with open face beholding as in a glass the glory of the Lord, are changed into the same image from glory to glory, even as by the Spirit of the Lord.—When that which is perfect is come, then that which is in part shall be done away.— For now we see through a glass, darkly; but then face to face: now I know in part; but then shall I know even as also I am known. Beloved, now are we the sons of God; and it doth not yet appear what we shall be: but we know that, when he shall appear, we shall be like him, for we shall see him as he is. And every man that hath this hope in him purifieth himself, even as he is pure.

PROV. 4. 18. *Phi.* 3. 12.—*Ho.* 6. 3. *Mat.* 13. 43.—2 *Co.* 3. 18.— 1 *Co.* 13. 10, 12.—1 *Jno.* 3. 2, 3.

Whosoever shall call upon the name of the Lord shall be saved.

Him that cometh to me I will in no wise cast out.—Lord, remember me when thou comest into thy kingdom. And Jesus said unto him, Verily I say unto thee, To day shalt thou be with me in paradise.—What will ye that I shall do unto you? They say unto him, Lord, that our eyes may be opened. So Jesus had compassion on them, and touched their eyes: and immediately their eyes received sight, and they followed him.

If ye . . . being evil, know how to give good gifts unto your children: how much more shall your heavenly Father give the Holy Spirit to them that ask him?—I will put my Spirit within you. Thus saith the Lord GOD; I will yet for this be enquired of.

This is the confidence that we have in him, that, if we ask any thing according to his will, he heareth us: and if we know that he hear us, whatsoever we ask, we know that we have the petitions that we desired of him.

ROM. 10. 13. *Jno.* 6. 37.—*Lu.* 23. 42, 43.—*Mat.* 20. 32-34. *Lu.* 11. 13— *Eze.* 36. 27, 37. 1 *Jno.* 5. 14, 15.

Thou art all fair, my love; there is no spot in thee.

The whole head is sick, and the whole heart faint. From the sole of the foot even unto the head there is no soundness in it; but wounds, and bruises, and putrifying sores: they have not been closed, neither bound up, neither mollified with ointment.— We are all as an unclean thing, and all our righteousnesses are as filthy rags.—I know that in me (that is, in my flesh,) dwelleth no good thing.

Ye are washed, . . . ye are sanctified, . . . ye are justified in the name of the Lord Jesus, and by the Spirit of our God.—The King's daughter is all glorious within.—Perfect through my comeliness, which I had put upon thee, saith the Lord GOD.

Let the beauty of the LORD our God be upon us.

These are they which . . . have washed their robes, and made them white in the blood of the Lamb.—A glorious church, not having spot, or wrinkle, or any such thing; but . . . holy and without blemish.—Ye are complete in him.

CANT. 4. 7. *Is.* 1. 5, 6.—*Is.* 64. 6.—*Ro.* 7. 18. 1 *Co.* 6. 11.—*Ps.* 45. 13.— *Eze.* 16. 14. *Ps.* 90. 17. *Re.* 7. 14.—*Ep.* 5. 27.—*Col.* 2. 10.

Broken cisterns, that can hold no water.

Eve . . . bare Cain, and said, I have gotten a man from the LORD.

Go to, let us build us a city and a tower, whose top may reach unto heaven. The LORD scattered them.—Lot chose him all the plain of Jordan; it was well watered every where, even as the garden of the LORD. But the men of Sodom were wicked and sinners before the LORD exceedingly.

I gave my heart to know wisdom, and to know madness and folly: I perceived that this also is vexation of spirit. For in much wisdom is much grief: and he that increaseth knowledge increaseth sorrow.—I made me great works; I builded me houses; I planted me vineyards: I gathered me also silver and gold. Then I looked on all, and, behold, all was vanity and vexation of spirit.

If any man thirst, let him come unto me, and drink.—He satisfieth the longing soul, and filleth the hungry soul with goodness.

Set your affection on things above, not on things on the earth.

JER. 2. 13. *Ge.* 4. 1. *Ge* 11. 4, 8.—*Ge.* 13. 11, 10, 13. *Ec.* 1. 17, 18. —*Ec.* 2. 4, 8. 11. *Jno.* 7. 37.—*Ps.* 107. 9. *Col.* 3. 2.

I pray not that thou shouldest take them out of the world, but thou shouldest keep them from the evil.

Blameless and harmless, the sons of God, without rebuke, in the midst of a crooked and perverse nation, among whom ye shine as lights in the world.—Ye are the salt of the earth, . . . the light of the world.—Let your light so shine before men, that they may see your good works, and glorify your Father which is in heaven.

I also withheld thee from sinning against me.

The Lord is faithful, who shall stablish you, and keep you from evil.—So did not I, because of the fear of God.—Who gave himself for our sins, that he might deliver us from this present evil world, according to the will of God and our Father.—Now unto him that is able to keep you from falling, and to present you faultless before the presence of his glory with exceeding joy, to the only wise God our Saviour, be glory and majesty, dominion and power, both now and ever. Amen.

JOHN 17. 15. *Phi.* 2. 15.—*Mat.* 5. 13, 14, 16. *Ge.* 20. 6. 2 *Thes.* 3. 3.—
Ne. 5. 15.—*Gal.* 1. 4.—*Jude* 24, 25.

Whoso putteth his trust in the Lord shall be safe. (*Or*, set on high.)

The LORD is exalted; for he dwelleth on high.—The LORD is high above all nations, and his glory above the heavens. He raiseth up the poor out of the dust, and lifteth the needy out of the dunghill; that he may set him with princes.

God, who is rich in mercy, for his great love wherewith he loved us, even when we were dead in sins, hath quickened us together with Christ, (by grace ye are saved;) and hath raised us up together and made us sit together in heavenly places in Christ Jesus.

He that spared not his own Son, but delivered him up for us all, how shall he not with him also freely give us all things? For I am persuaded, that neither death, nor life, nor angels, nor principalities, nor powers, nor things present, nor things to come, nor height, nor depth, nor any other creature, shall be able to separate us from the love of God, which is in Christ Jesus our Lord.

PROV. 29. 25. *Is.* 33. 5.—*Ps.* 113. 4, 7, 8. *Ep.* 2. 4-6. *Ro.* 8. 32, 38, 39.

That through death He might destroy him that had the power of death.

Our Saviour Jesus Christ . . . hath abolished death, and hath brought life and immortality to light through the gospel.—He will swallow up death in victory; and the Lord God shall wipe away tears from off all faces; and the rebuke of his people shall he take away from off all the earth: for the Lord hath spoken it. When this corruptible shall have put on incorruption, and this mortal shall have put on immortality, then shall be brought to pass the saying that is written, Death is swallowed up in victory. O death, where is thy sting? O grave, where is thy victory? The sting of death is sin; and the strength of sin is the law. But thanks be to God, which giveth us the victory through our Lord Jesus Christ.

God hath not given us the spirit of fear; but of power, and of love, and of a sound mind.—Yea, though I walk through the valley of the shadow of death, I will fear no evil: for thou art with me; thy rod and thy staff they comfort me.

HEB. 2. 14. 2 *Ti.* 1. 10.—*Is.* 25. 8.—1 *Co.* 15. 54-57. 2 *Ti.* 1. 7.—*Ps.* 23. 4.

Where is the way where light dwelleth?

God is light, and in him is no darkness at all.—As long as I am in the world, I am the light of the world.

If we say that we have fellowship with him, and walk in darkness, we lie, and do not the truth: but if we walk in the light, as he is in the light, we have fellowship one with another, and the blood of Jesus Christ his Son cleanseth us from all sin.—The Father . . . hath made us meet to be partakers of the inheritance of the saints in light, who hath delivered us from the power of darkness, and hath translated us into the kingdom of his dear Son; in whom we have redemption through his blood, even the forgiveness of sins.

Ye are all the children of light, and the children of the day: we are not of the night, nor of darkness.—Ye are the light of the world. A city that is set on an hill cannot be hid. Let your light so shine before men, that they may see your good works, and glorify your Father which is in heaven.

JOB 38. 19. 1 *Jno.* 1. 5.—*Jno.* 9. 5. 1 *Jno.* 1. 6, 7.—*Col.* 1. 12-14.
1 *Th.* 5. 5.—*Mat.* 5. 14, 16.

The Lord will not cast off for ever: but though he cause grief, yet will he have compassion.

Fear thou not, . . . saith the LORD: for I am with thee; . . . I will not make a full end of thee, but correct thee in measure.— For a small moment have I forsaken thee; but with great mercies will I gather thee. In a little wrath I hid my face from thee for a moment; but with everlasting kindness will I have mercy on thee, saith the LORD thy Redeemer. For the mountains shall depart, and the hills be removed; but my kindness shall not depart from thee, neither shall the covenant of my peace be removed, saith the LORD that hath mercy on thee. O thou afflicted, tossed with tempest, and not comforted, behold, I will lay thy stones with fair colours, and lay thy foundations with sapphires.

I will bear the indignation of the LORD, because I have sinned against him, until he plead my cause, and execute judgment for me: he will bring me forth to the light, and I shall behold his righteousness.

LAM. 3. 31, 32. *Je.* 46. 28.—*Is.* 54. 7, 8, 10, 11. *Mi.* 7. 9.

God hath chosen the weak things of the world to confound the things which are mighty.

When the children of Israel cried unto the LORD, the LORD raised them up a deliverer, Ehud, . . . a man lefthanded. After him was Shamgar, . . . which slew of the Philistines six hundred men with an ox goad: and he also delivered Israel.

The LORD looked upon [Gideon], and said, Go in this thy might: . . . have not I sent thee? And he said unto him, O my Lord, wherewith shall I save Israel? behold my family is poor in Manasseh, and I am the least in my father's house.

The LORD said unto Gideon, The people that are with thee are too many for me, . . . lest Israel vaunt themselves against me, saying, Mine own hand hath saved me.

Not by might, nor by power, but by my Spirit, saith the LORD of hosts.—My brethren, be strong in the Lord, and in the power of his might.

1 COR. 1. 27. *Ju.* 3. 15, 31. *Ju.* 7. 2. *Zec.* 4. 6. *Ep.* 6. 10.

He hath prepared for them a city.

If I go and prepare a place for you, I will come again, and receive you unto myself; that where I am, there ye may be also.—An inheritance incorruptible, and undefiled, and that fadeth not away, reserved in heaven for you.—Here have we no continuing city, but we seek one to come.

This same Jesus, which is taken up from you into heaven, shall so come in like manner as ye have seen him go into heaven.—Be patient therefore, brethren, unto the coming of the Lord. Behold, the husbandman waiteth for the precious fruit of the earth, and hath long patience for it, until he receive the early and latter rain. —Be ye also patient; stablish your hearts: for the coming of the Lord draweth nigh.—Yet a little while, and he that shall come will come, and will not tarry.

We which are alive and remain shall be caught up together with them in the clouds, to meet the Lord in the air: and so shall we ever be with the Lord. Wherefore comfort one another with these words.

HEB. 11. 16. *Jno.* 14. 3.—1 *Pe.* 1. 4.—*Heb.* 13. 14. *Ac.* 1. 11.—*Ja.* 5. 7, 8.— *He.* 10. 37. 1 *Thes.* 4. 17, 18.

Base things of the world hath God chosen.

Be not deceived: neither fornicators, nor idolators, nor adulterers, nor effeminate, nor abusers of themselves with mankind, nor thieves, nor covetous, nor drunkards, nor revilers, nor extortioners, shall inherit the kingdom of God. And such were some of you: but ye are washed, but ye are sanctified, but ye are justified in the name of the Lord Jesus, and by the Spirit of our God.

You hath he quickened, who were dead in trespasses and sins; wherein in time past ye walked according to the course of this world; among whom also we all had our conversation in times past in the lusts of our flesh, fulfilling the desires of the flesh and of the mind.

According to his mercy he saved us, by the washing of regeneration, and renewing of the Holy Ghost; which he shed on us abundantly through Jesus Christ our Saviour.

My thoughts are not your thoughts, neither are your ways my ways, saith the LORD.

1 *COR.* 1. 28. 1 *Co.* 6. 9-11. *Ep.* 2. 1-3. *Tit.* 3. 5, 6. *Is.* 55. 8.

The joy of the Lord is your strength.

Sing, O heavens; and be joyful, O earth; and break forth into singing, O mountains: for the LORD hath comforted his people, and will have mercy upon his afflicted.—Behold, God is my salvation; I will trust, and not be afraid: for the LORD JEHOVAH is my strength and my song; he also is become my salvation.—The LORD is my strength and my shield; my heart trusted in him, and I am helped: therefore my heart greatly rejoiceth; and with my song will I praise him.—My soul shall be joyful in my God; for he hath clothed me with the garments of salvation, he hath covered me with the robe of righteousness, as a bridegroom decketh himself with ornaments, and as a bride adorneth herself with her jewels.

I have therefore whereof I may glory through Jesus Christ in those things which pertain to God.—We . . . joy in God through our Lord Jesus Christ, by whom we have now received the atonement.—I will joy in the God of my salvation.

NEHE. 8. 10. *Is.* 49. 13.—*Is.* 12. 2.—*Ps.* 28. 7.—*Is.* 61. 10. *Ro.* 15. 17.— *Ro.* 5. 11.—*Hab.* 3. 18.

AUGUST 14

He hath made with me an everlasting covenant, ordered in all things, and sure.

I know whom I have believed, and am persuaded that he is able to keep that which I have committed unto him against that day.

Blessed be the God and Father of our Lord Jesus Christ, who hath blessed us with all spiritual blessings in heavenly places in Christ: according as he hath chosen us in him before the foundation of the world, that we should be holy and without blame before him in love: having predestinated us unto the adoption of children by Jesus Christ to himself, according to the good pleasure of his will.

We know that all things work together for good to them that love God, to them who are the called according to his purpose. For whom he did foreknow, he also did predestinate to be conformed to the image of his Son. Moreover whom he did predestinate, them he also called : and whom he called, them he also justified: and whom he justified, them he also glorified.

2 SAM. 23. 5. *2 Ti.* 1. 12. *Ep.* 1. 3-5. *Ro.* 8. 28-30.

The God of peace make you perfect in every good work to do his will.

Be perfect, be of good comfort, be of one mind, live in peace; and the God of love and peace shall be with you.

By grace are ye saved through faith; and that not of yourselves: it is the gift of God; not of works, lest any man should boast.— Every good gift and every perfect gift is from above, and cometh down from the Father of lights, with whom is no variableness neither shadow of turning.

Work out your own salvation with fear and trembling. For it is God which worketh in you both to will and to do of his good pleasure.—Be ye transformed by the renewing of your mind, that ye may prove what is that good, and acceptable, and perfect, will of God.—Being filled with the fruits of righteousness, which are by Jesus Christ, unto the glory and praise of God.

Not that we are sufficient of ourselves to think any thing as of ourselves; but our sufficiency is of God.

HEB. 13. 20, 21. 2 *Co.* 13. 11. *Ep.* 2. 8, 9.—*Ja.* 1. 17. *Phi.* 2. 12, 13.—
Ro. 12. 2.—*Phi.* 1. 11. 2 *Co.* 3. 5.

I will allure her, and bring her into the wilderness, and speak comfortably unto her.

Come out from among them, and be ye separate, saith the Lord, and touch not the unclean thing; and I will receive you, and will be a Father unto you, and ye shall be my sons and daughters, saith the Lord Almighty.—Having therefore these promises, dearly beloved, let us cleanse ourselves from all filthiness of the flesh and spirit, perfecting holiness in the fear of God.

Jesus, . . . that he might sanctify the people with his own blood, suffered without the gate. Let us go forth therefore unto him without the camp, bearing his reproach.

[Jesus] said, . . . Come ye yourselves apart into a desert place, and rest a while.—The LORD is my shepherd; I shall not want. He maketh me to lie down in green pastures: he leadeth me beside the still waters. He restoreth my soul: he leadeth me in the paths of righteousness for his name's sake.

HOSEA 2. 14. 2 *Co.* 6. 17, 18.—2 *Co.* 7. 1. *He.* 13. 12, 13.
Mar. 6. 31.—*Ps.* 23. 1-3.

The house that is to be builded for the Lord must be exceeding magnifical.

Ye . . . as lively stones, are built up a spiritual house.—Know ye not that ye are the temple of God, and that the Spirit of God dwelleth in you? If any man defile the temple of God, him shall God destroy; for the temple of God is holy, which temple ye are. —Your body is the temple of the Holy Ghost which is in you, which ye have of God, and ye are not your own. For ye are bought with a price: therefore glorify God in your body, and in your spirit, which are God's.—What agreement hath the temple of God with idols? for ye are the temple of the living God; as God hath said, I will dwell in them, and walk in them; and I will be their God, and they shall be my people.—Ye . . . are built upon the foundation of the apostles and prophets, Jesus Christ himself being the chief corner stone; in whom all the building fitly framed together groweth unto a holy temple in the Lord: in whom ye also are builded together for a habitation of God through the Spirit.

1 *CHRON.* 22. 5. 1 *Pe.* 2. 5.—1 *Co.* 3. 16, 17.—1 *Co.* 6. 19, 20.— 2 *Co.* 6. 16.—*Ep.* 2. 19-22.

He is before all things.

The Amen; the beginning of the creation of God.—The beginning, the firstborn from the dead; that in all things he might have the pre-eminence.

The LORD possessed me in the beginning of his way, before his works of old. I was set up from everlasting, from the beginning, or ever the earth was. When he prepared the heavens, I was there: when he set a compass upon the face of the depth: when he established the clouds above: when he strengthened the fountains of the deep; when he gave to the sea his decree, that the waters should not pass his commandment. I was daily his delight, rejoicing always before him.—Yea, before the day was I am he.

The Lamb slain from the foundation of the world.—The author and finisher of our faith; who for the joy that was set before him endured the cross, despising the shame, and is set down at the right hand of the throne of God.

COL. 1. 17. *Re.* 3. 14.—*Col.* 1. 18. *Pr.* 8. 22, 23, 27-30.—*Is.* 43. 13. *Re.* 13. 8.—*He.* 12. 2.

Pray one for another, that ye may be healed.

Abraham answered and said, Behold now, I have taken upon me to speak unto the Lord, which am but dust and ashes: peradventure there shall lack five cf the fifty righteous: wilt thou destroy all the city for lack of five? And he said, If I find there forty and five, I will not destroy it.

Father, forgive them; for they know not what they do.—Pray for them which despitefully use you, and persecute you.

I pray for them: I pray not for the world, but for them which thou hast given me; for they are thine. Neither pray I for these alone, but for them also which shall believe on me through their word.—Bear ye one another's burdens, and so fulfil the law of Christ.

The effectual fervent prayer of a righteous man availeth much. Elias was a man subject to like passions as we are, and he prayed earnestly that it might not rain: and it rained not on the earth by the space of three years and six months.

JAMES 5. 16. *Ge.* 18. 27, 28. *Lu.* 23. 34.—*Mat.* 5. 44. *Jno.* 17. 9, 20.—
Gal. 6. 2. *Jas.* 5. 16, 17.

As for man, his days are as grass: as a flower of the field, so he flourisheth. For the wind passeth over it, and it is gone; and the place therof shall know it no more.

So teach us to number our days, that we may apply our hearts unto wisdom.—What shall it profit a man, if he shall gain the whole world, and lose his own soul?

Surely the people is grass. The grass withereth, the flower fadeth: but the world of our God shall stand for ever.—The world passeth away, and the lust thereof: but he that doeth the will of God abideth for ever.

Behold, now is the accepted time; behold, now is the day of salvation.—Use this world, as not abusing it: for the fashion of this world passeth away.—Let us consider one another to provoke unto love and to good works: not forsaking the assembling of ourselves together, as the manner of some is; but exhorting one another; and so much the more, as ye see the day approaching.

PSA. 103. 15, 16. *Ps.* 90. 12.—*Mar.* 8. 36. *Is.* 40. 7, 8.—1 *Jno.* 2. 17.
2 *Co.* 6. 2.—1 *Co.* 7. 31.—*He.* 10. 24, 25

What God is there in heaven or in earth, that can do according to thy works, and according to thy might ?

Who in the heaven can be compared unto the LORD? who among the sons of the mighty can be likened unto the LORD? O LORD God of hosts, who is a strong LORD like unto thee? or to thy faithfulness round about thee?—Among the gods there is none like unto thee, O Lord; neither are there any works like unto thy works.—For thy word's sake, and according to thine own heart, hast thou done all these great things, to make thy servant know them. Wherefore thou art great, O LORD God: for there is none like thee, neither is there any God beside thee, according to all that we have heard with our ears.

Eye hath not seen, nor ear heard, neither have entered into the heart of man, the things which God hath prepared for them that love him. But God hath revealed them unto us by his Spirit.—The secret things belong unto the LORD our God: but those things which are revealed belong unto us and to our children.

DEUT. 3. 24. *Ps.* 89. 6, 8.—*Ps.* 86. 8.—2 *Sa.* 7. 21, 22. 1 *Co.* 2. 9, 10.—*De.* 29. 29.

He that glorieth, let him glory in the Lord.

Let not the wise man glory in his wisdom, neither let the mighty man glory in his might, let not the rich man glory in his riches: but let him that glorieth glory in this, that he understandeth and knoweth me, that I am the LORD.

I count all things but loss for the excellency of the knowledge of Christ Jesus my Lord : for whom I have suffered the loss of all things, and do count them but dung, that I may win Christ.—I am not ashamed of the gospel of Christ: for it is the power of God unto salvation to every one that believeth.—I have . . . whereof I may glory through Jesus Christ in those things which pertain to God.

Whom have I in heaven but thee? and there is none upon earth that I desire beside thee.—My heart rejoiceth in the LORD. . . . I rejoice in thy salvation.

Not unto us, O LORD, not unto us, but unto thy name give glory, for thy mercy, and for thy truth's sake.

1 *COR.* 1. 31. *Je.* 9. 23, 24. *Phi.* 3. 8.—*Ro.* 1. 16.—*Ro.* 15. 17. *Ps.* 73. 25.—1 *Sa.* 2. 1. *Ps.* 115. 1.

As he which hath called you is holy, so be ye holy in all manner of conversation.

Ye know how we exhorted . . . and charged every one of you, . . . that ye would walk worthy of God, who hath called you unto his kingdom and glory.—Ye should shew forth the praises of him who hath called you out of darkness into his marvellous light.

Ye were sometime darkness, but now are ye light in the Lord: walk as children of light: (for the fruit of the Spirit is in all goodness and righteousness and truth;) proving what is acceptable unto the Lord. And have no fellowship with the unfruitful works of darkness, but rather reprove them.—Being filled with the fruits of righteousness, which are by Jesus Christ, unto the glory and praise of God.

Let your light so shine before men, that they may see your good works, and glorify your Father which is in heaven.—Whether therefore ye eat, or drink, or whatsoever ye do, do all to the glory of God.

1 *PET*. 1. 15. 1 *Thes*. 2. 11, 12.—1 *Pe*. 2. 9. *Ep*. 5. 8-11.—*Phi*. 1. 11.
Mat. 5. 16.—1 *Co*. 10. 31.

Ask me of things to come concerning my sons, and concerning the work of my hands command ye me.

A new heart . . . will I give you, and a new spirit will I put within you: and I will take away the stony heart out of your flesh, and I will give you an heart of flesh. And I will put my Spirit within you, and cause you to walk in my statutes. Thus saith the Lord GOD; I will yet for this be enquired of by the house of Israel, to do it for them.

If two of you shall agree on earth as touching anything that they shall ask, it shall be done for them of my Father which is in heaven. For where two or three are gathered together in my name, there am I in the midst of them.

Have faith in God. Verily I say unto you, That whosoever shall say unto this mountain, Be thou removed, and be thou cast into the sea; and shall not doubt in his heart, but shall believe that those things which he saith shall come to pass; he shall have whatsoever he saith.

ISA. 45. 11. *Eze*. 36. 26, 27, 37. *Mat*. 18. 19, 20. *Mar*. 11. 22, 23.

**God is not a man, that he should lie; neither the son of man,
that he should repent.**

The Father of lights, with whom is no variableness, neither
shadow of turning.—Jesus Christ, the same yesterday, and to-day,
and for ever.

His truth shall be thy shield and buckler.

God, willing more abundantly to shew unto the heirs of promise
the immutability of his counsel, confirmed it by an oath; that
by two immutable things, in which it was impossible for God to
lie, we might have a strong consolation, who have fled for refuge
to lay hold upon the hope set before us.

The faithful God, which keepeth covenant and mercy with them
that love him and keep his commandments to a thousand generations.—All the paths of the LORD are mercy and truth unto such
as keep his covenant and his testimonies.—Happy is he that hath
the God of Jacob for his help, whose hope is in the LORD his
God . . . which keepeth truth for ever.

NUM. 23. 19. *Ja.* 1. 17.—*He.* 13. 8.—*Ps.* 91. 4. *He.* 6. 17, 18. *De.* 7. 9.—
Ps. 25. 10.—*Ps.* 146. 5, 6.

If thou faint in the day of adversity, thy strength is small.

He giveth power to the faint; and to them that have no might
he increaseth strength.—My grace is sufficient for thee: for my
strength is made perfect in weakness.—He shall call upon me,
and I will answer him: I will be with him in trouble; I will deliver
him.—The eternal God is thy refuge, and underneath are the everlasting arms: and he shall thrust out the enemy from before thee.

I looked for some to take pity, but there was none; and for
comforters, but I found none.

Every high priest taken from among men is ordained for men
in things pertaining to God, . . . who can have compassion on the
ignorant, and on them that are out of the way: so also Christ,
. . . though he were a Son, yet learned he obedience by the things
which he suffered; and being made perfect, he became the author
of eternal salvation unto all them that obey him.—Surely he hath
borne our griefs, and carried our sorrows.

PROV. 24. 10. *Is.* 40. 29.—*2 Co.* 12. 9.—*Ps.* 91. 15.—*De.* 33. 27. *Ps.* 69. 20.
He. 5. 1, 2, 5, 8, 9.—*Is.* 53. 4.

Thou art my portion, O Lord.

All things are yours; . . . and ye are Christ's; and Christ is God's.—Our Saviour Jesus Christ . . . gave himself for us.—God gave him to be the head over all things to the church.—Christ loved the church, and gave himself for it; that he might present it to himself a glorious church, not having spot, or wrinkle, or any such thing; but that it should be holy and without blemish.

My soul shall make her boast in the LORD.—I will greatly rejoice in the LORD, my soul shall be joyful in my God; for he hath clothed me with the garments of salvation, he hath covered me with the robe of righteousness.

Whom have I in heaven but thee? and there is none upon earth that I desire beside thee. My flesh and my heart faileth: but God is the strength of my heart, and my portion for ever.—O my soul, thou hast said unto the LORD, Thou art my Lord. The LORD is the portion of mine inheritance and of my cup: thou maintainest my lot. The lines are fallen unto me in pleasant places; yea, I have a goodly heritage.

PSA. 119. 57. *1 Co*. 3. 21, 23.—*Tit*. 2. 13, 14.—*Ep*. 1. 22.—*Ep*. 5. 25, 27. *Ps*. 34. 2.—*Is*. 61. 10. *Ps*. 73. 25, 26.—*Ps*. 16. 2, 5, 6.

There is a way which seemeth right unto a man, but the end thereof are the ways of death.

He that trusteth in his own heart is a fool.

Thy word is a lamp unto my feet, and a light unto my path.—Concerning the works of men, by the word of thy lips I have kept me from the paths of the destroyer.

If there arise among you a prophet, or a dreamer of dreams, saying, Let us go after other gods, which thou hast not known, and let us serve them; thou shalt not hearken unto the words of that prophet: for the LORD your God proveth you, to know whether ye love the LORD your God with all your heart and with all your soul. Ye shall walk after the LORD your God, and fear him, and keep his commandments, and obey his voice, and ye shall serve him, and cleave unto him.

I will instruct thee and teach thee in the way which thou shalt go; I will guide thee with mine eye.

PROV. 14. 12. *Pr*. 28. 26. *Ps*. 119. 105.—*Ps*. 17. 4. *De*. 13. 1-4. *Ps*. 32. 8.

None of us liveth to himself, and no man dieth to himself.

Whether we live, we live unto the Lord; and whether we die, we die unto the Lord: whether we live therefore, or die, we are the Lord's.—Let no man seek his own: but every man another's wealth.—Ye are bought with a price: therefore glorify God in your body, and in your spirit, which are God's.

Christ shall be magnified in my body, whether it be by life, or by death. For to me to live is Christ, and to die is gain. But if I live in the flesh, this is the fruit of my labour: yet what I shall choose I wot not. For I am in a strait betwixt two, having a desire to depart, and to be with Christ; which is far better.

I through the law am dead to the law, that I might live unto God. I am crucified with Christ: nevertheless I live; yet not I, but Christ liveth in me: and the life which I now live in the flesh I live by the faith of the Son of God, who loved me, and gave himself for me.

ROM. 14. 7. *Ro.* 14. 8.—1 *Co* 10. 24.—1 *Co.* 6. 20. *Phi.* 1. 20-23. *Gal.* 2. 19, 20.

God gave Solomon . . . largeness of heart, even as the sand that is on the sea shore.

Behold, a greater than Solomon is here.—The Prince of Peace.

Scarcely for a righteous man will one die: yet peradventure for a good man some would even dare to die. But God commendeth his love toward us, in that, while we were yet sinners, Christ died for us.—Who, being in the form of God, thought it not robbery to be equal with God: but made himself of no reputation, and took upon him the form of a servant, and was made in the likeness of men: and being found in fashion as a man, he humbled himself, and became obedient unto death, even the death of the cross. —The love of Christ passeth knowledge.

Christ the power of God, and the wisdom of God.—In whom are hid all the treasures of wisdom and knowledge.—The unsearchable riches of Christ.—Of him are ye in Christ Jesus, who of God is made unto us wisdom, and righteousness, and sanctification, and redemption.

1 *KINGS* 4. 29. *Mat.* 12. 42.—*Is.* 9. 6. *Ro.* 5. 7, 8.—*Phi.* 2. 6-8.—*Ep.* 3. 19. 1 *Co.* 1. 24.—*Col.* 2. 3.—*Ep.* 3. 8.—1 *Co.* 1. 30.

I have loved thee with an everlasting love: therefore with loving-kindness have I drawn thee.

We are bound to give thanks alway to God for you, brethren beloved of the Lord, because God hath from the beginning chosen you to salvation through sanctification of the Spirit and belief of the truth: whereunto he called you by our gospel, to the obtaining of the glory of our Lord Jesus Christ.—God . . . hath saved us, and called us with a holy calling, not according to our works, but according to his own purpose and grace, which was given us in Christ Jesus before the world began.—Thine eyes did see my substance, yet being unperfect; and in thy book all my members were written, which in continuance were fashioned, when as yet there was none of them.

God so loved the world, that he gave his only begotten Son, that whosoever believeth in him should not perish, but have everlasting life.

Herein is love, not that we loved God, but that he loved us, and sent his Son to be the propitiation for our sins.

JERE. 31. 3. 2 *Thes.* 2. 13, 14.—2 *Ti.* 1. 9.—*Ps.* 139. 16. *Jno.* 3. 16.
1 *Jno.* 4. 10.

I have made, and I will bear.

Thus saith the Lord that created thee, O Jacob, and he that formed thee, O Israel, Fear not: for I have redeemed thee, I have called thee by thy name; thou art mine. When thou passest through the waters, I will be with thee; and through the rivers, they shall not overflow thee.—Even to your old age I am he; and even to hoar hairs will I carry you.

As an eagle stirreth up her nest, fluttereth over her young, spreadeth abroad her wings, taketh them, beareth them on her wings: so the Lord alone did lead him.—He bare them, and carried them all the days of old.

Jesus Christ the same yesterday, and to-day, and for ever.—For I am persuaded, that neither . . . height, nor depth, nor any other creature, shall be able to separate us from the love of God, which is in Christ Jesus our Lord.

Can a woman forget her sucking child, that she should not have compassion on the son of her womb? yea, they may forget, yet will I not forget thee.

ISA. 46. 4. *Is.* 43. 1, 2.—*Is.* 46. 4. *De.* 32. 11. 12.—*Is.* 63. 9. *He.* 13. 8.—
Ro. 8. 38, 39. *Is.* 49. 15.

I know their sorrows.

A man of sorrows and acquainted with grief.—Touched with the feeling of our infirmities.

Himself took our infirmities, and bare our sicknesses.—Jesus . . . being wearied with his journey, sat thus on the well.

When Jesus . . . saw her weeping, and the Jews also weeping which came with her, he groaned in the spirit, and was troubled. Jesus wept.—For in that he himself hath suffered being tempted, he is able to succour them that are tempted.

He hath looked down from the height of his sanctuary; from heaven did the LORD behold the earth; to hear the groaning of the prisoner; to loose those that are appointed to death.—He knoweth the way that I take: when he hath tried me, I shall come forth as gold.—When my spirit was overwhelmed within me, then thou knewest my path.

He that toucheth you toucheth the apple of his eye.—In all their affliction he was afflicted; and the angel of his presence saved them.

EXOD. 3. 7. *Is.* 53. 3.—*He.* 4. 15. *Mat.* 8. 17.—*Jno.* 4. 6. *Jno.* 11. 33, 35.— *He.* 2. 18. *Ps.* 102. 19, 20.—*Job* 23. 10.—*Ps.* 142. 3. *Zec.* 2. 8.—*Is.* 63. 9.

AUGUST 24   EVENING
I must work the works of him that sent me, while it is day.

The soul of the sluggard desireth, and hath nothing: but the soul of the diligent shall be made fat.—He that watereth shall be watered.

My meat is to do the will of him that sent me, and to finish his work. Say not ye, There are yet four months, and then cometh harvest: behold, I say unto you, Lift up your eyes, and look on the fields; for they are white already to harvest. And he that reapeth receiveth wages, and gathereth fruit unto life eternal: that both he that soweth and he that reapeth may rejoice together.— The kingdom of heaven is like unto a man that is an householder, which went out early in the morning to hire labourers into his vineyard. And when he had agreed with the labourers for a penny a day, he sent them into his vineyard.

Preach the word; be instant in season, out of season.—Occupy till I come.

I laboured more abundantly than they all: yet not I, but the grace of God which was with me.

JOHN 9. 4. *Pr.* 13. 4.—*Pr.* 11. 25.- *Jno.* 4. 34-36.—*Mat.* 20. 1, 2. 2 *Ti.* 4. 2.—*Lu.* 19. 13. 1 *Co.* 15. 10.

Look unto the rock whence ye are hewn, and to the hole of the pit whence ye are digged.

Behold, I was shapen in iniquity.—None eye pitied thee, . . . but thou wast cast out in the open field, to the loathing of thy person, in the day that thou wast born. And when I passed by thee, and saw thee polluted in thine own blood, I said unto thee, . . . Live.

He brought me up . . . out of a horrible pit, out of the miry clay, and set my feet upon a rock, and established my goings. And he hath put a new song in my mouth, even praise unto our God.

When we were yet without strength, in due time Christ died for the ungodly. For scarcely for a righteous man will one die: yet peradventure for a good man some would even dare to die. But God commendeth his love toward us, in that, while we were yet sinners, Christ died for us.—God, who is rich in mercy, for his great love wherewith he loved us, even when we were dead in sins, hath quickened us together with Christ.

ISA. 51. 1. *Ps.* 51. 5.—*Eze.* 16. 5, 6. *Ps.* 40. 2, 3. *Ro.* 5. 6-8.—*Ep.* 2. 4, 5.

I will greatly rejoice in the Lord, my soul shall be joyful in my God.

I will bless the LORD at all times: his praise shall continually be in my mouth. My soul shall make her boast in the LORD: the humble shall hear thereof, and be glad. O magnify the LORD with me, and let us exalt his name together.—The LORD will give grace and glory: no good thing will he withhold from them that walk uprightly. O LORD of hosts, blessed is the man that trusteth in thee.—Bless the LORD, O my soul: and all that is within me, bless his holy name.

Is any merry? let him sing psalms.—Be filled with the Spirit; speaking to yourselves in psalms and hymns and spiritual songs, singing and making melody in your heart to the LORD; giving thanks always for all things.—Singing with grace in your hearts to the Lord.

At midnight Paul and Silas prayed, and sang praises unto God: and the prisoners heard them.—Rejoice in the Lord alway: and again, I say, Rejoice.

ISA. 61. 10. *Ps.* 34. 1-3.—*Ps.* 84. 11, 12.—*Ps.* 103. 1. *Ja.* 5. 13.—*Ep.* 5, 13-20. —*Col.* 3. 16. *Ac.* 16. 25.—*Phi.* 4. 4.

Thou shalt make a plate of pure gold, and grave upon it, like the engravings of a signet.

HOLINESS TO THE LORD

Holiness, without which no man can see the Lord.—God is a Spirit: and they that worship him must worship him in spirit and in truth.—But we are all as an unclean thing, and all our righteousnesses are as filthy rags.—I will be sanctified in them that come nigh me, and before all the people I will be glorified.

This is the law of the house: Upon the top of the mountain the whole limit thereof round about shall be most holy.—Holiness becometh thine house, O LORD, for ever.

For their sakes I sanctify myself, that they also might be sanctified through the truth.—Seeing . . . that we have a great high priest, that is passed into the heavens, Jesus the Son of God, let us . . . come boldly unto the throne of grace, that we may obtain mercy, and find grace to help in time of need.

EXOD. 28. 36. *He.* 12. 14.—*Jno.* 4. 24.—*Is.* 64. 6.—*Le.* 10. 3. *Eze.* 43. 12.—
Ps. 93. 5. *Jno.* 17. 19.—*He.* 4. 14, 16.

My cup runneth over.

O taste and see that the LORD is good: blessed is the man that trusteth in him. O fear the LORD, ye his saints: for there is no want to them that fear him. The young lions do lack, and suffer hunger: but they that seek the LORD shall not want any good thing.—His compassions fail not. They are new every morning: great is thy faithfulness.

The LORD is the portion of mine inheritance and of my cup: thou maintainest my lot. The lines are fallen unto me in pleasant places; yea, I have a goodly heritage.—Whether . . . the world, or life, or death, or things present, or things to come; all are your's.—Blessed be the God and Father of our Lord Jesus Christ, who hath blessed us with all spiritual blessings in heavenly places in Christ.

I have learned, in whatsoever state I am, therewith to be content.—Godliness with contentment is great gain.—My God shall supply all your need according to his riches in glory by Christ Jesus.

PSA. 23. 5. *Ps.* 34. 8-10.—*La.* 3. 22, 23. *Ps.* 16. 5, 6.—1 *Co.* 3. 22.—
Ep. 1. 3. *Phi.* 4. 11.—1 *Ti.* 6. 6.—*Phi.* 4. 19.

Thy word is a lamp unto my feet, and a light unto my path.

By the word of thy lips I have kept me from the paths of the destroyer. Hold up my goings in thy paths, that my footsteps slip not.—When thou goest, it shall lead thee; when thou sleepest, it shall keep thee; and when thou awakest, it shall talk with thee. For the commandment is a lamp; and the law is light.—Thine ears shall hear a word behind thee, saying, This is the way, walk ye in it, when ye turn to the right hand, and when ye turn to the left.

I am the light of the world: he that followeth me shall not walk in darkness, but shall have the light of life.—We have also a . . . sure word of prophecy; whereunto ye do well that ye take heed, as unto a light that shineth in a dark place.—Now we see through a glass, darkly; but then face to face: now I know in part; but then shall I know even as also I am known.—They need no candle, neither light of the sun; for the Lord God giveth them light: and they shall reign for ever and ever.

PSA. 119. 105. *Ps.* 17. 4, 5.—*Pr.* 6. 22, 23.—*Is.* 30. 21.
Jno. 8. 12.—2 *Pe.* 1. 19.—1 *Co.* 13. 12.—*Re.* 22. 5.

What meanest thou, O sleeper? arise.

This is not your rest: . . . it is polluted, it shall destroy you.— Set your affection on things above, not on things on the earth.— If riches increase, set not your heart upon them.—Set your heart and your soul to seek your God: arise therefore.

Why sleep ye? rise and pray, lest ye enter into temptation.— Take heed to yourselves, lest at any time your hearts be overcharged with surfeiting, and drunkenness, and cares of this life, and so that day come upon you unawares.

While the bridegroom tarried, they all slumbered and slept.— Yet a little while, and he that shall come will come, and will not tarry.—Now it is high time to awake out of sleep: for now is our salvation nearer than when we believed.—Watch ye therefore: for ye know not when the master of the house cometh, at even, or at midnight, or at the cockcrowing, or in the morning: lest coming suddenly he finds you sleeping.

JONAH 1. 6. *Mi.* 2. 10.—*Col.* 3. 2.—*Ps.* 62. 10.—1 *Ch.* 22. 19.
Lu. 22. 46.—*Lu.* 21. 34. *Mat.* 25. 5.—*He.* 10. 37.—*Ro.* 13. 11.—
Mar. 13. 35, 36.

The accuser of our brethren is cast down, which accused them before our God day and night.

They overcame him by the blood of the Lamb, and by the word of their testimony.—Who shall lay any thing to the charge of God's elect? It is God that justifieth. Who is he that condemneth? It is Christ that died, yea, rather, that is risen again, who is even at the right hand of God, who also maketh intercession for us.

Having spoiled principalities and powers, he made a shew of them openly.—That through death he might destroy him that had the power of death, that is, the devil; and deliver them who through fear of death were all their lifetime subject to bondage.— In all these things we are more than conquerors, through him that loved us.—Put on the whole armour of God, that ye may be able to stand against the wiles of the devil. And take the sword of the Spirit, which is the word of God.—Thanks be to God, which giveth us the victory through our Lord Jesus Christ.

REV. 12. 10. *Re.* 12. 11.—*Ro.* 8. 33, 34. *Col.* 2. 15.—*He.* 2. 14, 15.— *Ro.* 8. 37.—*Ep.* 6. 11, 17.—1 *Co.* 15. 57.

The tree of life.

God hath given to us eternal life, and this life is in his Son.— He gave his only begotten Son, that whosoever·believeth in him should not perish, but have everlasting life.—As the Father raiseth up the dead, and quickeneth them; even so the Son quickeneth whom he will. As the Father hath life in himself; so hath he given to the Son to have life in himself.

To him that overcometh will I give to eat of the tree of life, which is in the midst of the paradise of God.—In the midst of the street of it, and on either side of the river, was there the tree of life, which bare twelve manner of fruits, and yielded her fruit every month: and the leaves of the tree were for the healing of the nations.

Happy is the man that findeth wisdom. Length of days is in her right hand. She is a tree of life to them that lay hold upon her: and happy is every one that retaineth her.—Christ Jesus, . . . is made unto us wisdom.

GEN. 2. 9. 1 *Jno.* 5. 11.—*Jno.* 3. 16.—*Jno.* 5. 21, 26. *Re.* 2. 7.—*Re.* 22. 2. *Pr.* 3. 13, 16, 18.—1 *Co.* 1. 30.

Whoso trusteth in the Lord, happy is he.

[Abraham] staggered not at the promise of God through unbelief; but was strong in faith, giving glory to God; and being fully persuaded that, what he had promised, he was able also to perform.—The children of Judah prevailed, because they relied upon the LORD God of their fathers.

God is our refuge and strength, a very present help in trouble. Therefore will not we fear, though the earth be removed, and though the mountains be carried into the midst of the sea.—It is better to trust in the LORD than to put confidence in man. It is better to trust in the LORD than to put confidence in princes.—The steps of a good man are ordered by the LORD: and he delighteth in his way. Though he fall, he shall not be utterly cast down: for the LORD upholdeth him with his hand.

O taste and see that the LORD is good: blessed is the man that trusteth in him. O fear the LORD, ye his saints: for there is no want to them that fear him.

PRO. 16. 20. *Ro.* 4. 20, 21.—2 *Ch.* 13. 18. *Ps.* 46, 1, 2.—*Ps.* 118. 8, 9. *Ps.* 37. 23, 24. *Ps.* 34. 8, 9.

I will both lay me down in peace, and sleep: for thou, Lord, only makest me dwell in safety.

Thou shalt not be afraid for the terror by night. He shall cover thee with his feathers, and under his wings shalt thou trust.—Even as a hen gathereth her chickens under her wings.—He will not suffer thy foot to be moved: he that keepeth thee will not slumber. Behold, he that keepeth Israel shall neither slumber nor sleep. The LORD is thy keeper: the LORD is thy shade upon thy right hand.

I will abide in thy tabernacle for ever: I will trust in the covert of thy wings.—The darkness hideth not from thee; but the night shineth as the day: the darkness and the light are both alike to thee.

He that spared not his own Son, but delivered him up for us all, how shall he not with him also freely give us all things?—Ye are Christ's; and Christ is God's.—I will trust, and not be afraid.

PSA. 4. 8. *Ps.* 91. 5, 4.—*Mat.* 23. 37.—*Ps.* 121. 3-5. *Ps.* 61. 4.—*Ps.* 139. 12. *Ro.* 8. 32.—1 *Co.* 3. 23.—*Is.* 12. 2.

The king held out . . . the golden sceptre. So Esther drew near, and touched the top of the sceptre.

It shall come to pass, when he crieth unto me, that I will hear; for I am gracious.

We have known and believed the love that God hath to us. God is love; and he that dwelleth in love dwelleth in God, and God in him. Herein is our love made perfect, that we may have boldness in the day of judgment: because as he is, so are we in this world. There is no fear in love; but perfect love casteth out fear: because fear hath torment. He that feareth is not made perfect in love. We love him, because he first loved us.

Let us draw near with a true heart. in full assurance of faith, having our hearts sprinkled from an evil conscience, and our bodies washed with pure water.—For through him we . . . have access by one Spirit unto the Father.—We have boldness and access with confidence by the faith of him.—Let us therefore come boldly unto the throne of grace, that we may obtain mercy, and find grace to help in time of need.

EST. 5. 2. *Ex.* 22. 27. 1 *Jno.* 4. 16-19. *He.* 10. 22.—*Ep.* 2. 18.— *Ep.* 3. 12.—*He.* 4. 16.

They said, . . . It is manna: for they wist not what it was.

Without controversy great is the mystery of godliness: God was manifest in the flesh.—The bread of God is he which cometh down from heaven, and giveth life unto the world.

Your fathers did eat manna in the wilderness, and are dead.— If any man eat of this bread, he shall live for ever: and the bread that I will give is my flesh, which I will give for the life of the world.—My flesh is meat indeed, and my blood is drink indeed.

The children of Israel . . . gathered, some more, some less. He that gathered much had nothing over, and he that gathered little had no lack. They gathered it every morning, every man according to his eating.

Take no thought, saying, What shall we eat: or, What shall we drink? Your heavenly Father knoweth that ye have need of all these things. But seek ye first the kingdom of God and his righteousness; and all these things shall be added unto you.

EXOD. 16. 15. 1 *Ti.* 3. 16.—*Jno.* 6. 33. *Jno.* 6. 49, 51, 55. *Ex.* 16. 17, 18, 21. *Mat.* 6. 31-33.

The free gift is of many offences unto justification.

Though your sins be as scarlet, they shall be as white as snow; though they be red like crimson, they shall be as wool.—I, even I, am he that blotteth out thy transgressions for mine own sake, and will not remember thy sins. Put me in remembrance: let us plead together: declare thou, that thou mayest be justified.—I have blotted out, as a thick cloud, thy transgressions, and, as a cloud, thy sins: return unto me; for I have redeemed thee.

God so loved the world, that he gave his only begotten Son, that whosoever believeth in him should not perish, but have everlasting life.—Not as the offence, so also is the free gift. For if through the offence of one many be dead, much more the grace of God, and the gift by grace, which is by one man, Jesus Christ, hath abounded unto many.—And such were some of you: but ye are washed, but ye are sanctified, but ye are justified in the name of the Lord Jesus, and by the Spirit of our God.

ROM. 5. 16. Is. 1. 18.—Is. 43. 25, 26.—Is. 44. 22. Jno. 3. 16.— Ro. 5. 15.—1 Co. 6. 11.

Occupy till I come.

The Son of man is as a man taking a far journey, who left his house, and gave authority to his servants, and to every man his work, and commanded the porter to watch.—Unto one he gave five talents, to another two, and to another one; to every man according to his several ability; and straightway took his journey.

I must work the works of him that sent me, while it is day: the night cometh, when no man can work.—Wist ye not that I must be about my Father's business?—Leaving us an example, that ye should follow his steps.

Preach the word; be instant in season, out of season; reprove, rebuke, exhort with all long-suffering and doctrine.—Every man's work shall be made manifest: for the day shall declare it.—Therefore, my beloved brethren, be ye stedfast, unmoveable, always abounding in the work of the Lord, forasmuch as ye know that your labour is not in vain in the Lord.

LUKE 19. 13. Mar. 13. 34.—Mat. 25. 15. Jno. 9. 4.—Lu. 2. 49.— 1 Pe. 2. 21. 2 Ti. 4. 2.—1 Co. 3. 13.—1 Co. 15. 58.

The fruit of the Spirit is meekness.

The meek . . . shall increase their joy in the LORD, and the poor among men shall rejoice in the Holy One of Israel.—Except ye be converted, and become as little children, ye shall not enter into the kingdom of heaven. Whosoever therefore shall humble himself as this little child, the same is greatest in the kingdom of heaven.—The ornament of a meek and quiet spirit, . . . is in the sight of God of great price.—Charity vaunteth not itself, is not puffed up.

Follow after meekness. Take my yoke upon you and learn of me, for I am meek and lowly in heart.—He was oppressed, and he was afflicted, yet he opened not his mouth: he is brought as a lamb to the slaughter, and as a sheep before her shearers is dumb, so he openeth not his mouth.—Christ also suffered for us, leaving us an example, that ye should follow his steps: who did no sin, neither was guile found in his mouth: who, when he was reviled, reviled not again, . . . but committed himself to him that judgeth righteously.

GAL. 5. 22. Is. 29. 19.—Mat. 18. 3, 4.—1 Pe. 3. 4.—1 Co. 13. 4.
1 Ti. 6. 11.—Mat. 11. 29.—Is. 53. 7.—1 Pe. 2. 21-23.

If any man will come after me, let him deny himself, and take up his cross daily, and follow me.

By honour and dishonour, by evil report and good report.—All that will live godly in Christ Jesus shall suffer persecution.—The offence of the cross.

If I yet pleased men, I should not be the servant of Christ.

If ye be reproached for the name of Christ, happy are ye: but let none of you suffer as a murderer, or as a thief, or as an evil-doer, or as a busybody in other men's matters. Yet if any man suffer as a Christian, let him not be ashamed; but let him glorify God on this behalf.

Unto you it is given in the behalf of Christ, not only to believe on him, but also to suffer for his sake.—If one died for all, then were all dead: and that he died for all, that they which live should not henceforth live unto themselves, but unto him which died for them, and rose again.—If we suffer, we shall also reign with him.

LUKE 9. 23. 2 Co. 6. 8.—2 Ti. 3. 12.—Ga. 5. 11. Ga. 1. 10.
1 Pe. 4. 14-16. Phi. 1. 29.—2 Co. 5. 14, 15.—2 Ti. 2. 12.

Wait on the Lord: be of good courage, and he shall strengthen thine heart.

Hast thou not known? hast thou not heard, that the everlasting God, the LORD, the Creator of the ends of the earth, fainteth not, neither is weary? He giveth power to the faint; and to them that have no might he increaseth strength.—Fear thou not; for I am with thee: be not dismayed; for I am thy God: I will strengthen thee; yea, I will help thee; yea, I will uphold thee with the right hand of my righteousness.—Thou hast been a strength to the poor, a strength to the needy in distress, a refuge from the storm, a shadow from the heat, when the blast of the terrible ones is as a storm against the wall.

The trying of your faith worketh patience. But let patience have her perfect work, that ye may be perfect and entire, wanting nothing.—Cast not away therefore your confidence, which hath great recompence of reward. For ye have need of patience, that, after ye have done the will of God, ye might receive the promise.

PSA. 27. 14. *Is.* 40. 28, 29.—*Is.* 41. 10.—*Is.* 25. 4. *Ja.* 1. 3, 4.—
He. 10. 35, 36.

He maketh me to lie down in green pastures.

The wicked are like the troubled sea, when it cannot rest. There is no peace, saith my God, to the wicked.

Come unto me, all ye that labour and are heavy laden, and I will give you rest.—Rest in the LORD. He that is entered into his rest, he also hath ceased from his own works.

Be not carried about with divers and strange doctrines. For it is a good thing that the heart be established with grace.—That we . . . be no more children, tossed to and fro, and carried about with every wind of doctrine, by the sleight of men, and cunning craftiness, whereby they lie in wait to deceive; but speaking the truth in love, may grow up into him in all things, which is the head, even Christ.

I sat down under his shadow with great delight, and his fruit was sweet to my taste. He brought me to the banqueting house, and his banner over me was love.

PSA. 23. 2. *Is.* 57. 20, 21. *Mat.* 11. 28.—*Ps.* 37. 7.—*He.* 4. 10. *He.* 13. 9.—
Ep. 4. 14, 15. *Ca.* 2. 3, 4.

Neither shall there be leaven seen with thee in all thy quarters.

The fear of the LORD is to hate evil.—Abhor that which is evil. —Abstain from all appearance of evil.—Looking diligently lest any man fail of the grace of God; lest any root of bitterness springing up trouble you, and thereby many be defiled.

If I regard iniquity in my heart, the Lord will not hear me.

Know ye not that a little leaven leaveneth the whole lump? Purge out therefore the old leaven, that ye may be a new lump, as ye are unleavened. For even Christ our passover is sacrificed for us: therefore let us keep the feast, not with old leaven, neither with the leaven of malice and wickedness; but with the unleavened bread of sincerity and truth.—Let a man examine himself, and so let him eat of that bread, and drink of that cup.

Let every one that nameth the name of Christ depart from iniquity.—Such an high priest became us, who is holy, harmless, undefiled, separate from sinners.—In him is no sin.

EXOD. 13. 7. *Pr.* 8. 13.—*Ro.* 12. 9.—1 *Thes.* 5. 22.—*He.* 12. 15. *Ps.* 66. 18. 1 *Co.* 5. 6-8. 1 *Co.* 11. 28.—2 *Ti.* 2. 19.—*He.* 7. 26.—1 *Jno.* 3. 5.

The serpent said unto the woman, Ye shall not surely die: . . . your eyes shall be opened, and ye shall be as gods, knowing good and evil.

I fear, lest by any means, as the serpent beguiled Eve through his subtilty, so your minds should be corrupted from the simplicity that is in Christ.

My brethren, be strong in the Lord, and in the power of his might. Put on the whole armour of God, that ye may be able to stand against the wiles of the devil. Take unto you the whole armour of God, that ye may be able to withstand in the evil day, and having done all, to stand. Stand therefore, having your loins girt about with truth, and having on the breastplate of righteousness; and your feet shod with the preparation of the gospel of peace; above all, taking the shield of faith, wherewith ye shall be able to quench all the fiery darts of the wicked. And take the helmet of salvation, and the sword of the Spirit, which is the word of God.—Lest Satan should get an advantage of us; for we are not ignorant of his devices.

GEN. 3. 4, 5. 2 *Co.* 11. 3. *Ep.* 6. 10, 11, 13-17.—2 *Co.* 2. 11.

Sit still, my daughter.

Take heed, and be quiet; fear not, neither be fainthearted.—Be still, and know that I am God.—Said I not unto thee, that, if thou wouldest believe, thou shouldest see the glory of God?—The loftiness of man shall be bowed down, and the haughtiness of men shall be made low: and the LORD alone shall be exalted in that day.

Mary . . . sat at Jesus' feet, and heard his word.—Mary hath chosen that good part, which shall not be taken away from her.—In returning and rest shall ye be saved; in quietness and in confidence shall be your strength.—Commune with your own heart upon your bed, and be still.

Rest in the LORD, and wait patiently for him: fret not thyself because of him who prospereth in his way, because of the man who bringeth wicked devices to pass.

He shall not be afraid of evil tidings: his heart is fixed, trusting in the LORD. His heart is established.

He that believeth shall not make haste.

RUTH 3. 18. *Is.* 7. 4.—*Ps.* 46. 10.—*Jno.* 11. 40.—*Is.* 2. 17.
Lu. 10. 39, 42.—*Is.* 30. 15.—*Ps.* 4. 4. *Ps.* 37. 7. *Ps.* 112. 7, 8.
Is. 28. 16.

What I do thou knowest not now; but thou shalt know hereafter.

Thou shalt remember all the way which the LORD thy God led thee these forty years in the wilderness, to humble thee, and to prove thee, to know what was in thine heart, whether thou wouldest keep his commandments, or no.

When I passed by thee, and looked upon thee, behold, thy time was the time of love; yea, I sware unto thee, and entered into a covenant with thee, saith the Lord GOD, and thou becamest mine.—Whom the Lord loveth he chasteneth.

Beloved, think it not strange concerning the fiery trial which is to try you, as though some strange thing happened unto you: but rejoice, inasmuch as ye are partakers of Christ's sufferings; that, when his glory shall be revealed, ye may be glad also with exceeding joy.—Our light affliction, which is but for a moment, worketh for us a far more exceeding and eternal weight of glory; while we look not at the things which are seen, but at the things which are not seen.

JOHN 13. 7. *De.* 8. 2. *Eze.* 16. 8.—*He.* 12. 6. 1 *Pe.* 4. 12, 13.—
2 *Co.* 4. 17. 18.

As the body is one, and hath many members, ... so also is Christ.

He is the head of the body, the church.—The head over all things to the church, which is his body, the fulness of him that filleth all in all.—We are members of his body, of his flesh, and of his bones.

A body hast thou prepared me.—Thine eyes did see my substance, yet being unperfect; and in thy book all my members were written, which in continuance were fashioned, when as yet there was none of them.

Thine they were, and thou gavest them me.—He hath chosen us in him before the foundation of the world.—Whom he did foreknow, he also did predestinate to be conformed to the image of his Son.

Grow up into him in all things, which is the head, even Christ: from whom the whole body fitly joined together, and compacted by that which every joint supplieth, . . . maketh increase of the body unto the edifying of itself in love.

1 COR. 12. 12. Col. 1. 18.—Ep. 1. 22, 23.—Ep. 5. 30. He. 10. 5.—
Ps. 139. 16. Jno. 17. 6.—Ep. 1. 4.—Ro. 8. 29. Ep. 4. 15, 16.

The fountain of living waters.

How excellent is thy lovingkindness, O God! therefore the children of men put their trust under the shadow of thy wings. They shall be abundantly satisfied with the fatness of thy house; and thou shalt make them drink of the river of thy pleasures. For with thee is the fountain of life.

Thus saith the Lord GOD, Behold, my servants shall eat, but ye shall be hungry: behold, my servants shall drink, but ye shall be thirsty.—Whosoever drinketh of the water that I shall give him shall never thirst; but the water that I shall give him shall be in him a well of water springing up into everlasting life.—This spake he of the Spirit, which they that believe on him should receive.

Ho, every one that thirsteth, come ye to the waters.—The Spirit and the bride say, Come. And let him that heareth say, Come. And let him that is athirst come. And whosoever will, let him take the water of life freely.

JER. 2. 13. Ps. 36. 7-9. Is. 65. 13.—Jno. 4. 14.—Jno. 7. 39. Is. 55. 1.—
Re. 22. 17.

Let us lift up our heart with our hands unto God in the heavens.

Who is like unto the LORD our God, who dwelleth on high, who humbleth himself to behold the things that are in heaven, and in the earth!—Unto thee, O LORD, do I lift up my soul.—I stretch forth my hands unto thee: my soul thirsteth after thee, as a thirsty land. Hide not thy face from me, lest I be like unto them that go down into the pit. Cause me to hear thy lovingkindness in the morning; for in thee do I trust: cause me to know the way wherein I should walk; for I lift up my soul unto thee.

Because thy lovingkindness is better than life, my lips shall praise thee. Thus will I bless thee while I live: I will lift up my hands in thy name.—Rejoice the soul of thy servant: for unto thee, O Lord, do I lift up my soul. For thou, Lord, art good, and ready to forgive; and plenteous in mercy unto all them that call upon thee.

Whatsoever ye shall ask in my name, that will I do.

LAM. 3. 41. *Ps.* 113. 5, 6.—*Ps.* 25. 1.—*Ps.* 143. 6-8. *Ps.* 63. 3, 4.— *Ps.* 86. 4, 5. *Jno.* 14. 13.

Watchman, what of the night?

It is high time to awake out of sleep: for now is our salvation nearer than when we believed. The night is far spent, the day is at hand: let us therefore cast off the works of darkness, and let us put on the armour of light.

Learn a parable of the fig tree; When his branch is yet tender, and putteth forth leaves, ye know that summer is nigh: so likewise ye, when ye shall see all these things, know that it is near, even at the doors. Heaven and earth shall pass away, but my words shall not pass away.

I wait for the LORD, my soul doth wait, and in his word do I hope. My soul waiteth for the Lord more than they that watch for the morning: I say, more than they that watch for the morning.

He which testifieth these things saith, Surely I come quickly. Amen. Even so, come, Lord Jesus.

Watch, . . . for ye know neither the day nor the hour wherein the Son of man cometh.

ISA. 21. 11. *Ro.* 13. 11, 12. *Mat.* 24. 32, 33, 35. *Ps.* 130. 5, 6. *Re.* 22. 20. *Mat.* 25. 13.

Rejoicing in hope.

The hope which is laid up for you in heaven.—If in this life only we have hope in Christ, we are of all men most miserable.—We must through much tribulation enter into the kingdom of God.—Whosoever doth not bear his cross, and come after me, cannot be my disciple.—No man should be moved by these afflictions: for yourselves know that we are appointed thereunto.

Rejoice in the Lord alway: and again I say, Rejoice.—The God of hope fill you with all joy and peace in believing, that ye may abound in hope, through the power of the Holy Ghost.—Blessed be the God and Father of our Lord Jesus Christ, which according to his abundant mercy hath begotten us again unto a lively hope by the resurrection of Jesus Christ from the dead.—Whom having not seen, ye love; in whom, though now ye see him not, yet believing, ye rejoice with joy unspeakable and full of glory.—By whom also we have access by faith into this grace wherein we stand, and rejoice in hope of the glory of God.

ROM. 12. 12. *Col.* 1. 5.—1 *Co.* 15. 19.—*Ac.* 14. 22.—*Lu.* 14. 27.—
1 *Thes.* 3. 3. *Phi.* 4. 4.—*Ro.* 15. 13.—1 *Pe.* 1. 3.—1 *Pe.* 1. 8.—*Ro.* 5. 2.

SEPTEMBER 7

EVENING

I am poor and needy; yet the Lord thinketh upon me.

I know the thoughts that I think toward you, saith the LORD, thoughts of peace, and not of evil.—My thoughts are not your thoughts, neither are your ways my ways, saith the LORD. For as the heavens are higher than the earth, so are my ways higher than your ways, and my thoughts than your thoughts.

How precious . . . are thy thoughts unto me, O God! how great is the sum of them! If I should count them, they are more in number than the sand: when I awake, I am still with thee.—O LORD, how great are thy works! and thy thoughts are very deep.—Many, O LORD my God, are thy wonderful works which thou hast done, and thy thoughts which are to us-ward.

Not many mighty, not many noble, are called.—Hath not God chosen the poor of this world rich in faith, and heirs of the kingdom? Having nothing, and yet possessing all things.—The unsearchable riches of Christ.

PSA. 40. 17. *Je.* 29. 11.—*Is.* 55. 8, 9. *Ps.* 139. 17, 18.—*Ps.* 92. 5.—
Ps. 40. 5. 1 *Co.* 1. 26.—*Ja.* 2. 5.—2 *Co.* 6. 10.—*Ep.* 3, 8.

Thou art weighed in the balances, and art found wanting.

The LORD is a God of knowledge, and by him, actions are weighed.—That which is highly esteemed among men is abomination in the sight of God.—The LORD seeth not as man seeth; for man looketh on the outward appearance, but the LORD looketh on the heart.—Be not deceived; God is not mocked: for whatsoever a man soweth, that shall he also reap. For he that soweth to his flesh shall of the flesh reap corruption; but he that soweth to the Spirit shall of the Spirit reap life everlasting.

What is a man profited, if he shall gain the whole world, and lose his own soul? or what shall a man give in exchange for his soul?—What things were gain to me, those I counted loss for Christ.

Behold, thou desirest truth in the inward parts.—Thou hast proved mine heart; thou hast visited me in the night; thou hast tried me, and shalt find nothing.

DAN. 5. 27. 1 *Sa.* 2. 3.—*Lu.* 16. 15.—1 *Sa.* 16. 7.—*Gal.* 6. **7, 8.**
Mat. 16. 26.—*Phi.* 3. 7. *Ps.* 51. 6.—*Ps.* 17. 3.

Christ the firstfruits.

Except a corn of wheat fall into the ground and die, it abideth alone: but if it die, it bringeth forth much fruit.—If the firstfruit be holy, the lump is also holy: and if the root be holy, so are the branches.—Now is Christ risen from the dead, and become the firstfruits of them that slept.—If we have been planted together in the likeness of his death, we shall be also in the likeness of his resurrection.—The Lord Jesus Christ . . . shall change our vile body, that it may be fashioned like unto his glorious body, according to the working whereby he is able even to subdue all things unto himself.

The firstborn from the dead.—If the Spirit of him that raised up Jesus from the dead dwell in you, he that raised up Christ from the dead shall also quicken your mortal bodies by his Spirit that dwelleth in you.

I am the resurrection, and the life: he that believeth in me, though he were dead, yet shall he live.

1 *COR.* 15. 23. *Jno.* 12. 24.—*Ro.* 11. 16.—1 *Co.* 15. 20.—*Ro.* 6. **5.**—
Phi. 3. 20, 21. *Col.* 1. 18.—*Ro.* 8. 11. *Jno.* 11. 25.

He hath filled the hungry with good things; and the rich he hath sent empty away.

Thou sayest, I am rich, and increased with goods, and have need of nothing; and knowest not that thou art wretched, and miserable, and poor, and blind, and naked: I counsel thee to buy of me gold tried in the fire, that thou mayest be rich. As many as I love, I rebuke and chasten: be zealous therefore and repent.

Blessed are they which do hunger and thirst after righteousness: for they shall be filled.—When the poor and needy seek water, and there is none, and their tongue faileth for thirst, I the LORD will hear them, I the God of Israel will not forsake them.—I am the LORD thy God, . . . open thy mouth wide, and I will fill it.

Wherefore do ye spend money for that which is not bread? and your labour for that which satisfieth not? hearken diligently unto me, and eat ye that which is good, and let your soul delight itself in fatness.—I am the bread of life: he that cometh to me shall never hunger; and he that believeth on me shall never thirst.

LUKE 1. 53. *Re.* 3. 17-19. *Mat.* 5. 6.—*Is.* 41. 17.—*Ps.* 81. 10. *Is.* 55. 2.— *Jno.* 6. 35.

My feet were almost gone; my steps had well nigh slipped.

When I said, My foot slippeth; thy mercy, O LORD, help me up.

The Lord said, Simon, Simon, behold Satan hath desired to have you, that he may sift you as wheat: but I have prayed for thee, that thy faith fail not.

A just man falleth seven times, and riseth up again.—Though he fall, he shall not be utterly cast down: for the LORD upholdeth him with his hand.

Rejoice not against me, O mine enemy: when I fall, I shall arise; when I sit in darkness, the LORD shall be a light unto me. —He shall deliver thee in six troubles: yea, in seven there shall no evil touch thee.

If any man sin, we have an advocate with the Father, Jesus Christ the righteous.—Wherefore he is able also to save them to the uttermost that come unto God by him, seeing he ever liveth to make intercession for them.

PSA. 73. 2. *Ps.* 94. 18. *Lu.* 22. 31, 32. *Pr.* 24. 16.—*Ps.* 37. 24. *Mi.* 7. 8.— *Job* 5. 19. 1 *Jno.* 2. 1.—*He.* 7. 25.

I will give them one heart, and one way, that they may fear me for ever, for the good of them, and of their children after them.

A new heart . . . will I give you, and a new spirit will I put within you.—Good and upright is the LORD: therefore will he teach sinners in the way. The meek will he guide in judgment: and the meek will he teach his way. All the paths of the LORD are mercy and truth unto such as keep his covenant and his testimonies.

That they all may be one; as thou, Father, art in me, and I in thee, that they also may be one in us: that the world may believe that thou hast sent me.

I . . . beseech you that ye walk worthy of the vocation wherewith ye are called, with all lowliness and meekness, . . . endeavouring to keep the unity of the Spirit in the bond of peace. There is one body, and one Spirit, even as ye are called in one hope of your calling; one Lord, one faith, one baptism, one God and Father of all, who is above all, and through all, and in you all.

JER. 32. 39. *Eze.* 36. 26.—*Ps.* 25. 8-10. *Jno.* 17. 21. *Ep.* 4. 1-6.

They that wait upon the Lord shall renew their strength.
(*Or*, change strength.)

When I am weak, then am I strong.—My God shall be my strength.—He said unto me, My grace is sufficient for thee: for my strength is made perfect in weakness. Most gladly therefore will I rather glory in my infirmities, that the power of Christ may rest upon me.—Let him take hold of my strength.

Cast thy burden upon the LORD, and he shall sustain thee.— The arms of his hands were made strong by the hands of the mighty God of Jacob.

I will not let thee go, except thou bless me.

Thou comest to me with a sword, and with a spear, and with a shield: but I come to thee in the name of the LORD of hosts, the God of the armies of Israel, whom thou hast defied.—Plead my cause, O LORD, with them that strive with me: fight against them that fight against me. Take hold of shield and buckler, and stand up for mine help.

ISA. 40. 31. 2 *Co.* 12. 10.—*Is.* 49. 5.—2 *Co.* 12. 9.—*Is.* 27. 5. *Ps.* 55. 22.— *Ge.* 49. 24. *Ge.* 32. 26. 1 *Sa.* 17. 45.—*Ps.* 35. 1, 2.

Be not conformed to this world: but be ye transformed by the renewing of your mind.

Thou shalt not follow a multitude to do evil.

Know ye not that the friendship of the world is enmity with God? whosoever therefore will be a friend of the world is the enemy of God.

What fellowship hath righteousness with unrighteousness? and what communion hath light with darkness? And what concord hath Christ with Belial? or what part hath he that believeth with an infidel? And what agreement hath the temple of God with idols?—Love not the world, neither the things that are in the world. If any man love the world, the love of the Father is not in him. The world passeth away, and the lust thereof: but he that doeth the will of God abideth for ever.

In time past ye walked according to the course of this world, according to the prince of the power of the air, the spirit that now worketh in the children of disobedience.—Ye have not so learned Christ; if so be that ye have heard him, . . . as the truth is in Jesus.

ROM. 12. 2. *Ex.* 23. 2. *Ja.* 4. 4. *2 Co.* 6. 14-16.—*1 Jno.* 2. 15, 17.
Ep. 2. 2.—*Ep.* 4. 20, 21.

Man goeth forth unto his work and to his labour until the evening.

In the sweat of thy face shalt thou eat bread, till thou return unto the ground.—We commanded you, that if any would not work, neither should he eat.—Study to be quiet, and to do your own business, and to work with your own hands.

Whatsoever thy hand findeth to do, do it with thy might; for there is no work, nor device, nor knowledge, nor wisdom, in the grave, whither thou goest.—The night cometh when no man can work.

Let us not be weary in well doing: for in due season we shall reap, if we faint not.—Always abounding in the work of the Lord, forasmuch as ye know that your labour is not in vain in the Lord.

There remaineth . . . a rest to the people of God.—Unto us, which have borne the burden and heat of the day.—This is the rest wherewith ye may cause the weary to rest; and this is the refreshing.

PSA. 104. 23. *Ge.* 3. 19.—*2 Th.* 3. 10.—*1 Th.* 4. 11. *Ec.* 9. 10.—*Jno.* 9. 4.
Ga. 6. 9.—*1 Co.* 15. 58. *He.* 4. 9.—*Mat.* 20. 12.—*Is.* 28. 12.

I have seen his ways, and will heal him.

I am the LORD that healeth thee.

O LORD, thou hast searched me, and known me. Thou knowest my downsitting and mine uprising, thou understandest my thought afar off. Thou compassest my path and my lying down, and art acquainted with all my ways.—Thou hast set our iniquities before thee, our secret sins in the light of thy countenance.—All things are naked and opened unto the eyes of him with whom we have to do.

Come now, and let us reason together, saith the LORD: though your sins be as scarlet, they shall be as white as snow; though they be red like crimson, they shall be as wool.—He is gracious unto him, and saith, Deliver him from going down to the pit: I have found a ransom.—He was wounded for our transgressions, he was bruised for our iniquities: the chastisement of our peace was upon him; and with his stripes we are healed.—He hath sent me to bind up the brokenhearted.—Thy faith hath made thee whole; go in peace, and be whole of thy plague.

ISA. 57. 18. *Ex.* 15. 26. *Ps.* 139. 1-3.—*Ps.* 90. 8.—*He.* 4. 13. *Is.* 1. 18.—
Job 33. 24.—*Is.* 53. 5 *Is.* 61. 1.—*Mar.* 5. 34.

The Lord taketh my part.

The LORD hear thee in the day of trouble; the name of the God of Jacob defend thee; send thee help from the sanctuary, and strengthen thee out of Zion. We will rejoice in thy salvation, and in the name of our God we will set up our banners. Some trust in chariots, and some in horses: but we will remember the name of the LORD our God. They are brought down and fallen: but we are risen, and stand upright.

When the enemy shall come in like a flood, the Spirit of the LORD shall lift up a standard against him.—There hath no temptation taken you but such as is common to man: but God is faithful, who will not suffer you to be tempted above that ye are able; but will with the temptation also make a way to escape, that ye may be able to bear it.

If God be for us, who can be against us?—The LORD is on my side; I will not fear.

Our God whom we serve is able to deliver us, and he will deliver us.

PSA. 118. 7. *Ps.* 20. 1, 2, 5, 7, 8. *Is.* 59. 19.—1 *Co.* 10. 13. *Ro.* 8. 31.—
Ps. 118. 6. *Da.* 3. 17.

If any man thirst, let him come unto me, and drink.

My soul longeth, yea, even fainteth for the courts of the LORD: my heart and my flesh crieth out for the living God.—O God, thou art my God; early will I seek thee: my soul thirsteth for thee, my flesh longeth for thee in a dry and thirsty land where no water is; to see thy power and thy glory, so as I have seen thee in the sanctuary.

Ho, every one that thirsteth, come ye to the waters, and he that hath no money; come ye, buy, and eat; yea, come, buy wine and milk without money and without price.—The Spirit and the bride say, Come. And let him that heareth say, Come. And let him that is athirs come. And whosoever will, let him take the water of life freely.—Whosoever drinketh of the water that I shall give him shall never thirst; but the water that I shall give him shall be in him a well of water springing up into everlasting life.—My blood is drink indeed.

Eat, O friends; drink, yea, drink abundantly, O beloved.

JOHN 7. 37. *Ps.* 84. 2.—*Ps.* 63. 1, 2. *Is.* 55. 1.—*Re.* 22. 17.—*Jno.* 4. 14.— *Jno.* 6. 55. *Ca.* 5. 1.

Ye are the salt of the earth.

That which is not corruptible.—Being born again, not of corruptible seed, but of incorruptible, by the word of God, which liveth and abideth for ever.—He that believeth in me, though he were dead, yet shall he live.—The children of God, being the children of the resurrection.—The uncorruptible God.

If any man have not the Spirit of Christ, he is none of his. And if Christ be in you, the body is dead because of sin; but the Spirit is life because of righteousness. But if the Spirit of him that raised up Jesus from the dead dwell in you, he that raised up Christ from the dead shall also quicken your mortal bodies by his Spirit that dwelleth in you.—It is sown in corruption; it is raised in incorruption.

Have salt in yourselves, and have peace one with another.—Let no corrupt communication proceed out of your mouth, but that which is good to the use of edifying, that it may minister grace unto the hearers.

MAT. 5. 13. *1 Pe.* 3. 4.—*1 Pe.* 1. 23.—*Jno.* 11. 25.—*Lu.* 20. 36.—*Ro.* 1. 23. *Ro.* 8. 9-11.—*1 Co.* 15. 42. *Mar.* 9. 50.—*Ep.* 4. 29.

I, even I, am he that comforteth you.

Blessed be God, even the Father of our Lord Jesus Christ, the Father of mercies, and the God of all comfort; who comforteth us in all our tribulation, that we may be able to comfort them which are in any trouble, by the comfort wherewith we ourselves are comforted of God.—Like as a father pitieth his children, so the LORD pitieth them that fear him. For he knoweth our frame; he remembereth that we are dust.—As one whom his mother comforteth, so will I comfort you.—Casting all your care upon him, for he careth for you.

Thou, O Lord, art a God full of compassion, and gracious, longsuffering, and plenteous in mercy and truth.

Another Comforter . . . even the Spirit of truth. The Spirit . . . helpeth our infirmities.

God shall wipe away all tears from their eyes; and there shall be no more death, neither sorrow, nor crying, neither shall there be any more pain: for the former things are passed away.

ISA. 51. 12. 2 *Co.* 1. 3, 4.—*Ps.* 103. 13, 14.—*Is.* 66. 13.—1 *Pe.* 5. 7. *Ps.* 86. 15. *Jno.* 14. 16, 17.—*Ro.* 8. 26. *Re.* 21. 4.

Ye were called unto the fellowship of his Son.

He received from God the Father honour and glory, when there came such a voice to him from the excellent glory, This is my beloved Son, in whom I am well pleased.—Behold, what manner of love the Father hath bestowed upon us, that we should be called the sons of God.

Be ye . . . followers of God, as dear children.—If children, then heirs; heirs of God, and joint-heirs with Christ.

The brightness of his glory, and the express image of his person.—Let your light so shine before men, that they may see your good works, and glorify your Father which is in heaven.

Jesus the author and finisher of our faith; who for the joy that was set before him endured the cross, despising the shame.—These things I speak in the world, that they might have my joy fulfilled in themselves.—As the sufferings of Christ abound in us, so our consolation also aboundeth by Christ.

1 *COR.* 1. 9. 2 *Pe.* 1. 17.—1 *Jno.* 3. 1. *Ep.* 5. 1.—*Ro.* 8. 17. *He.* 1. 3.— *Mat.* 5. 16. *He.* 12. 2.—*Jno.* 17. 13.—2 *Co.* 1. 5.

Sin shall not have dominion over you: for ye are not under the law, but under grace.

What then? shall we sin, because we are not under the law, but under grace? God forbid.—My brethren, ye . . . are become dead to the law by the body of Christ; that ye should be married to another, even to him who is raised from the dead, that we should bring forth fruit unto God.—Being not without law to God, but under the law to Christ.—The sting of death is sin; and the strength of sin is the law. But thanks be to God, which giveth us the victory through our Lord Jesus Christ.

The law of the Spirit of life in Christ Jesus hath made me free from the law of sin and death.—Whosoever committeth sin is the servant of sin.—If the Son . . . shall make you free, ye shall be free indeed.

Stand fast therefore in the liberty wherewith Christ hath made us free, and be not entangled again with the yoke of bondage.

ROM. 6. 14. *Ro.* 6. 15.—*Ro.* 7. 4.—1 *Co.* 9. 21.—1 *Co.* 15. 56, 57. *Ro.* 8. 2.—*Jno.* 8. 34, 36. *Gal.* 5. 1.

A double minded man is unstable in all his ways.

No man, having put his hand to the plough, and looking back, is fit for the kingdom of God.

He that cometh to God must believe that he is, and that he is a rewarder of them that diligently seek him.—Let him ask in faith, nothing wavering. For he that wavereth is like a wave of the sea driven with the wind and tossed. For let not that man think that he shall receive any thing of the Lord.—What things soever ye desire, when ye pray, believe that ye receive them, and ye shall have them.

Be no more children, tossed to and fro, and carried about with every wind of doctrine, by the sleight of men, and cunning craftiness, whereby they lie in wait to deceive; but speaking the truth in love, . . . grow up into him in all things which is the head, even Christ.

Abide in me.—Be ye steadfast, unmoveable, always abounding in the work of the Lord, forasmuch as ye know that your labour is not in vain in the Lord.

JAMES 1. 8. *Lu.* 9. 62. *He.* 11. 6.—*Ja.* 1. 6, 7.—*Màr.* 11. 24. *Ep.* 4. 14, 15. *Jno.* 15. 4.—1 *Co.* 15. 58.

The Lord pondereth the hearts.

The LORD knoweth the way of the righteous: but the way of the ungodly shall perish.—The LORD will shew who are his, and who is holy.—Thy Father which seeth in secret himself shall reward thee openly.

Search me, O God, and know my heart: try me, and know my thoughts: and see if there be any wicked way in me, and lead me in the way everlasting.—There is no fear in love; but perfect love casteth out fear.

Lord, all my desire is before thee; and my groaning is not hid from thee.—When my spirit was overwhelmed within me, then thou knewest my path.—He that searcheth the hearts knoweth what is the mind of the Spirit, because he maketh intercession for the saints according to the will of God.

The foundation of God standeth sure, having this seal, The Lord knoweth them that are his. And, Let every one that nameth the name of Christ depart from iniquity.

PROV. 21. 2. *Ps.* 1. 6.—*Nu.* 16. 5.—*Mat.* 6. 4.—*Ps.* 139. 23, 24.—
1 *Jno.* 4. 18. *Ps.* 38. 9.—*Ps.* 142. 3.—*Ro.* 8. 27. 2 *Ti.* 2. 19.

Weeping may endure for a night, but joy cometh in the morning.

No man should be moved by these afflictions: for yourselves know that we are appointed thereunto. For verily, when we were with you, we told you before that we should suffer tribulation.—In me ye . . . have peace. In the world ye shall have tribulation: but be of good cheer; I have overcome the world.

I shall be satisfied, when I awake, with thy likeness.—The night is far spent, the day is at hand.—He shall be as the light of the morning, when the sun riseth, even a morning without clouds; as the tender grass springing out of the earth by clear shining after rain.

He will swallow up death in victory; and the Lord GOD will wipe away tears from off all faces.—There shall be no more death, neither sorrow, nor crying, neither shall there be any more pain: for the former things are passed away.—We which are alive and remain shall be caught up together with them in the clouds, to meet the Lord in the air. Wherefore comfort one another with these words.

PSA. 30. 5. 1 *Th.* 3. 3, 4.—*Jno.* 16. 33. *Ps.* 17. 15.—*Ro.* 13. 12.—
2 *Sa.* 23. 4. *Is.* 25. 8.—*Re.* 21. 4.—1 *Th.* 4. 17, 18.

A bruised reed shall he not break.

The sacrifices of God are a broken spirit: a broken and a contrite heart, O God, thou wilt not despise.—He healeth the broken in heart, and bindeth up their wounds.—Thus saith the high and lofty One that inhabiteth eternity, whose name is Holy; I dwell in the high and holy place, with him also that is of a contrite and humble spirit, to revive the spirit of the humble, and to revive the heart of the contrite ones. For I will not contend for ever, neither will I be always wroth: for the spirit should fail before me, and the souls which I have made.

I will seek that which was lost, and bring again that which was driven away, and will bind up that which was broken, and will strengthen that which was sick.—Wherefore lift up the hands which hang down, and the feeble knees; and make straight paths for your feet, lest that which is lame be turned out of the way; but let it rather be healed.—Behold, your God . . . will come and save you.

MAT. 12. 20. *Ps.* 51. 17.—*Ps.* 147. 3.—*Is.* 57. 15, 16. *Eze.* 34. 16.— *He.* 12. 12, 13.—*Is.* 35. 4.

O taste and see that the Lord is good: blessed is the man that trusteth in him.

When the ruler of the feast had tasted the water that was made wine, and knew not whence it was: he saith, . . . Every man at the beginning doth set forth good wine; and when men have well drunk, then that which is worse: but thou hast kept the good wine until now.

The ear trieth words, as the mouth tasteth meat.—I believed, and therefore have I spoken.—I know whom I have believed.— I sat down under his shadow with great delight, and his fruit was sweet to my taste.

The goodness of God.—He that spared not his own Son, but delivered him up for us all, how shall he not with him also freely give us all things?

As newborn babes, desire the sincere milk of the word, that ye may grow thereby: if so be ye have tasted that the Lord is gracious.

Let all those that put their trust in thee rejoice: let them ever shout for joy.

PSA. 34. 8. *Jno.* 2. 9, 10. *Job* 34. 3.—2 *Co.* 4. 13.—2 *Ti.* 1. 12.— *Ca.* 2. 3. *Ro.* 2. 4.—*Ro.* 8. 32. 1 *Pe.* 2. 2, 3. *Ps.* 5. 11.

**Open thou mine eyes, that I may behold wondrous things
out of thy law.**

Then opened he their understanding, that they might understand
the scriptures.—It is given unto you to know the mysteries of the
kingdom of heaven, but to them it is not given. I thank thee, O
Father, Lord of heaven and earth, because thou hast hid these
things from the wise and prudent, and hast revealed them unto
babes. Even so, Father: for so it seemed good in thy sight.—We
have received, not the spirit of the world, but the spirit which is
of God; that we might know the things that are freely given to us
of God.—How precious also are thy thoughts unto me, O God!
how great is the sum of them! If I should count them, they are
more in number than the sand.—O the depth of the riches both of
the wisdom and knowledge of God! how unsearchable are his
judgments, and his ways past finding out! For who hath known
the mind of the Lord? or who hath been his counsellor? For of
him, and through him, and to him are all things: to whom be
glory for ever. Amen.

PSA. 119. 18. *Lu.* 24. 45. *Mat.* 13. 11.—*Mat.* 11. 25, 26.—1 *Co.* 2. 12.—
Ps. 139. 17, 18.—*Ro.* 11. 33, 34, 36.

En-hakkore. (*Or*, **The well of him that cried.**)

If thou knewest the gift of God, and who it is that saith unto
thee, Give me to drink; thou wouldest have asked of him, and
he would have given thee living water.—If any man thirst, let
him come unto me and drink. This spake he of the Spirit, which
they that believe on him should receive.

Prove me now herewith, saith the LORD of hosts, if I will not
open you the windows of heaven, and pour you out a blessing,
that there shall not be room enough to receive it.—If ye, . . . being
evil, know how to give good gifts unto your children: how much
more shall your heavenly Father give the Holy Spirit to them that
ask him?—Ask, and it shall be given you; seek, and ye shall
find.

Because ye are sons, God hath sent forth the Spirit of his Son
into your hearts, crying, Abba, Father.—Ye have not received
the spirit of bondage again to fear; but ye have received the Spirit
of adoption, whereby we cry, Abba, Father.

JUDGES 15. 19. *Jno.* 4. 10.—*Jno.* 7. 37, 39. *Mal.* 3. 10.—*Lu.* 11. 13.—
Lu. 11. 9. *Ga.* 4. 6.—*Ro.* 8. 15.

The God of all grace.

I will proclaim the name of the LORD before thee; and will be gracious to whom I will be gracious.—He is gracious unto him, and saith, Deliver him from going down to the pit: I have found a ransom.—Being justified freely by his grace, through the redemption that is in Christ Jesus: whom God hath set forth to be a propitiation through faith in his blood, to declare his righteousness for the remission of sins that are past, through the forbearance of God.—Grace and truth came by Jesus Christ.

By grace are ye saved through faith; and that not of yourselves: it is the gift of God.—Grace, mercy, and peace, from God our Father and Jesus Christ our Lord.—Unto every one of us is given grace according to the measure of the gift of Christ.—As every man hath received the gift, even so minister the same one to another, as good stewards of the manifold grace of God.—He giveth more grace.

Grow in grace, and in the knowledge of our Lord and Saviour Jesus Christ. To him be glory both now and for ever.

1 PET. 5. 10. *Ex.* 33. 19.—*Job* 33. 24.—*Ro.* 3. 24, 25.—*Jno.* 1. 17. *Ep.* 2. 8.—1 *Ti.* 1. 2.—*Ep.* 4. 7.—1 *Pe.* 4. 10.—*Ja.* 4. 6. 2 *Pe.* 3. 18.

I will lift up mine eyes unto the hills, from whence cometh my help. My help cometh from the Lord.

As the mountains are round about Jerusalem, so the LORD is round about his people from henceforth even for ever.

Unto thee lift I up mine eyes, O thou that dwellest in the heavens. Behold, as the eyes of servants look unto the hand of their masters, and as the eyes of a maiden unto the hand of her mistress; so our eyes wait upon the LORD our God, until that he have mercy upon us.—Because thou hast been my help, therefore in the shadow of thy wings will I rejoice.

O our God, wilt thou not judge them? for we have no might against this great company that cometh against us; neither know we what to do: but our eyes are upon thee.—Mine eyes are ever toward the LORD; for he shall pluck my feet out of the net.—Our help is in the name of the LORD, who made heaven and earth.

PSA. 121. 1, 2. *Ps.* 125. 2. *Ps.* 123. 1, 2.—*Ps.* 63. 7. 2 *Ch.* 20. 12.— *Ps.* 25. 15.—*Ps.* 124. 8.

Happy is the man that findeth wisdom, and the man that getteth understanding.

Whoso findeth me findeth life, and shall obtain favour of the LORD.

Thus saith the LORD, Let not the wise man glory in his wisdom, neither let the mighty man glory in his might: . . . but let him that glorieth glory in this, that he understandeth and knoweth me, that I am the LORD.—The fear of the LORD is the beginning of wisdom.

What things were gain to me, those I counted loss for Christ. Yea doubtless, and I count all things but loss for the excellency of the knowledge of Christ Jesus my Lord: for whom I have suffered the loss of all things, and do count them but dung, that I may win Christ.—In whom are hid all the treasures of wisdom and knowledge.—Counsel is mine, and sound wisdom: I am understanding; I have strength.

Christ Jesus, . . . is made unto us wisdom, and righteousness, and sanctification, and redemption.

He that winneth souls is wise.

PROV. 3. 13. *Pr.* 8. 35. *Je.* 9. 23, 24.—*Pr.* 9. 10. *Phi.* 3. 7, 8.—
Col. 2. 3.—*Pr.* 8. 14. 1 *Co.* 1. 30. *Pr.* 11. 30.

Poor, yet making many rich.

Ye know the grace of our Lord Jesus Christ, that, though he was rich, yet for your sakes he became poor, that ye through his poverty might be rich.—Of his fulness have all we received, and grace for grace.—My God shall supply all your need according to his riches in glory by Christ Jesus.—God is able to make all grace abound toward you; that ye, always having all sufficiency in all things, may abound to every good work.

Hath not God chosen the poor of this world rich in faith, and heirs of the kingdom which he hath promised to them that love him?—Not many wise men after the flesh, not many mighty, not many noble, are called: but God hath chosen the foolish things of the world to confound the wise; and God hath chosen the weak things of the world to confound the things which are mighty.

We have this treasure in earthen vessels, that the excellency of the power may be of God, and not of us.

2 *COR.* 6. 10. 2 *Co.* 8. 9.—*Jno.* 1. 16.—*Phi.* 4. 19.—2 *Co.* 9. 8. *Ja.* 2. 5.—
1 *Co.* 1. 26, 27. 2 *Co.* 4. 7.

We know that all things work together for good to them that love God.

Surely the wrath of man shall praise thee: the remainder of wrath shalt thou restrain.—Ye thought evil against me: but God meant it unto good.

All things are your's; whether . . . the world, or life, or death, or things present, or things to come; all are your's; and ye are Christ's; and Christ is God's.—All things are for your sakes, that the abundant grace might through the thanksgiving of many redound to the glory of God. For which cause we faint not; but though our outward man perish, yet the inward man is renewed day by day. For our light affliction, which is but for a moment, worketh for us a far more exceeding and eternal weight of glory.

My brethren, count it all joy when ye fall into divers temptations; knowing this, that the trying of your faith worketh patience. But let patience have her perfect work, that ye may be perfect and entire, wanting nothing.

ROM. 8. 28. *Ps.* 76. 10.—*Ge.* 50. 20. 1 *Co.* 3. 21-23.—2 *Co.* 4. 15-17. *Ja.* 1. 2-4.

The communion of the Holy Ghost be with you all.

I will pray the Father, and he shall give you another Comforter, that he may abide with you for ever; even the Spirit of truth; whom the world cannot receive, because it seeth him not, neither knoweth him: but ye know him; for he dwelleth with you, and shall be in you.—He shall not speak of himself. He shall glorify me: for he shall receive of mine, and shall shew it unto you.

The love of God is shed abroad in our hearts by the Holy Ghost which is given unto us.

He that is joined unto the Lord is one spirit, Know ye not that your body is the temple of the Holy Ghost which is in you, which ye have of God, and ye are not your own?

Grieve not the holy Spirit of God, whereby ye are sealed unto the day of redemption.—The Spirit also helpeth our infirmities: for we know not what we would pray for as we ought: but the Spirit itself maketh intercession for us with groanings which cannot be uttered.

2 *COR.* 13. 14. *Jno.* 14. 16, 17.—*Jno.* 16. 13, 14. *Ro.* 5. 5. 1 *Co.* 6. 17, 19. *Ep.* 4. 30.—*Ro.* 8. 26.

My meditation of him shall be sweet: I will be glad in the Lord.

As the apple tree among the trees of the wood, so is my beloved among the sons. I sat down under his shadow with great delight, and his fruit was sweet to my taste.—For who in the heaven can be compared unto the LORD? who among the sons of the mighty can be likened unto the LORD?

My beloved is white and ruddy, the chiefest among ten thousand. —One pearl of great price.—The prince of the kings of the earth.

His head is as the most fine gold, his locks are bushy, and black as a raven.—The head over all things.—He is the head of the body, the church.

His cheeks are as a bed of spices, as sweet flowers.—He could not be hid.

His lips like lilies, dropping sweet smelling myrrh.—Never man spake like this man.

His countenance is as Lebanon, excellent as the cedars.—Make thy face to shine upon thy servant.—LORD, lift thou up the light of thy countenance upon us.

PSA. 104. 34. *Ca.* 2. 3.—*Ps.* 89. 6.—*Ca.* 5. 10.—*Mat.* 13. 46.—*Re.* 1. 5. *Ca.* 5. 11.—*Ep.* 1. 22.—*Col.* 1. 18. *Ca.* 5. 13.—*Mar.* 7. 24. *Ca.* 5. 13.— *Jno.* 7. 46. *Ca.* 5. 15.—*Ps.* 31. 16.— *Ps.* 4. 6.

O my Father, if it be possible, let this cup pass from me: nevertheless not as I will, but as thou wilt.

Now is my soul troubled; and what shall I say? Father, save me from this hour: but for this cause came I unto this hour.

I came down from heaven, not to do mine own will, but the will of him that sent me.—He . . . became obedient unto death, even the death of the cross.—In the days of his flesh, when he had offered up prayers and supplications with strong crying and tears unto him that was able to save him from death, and was heard in that he feared; though he were a Son, yet learned he obedience by the things which he suffered.

Thinkest thou that I cannot now pray to my Father, and he shall presently give me more than twelve legions of angels?— Thus it is written, and thus it behoved Christ to suffer, and to rise from the dead the third day: and that repentance and remission of sins should be preached in his name among all nations, beginning at Jerusalem.

MAT. 26. 39. *Jno.* 12. 27. *Jno.* 6. 38.—*Phi.* 2. 8.—*He.* 5. 7, 8. *Mat.* 26. 53.—*Lu.* 24. 46, 47.

Our God hath not forsaken us.

Beloved, think it not strange concerning the fiery trial which is to try you, as though some strange thing happened unto you.— If ye endure chastening, God dealeth with you as with sons; for what son is he whom the father chasteneth not? But if ye be without chastisement, whereof all are partakers, then are ye bastards, and not sons.

The LORD your God proveth you, to know whether ye love the LORD your God with all your heart and with all your soul.

The LORD will not forsake his people for his great name's sake: because it hath pleased the LORD to make you his people.—Can a woman forget her sucking child, that she should not have compassion on the son of her womb? yea, they may forget, yet will I not forget thee.—Happy is he that hath the God of Jacob for his help, whose hope is in the LORD his God.

Shall not God avenge his own elect, which cry day and night unto him, though he bear long with them? I tell you that he will avenge them speedily.

EZRA 9. 9. 1 Pe. 4. 12.—He. 12, 7, 8. De. 13. 3. 1 Sa. 12. 22.— Is. 49. 15.—Ps. 146. 5. Lu. 18. 7, 8.

He that overcometh shall inherit all things.

If in this life only we have hope in Christ, we are of all men most miserable.—Now they desire a better country, that is, an heavenly: wherefore God is not ashamed to be called their God; for he hath prepared for them a city.—An inheritance incorruptible, and undefiled, and that fadeth not away, reserved in heaven for you.

All things are your's; . . . the world, or life, or death, or things present, or things to come; all are your's.—Eye hath not seen, nor ear heard, neither have entered into the heart of man, the things which God hath prepared for them that love him. But God hath revealed them unto us by his Spirit.

Look to yourselves, that we lose not those things which we have wrought, but that we receive a full reward.—Let us lay aside every weight, and the sin which doth so easily beset us, and let us run with patience the race that is set before us.

REV. 21. 7. 1 Co. 15. 19.—He. 11. 16.—1 Pe. 1. 4. 1 Co. 3. 21, 22. 1 Co. 2. 9, 10. 2 Jno. 8.—He. 12. 1.

It is good for me to draw near to God.

LORD, I have loved the habitation of thy house, and the place where thine honour dwelleth.—A day in thy courts is better than a thousand. I had rather be a door-keeper in the house of my God, than to dwell in the tents of wickedness.—Blessed is the man whom thou choosest, and causest to approach unto thee, that he may dwell in thy courts: we shall be satisfied with the goodness of thy house, even of thy holy temple.

The LORD is good unto them that wait for him, to the soul that seeketh him.—Therefore will the LORD wait that he may be gracious unto you, and therefore will he be exalted that he may have mercy upon you: for the LORD is a God of judgment: blessed are all they that wait for him.

Having therefore, brethren, boldness to enter into the holiest by the blood of Jesus, by a new and living way, which he hath consecrated for us; . . . let us draw near with a true heart in full assurance of faith, having our hearts sprinkled from an evil conscience.

PSA. 73. 28. *Ps.* 26. 8.—*Ps.* 84. 10.—*Ps.* 65. 4. *La.* 3. 25.—*Is.* 30. 18.
He. 10. 19, 20, 22.

Ye know the grace of our Lord Jesus Christ.

The Word was made flesh, and dwelt among us, (and we beheld his glory, the glory as of the only begotten of the Father,) full of grace and truth.—Thou are fairer than the children of men: grace is poured into thy lips.—All bare him witness, and wondered at the gracious words which proceeded out of his mouth.

Ye have tasted that the Lord is gracious.—He that believeth on the Son of God hath the witness in himself.—We speak that we do know, and testify that we have seen.

O taste and see that the LORD is good: blessed is the man that trusteth in him.—I sat down under his shadow with great delight, and his fruit was sweet to my taste.

He said unto me, My grace is sufficient for thee: for my strength is made perfect in weakness.—Unto every one of us is given grace according to the measure of the gift of Christ.—As every man hath received the gift, even so minister the same one to another, as good stewards of the manifold grace of God.

2 *COR.* 8. 9. *Jno.* 1. 14.—*Ps.* 45. 2.—*Lu.* 4. 22. 1 *Pe.* 2. 3.—1 *Jno.* 5. 10.—
Jno. 3. 11. *Ps.* 34. 8.—*Ca.* 2. 3. 2 *Co.* 12. 9.—*Ep.* 4. 7.—1 *Pe.* 4. 10.

Let patience have her perfect work, that ye may be perfect and entire, wanting nothing.

Now for a season, if need be, ye are in heaviness through manifold temptations: that the trial of your faith, being much more precious than of gold that perisheth, though it be tried with fire, might be found unto praise and honour and glory at the appearing of Jesus Christ.—We glory in tribulations: . . . knowing that tribulation worketh patience; and patience, experience; and experience, hope.

It is good that a man should both hope and quietly wait for the salvation of the LORD.—Ye have in heaven a better and an enduring substance. Cast not away therefore your confidence, which hath great recompence of reward. For ye have need of patience, that, after ye have done the will of God, ye might receive the promise.—Our Lord Jesus Christ himself, and God, even our Father, which hath loved us, and hath given us everlasting consolation and good hope through grace, comfort your hearts.

JAMES 1. 4. 1 *Pe.* 1. 6, 7.—*Ro.* 5. 3, 4. *La.* 3. 26.—*He.* 10. 34-36.—
2 *Thes.* 2. 16, 17.

God shall judge the secrets of men by Jesus Christ.

Judge nothing before the time, until the Lord come, who both will bring to light the hidden things of darkness, and will make manifest the counsels of the hearts: and then shall every man have praise of God.—The Father judgeth no man, but hath committed all judgment unto the Son: because he is the Son of man.—The Son of God . . . hath his eyes like unto a flame of fire.

They say, How doth God know? and is there knowledge in the most High?—These things thou hast done, and I kept silence; thou thoughtest that I was altogether such an one as thyself: but I will reprove thee, and set them in order before thine eyes.—There is nothing covered, that shall not be revealed; neither hid, that shall not be known.

Lord, all my desire is before thee; and my groaning is not hid from thee.—Examine me, O LORD, and prove me; try my reins and my heart.

ROM. 2. 16. 1 *Co.* 4. 5.—*Jno.* 5. 22, 27.—*Re.* 2. 18. *Ps.* 73. 11.—
Ps. 50. 21.—*Lu.* 12. 2. *Ps.* 38. 9.—*Ps.* 26. 2.

A God of truth and without iniquity, just and right is he.

Him that judgeth righteously.—We must all appear before the judgment seat of Christ; that every one may receive the things done in his body, according to that he hath done, whether it be good or bad.—Every one of us shall give account of himself to God.—The soul that sinneth it shall die.

Awake, O sword, against my shepherd, and against the man that is my fellow, saith the LORD of hosts: smite the shepherd.— The LORD hath laid on him the iniquity of us all.—Mercy and truth are met together: righteousness and peace have kissed each other.—Mercy rejoiceth against judgment.—The wages of sin is death; but the gift of God is eternal life through Jesus Christ our Lord.

A just God and a Saviour; there is none beside me.—Just, and the justifier of him which believeth in Jesus.—Justified freely by his grace through the redemption that is in Christ Jesus.

DEUT. 32. 4. 1 *Pe.* 2. 23.—2 *Co.* 5. 10.—*Ro.* 14. 12.—*Eze.* 18. 4. *Zec.* 13. 7. *Is.* 53. 6.—*Ps.* 85. 10.—*Ja.* 2. 13.—*Ro.* 6. 23. *Is.* 45. 21.—*Ro.* 3. 26.—*Ro.* 3. 24.

Death is swallowed up in victory.

Thanks be to God, which giveth us the victory through our Lord Jesus Christ.

Forasmuch . . . as the children are partakers of flesh and blood, he also himself likewise took part of the same; that through death he might destroy him that had the power of death, that is, the devil; and deliver them who through fear of death were all their lifetime subject to bondage.

If we be dead with Christ, we believe that we shall also live with him: knowing that Christ being raised from the dead dieth no more; death hath no more dominion over him. For in that he died, he died unto sin once: but in that he liveth, he liveth unto God.

Likewise reckon ye also yourselves to be dead indeed unto sin, but alive unto God through Jesus Christ our Lord.

In all these things we are more than conquerors through him that loved us.

1 *COR.* 15. 54. 1 *Co.* 15. 57.—*He.* 2. 14, 15. *Ro.* 6. 8-11. *Ro.* 8. 37.

**Humble yourselves under the mighty hand of God, that he may
exalt you in due time.**

Every one that is proud in heart is an abomination to the LORD:
though hand join in hand, he shall not be unpunished.

O LORD, thou art our father; we are the clay, and thou our
potter; and we all are the work of thy hand. Be not wroth very
sore, O LORD, neither remember iniquity for ever: behold, see,
we beseech thee, we are all thy people.—Thou hast chastised me,
and I was chastised, as a bullock unaccustomed to the yoke: turn
thou me, and I shall be turned; for thou art the LORD my God.
Surely after that I was turned, I repented; and after that I was
instructed, I smote upon my thigh: I was ashamed, yea, even
confounded, because I did bear the reproach of my youth.—It is
good for a man that he bear the yoke in his youth.

Affliction cometh not forth of the dust, neither doth trouble
spring out of the ground; yet man is born unto trouble, as the
sparks fly upward.

1 *PET.* 5. 6. *Pr.* 16. 5. *Is.* 64. 8, 9.—*Je.* 31. 18, 19.—*La.* 3. 27. *Job* 5. 6, 7.

Yea, hath God said?

When the tempter came to Jesus, he said, If thou be the Son of
God.—Jesus said unto him, It is written, . . . it is written, . . . it
is written.—Then the devil leaveth him.

I may not return with thee. For it was said to me by the word
of the LORD, Thou shalt eat no bread nor drink water there. He
said unto him, I am a prophet also as thou art; and an angel spake
unto me by the word of the LORD, saying, Bring him back with thee
into thine house, that he may eat bread and drink water. But he
lied unto him. So he went back with him. The man of God, . . .
was disobedient unto the word of the LORD: therefore the LORD
hath delivered him unto the lion, which hath torn him, and slain
him, according to the word of the LORD.—Though we, or an angel
from heaven, preach any other gospel unto you than that which
we have preached unto you, let him be accursed.—Thy word have
I hid in mine heart, that I might not sin against thee.

GEN. 3. 1. *Mat.* 4. 3, 4, 7, 10, 11. 1 *Ki.* 13. 16-19, 26.—*Ga.* 1. 8.—
Ps. 119. 11.

**They shall put my name upon the childen of Isael; and
I will bless them.**

O LORD our God, other lords beside thee have had dominion
over us: but by thee only will we make mention of thy name.—
We are thine: thou never barest rule over them; they were not
called by thy name.

All people of the earth shall see that thou art called by the
name of the LORD; and they shall be afraid of thee.—The LORD
will not forsake his people for his great name's sake: because it
hath pleased the LORD to make you his people.

O Lord, hear; O Lord, forgive; O Lord, hearken and do; defer
not, for thine own sake, O my God: for thy city and thy people
are called by thy name.—Help us, O God of our salvation, for the
glory of thy name: and deliver us, and purge away our sins, for
thy name's sake. Wherefore should the heathen say, Where is their
God?—The name of the LORD is a strong tower; the righteous
runneth into it, and is safe.

NUM. 6. 27. *Is.* 26. 13.—*Is.* 63. 19. *De.* 28. 10.—1 *Sa.* 12. 22. *Da.* 9. 19.—
Ps. 79. 9, 10.—*Pr.* 18. 10.

**The heavens declare the glory of God; and the firmament
sheweth his handywork.**

The invisible things of him from the creation of the world are
clearly seen, being understood by the things that are made, even
his eternal power and Godhead.—He left not himself without witness.—Day unto day uttereth speech, and night unto night sheweth
knowledge. There is no speech nor language, where their voice is
not heard.

When I consider thy heavens, the work of thy fingers, the moon
and the stars, which thou hast ordained; what is man, that thou
art mindful of him? and the son of man, that thou visitest him?

There is one glory of the sun, and another glory of the moon,
and another glory of the stars: for one star differeth from another
star in glory. So also is the resurrection of the dead.—They that
be wise shall shine as the brightness of the firmament; and they
that turn many to righteousness as the stars for ever and ever.

PSA. 19. 1. *Ro.* 1. 20.—*Ac.* 14. 17.—*Ps.* 19. 2, 3. *Ps.* 8. 3, 4.
1 *Co.* 15. 41, 42.—*Da.* 12. 3.

Hereby perceive we the love of God, because he laid down his life for us.

The love of Christ, which passeth knowledge.—Greater love hath no man than this, that a man lay down his life for his friends. —Ye know the grace of our Lord Jesus Christ, that, though he was rich, yet for your sakes he became poor, that ye through his poverty might be rich.—Beloved, if God so loved us, we ought also to love one another.—Be ye kind one to another, tenderhearted, forgiving one another, even as God for Christ's sake hath forgiven you.—Forbearing one another, and forgiving one another, if any man have a quarrel against any: even as Christ forgave you, so also do ye.—For even the Son of man came not to be ministered unto, but to minister, and to give his life a ransom for many.— Christ . . . suffered for us, leaving us an example, that ye should follow his steps.

Ye also ought to wash one another's feet. For I have given you an example, that ye should do as I have done to you.—We ought to lay down our lives for the brethren.

1 *JOHN* 3. 16. *Ep.* 3. 19.—*Jno.* 15. 13.—2 *Co.* 8. 9.—1 *Jno.* 4. 11.— *Ep.* 4. 32.—*Col.* 3. 13.—*Mar.* 10. 45.—1 *Pe.* 2. 21. *Jno.* 13. 14, 15.— 1 *Jno.* 3. 16.

What things soever the Father doeth, these also doeth the Son likewise.

The LORD giveth wisdom: out of his mouth cometh knowledge and understanding.—I will give you a mouth and wisdom, which all your adversaries shall not be able to gainsay nor resist.

Wait on the LORD: be of good courage, and he shall strengthen thine heart.—My grace is sufficient for thee: for my strength is made perfect in weakness.

Them that are sanctified by God the Father.—He that sanctifieth and they who are sanctified are all of one: for which cause he is not ashamed to call them brethren.

Do not I fill heaven and earth? saith the LORD.—The fulness of him that filleth all in all.

I, even I, am the LORD; and beside me there is no saviour.— This is indeed the Christ, the Saviour of the world.

Grace, mercy, and peace, from God the Father and the Lord Jesus Christ our Saviour.

JOHN 5. 19. *Pr.* 2. 6.—*Lu.* 21. 15. *Ps.* 27. 14.—2 *Co.* 12. 9. *Jude* 1.— *He.* 2. 11. *Je.* 23. 24.—*Ep.* 1. 23. *Is.* 43. 11.—*Jno.* 4. 42. *Tit.* 1. 4.

**He knoweth the way that I take: when he hath tried me,
I shall come forth as gold.**

He knoweth our frame.—He doth not afflict willingly nor grieve the children of men.

The foundation of God standeth sure, having this seal, The Lord knoweth them that are his. And, Let every one that nameth the name of Christ depart from iniquity. But in a great house there are not only vessels of gold and of silver, but also of wood and of earth; and some to honour, and some to dishonour. If a man therefore purge himself from these, he shall be a vessel unto honour, sanctified, and meet for the master's use, and prepared unto every good work.

He shall sit as a refiner and purifier of silver: and he shall purify the sons of Levi, and purge them as gold and silver, that they may offer unto the LORD an offering in righteousness.—I . . . will refine them as silver is refined, . . . they shall call on my name, and I will hear them: I will say, It is my people: and they shall say, The LORD is my God.

JOB 23. 10. *Ps.* 103. 14.—*La.* 3. 33. 2 *Ti.* 2. 19-21. *Mal.* 3. 3.—*Zec.* 13. 9.

Shew me thy ways, O Lord; teach me thy paths.

Moses said unto the LORD, I pray thee, if I have found grace in thy sight, shew me now thy way, that I may know thee. And he said, My presence shall go with thee, and I will give thee rest.—He made known his ways unto Moses, his acts unto the children of Israel.

The meek will he guide in judgment; and the meek will he teach his way. What man is he that feareth the LORD? him shall he teach in the way that he shall choose.—Trust in the LORD with all thine heart; and lean not unto thine own understanding. In all thy ways acknowledge him, and he shall direct thy paths.

Thou wilt shew me the path of life: in thy presence is fulness of joy; at thy right hand there are pleasures for evermore.—I will instruct thee and teach thee in the way which thou shalt go: I will guide thee with mine eye.—The path of the just is as the shining light, that shineth more and more unto the perfect day.

PSA. 25. 4. *Ex.* 33. 12-14.—*Ps.* 103. 7. *Ps.* 25. 9, 12.—*Ps.* 3. 5, 6.
Ps. 16. 11.—*Ps.* 32. 8.—*Pr.* 4. 18.

The fruit of the Spirit is temperance.

Every man that striveth for the mastery is temperate in all things. Now they do it to obtain a corruptible crown; but we an incorruptible. I therefore so run, not as uncertainly; so fight I, not as one that beateth the air: but I keep under my body, and bring it into subjection: lest that by any means, when I have preached to others, I myself should be a castaway.

Be not drunk with wine, wherein is excess; but be filled with the Spirit.

If any man will come after me, let him deny himself, and take up his cross, and follow me.

Let us not sleep, as do others; but let us watch and be sober. For they that sleep sleep in the night; and they that be drunken are drunken in the night. But let us, who are of the day, be sober.—Denying ungodliness and worldly lusts, we should live soberly, righteously, and godly, in this present world; looking for that blessed hope, and the glorious appearing of the great God and our Saviour Jesus Christ.

GAL. 5. 22. 1 *Co.* 9. 25-27. *Ep.* 5. 18. *Mat.* 16. 24. 1 *Thes.* 5. 6-8.—
Tit. 2. 12, 13.

Grow up into him in all things, which is the head, even Christ.

First the blade, then the ear, after that the full corn in the ear.—Till we all come in the unity of the faith, and of the knowledge of the Son of God, unto a perfect man, unto the measure of the stature of the fulness of Christ.

They measuring themselves by themselves, and comparing themselves among themselves, are not wise. But he that glorieth, let him glory in the Lord. For not he that commendeth himself is approved, but whom the Lord commendeth.

The body is of Christ. Let no man beguile you of your reward in a voluntary humility and worshipping of angels, intruding into those things which he hath not seen, vainly puffed up by his fleshly mind, and not holding the Head, from which all the body by joints and bands having nourishment ministered, and knit together, increaseth with the increase of God.

Grow in grace, and in the knowledge of our Lord and Saviour Jesus Christ.

EPH. 4. 15. *Mar.* 4. 28.—*Ep.* 4. 13. 2 *Co.* 10. 12, 17, 18. *Col.* 2. 17-19.
2 *Pe.* 3. 18.

The goat shall bear upon him all their iniquities unto a land not inhabited: and he shall let go the goat in the wilderness.

As far as the east is from the west, so far hath he removed our transgressions from us.—In those days, and in that time, saith the LORD, the iniquity of Israel shall be sought for, and there shall be none; and the sins of Judah, and they shall not be found: for I will pardon them whom I reserve.—Thou wilt cast all their sins into the depths of the sea.—Who is a God like unto thee, that pardoneth iniquity?

All we like sheep have gone astray; we have turned every one to his own way; and the LORD hath laid on him the iniquity of us all.—He shall bear their iniquities. Therefore will I divide him a portion with the great, and he shall divide the spoil with the strong, because he hath poured out his soul unto death; and he was numbered with the transgressors; and he bare the sin of many, and made intercession for the transgressors.—The Lamb of God, which taketh away the sin of the world.

LEV. 16. 22. *Ps.* 103. 12.—*Je.* 50. 20.—*Mi.* 7. 19, 18. *Is.* 53. 6.—
Is. 53. 11, 12.—*Jno.* 1. 29.

Who maketh thee to differ from another? and what hast thou that thou didst not receive?

By the grace of God I am what I am.—Of his own will begat he us with the word of truth.—It is not of him that willeth, nor of him that runneth, but of God that sheweth mercy.—Where is boasting then? It is excluded.—Christ Jesus, . . . is made unto us wisdom, and righteousness, and sanctification, and redemption: . . . He that glorieth let him glory in the Lord.

You hath he quickened, who were dead in trespasses and sins; wherein in time past ye walked according to the course of this world, according to the prince of the power of the air, the spirit that now worketh in the children of disobedience: among whom also we all had our conversation in times past in the lusts of our flesh, fulfilling the desires of the flesh and of the mind; and were by nature the children of wrath, even as others.—Ye are washed, . . . ye are sanctified, . . . ye are justified in the name of the Lord Jesus, and by the Spirit of our God.

1 COR. 4. 7. 1 *Co.* 15. 10.—*Ja.* 1. 18.—*Ro.* 9. 16. *Ro.* 3. 27.—
1 *Co.* 1. 30, 31. *Ep.* 2. 1-3.—1 *Co.* 6. 11.

Unto him that loved us, and washed us from our sins in his own blood.

Many waters cannot quench love, neither can the floods drown it. Love is strong as death.—Greater love hath no man than this, that a man lay down his life for his friends.

Who his own self bare our sins in his own body on the tree, that we, being dead to sins, should live unto righteousness: by whose stripes ye were healed.—In whom we have redemption through his blood, the forgiveness of sins, according to the riches of his grace.

Ye are washed, . . . ye are sanctified, . . . ye are justified in the name of the Lord Jesus, and by the Spirit of our God.—Ye are a chosen generation, a royal priesthood, a holy nation, a peculiar people; that ye should shew forth the praises of him who hath called you out of darkness into his marvellous light.—I beseech you . . . brethren, by the mercies of God, that ye present your bodies a living sacrifice, holy, acceptable unto God, which is your reasonable service.

REV. 1. 5. *Ca.* 8. 7, 6.—*Jno.* 15. 13. 1 *Pe.* 2. 24.—*Ep.* 1. 7. 1 *Co.* 6. 11.—
1 *Pe.* 2. 9.—*Ro.* 12. 1.

There are differences of administrations, but the same Lord.

Over the king's treasures was Azmaveth the son of Adiel: and over the storehouses . . . Jehonathan: and over them that did the work of the field for tillage of the ground was Ezri: and over the vineyards was Shimei. These were the rulers of the substance which was king David's.

God hath set some in the church, first apostles, secondarily prophets, thirdly teachers, after that miracles, then gifts of healings, helps, governments, diversities of tongues. All these worketh that one and the selfsame Spirit, dividing to every man severally as he will.

As every man hath received the gift, even so minister the same one to another, as good stewards of the manifold grace of God. If any man speak, let him speak as the oracles of God; if any man minister, let him do it as of the ability which God giveth: that God in all things may be glorified through Jesus Christ, to whom be praise and dominion for ever and ever.

1 *COR.* 12. 5. 1 *Ch.* 27. 25-27, 31. 1 *Co.* 12. 28, 11. 1 *Pe.* 4. 10, 11.

Moses wist not that the skin of his face shone while he talked with him.

Not unto us, O LORD, not unto us, but unto thy name give glory.—Lord, when saw we thee a hungred, and fed thee? or thirsty, and gave thee drink?—In lowliness of mind, let each esteem other better than themselves.—Be clothed with humility.

[Jesus] was transfigured before them: and his face did shine as the sun, and his raiment was white as the light.—All that sat in the council, looking stedfastly on [Stephen], saw his face as it had been the face of an angel.—The glory which thou gavest me, I have given them.—We all, with open face beholding as in a glass the glory of the Lord, are changed into the same image from glory to glory, even as by the Spirit of the Lord.

Ye are the light of the world. A city that is set on a hill cannot be hid. Neither do men light a candle, and put it under a bushel, but on a candlestick; and it giveth light unto all that are in the house.

EXOD. 34. 29. *Ps.* 115. 1.—*Mat.* 25. 37.—*Phi.* 2. 3.—1 *Pe.* 5. 5. *Mat.* 17. 2.—*Ac.* 6. 15.—*Jno.* 17. 22.—2 *Co.* 3. 18. *Mat.* 5. 14, 15.

There are diversities of operations, but it is the same God which worketh all in all.

There fell some of Manasseh to David. And they helped David against the band of the rovers: for they were all mighty men of valour.—The manifestation of the Spirit is given to every man to profit withal.

Of the children of Issachar, which were men that had understanding of the times, to know what Israel ought to do.—To one is given by the Spirit the word of wisdom; to another the word of knowledge by the same Spirit.

Of Zebulun, such as went forth to battle, expert in war, with all instruments of war, fifty thousand, which could keep rank: they were not of double heart.—A double minded man is unstable in all his ways.

There should be no schism in the body; but . . . the members should have the same care one for another. And whether one member suffer, all the members suffer with it; or one member be honoured, all the members rejoice with it.

One Lord, one faith, one baptism.

1 *COR.* 12. 6. 1 *Ch.* 12. 19, 21.—1 *Co.* 12. 7.—1 *Ch.* 12. 32.—1 *Co.* 12. 8. 1 *Ch.* 12. 33.—*Ja.* 1. 8. 1 *Co.* 12. 25, 26. *Ep.* 4. 5.

Call upon me in the day of trouble: I will deliver thee, and thou shalt glorify me.

Why art thou cast down, O my soul? and why art thou disquieted within me? hope thou in God: for I shall yet praise him, who is the health of my countenance, and my God.—LORD, thou hast heard the desire of the humble: thou wilt prepare their heart, thou wilt cause thine ear to hear.—For thou, Lord, art good, and ready to forgive; and plenteous in mercy unto all them that call upon thee.

Jacob said unto his household, . . . Let us arise, and go up to Beth-el; and I will make there an altar unto God, who answered me in the day of my distress, and was with me in the way which I went.—Bless the LORD, O my soul, and forget not all his benefits.

I love the LORD, because he hath heard my voice and my supplications. Because he hath inclined his ear unto me, therefore will I call upon him as long as I live. The sorrows of death compassed me, and the pains of hell gat hold upon me: I found trouble and sorrow. Then called I on the name of the LORD.

PSA. 50. 15. *Ps.* 42. 11.—*Ps.* 10. 17.—*Ps.* 86. 5. *Ge.* 35. 2, 3.—*Ps.* 103. 2. *Ps.* 116. 1-4.

Yet a little while, (*Gr.* how little, how little,) and he that shall come will come, and will not tarry.

Write the vision, and make it plain upon tables, that he may run that readeth it. For the vision is yet for an appointed time, but at the end it shall speak, and not lie: though it tarry, wait for it; because it will surely come, it will not tarry.

Beloved, be not ignorant of this one thing, that one day is with the Lord as a thousand years, and a thousand years as one day. The Lord is not slack concerning his promise, as some men count slackness; but is longsuffering to us-ward, not willing that any should perish, but that all should come to repentence.—Thou, O Lord, art a God full of compassion, and gracious, longsuffering, and plenteous in mercy and truth.—Oh that thou wouldest rend the heavens, that thou wouldest come down. For since the beginning of the world men have not heard, nor perceived by the ear, neither hath the eye seen, O God, beside thee, what he hath prepared for him that waiteth for him.

HEB. 10. 37. *Hab.* 2. 2, 3. 2 *Pe.* 3. 8, 9.—*Ps.* 86. 15.—*Is.* 64. 1, 4

The Lord God omnipotent reigneth.

I know that thou canst do every thing.—The things which are impossible with men are possible with God.—He doeth according to his will in the army of heaven, and among the inhabitants of the earth: and none can stay his hand, or say unto him, What doest thou?—There is none that can deliver out of my hand: I will work, and who shall let it?—Abba, Father, all things are possible unto thee.

Believe ye that I am able to do this? They said unto him, Yea, Lord. Then touched he their eyes, saying, According to your faith be it unto you.—Lord, if thou wilt, thou canst make me clean. And Jesus put forth his hand and touched him, saying, I will; be thou clean.—The mighty God.—All power is given unto me in heaven and in earth.

Some trust in chariots, and some in horses: but we will remember the name of the LORD our God.—Be strong and courageous, be not afraid nor dismayed, . . . there be more with us than with him.

REV. 19. 6. *Job* 42. 2.—*Lu.* 18. 27.—*Da.* 4. 35.—*Is.* 43. 13.—*Mar.* 14. 36. *Mat.* 9. 28, 29.—*Mat.* 8. 2, 3.—*Is.* 9. 6.—*Mat.* 28. 18. *Ps.* 20. 7.—*2 Ch.* 32. 7.

What is the thing that the Lord hath said unto thee?

He hath shewed thee, O man, what is good; and what doth the LORD require of thee, but to do justly, and to love mercy, and to walk humbly with thy God?—To keep the commandments of the LORD, and his statutes, which I command thee this day for thy good.

As many as are of the works of the law are under the curse: for it is written, Cursed is every one that continueth not in all things which are written in the book of the law to do them. But that no man is justified by the law in the sight of God, it is evident: for The just shall live by faith. Wherefore then serveth the law? It was added because of transgressions, till the seed should come to whom the promise was made.

God, who at sundry times and in divers manners spake in time past unto the fathers by the prophets, hath in these last days spoken unto us by his Son.

Speak, LORD; for thy servant heareth.

1 SAM. 3. 17. *Mi.* 6. 8.—*De.* 10. 13. *Ga.* 3. 10, 11, 19.—*He.* 1. 1, 2. *1 Sa.* 3. 9.

The meek will he teach his way.

Blessed are the meek.

I returned, and saw under the sun, that the race is not to the swift, nor the battle to the strong, neither yet bread to the wise, nor yet riches to men of understanding, nor yet favour to men of skill.—A man's heart deviseth his way: but the LORD directeth his steps.

Unto thee lift I up mine eyes, O thou that dwellest in the heavens. Behold, as the eyes of servants look unto the hand of their masters, and as the eyes of a maiden unto the hand of her mistress; so our eyes wait upon the LORD our God.—Cause me to know the way wherein I should walk; for I lift up my soul unto thee.

O our God, wilt thou not judge them? for we have no might against this great company that cometh against us; neither know we what to do: but our eyes are upon thee.

If any of you lack wisdom, let him ask of God, that giveth to all men liberally, and upbraideth not; and it shall be given him.

When he, the Spirit of truth, is come, he will guide you into all truth.

PSA. 25. 9. Mat. 5. 5. Ec. 9. 11.—Pr. 16. 9. Ps. 123. 1, 2.—Ps. 143. 8. 2 Ch. 20. 12. Ja. 1. 5. Jno. 16. 13.

OCTOBER 7

EVENING

O Lord God, . . . with thy blessing let the house of thy servant be blessed for ever.

Thou blessest, O LORD, and it shall be blessed for ever.—The blessing of the LORD, it maketh rich, and he addeth no sorrow with it.

Remember the words of the Lord Jesus, how he said, It is more blessed to give than to receive.—When thou makest a feast, call the poor, the maimed, the lame, the blind: and thou shalt be blessed; for they cannot recompense thee: for thou shalt be recompensed at the resurrection of the just.—Come, ye blessed of my Father, inherit the kingdom prepared for you from the foundation of the world: for I was an hungred, and ye gave me meat: I was thirsty, and ye gave me drink: I was a stranger, and ye took me in: naked, and ye clothed me: I was sick, and ye visited me: I was in prison, and ye came unto me.

Blessed is he that considereth the poor: the LORD will deliver him in time of trouble.

The LORD God is a sun and shield.

2 SAM. 7. 29. 1 Ch. 17. 27.—Pr. 10. 22. Ac. 20. 35.—Lu. 14. 13, 14.— Mat. 25. 34-36. Ps. 41. 1. Ps. 84. 11.

I will not fear what man shall do unto me.

Who shall separate us from the love of Christ? shall tribulation, or distress, or persecution, or famine, or nakedness, or peril, or sword? Nay, in all these things we are more than conquerors through him that loved us.

Be not afraid of them that kill the body, and after that have no more that they can do. But I will forewarn you whom ye shall fear: Fear him, which after he hath killed hath power to cast into hell: yea, I say unto you, Fear him.

Blessed are they which are persecuted for righteousness' sake: for their's is the kingdom of heaven. Blessed are ye, when men shall revile you, and persecute you, and shall say all manner of evil against you falsely, for my sake. Rejoice, and be exceeding glad: for great is your reward in heaven.—None of these things move me, neither count I my life dear unto myself, so that I might finish my course with joy.—I will speak of thy testimonies . . . before kings, and will not be ashamed.

HEB. 13. 6.　*Ro.* 8. 35, 37.　*Lu.* 12. 4, 5.　*Mat.* 5. 10-12.—
Ac. 20. 24.—*Ps.* 119. 46.

He set my feet upon a rock.

That Rock was Christ.—Simon Peter . . . said, Thou art the Christ the Son of the living God. Upon this rock I will build my church; and the gates of hell shall not prevail against it.— Neither is there salvation in any other: for there is none other name under heaven given among men, whereby we must be saved.

Full assurance of faith. Faith without wavering.—Faith, nothing wavering. . . . He that wavereth is like a wave of the sea driven with the wind and tossed.

Who shall separate us from the love of Christ? shall tribulation, or distress, or persecution, or famine, or nakedness, or peril, or sword? Nay, in all these things we are more than conquerors through him that loved us. For I am persuaded, that neither death, nor life, nor angels, nor principalities, nor powers, nor things present, nor things to come, nor height, nor depth, nor any other creature, shall be able to separate us from the love of God, which is in Christ Jesus our Lord.

PSA. 40. 2.　1 *Co.* 10. 4.—*Mat.* 16. 16, 18.—*Ac.* 4. 12.　*Heb.* 10. 22, 23.—
Ja. 1. 6.　*Ro.* 8. 35, 37, 39.

OCTOBER 9

Thou art a God ready to pardon, gracious and merciful.

The Lord is not slack concerning his promise, as some men count slackness; but is longsuffering to us-ward, not willing that any should perish, but that all should come to repentance.—The longsuffering of our Lord is salvation.

For this cause I obtained mercy, that in me first Jesus Christ might shew forth all longsuffering, for a pattern to them which should hereafter believe on him to life everlasting.—Whatsoever things were written aforetime were written for our learning, that we through patience and comfort of the scriptures might have hope.

Despisest thou the riches of his goodness and forbearance and longsuffering; not knowing that the goodness of God leadeth thee to repentance?—Rend your heart, and not your garments, and turn unto the LORD your God: for he is gracious and merciful, slow to anger, and of great kindness, and repenteth him of the evil.

NEHE. 9. 17. 2 Pe. 3. 9.—2 Pe. 3. 15. 1 Ti. 1. 16.—Ro. 15. 4. Ro. 2. 4.—
Joel 2. 13.

OCTOBER 9

The words of the Lord are pure words.

Thy word is very pure: therefore thy servant loveth it.—The statutes of the LORD are right, rejoicing the heart: the commandment of the LORD is pure, enlightening the eyes.—Every word of God is pure: he is a shield unto them that put their trust in him. Add thou not unto his words, lest he reprove thee, and thou be found a liar.

Thy word have I hid in mine heart, that I might not sin against thee. I will meditate in thy precepts, and have respect unto thy ways.—Brethren, whatsoever things are true, whatsoever things are honest, whatsoever things are just, whatsoever things are pure, whatsoever things are lovely, whatsoever things are of good report; if there be any virtue, and if there be any praise, think on these things.—As newborn babes, desire the sincere milk of the word, that ye may grow thereby.

We are not as many, which corrupt the word of God: but as of sincerity, but as of God, in the sight of God speak we in Christ. Nor handling the word of God deceitfully.

PSA. 12. 6. Ps. 119. 140.—Ps. 19. 8.—Pr. 30. 5, 6.—Ps. 119. 11, 15.—
Phi. 4. 8.—1 Pe. 2. 2. 2 Co. 2. 17.—2 Co. 4. 2.

The whole family in heaven and earth.

One God and Father of all, who is above all, and through all, and in you all.—Ye are all the children of God by faith in Christ Jesus.—That in the dispensation of the fulness of times, he might gather together in one all things in Christ, both which are in heaven, and which are on earth; even in him.

He is not ashamed to call them brethren.—Behold my mother and my brethren! Whosoever shall do the will of my Father which is in heaven, the same is my brother, and sister, and mother.—Go to my brethren, and say unto them, I ascend unto my Father, and your Father.

I saw under the altar the souls of them that were slain for the word of God, and for the testimony which they held: . . . and white robes were given unto every one of them; and it was said unto them, that they should rest for a little season, until their fellow-servants also and their brethren, that should be killed as they were, should be fulfilled.—That they without us should not be made perfect.

EPH. 3. 15. Ep. 4. 6.—Gal. 3. 26.—Ep. 1. 10. He. 2. 11.—Mat. 12. 49, 50.—Jno. 20. 17. Re. 6. 9-11—He. 11. 40.

After this manner . . . pray ye: Our Father which art in heaven.

Jesus lifted up his eyes to heaven, and said, Father.—My Father, and your Father.

Ye are all the children of God by faith in Christ Jesus.—Ye have not received the spirit of bondage again to fear; but ye have received the Spirit of adoption, whereby we cry, Abba, Father. The Spirit itself beareth witness with our spirit, that we are the children of God.

Because ye are sons, God hath sent forth the Spirit of his Son into your hearts, crying, Abba, Father. Wherefore thou art no more a servant, but a son.

Verily, verily, I say unto you, Whatsoever ye shall ask the Father in my name, he will give it you. Hitherto have ye asked nothing in my name: ask, and ye shall receive, that your joy may be full.

I will receive you, and will be a Father unto you, and ye shall be my sons and daughters, saith the Lord Almighty.

MAT. 6. 9. Jno. 17. 1.—Jno. 20. 17. Ga. 3. 26.—Ro. 8. 15, 16. Ga. 4. 6, 7. Jno. 16. 23, 24. 2 Co. 6. 17, 18.

Be not far from me; for trouble is near.

How long wilt thou forget me, O LORD? for ever? how long wilt thou hide thy face from me? How long shall I take counsel in my soul, having sorrow in my heart daily?—Hide not thy face far from me; put not thy servant away in anger: thou hast been my help; leave me not, neither forsake me, O God of my salvation.

He shall call upon me, and I will answer him: I will be with him in trouble; I will deliver him, and honour him.—The LORD is nigh unto all them that call upon him, to all that call upon him in truth. He will fulfil the desire of them that fear him: he also will hear their cry, and will save them.

I will not leave you comfortless: I will come to you.—Lo, I am with you alway, even unto the end of the world.

God is our refuge and strength, a very present help in trouble.—Truly my soul waiteth upon God: from him cometh my salvation.—My soul, wait thou only upon God; for my expectation is from him.

PSA. 22. 11. *Ps.* 13. 1, 2.—*Ps.* 27. 9. *Ps.* 91. 15.—*Ps.* 145. 18, 19. *Jno.* 14. 18.—*Mat.* 28. 20. *Ps.* 46. 1.—*Ps.* 62. 1, 5.

Hallowed be thy name.

Thou shalt worship no other god: for the LORD, whose name is Jealous, is a jealous God.

Who is like unto thee, O LORD, among the gods? who is like thee, glorious in holiness, fearful in praises, doing wonders?—Holy, holy, holy, Lord God Almighty.

Worship the LORD in the beauty of holiness.—I saw . . . the Lord sitting upon a throne, high and lifted up, and his train filled the temple. Above it stood the seraphims. And one cried unto another, and said, Holy, holy, holy, is the LORD of hosts; the whole earth is full of his glory. Then said I, Woe is me! for I am undone.—I have heard of thee by the hearing of the ear: but now mine eye seeth thee. Wherefore I abhor myself.

The blood of Jesus Christ his Son cleanseth us from all sin.—That we might be partakers of his holiness.—Having therefore, brethren, boldness to enter into the holiest by the blood of Jesus, let us draw near with a true heart.

MAT. 6. 9. *Ex.* 34. 14. *Ex.* 15. 11.—*Re.* 4. 8. *1 Ch.* 16. 29.—*Is.* 6. 1-3, 5.— *Job* 42. 5, 6. *1 Jno.* 1. 7.—*He.* 12. 10.—*He.* 10. 19, 22.

God was in Christ, reconciling the world unto himself, not imputing their trespasses unto them.

It pleased the Father, that in him should all fulness dwell; and, having made peace through the blood of his cross, by him to reconcile all things unto himself.—Mercy and truth are met together; righteousness ànd peace have kissed each other.

I know the thoughts that I think toward you, saith the LORD, thoughts of peace, and not of evil.—Come now, and let us reason together, saith the LORD: though your sins be as scarlet, they shall be as white as snow; though they be red like crimson, they shall be as wool.

Who is a God like unto thee, that pardoneth iniquity?

Acquaint now thyself with him, and be at peace.—Work out your own salvation with fear and trembling. For it is God which worketh in you both to will and to do of his good pleasure.—LORD, thou wilt ordain peace for us: for thou also hast wrought all our works in us.

2 *COR.* 5. 19. *Col.* 1. 19, 20.—*Ps.* 85. 10. *Je.* 29. 11.—*Is.* 1. 18. *Mi.* 7. 18. *Job* 22. 21.—*Phi.* 2. 12, 13.—*Is.* 26. 12.

Thy kingdom come.

In the days of these kings shall the God of heaven set up a kingdom, which shall never be destroyed: and the kingdom shall not be left to other people, but it shall break in pieces and consume all these kingdoms, and it shall stand for ever.—A stone . . . cut out without hands.—Not by might, nor by power, but my Spirit, saith the LORD of hosts.—The kingdom of God cometh not with observation: neither shall they say, Lo here! or, lo there! for, behold, the kingdom of God is within you.

Unto you it is given to know the mystery of the kingdom of God. So is the kingdom of God, as if a man should cast seed into the ground; and should sleep, and rise night and day, and the seed should spring and grow up, he knoweth not how. But when the fruit is brought forth, immediately he putteth in the sickle, because the harvest is come.

Be ye . . . ready: for in such an hour as ye think not, the Son of man cometh.

The Spirit and the bride say, Come. And let him that heareth say, Come.

MAT. 6. 10. *Da.* 2. 44.—*Da.* 2. 34.—*Zec.* 4. 6.—*Lu.* 17. 20, 21. *Mar.* 4. 11, 26, 27, 29. *Mat.* 24 14. *Re.* 22. 17.

From the first day that thou didst set thine heart to understand, and to chasten thyself before thy God, thy words were heard.

Thus saith the high and lofty One that inhabiteth eternity, whose name is Holy; I dwell in the high and holy place, with him also that is of a contrite and humble spirit, to revive the spirit of the humble, and to revive the heart of the contrite ones.—The sacrifices of God are a broken spirit: a broken and a contrite heart, O God, thou wilt not despise.—Though the LORD be high, yet hath he respect unto the lowly: but the proud he knoweth afar off.—Humble yourselves therefore under the mighty hand of God, that he may exalt you in due time.—God resisteth the proud, but giveth grace unto the humble. Submit yourselves therefore to God.

Thou, Lord, art good, and ready to forgive; and plenteous in mercy unto all them that call upon thee. Give ear, O LORD, unto my prayer; and attend to the voice of my supplications. In the day of my trouble I will call upon thee: for thou wilt answer me.

DAN. 10. 12. *Is.* 57. 15.—*Ps.* 51. 17.—*Ps.* 138. 6.—1 *Pe.* 5. 6.—*Ja.* 4. 6, 7. *Ps.* 86. 5-7.

Thy will be done in earth, as it is in heaven.

Understanding what the will of the Lord is.

It is not the will of your Father which is in heaven, that one of these little ones should perish.

This is the will of God, even your sanctification.—That he no longer should live the rest of his time in the flesh to the lusts of men, but to the will of God.—Of his own will begat he us with the word of truth: wherefore lay apart all filthiness.

Be ye holy; for I am holy.—[Jesus] said, Whosoever shall do the will of God, the same is my brother, and my sister, and mother. —Whosoever heareth these sayings of mine, and doeth them, I will liken him unto a wise man, which built his house upon a rock: and the rain descended, and the floods came, and the winds blew, and beat upon that house; and it fell not; for it was founded upon a rock.—The world passeth away, and the lust thereof: but he that doeth the will of God abideth for ever.

MAT. 6. 10. *Ep.* 5. 17. *Mat.* 18. 14. 1 *Thes.* 4. 3.—1 *Pe.* 4. 2.—*Ja.* 1. 18, 21. 1 *Pe.* 1. 16.—*Mar.* 3. 34, 35.—*Mat.* 7. 24, 25.—1 *Jno.* 2. 17.

Christ both died, and rose, and revived, that he might be Lord both of the dead and living.

It pleased the LORD to bruise him; he hath put him to grief: when thou shalt make his soul an offering for sin, he shall see his seed, he shall prolong his days, and the pleasure of the LORD shall prosper in his hand. He shall see of the travail of his soul, and shall be satisfied: by his knowledge shall my righteous servant justify many; for he shall bear their iniquities.—Ought not Christ to have suffered these things, and to enter into his glory?—We thus judge, that if one died for all, then were all dead: and that he died for all, that they which live should not henceforth live unto themselves, but unto him which died for them, and rose again.

Let all the house of Israel know assuredly, that God hath made that same Jesus, whom ye have crucified, both Lord and Christ.— Who verily was foreordained before the foundation of the world, but was manifest in these last times for you, who by him do believe in God.

ROM. 14. 9. *Is.* 53. 10, 11.—*Lu.* 24. 26.—2 *Co.* 5. 14, 15. *Ac.* 2. 36.— 1 *Pe.* 1. 20, 21.

Give us this day our daily bread.

I have been young, and now am old; yet have I not seen the righteous forsaken, nor his seed begging bread.—His bread shall be given him; his waters shall be sure.—The ravens brought him bread and flesh in the morning, and bread and flesh in the evening; and he drank of the brook.

My God shall supply all your need according to his riches in glory by Christ Jesus.—Be content with such things as ye have: for he hath said, I will never leave thee, nor forsake thee.

He humbled thee, and suffered thee to hunger, and fed thee with manna, . . . that he might make thee know that man doth not live by bread only, but by every word that proceedeth out of the mouth of the LORD doth man live.—Jesus said unto them, Verily, verily, I say unto you, Moses gave you not that bread from heaven; but my Father giveth you the true bread from heaven. For the bread of God is he which cometh down from heaven, and giveth life unto the world. Then said they unto him, Lord, evermore give us this bread.

MAT. 6. 11. *Ps.* 37. 25.—*Is.* 33. 16.—1 *Ki.* 17. 6. *Phi.* 4. 19.—*He.* 13. 5. *De.* 8. 3.—*Jno.* 6. 32-34.

God is my defence.

The LORD is my rock, and my fortress, and my deliverer; the God of my rock; in him will I trust: he is my shield, and the horn of my salvation, my high tower, and my refuge, my saviour.—The LORD is my strength and my shield; my heart trusted in him, and I am helped: therefore my heart greatly rejoiceth; and with my song will I praise him.

When the enemy shall come in like a flood, the Spirit of the LORD shall lift up a standard against him.—We may boldly say, The LORD is my helper, and I will not fear what man shall do unto me.

The LORD is my light and my salvation; whom shall I fear? the LORD is the strength of my life; of whom shall I be afraid?

As the mountains are round about Jerusalem, so the LORD is round about his people from henceforth even for ever.—Because thou hast been my help, therefore in the shadow of thy wings will I rejoice.

For thy name's sake lead me, and guide me.

PSA. 59. 9. *2 Sa.* 22. 2, 3.—*Ps.* 28. 7. *Is.* 59. 19.—*He.* 13. 6. *Ps.* 27. 1. *Ps.* 125. 2.—*Ps.* 63. 7. *Ps.* 31. 3.

Forgive us our debts, as we forgive our debtors.

Lord, how oft shall my brother sin against me, and I forgive him? till seven times? Jesus saith unto him, I say not unto thee, Until seven times: but, Until seventy times seven.—O thou wicked servant, I forgave thee all that debt, because thou desiredst me: shouldest not thou also have had compassion on thy fellow-servant, even as I had pity on thee? And his lord was wroth, and delivered him to the tormentors, till he should pay all that was due unto him. So likewise shall my heavenly Father do also unto you, if ye from your hearts forgive not every one his brother their trespasses.—Be ye kind one to another, tenderhearted, forgiving one another, even as God for Christ's sake hath forgiven you.— You, . . . hath he quickened, . . . having forgiven you all trespasses; blotting out the handwriting of ordinances that was against us, which was contrary to us, and took it out of the way, nailing it to his cross.—Even as Christ forgave you, so also do ye.

MAT. 6. 12. *Mat.* 18. 21, 22, 32-35.—*Ep.* 4. 32.—*Col.* 2. 13, 14.—*Col.* 3. 13.

Not slothful in business; fervent in spirit; serving the Lord.

Whatsoever thy hand findeth to do, do it with thy might; for there is no work, nor device, nor knowledge, nor wisdom, in the grave, whither thou goest.—Whatsoever ye do, do it heartily, as to the Lord, and not unto men; knowing that of the Lord ye shall receive the reward of the inheritance: for ye serve the Lord Christ.—Whatsoever good thing any man doeth, the same shall he receive of the Lord.

I must work the works of him that sent me, while it is day: the night cometh, when no man can work.—Wist ye not that I must be about my Father's business?—The zeal of thine house hath eaten me up.

Brethren, give diligence to make your calling and election sure: for if ye do these things, ye shall never fall.—We desire that every one of you do shew the same diligence to the full assurance of hope unto the end; that ye be not slothful, but followers of them who through faith and patience inherit the promises.—So run, that ye may obtain.

ROM. 12. 11.—*Ec.* 9. 10.—*Col.* 3. 23, 24.—*Ep.* 6. 8. *Jno.* 9. 4.—*Lu.* 2. 49.—
       Jno. 2. 17. 2 *Pe.* 1. 10.—*He.* 6. 11, 12.—1 *Co.* 9. 24.

Lead us not into temptation, but deliver us from evil.

He that trusteth in his own heart is a fool: but whoso walketh wisely, he shall be delivered.

Let no man say when he is tempted, I am tempted of God: for God cannot be tempted with evil, neither tempteth he any man: but every man is tempted, when he is drawn away of his own lust, and enticed.—Wherefore come out from among them, and be ye separate, saith the Lord, and touch not the unclean thing; and I will receive you.

Lot lifted up his eyes, and beheld all the plain of Jordan, that it was well watered every where, . . . even as the garden of the LORD. Then Lot chose him all the plain of Jordan; but the men of Sodom were wicked and sinners before the LORD exceedingly.— [The Lord] delivered just Lot, vexed with the filthy conversation of the wicked. The Lord knoweth how to deliver the godly out of temptations.—Yea, he shall be holden up: for God is able to make him stand.

MAT. 6. 13. *Pr.* 28. 26. *Ja.* 1. 13, 14.—2 *Co.* 6. 17. *Ge.* 13. 10, 11, 13.—
       2 *Pe.* 2. 7, 9.—*Ro.* 14. 4.

In thy name shall they rejoice all the day; and in thy righteousness shall they be exalted.

In the LORD have I righteousness and strength: even to him shall men come; and all that are incensed against him shall be ashamed. In the LORD shall all the seed of Israel be justified, and shall glory.—Be glad in the LORD, and rejoice, ye righteous: and shout for joy, all ye that are upright in heart.

The righteousness of God without the law is manifested, being witnessed by the law and the prophets; even the righteousness of God which is by faith of Jesus Christ unto all and upon all them that believe. To declare . . . at this time his righteousness: that he might be just, and the justifier of him which believeth in Jesus.

Rejoice in the Lord alway: and again I say, Rejoice.—Whom having not seen, ye love; in whom, though now ye see him not, yet believing, ye rejoice with joy unspeakable and full of glory.

PSA. 89. 16. *Is.* 45. 24, 25.—*Ps.* 32. 11. *Ro.* 3. 21, 22, 26. *Phi.* 4. 4.— 1 *Pe.* 1. 8.

Thine is the kingdom, and the power, and the glory, for ever.

The LORD reigneth, he is clothed with majesty: thy throne is established of old: thou art from everlasting.

The LORD is . . . great in power.—If God be for us, who can be against us?—Our God whom we serve is able to deliver us, . . . and he will deliver us.—My Father, which gave them me, is greater than all; and no man is able to pluck them out of my Father's hand.—Greater is he that is in you, than he that is in the world.

Not unto us, O LORD, not unto us, but unto thy name give glory. —Thine, O LORD, is the greatness, and the power, and the glory, and the victory, and the majesty: for all that is in the heaven and in the earth is thine; thine is the kingdom, O LORD, and thou art exalted as head above all. Now therefore, our God, we thank thee, and praise thy glorious name. But who am I, and what is my people, that we should be able to offer so willingly after this sort? for all things come of thee, and of thine own have we given thee.

MAT. 6. 13. *Ps.* 93. 1, 2. *Na.* 1. 3.—*Ro.* 8. 31.—*Da.* 3. 17.—*Jno.* 10. 29.— 1 *Jno.* 4. 4. *Ps.* 115. 1.—1 *Ch.* 29. 11, 13, 14.

One of the soldiers with a spear pierced his side, and forthwith came there out blood and water.

Behold the blood of the covenant, which the LORD hath made with you.—The life of the flesh is in the blood: and I have given it to you upon the altar to make an atonement for your souls.—It is not possible that the blood of bulls and of goats should take away sins.

Jesus said unto them, This is my blood of the new testament, which is shed for many.—By his own blood he entered in once into the holy place, having obtained eternal redemption for us.—Peace through the blood of his cross.

Ye know that ye were not redeemed with corruptible things, as silver and gold, . . . but with the precious blood of Christ, as of a lamb without blemish and without spot, . . . manifest in these last times for you.

Then will I sprinkle clean water upon you, and ye shall be clean: . . . from all your idols, will I cleanse you.—Let us draw near with a true heart in full assurance of faith, having our hearts sprinkled from an evil conscience.

JOHN 19. 34. *Ex.* 24. 8.—*Le.* 17. 11.—*He.* 10. 4. *Mark* 14. 24.—*He.* 9. 12. —*Col.* 1. 20. 1 *Pe.* 1. 18-20. *Eze.* 36. 25.—*He.* 10. 22.

Amen.

Amen: the LORD God . . . say so too.—He who blesseth himself in the earth shall bless himself in the God of truth (*Heb.* The Amen) ; and he that sweareth in the earth shall swear by the God of truth (The Amen).

When God made promise to Abraham, because he could swear by no greater, he sware by himself. For men verily swear by the greater: and an oath for confirmation is to them an end of all strife. Wherein God, willing more abundantly to shew unto the heirs of promise the immutability of his counsel, confirmed it by an oath: that by two immutable things, in which it was impossible for God to lie, we might have a strong consolation, who have fled for refuge to lay hold upon the hope set before us.

These things saith the Amen, the faithful and true witness.—For all the promises of God in him are yea, and in him Amen, unto the glory of God by us.

Blessed be the LORD God, the God of Israel, who only doeth wondrous things. And blessed be his glorious name for ever. Amen, and Amen.

MAT. 6. 13. 1 *Ki.* 1. 36.—*Is.* 65. 16. *He.* 6. 13, 16-18. *Re.* 3. 14.— 2 *Co.* 1. 20. *Ps.* 72. 18, 19.

The Lord shall be thy confidence, and shall keep thy foot from being taken.

Surely the wrath of man shall praise thee: the remainder of wrath shalt thou restrain.—The king's heart is in the hand of the LORD, as the rivers of water: he turneth it whithersoever he will.—When a man's ways please the LORD, he maketh even his enemies to be at peace with him.

I wait for the LORD, my soul doth wait, and in his word do I hope. My soul waiteth for the Lord more than they that watch for the morning: I say, more than they that watch for the morning.—I sought the LORD, and he heard me, and delivered me from all my fears.

The eternal God is thy refuge, and underneath are the everlasting arms: and he shall thrust out the enemy from before thee; and shall say, Destroy them.—Blessed is the man that trusteth in the LORD, and whose hope the LORD is.

What shall we then say to these things? If God be for us, who can be against us?

PROV. 3. 26. *Ps.* 76. 10.—*Pr.* 21. 1.—*Pr.* 16. 7. *Ps.* 130. 5, 6.—*Ps.* 34. 4. *De.* 33. 27.—*Je.* 17. 7. *Ro.* 8. 31.

Consolation in Christ, . . . comfort of love, . . . fellowship of the Spirit.

Man that is born of a woman is of few days, and full of trouble. He cometh forth like a flower, and is cut down; he fleeth also as a shadow, and continueth not.—My flesh and my heart faileth: but God is the strength of my heart, and my portion for ever.

The Father . . . shall give you another Comforter, that he may abide with you for ever: the Holy Ghost, whom the Father will send in my name.—Blessed be God, even the Father of our Lord Jesus Christ, the Father of mercies, and the God of all comfort; who comforteth us in all our tribulation, that we may be able to comfort them which are in any trouble, by the comfort wherewith we ourselves are comforted of God.

If we believe that Jesus died and rose again, even so them also which sleep in Jesus will God bring with him. And so shall we ever be with the Lord. Wherefore comfort one another with these words.

PHIL. 2. 1. *Job* 14. 1, 2.—*Ps.* 73. 26. *Jno.* 14. 16, 26. 2 *Co.* 1. 3, 4. 1. *Thes.* 4. 14, 17, 18.

I delight in the law of God after the inward man.

O how love I thy law! it is my meditation all the day.—Thy words were found, and I did eat them; and thy word was unto me the joy and rejoicing of mine heart.—I sat down under his shadow with great delight, and his fruit was sweet to my taste.—I have esteemed the words of his mouth more than my necessary food.

I delight to do thy will, O my God: yea, thy law is within my heart.—My meat is to do the will of him that sent me, and to finish his work.

The statutes of the Lord are right, rejoicing the heart: the commandment of the Lord is pure, enlightening the eyes. More to be desired are they than gold, yea, than much fine gold: sweeter also than honey and the honeycomb.—Be ye doers of the word, and not hearers only, deceiving your own selves. For if any be a hearer of the word, and not a doer, he is like unto a man beholding his natural face in a glass.

ROM. 7. 22. *Ps.* 119. 97.—*Je.* 15. 16.—*Ca.* 2. 3.—*Job* 23. 12. *Ps.* 40. 8. *Jno.* 4. 34. *Ps.* 19. 8, 10.—*Ja.* 1. 22, 23.

The Lord thy God accept thee.

Wherewith shall I come before the Lord, and bow myself before the high God? shall I come before him with burnt offerings, with calves of a year old? Will the Lord be pleased with thousands of rams, or with ten thousands of rivers of oil? shall I give my firstborn for my transgression, the fruit of my body for the sin of my soul? He hath shewed thee, O man, what is good; and what doth the Lord require of thee, but to do justly, and to love mercy, and to walk humbly with thy God?

We are all as an unclean thing, and all our righteousnesses are as filthy rags.—There is none righteous, no, not one. For all have sinned, and come short of the glory of God; being justified freely by his grace through the redemption that is in Christ Jesus: whom God hath set forth to be a propitiation through faith in his blood. To declare . . . at this time his righteousness: that he might be just, and the justifier of him which believeth in Jesus.

Accepted in the Beloved.—Ye are complete in him.

2 *SAM.* 24. 23. *Mi.* 6. 6-8. *Is.* 64. 6.—*Ro.* 3. 10, 23-26. *Ep.* 1. 6.—*Col.* 2. 10.

Of his fulness have all we received, and grace for grace.

This is my beloved Son, in whom I am well pleased.—Behold, what manner of love the Father hath bestowed upon us, that we should be called the sons of God.

His Son, whom he hath appointed heir of all things.—If children, then heirs; heirs of God, and joint-heirs with Christ; if so be that we suffer with him, that we may be also glorified together.

I and my Father are one. The Father is in me, and I in him.— My Father, and your Father; and . . . my God, and your God.—I in them, and thou in me, that they may be made perfect in one.

The Church, which is his body, the fulness of him that filleth all in all.

Having . . . these promises, dearly beloved, let us cleanse ourselves from all filthiness of the flesh and spirit, perfecting holiness in the fear of God.

JOHN 1. 16. *Mat.* 17. 5.—1 *Jno.* 3. 1. *He.* 1. 2.—*Ro.* 8. 17. *Jno.* 10. 30, 38.
    —*Jno.* 20. 17.—*Jno.* 17. 23. *Ep.* 1. 22, 23. 2 *Co.* 7. 1.

OCTOBER 21

EVENING

The servant is not greater than his lord; neither he that is sent greater than he that sent him. If ye know these things, happy are ye if ye do them.

There was . . . a strife among them, which of them should be accounted the greatest. And he said unto them, The kings of the Gentiles exercise lordship over them; and they that exercise authority upon them are called benefactors. But ye shall not be so: but he that is greatest among you, let him be as the younger; and he that is chief, as he that doth serve. For whether is greater, he that sitteth at meat, or he that serveth? is not he that sitteth at meat? but I am among you as he that serveth.—Even the Son of man came not to be ministered unto, but to minister, and to give his life a ransom for many.

Jesus riseth from supper, and laid aside his garments; and took a towel, and girded himself. After that he poureth water into a basin, and began to wash the disciples' feet, and to wipe them with the towel wherewith he was girded.

JOHN 13. 16, 17. *Lu.* 22. 24-27.—*Mat.* 20. 28. *Jno.* 13. 3-5.

O God, my heart is fixed.

The LORD is my light and my salvation; whom shall I fear? the LORD is the strength of my life; of whom shall I be afraid?

Thou wilt keep him in perfect peace, whose mind is stayed on thee: because he trusteth in thee.—He shall not be afraid of evil tidings: his heart is fixed, trusting in the LORD. His heart is established, he shall not be afraid, until he see his desire upon his enemies.

What time I am afraid, I will trust in thee. In the time of trouble he shall hide me in his pavilion: in the secret of his tabernacle shall he hide me; he shall set me up upon a rock. And now shall mine head be lifted up above mine enemies round about me: therefore will I offer in his tabernacle sacrifices of joy: I will sing, yea, I will sing praises unto the LORD.

The God of all grace, who hath called us unto his eternal glory by Christ Jesus, after that ye have suffered awhile, make you perfect, stablish, strengthen, settle you. To him be glory and dominion for ever and ever.

PSA. 108. 1. *Ps*. 27. 1. *Is*. 26. 3.—*Ps*. 112. 7, 8. *Ps*. 56. 3.—*Ps*. 27. 5, 6.
1 *Pe*. 5. 10, 11.

The Lord hath prepared his throne in the heavens; and his kingdom ruleth over all.

The lot is cast into the lap; but the whole disposing thereof is of the LORD.—Shall there be evil in a city, and the LORD hath not done it?

I am the LORD, and there is none else, there is no God beside me: I girded thee, though thou hast not known me: that they may know from the rising of the sun, and from the west, that there is none beside me. I am the LORD, and there is none else. I form the light, and create darkness: I make peace, and create evil: I the LORD do all these things.

He doeth according to his will in the army of heaven, and among the inhabitants of the earth: and none can stay his hand, or say unto him, What doest thou?—If God be for us, who can be against us?

He must reign, till he hath put all enemies under his feet.—Fear not, little flock; for it is your Father's good pleasure to give you the kingdom.

PSA. 103. 19. *Pr*. 16. 33.—*Am*. 3. 6. *Is*. 45. 5-7. *Da*. 4. 35.—*Ro*. 8. 31.
1 *Co*. 15. 25.—*Lu*. 12. 32.

A man's life consisteth not in the abundance of the things which he possesseth.

A little that a righteous man hath is better than the riches of many wicked.—Better is little with the fear of the LORD than great treasure and trouble therewith.—Godliness with contentment is great gain. Having food and raiment let us be therewith content.

Give me neither poverty nor riches; feed me with food convenient for me: lest I be full, and deny thee, and say, Who is the LORD? or lest I be poor, and steal, and take the name of my God in vain.—Give us this day our daily bread.

Take no thought for your life, what ye shall eat, or what ye shall drink; nor yet for your body, what ye shall put on. Is not the life more than meat, and the body than raiment? When I sent you without purse, and scrip, and shoes, lacked ye any thing? And they said, Nothing.—Let your conversation be without covetousness: and be content with such things as ye have: for he hath said, I will never leave thee, nor forsake thee.

LUKE 12. 15. *Ps.* 37. 16.—*Pr.* 15. 16.—1 *Ti.* 6. 6, 8. *Pr.* 30. 8, 9.—
Mat. 6. 11. *Mat.* 6. 25.—*Lu.* 22. 35. *He.* 13. 5.

It is the spirit that quickeneth.

The first man Adam was made a living soul; the last Adam was made a quickening spirit.—That which is born of the flesh is flesh; and that which is born of the Spirit is spirit.—Not by works of righteousness which we have done, but according to his mercy he saved us, by the washing of regeneration, and renewing of the Holy Ghost.

If any man have not the Spirit of Christ, he is none of his. And if Christ be in you, the body is dead because of sin; but the Spirit is life because of righteousness. But if the Spirit of him that raised up Jesus from the dead dwell in you, he that raised up Christ from the dead shall also quicken your mortal bodies by his Spirit that dwelleth in you.

I live; yet not I, but Christ liveth in me: and the life which I now live in the flesh I live by the faith of the Son of God.—Reckon ye . . . yourselves to be dead indeed unto sin, but alive unto God through Jesus Christ our Lord.

JOHN 6. 63. 1 *Co.* 15. 45.—*Jno.* 3. 6.—*Tit.* 3. 5. *Ro.* 8. 9-11 *Ga.* 2. 20.—
Ro. 6. 11.

I am cast out of thy sight; yet I will look again toward thy holy temple.

Zion said, The LORD hath forsaken me, and my Lord hath forgotten me. Can a woman forget her sucking child, that she should not have compassion on the son of her womb? yea, they may forget, yet will I not forget thee.

I forgat prosperity. And I said, My strength and my hope is perished from the LORD.—Awake, why sleepest thou, O Lord? arise, cast us not off for ever.—Why sayest thou, O Jacob, and speakest, O Israel, My way is hid from the LORD, and my judgment is passed over from my God? In a little wrath I hid my face from thee for a moment; but with everlasting kindness will I have mercy on thee, saith the LORD thy Redeemer.

Why art thou cast down, O my soul? and why art thou disquieted within me? hope in God: for I shall yet praise him, who is the health of my countenance.—We are troubled on every side, yet not distressed; we are perplexed, but not in despair; persecuted, but not forsaken; cast down, but not destroyed.

JONAH 2. 4. *Is.* 49. 14, 15. *La.* 3. 17, 18.—*Ps.* 44. 23.—*Is.* 40. 27.—
Is. 54. 8. *Ps.* 43. 5.—2 *Co.* 4. 8, 9.

When the poor and needy seek water, and there is none, and their tongue faileth for thirst, I the Lord will hear them.

There be many that say, Who will shew us any good?—What hath man of all his labour, and of the vexation of his heart, wherein he hath laboured under the sun? For all his days are sorrows, and his travail grief; yea, his heart taketh not rest in the night. All is vanity and vexation of spirit.—They have forsaken me the fountain of living waters, and hewed them out cisterns, broken cisterns, that can hold no water.

Him that cometh to me I will in no wise cast out.—I will pour water upon him that is thirsty.—Blessed are they which do hunger and thirst after righteousness: for they shall be filled.

O God, thou art my God; early will I seek thee: my soul thirsteth for thee, my flesh longeth for thee in a dry and thirsty land, where no water is.

ISA. 41. 17. *Ps.* 4. 6.—*Ec.* 2. 22, 23, 17.—*Je.* 2. 13. *Jno.* 6. 37.—*Is.* 44. 3.—
Mat. 5. 6. *Ps.* 63. 1.

Lo, I am with you alway, even unto the end of the world.

If two of you shall agree on earth as touching any thing that they shall ask, it shall be done for them of my Father which is in heaven. For where two or three are gathered together in my name, there am I in the midst of them.—He that hath my commandments, and keepeth them, he it is that loveth me: and he that loveth me shall be loved of my Father, and I will love him, and will manifest myself to him.

Lord, how is it that thou wilt manifest thyself unto us, and not unto the world? . . . If a man love me, he will keep my words: and my Father will love him, and we will come unto him, and make our abode with him.

Unto him that is able to keep you from falling, and to present you faultless before the presence of his glory with exceeding joy, to the only wise God our Saviour, be glory and majesty, dominion and power, both now and ever. Amen.

MAT. 28. 20. *Ma.* 18. 19, 20.—*Jno.* 14. 21. *Jno.* 14. 22, 23. *Jude* 24, 25.

The end of all things is at hand.

I saw a great white throne, and him that sat on it, from whose face the earth and the heaven fled away.—The heavens and the earth, which are now, . . . are kept in store, reserved unto fire against the day of judgment.

God is our refuge and strength, a very present help in trouble. Therefore will not we fear, though the earth be removed, and though the mountains be carried into the midst of the sea; though the waters thereof roar and be troubled, though the mountains shake with the swelling thereof.—Ye shall hear of wars and rumours of wars: see that ye be not troubled.

We have a building of God, an house not made with hands, eternal in the heavens.—We . . . look for new heavens and a new earth, wherein dwelleth righteousness. Wherefore, beloved, seeing that ye look for such things, be diligent that ye may be found of him in peace, without spot, and blameless.

1 *PET.* 4. 7. *Re.* 20. 11.—2 *Pe.* 3. 7. *Ps.* 46. 1-3.—*Mat.* 24. 6. 2 *Co.* 5. 1.—
2 *Pe.* 3. 13, 14.

The Lord reigneth.

Fear ye not me? saith the LORD: will ye not tremble at my presence, which have placed the sand for the bound of the sea by a perpetual decree, that it cannot pass it: and though the waves thereof toss themselves, yet can they not prevail; though they roar, yet can they not pass over it?—Promotion cometh neither from the east, nor from the west, nor from the south. But God is the judge: he putteth down one, and setteth up another.

He changeth the times and the seasons: he removeth kings, and setteth up kings: he giveth wisdom unto the wise, and knowledge to them that know understanding.—Ye shall hear of wars and rumours of wars : see that ye be not troubled.

If God be for us, who can be against us?—Are not two sparrows sold for a farthing? and one of them shall not fall on the ground without your Father. The very hairs of your head are all numbered. Fear ye not therefore, ye are of more value than many sparrows.

PSA. 99. 1. *Je.* 5. 22.—*Ps.* 75. 6, 7. *Da.* 2. 21.—*Mat.* 24. 6. *Ro.* 8. 31.—
Mat. 10. 29-31.

Take heed to your spirit.

Master, we saw one casting out devils in thy name; and we forbad him, because he followeth not with us. And Jesus said unto him, Forbid him not: for he that is not against us is for us. Lord, wilt thou that we command fire to come down from heaven, and consume them, even as Elias did? But he . . . rebuked them, and said, Ye know not what manner of spirit ye are of.

Eldad and Medad do prophesy in the camp. And Joshua the son of Nun . . . answered and said, My lord Moses, forbid them. And Moses said unto him, Enviest thou for my sake? would God that all the LORD's people were prophets, and that the LORD would put his spirit upon them!

The fruit of the Spirit is love, joy, peace, longsuffering, gentleness, goodness, faith, meekness, temperance.—And they that are Christ's have crucified the flesh with the affections and lusts. If we live in the Spirit, let us also walk in the Spirit. Let us not be desirous of vain glory, provoking one another, envying one another.

MAL. 2. 15. *Lu.* 9. 49, 50, 54, 55.—*Nu.* 11. 27-29. *Ga.* 5. 22-26.

Himself took our infirmities, and bare our sicknesses.

Then shall the priest command to take for him that is to be cleansed two birds alive and clean, and cedar wood, and scarlet, and hyssop: and the priest shall command that one of the birds be killed in an earthen vessel over running water: as for the living bird, he shall take it, and the cedar wood, and the scarlet, and the hyssop, and shall dip them and the living bird in the blood of the bird that was killed over the running water: and he shall sprinkle upon him that is to be cleansed from the leprosy seven times, and shall pronounce him clean, and shall let the living bird loose into the open field.

Behold a man full of leprosy: who seeing Jesus fell on his face, and besought him, saying, Lord, if thou wilt, thou canst make me clean.—And Jesus, moved with compassion, put forth his hand, and touched him, and saith unto him, I will; be thou clean. And as soon as he had spoken, immediately the leprosy departed from him, and he was cleansed.

MAT. 8. 17. *Le.* 14. 4-7. *Lu.* 5. 12.—*Mar.* 1. 41, 42.

He whom thou blessest is blessed.

Blessed are the poor in spirit: for their's is the kingdom of heaven.

Blessed are they that mourn: for they shall be comforted. Blessed are the meek: for they shall inherit the earth. Blessed are they which do hunger and thirst after righteousness: for they shall be filled. Blessed are the merciful: for they shall obtain mercy. Blessed are the pure in heart: for they shall see God. Blessed are the peacemakers: for they shall be called the children of God. Blessed are they which are persecuted for righteousness' sake: for their's is the kingdom of heaven. Blessed are ye, when men shall revile you, and persecute you, and shall say all manner of evil against you falsely, for my sake. Rejoice, and be exceeding glad: for great is your reward in heaven.—Blessed are they that hear the word of God, and keep it.

Blessed are they that do his commandments, that they may have right to the tree of life, and may enter in through the gates into the city.

NUM. 22. 6. *Mat.* 5. 3-12. *Lu.* 11. 28. *Re.* 22. 14.

He saw that there was no man, and wondered that there was no intercessor: therefore his arm brought salvation unto him.

Sacrifice and offering thou didst not desire: mine ears hast thou opened: burnt offering and sin offering hast thou not required. Then said I, Lo, I come: in the volume of the book it is written of me, I delight to do thy will, O my God: yea, thy law is within my heart.—I lay down my life, that I might take it again. No man taketh it from me, but I lay it down of myself. I have power to lay it down, and I have power to take it again.

There is no God else beside me: a just God and a Saviour; there is none beside me. Look unto me, and be ye saved, all the ends of the earth: for I am God, and there is none else.—There is none other name under heaven given among men, whereby we must be saved.

Ye know the grace of our Lord Jesus Christ, that, though he was rich, yet for your sakes he became poor, that ye through his poverty might be rich.

ISA. 59. 16. *Ps.* 40. 6-8.—*Jno.* 10. 17, 18. *Is.* 45. 21, 22.—*Ac.* 4. 12.
2 *Cor.* 8. 9.

The Enemy.

Be sober, be vigilant; because your adversary the devil, as a roaring lion, walketh about, seeking whom he may devour.—Resist the devil, and he will flee from you.

Put on the whole armour of God, that ye may be able to stand against the wiles of the devil. For we wrestle not against flesh and blood, but against principalities, against powers, against the rulers of the darkness of this world, against spiritual wickedness in high places. Wherefore take unto you the whole armour of God, that ye may be able to withstand in the evil day, and having done all, to stand. Stand therefore, having your loins girt about with truth, and having on the breastplate of righteousness; and your feet shod with the preparation of the gospel of peace; above all, taking the shield of faith, wherewith ye shall be able to quench all the fiery darts of the wicked.

Rejoice not against me, O mine enemy: when I fall, I shall arise; when I sit in darkness, the LORD shall be a light unto me.

LUKE 10. 19. 1 *Pe.* 5. 8.—*Ja.* 4. 7. *Ep.* 6. 11-16. *Mi.* 7. 8.

He is altogether lovely.

My meditation of him shall be sweet.—My beloved is . . . the chiefest among ten thousand.—A chief corner stone, elect, precious: and he that believeth on him shall not be confounded.—Thou art fairer than the children of men: grace is poured into thy lips.—God . . . hath highly exalted him, and given him a name which is above every name.—It pleased the Father that in him should all fulness dwell.

Whom having not seen, ye love; in whom, though now ye see him not, yet believing, ye rejoice with joy unspeakable and full of glory.

I count all things but loss, for the excellency of the knowledge of Christ Jesus my Lord: for whom I have suffered the loss of all things, and do count them but dung, that I may win Christ, and be found in him, not having mine own righteousness which is of the law, but that which is through the faith of Christ, the righteousness which is of God by faith.

CANT. 5. 16. *Ps.* 104. 34.—*Ca.* 5. 10.—1 *Pe* 2. 6.—*Ps.* 45. 2.—*Phi.* 2. 9.—
Col. 1. 19. 1 *Pe.* 1. 8. *Phi.* 3. 8, 9.

David encouraged himself in the Lord his God.

Lord, to whom shall we go? thou hast the words of eternal life. —I know whom I have believed, and am persuaded that he is able to keep that which I have committed unto him against that day.

In my distress I called upon the LORD, and cried unto my God: he heard my voice out of his temple, and my cry came before him, even into his ears. They prevented me in the day of my calamity: but the LORD was my stay. He brought me forth also into a large place; he delivered me, because he delighted in me.

I will bless the LORD at all times: his praise shall continually be in my mouth. My soul shall make her boast in the LORD: the humble shall hear thereof, and be glad. O magnify the LORD with me, and let us exalt his name together. I sought the LORD, and he heard me, and delivered me from all my fears. O taste and see that the LORD is good: blessed is the man that trusteth in him.

1 *SAM.* 30. 6. *Jno.* 6. 68.—2 *Ti.* 1. 12. *Ps.* 18. 6, 18, 19. *Ps.* 34. 1-4, 8.

It is good that a man should both hope and quietly wait for the salvation of the Lord.

Hath God forgotten to be gracious? hath he in anger shut up his tender mercies?—I said in my haste, I am cut off from before thine eyes: nevertheless thou heardest the voice of my supplications when I cried unto thee.

Shall not God avenge his own elect, which cry day and night unto him, though he bear long with them? I tell you that he will avenge them speedily.—Wait on the LORD, and he shall save thee.—Rest in the LORD, and wait patiently for him: fret not thyself because of him who prospereth in his way, because of the man who bringeth wicked devices to pass.

Ye shall not need to fight in this battle: set yourselves, stand ye still, and see the salvation of the LORD.

Let us not be weary in well doing: . . . in due season we shall reap, if we faint not.—Behold, the husbandman waiteth for the precious fruit of the earth, and hath long patience for it, until he receive the early and latter rain.

LAM. 3. 26. Ps. 77. 9.—Ps. 31. 22. Lu. 18. 7, 8.—Pr. 20. 22.—Ps. 37. 7. 2 Ch. 20. 17. Gal. 6. 9.—Ja. 5. 7.

Take us the foxes, the little foxes, that spoil the vines: for our vines have tender grapes.

Who can understand his errors? cleanse thou me from secret faults.—Looking diligently lest any man fail of the grace of God; lest any root of bitterness springing up trouble you, and thereby many be defiled.—Ye did run well; who did hinder you that ye should not obey the truth?

He which hath begun a good work in you will perform it until the day of Jesus Christ: only let your conversation be as it becometh the gospel of Christ.—The tongue is a little member, and boasteth great things. Behold, how great a matter a little fire kindleth! And the tongue is a fire, a world of iniquity: so is the tongue among our members, that it defileth the whole body, and setteth on fire the course of nature; and it is set on fire of hell. The tongue can no man tame; it is an unruly evil, full of deadly poison.—Let your speech be alway with grace, seasoned with salt.

CANT. 2. 15. Ps. 19. 12.—He. 12. 15.—Ga. 5. 7. Phi. 1. 6, 27.— Ja. 3. 5, 6, 8.—Col. 4. 6.

Not by might, nor by power, but by my Spirit, saith the Lord of hosts.

Who hath directed the Spirit of the LORD, or being his counsellor hath taught him?

God hath chosen the foolish things of the world to confound the wise; and God hath chosen the weak things of the world to confound the things which are mighty; and base things of the world, and things which are despised, hath God chosen, yea, and things which are not, to bring to nought things that are: that no flesh should glory in his presence.

The wind bloweth where it listeth, and thou hearest the sound thereof, but canst not tell whence it cometh, and whither it goeth: so is every one that is born of the Spirit.—Born not of blood, nor of the will of the flesh, nor of the will of man, but of God.

My Spirit remaineth among you: fear ye not.—The battle is not your's, but God's.

The LORD saveth not with sword and spear: for the battle is the LORD's.

ZEC. 4. 6. *Is.* 40. 13. 1 *Co.* 1. 27-29. *Jno.* 3. 8.—*Jno.* 1. 13. *Hag.* 2. 5.— 2 *Ch.* 20. 15. 1 *Sa.* 17. 47.

Do as thou hast said.

Stablish thy word unto thy servant, who is devoted to thy fear. So shall I have wherewith to answer him that reproacheth me: for I trust in thy word. Remember the word unto thy servant, upon which thou hast caused me to hope. Thy statutes have been my songs in the house of my pilgrimage. The law of thy mouth is better unto me than thousands of gold and silver. For ever, O LORD, thy word is settled in heaven. Thy faithfulness is unto all generations.

God, willing more abundantly to shew unto the heirs of promise the immutability of his counsel, confirmed it by an oath; that by two immutable things, in which it was impossible for God to lie, we might have a strong consolation, who have fled for refuge to lay hold upon the hope set before us: which hope we have as an anchor of the soul, both sure and stedfast, and which entereth into that within the veil; whither the forerunner is for us entered, even Jesus.

Exceeding great and precious promises.

2 *SAM.* 7. 25. *Ps.* 119. 38, 42, 49, 54, 72, 89, 90. *He.* 6. 17-26. 2 *Pe.* 1. 4.

Blessed is the man that heareth me, watching daily at my gates, waiting at the posts of my doors.

Behold, as the eyes of servants look unto the hand of their masters, and as the eyes of a maiden unto the hand of her mistress; so our eyes wait upon the LORD our God, until that he have mercy upon us.

A continual burnt offering throughout your generations at the door of the tabernacle of the congregation before the LORD: where I will meet you, to speak there unto thee.—In all places where I record my name I will come unto thee, and I will bless thee.

Where two or three are gathered together in my name, there am I in the midst of them.

The hour cometh, and now is, when the true worshippers shall worship the Father in spirit and in truth: for the Father seeketh such to worship him. God is a Spirit: and they that worship him must worship him in spirit and in truth.

Praying always with all prayer and supplication in the Spirit.—Pray without ceasing.

PROV. 8. 34. *Ps.* 123. 2.—*Ex.* 29. 42.—*Ex.* 20. 24. *Mat.* 18. 20.
Jno. 4. 23, 24. *Ep.* 6. 18.—1 *Thes.* 5. 17.

His name shall be called Counsellor.

The Spirit of the LORD shall rest upon him, the spirit of wisdom and understanding, the spirit of counsel and might, the spirit of knowledge, and of the fear of the LORD. And shall make him of quick understanding in the fear of the LORD.

Doth not wisdom cry? and understanding put forth her voice? Unto you, O men, I call; and my voice is to the sons of man. O ye simple, understand wisdom: and ye fools, be ye of an understanding heart. Hear; for I will speak of excellent things; and the opening of my lips shall be right things. Counsel is mine, and sound wisdom: I am understanding; I have strength.

The LORD of hosts . . . is wonderful in counsel, and excellent in working.—If any of you lack wisdom, let him ask of God, that giveth to all men liberally, and upbraideth not; and it shall be given him.—Trust in the LORD with all thine heart; and lean not unto thine own understanding. In all thy ways acknowledge him, and he shall direct thy paths.

ISA. 9. 6. *Is.* 11. 2, 3. *Pr.* 8. 1, 4-6, 14. *Is.* 28. 29.—*Ja.* 1. 5. *Pr.* 3. 5, 6.

Ever follow that which is good.

For even hereunto were ye called: because Christ also suffered for us, leaving us an example, that ye should follow his steps: who did no sin, neither was guile found in his mouth: who, when he was reviled, reviled not again; . . . but committed himself to him that judgeth righteously.—Consider him that endured such contradiction of sinners against himself, lest ye be wearied and faint in your minds.

Let us lay aside every weight, and the sin which doth so easily beset us, and let us run with patience the race that is set before us, looking unto Jesus the author and finisher of our faith; who for the joy that was set before him endured the cross, despising the shame, and is set down at the right hand of the throne of God.

Finally, brethren, whatsoever things are true, whatsoever things are honest, whatsoever things are just, whatsoever things are pure, whatsoever things are lovely, whatsoever things are of good report; if there be any virtue, and if there be any praise, think on these things.

1 *THES.* 5. 15. 1 *Pe.* 2. 21-23.—*He.* 12. 3. *He.* 12. 1, 2. *Phi.* 4. 8.

The mighty God.

Thou art fairer than the children of men: grace is poured into thy lips: therefore God hath blessed thee for ever. Gird thy sword upon thy thigh, O most Mighty, with thy glory and thy majesty. And in thy majesty ride prosperously. . . . Thy throne, O God, is for ever and ever: the sceptre of thy kingdom is a right sceptre.— Thou spakest in vision to thy Holy One, and saidst, I have laid help upon one that is mighty.—The man that is my fellow, saith the LORD of hosts.

Behold, God, is my salvation; I will trust, and not be afraid: for the LORD JEHOVAH is my strength and my song; he also is become my salvation.—Thanks be unto God, which always causes us to triumph in Christ.

Now unto him that is able to keep you from falling, and to present you faultless before the presence of his glory with exceeding joy. To the only wise God our Saviour, be glory and majesty, dominion and power, both now and ever.

ISA. 9. 6. *Ps.* 45. 2-4, 6.—*Ps.* 89. 19.—*Ze.* 13. 7. *Is.* 12. 2.—2 *Co.* 2. 14.
Jude 24, 25.

The ways of the Lord are right, and the just shall walk in them: but the transgressors shall fall therein.

Unto you . . . which believe he is precious: but unto them which be disobedient, . . . a stone of stumbling, and a rock of offence.—The way of the LORD is strength to the upright: but destruction shall be to the workers of iniquity.

He that hath ears to hear, let him hear.—Whoso is wise, and will observe these things, even they shall understand the lovingkindness of the LORD.—The light of the body is the eye: if therefore thine eye be single, thy whole body shall be full of light.—If any man will do his will, he shall know of the doctrine, whether it be of God.—Whosoever hath, to him shall be given, and he shall have more abundance.

He that is of God heareth God's words: ye therefore hear them not, because ye are not of God.—Ye will not come unto me, that ye might have life.—My sheep hear my voice, and I know them, and they follow me.

HOS. 14. 9. 1 Pe. 2. 7, 8.—Pr. 10. 29. Mat. 11. 15.—Ps. 107. 43.—Mat. 6. 22.—Jno. 7. 17.—Mat. 13. 12. Jno. 8. 47.—Jno. 5. 40.—Jno. 10. 27.

The everlasting Father.

Hear, O Israel: The LORD our God is one LORD.

I and my Father are one, the Father is in me, and I in him.—If ye had known me, ye should have known my Father also.—Philip saith unto him, Lord, shew us the Father, and it sufficeth us. Jesus saith unto him, Have I been so long time with you, and yet hast thou not known me, Philip? he that hath seen me hath seen the Father.—Behold I and the children which God hath given me.—He shall see of the travail of his soul, and shall be satisfied.—I am Alpha and Omega, the beginning and the ending, saith the Lord, which is, and which was, and which is to come, the Almighty.—Before Abraham was, I am.—God said unto Moses, I AM THAT I AM: and he said, Thus shalt thou say unto the children of Israel, I AM hath sent me unto you.

Unto the Son he saith, Thy throne, O God, is for ever and ever.—He is before all things, and by him all things consist.—In him dwelleth all the fulness of the Godhead bodily.

ISA. 9. 6. De. 6. 4. Jno. 10. 30, 38.—Jno. 8. 19.—Jno. 14. 8, 9.—He. 2. 13. Is. 53. 11.—Rev. 1. 8.—Jno. 8. 58.—Ex. 3. 14. He. 1. 8.—Col. 1. 17.—Col. 2. 9.

Now for a season, if need be, ye are in heaviness through manifold temptations.

Beloved, think it not strange concerning the fiery trial which is to try you, as though some strange thing happened unto you: but rejoice, inasmuch as ye are partakers of Christ's sufferings; that, when his glory shall be revealed, ye may be glad also with exceeding joy.—The exhortation . . . speaketh unto you as unto children, My son, despise not thou the chastening of the Lord, nor faint when thou art rebuked of him.—Now no chastening for the present seemeth to be joyous, but grievous: nevertheless, afterward it yieldeth the peaceable fruit of righteousness unto them which are exercised thereby.

We have not a high priest which cannot be touched with the feeling of our infirmities; but was in all points tempted like as we are, yet without sin.—For in that he himself hath suffered being tempted, he is able to succour them that are tempted.—God is faithful, who will not suffer you to be tempted above that ye are able.

1 *PETER* 1. 6. 1 *Pe.* 4. 12, 13.—*He.* 12. 5.—*He.* 12. 11. *He.* 4. 15.—
He. 2. 18.—1 *Co.* 10. 13.

The Prince of Peace.

He shall judge thy people with righteousness, and thy poor with judgment. The mountains shall bring peace to the people, and the little hills, by righteousness. He shall come down like rain upon the mown grass; as showers that water the earth. In his days shall the righteous flourish ; and abundance of peace so long as the moon endureth.—Glory to God . . . on earth peace, good will toward men.

Through the tender mercy of our God; . . . the dayspring from on high hath visited us. To give light to them that sit in darkness and in the shadow of death, to guide our feet into the way of peace;—peace by Jesus Christ: (he is Lord of all).

These things I have spoken unto you, that in me ye might have peace. In the world ye shall have tribulation: but be of good cheer; I have overcome the world.—Peace I leave with you, my peace I give unto you: not as the world giveth, give I unto you.—The peace of God, which passeth all understanding, shall keep your hearts and minds through Christ Jesus.

ISA. 9. 6. *Ps.* 72. 2-7.—*Lu.* 2. 14. *Lu.* 1. 78, 79.—*Ac.* 10. 36. *Jno.* 16. 33.
Jno. 14. 27.—*Ph.* 4. 7.

Take thou also unto thee principal spices, and thou shalt make it an oil of holy ointment.

Upon man's flesh shall it not be poured, neither shall ye make any other like it, after the composition of it: it is holy, and it shall be holy unto you.—One Spirit.—Diversities of gifts, but the same Spirit.

Thy God hath anointed thee with the oil of gladness above thy fellows.—God anointed Jesus of Nazareth with the Holy Ghost and with power.—God giveth not the Spirit by measure unto him.

Of his fulness have all we received.—As the same anointing teacheth you of all things, and is truth, and is no lie, and even as it hath taught you, ye shall abide in him.—He which . . . hath anointed us, is God; who hath also sealed us, and given the earnest of the Spirit in our hearts.

The fruit of the Spirit is love, joy, peace, longsuffering, gentleness, goodness, faith, meekness, temperance: against such there is no law.

EXOD. 30. 23, 25. *Ex.* 30. 32.—*Ep.* 4. 4.—1 *Co.* 12. 4. *Ps.* 45. 7.— *Ac.* 10. 38.—*Jno.* 3. 34. *Jno.* 1. 16.—1 *Jno.* 2. 27.—2 *Co.* 1. 21, 22. *Gal.* 5. 22, 23.

The fashion of this world passeth away.

All the days of Methuselah were nine hundred sixty and nine years: and he died.

Let the brother of low degree rejoice in that he is exalted: but the rich, in that he is made low: because as the flower of the grass he shall pass away. For the sun is no sooner risen with a burning heat, but it withereth the grass, and the flower thereof falleth, and the grace of the fashion of it perisheth: so also shall the rich man fade away in his ways.—For what is your life? It is even a vapour that appeareth for a little time, and then vanisheth away.—The world passeth away, and the lust thereof: but he that doeth the will of God abideth for ever.

LORD, make me to know mine end, and the measure of my days, what it is; that I may know how frail I am.—When they shall say, Peace and safety; then sudden destruction cometh upon them, as travail upon a woman with child; and they shall not escape. But ye, brethren, are not in darkness, that that day should overtake you as a thief.

1 *COR.* 7. 31. *Gen.* 5. 27. *Ja.* 1. 9-11.—*Ja.* 4. 14.—1 *Jno.* 2. 17. *Ps.* 39. 4.— 1 *Thes.* 5. 3, 4.

When Christ, who is our life, shall appear, then shall ye also appear with him in glory.

I am the resurrection, and the life: he that believeth in me, though he were dead, yet shall he live.—God hath given to us eternal life, and this life is in his Son. He that hath the Son hath life; and he that hath not the Son of God hath not life.

The Lord himself shall descend from heaven with a shout, with the voice of the archangel, and with the trump of God: and the dead in Christ shall rise first: then we which are alive and remain shall be caught up together with them in the clouds, to meet the Lord in the air: and so shall we ever be with the Lord. Wherefore comfort one another with these words.—When he shall appear, we shall be like him; for we shall see him as he is.—It is sown in dishonour; it is raised in glory; it is sown in weakness; it is raised in power.

If I go and prepare a place for you, I will come again, and receive you unto myself; that where I am, there ye may be also.

COL. 3. 4. *Jno.* 11. 25.—1 *Jno.* 5. 11, 12. 1 *Thes.* 4. 16-18.—1 *Jno.* 3. 2.—
1 *Co.* 15. 43. *Jno.* 14. 3.

Lead me in thy truth, and teach me.

When . . . the Spirit of truth is come, he will guide you into all truth.—Ye have an unction from the Holy One, and ye know all things.

To the law and to the testimony: if they speak not according to this word, it is because there is no light in them.—All scripture is given by inspiration of God, and is profitable for doctrine, for reproof, for correction, for instruction in righteousness; That the man of God may be perfect, throughly furnished unto all good works.—The holy Scriptures . . . are able to make thee wise unto salvation through faith which is in Christ Jesus.

I will instruct thee and teach thee in the way which thou shalt go: I will guide thee with mine eye.—The light of the body is the eye: if therefore thine eye be single, thy whole body shall be full of light.—If any man will do his will, he shall know of the doctrine, whether it be of God.—The wayfaring men, though fools, shall not err therein.

PSA. 25. 5. *Jno.* 16. 13.—1 *Jno.* 2. 20. *Is.* 8. 20.—2 *Ti.* 3. 16, 17. 2 *Ti.* 3. 15.
Ps. 32. 8.—*Mat.* 6. 22.—*Jno.* 7. 17.—*Is.* 35. 8.

Oh that men would praise the Lord for his goodness, and for his wonderful works to the children of men!

O taste and see that the LORD is good: blessed is the man that trusteth in him.—How great is thy goodness, which thou hast laid up for them that fear thee!

This people have I formed for myself; they shall shew forth my praise.—Having predestinated us unto the adoption of children by Jesus Christ to himself, according to the good pleasure of his will, to the praise of the glory of his grace, wherein he hath made us accepted in the beloved. That we should be to the praise of his glory, who first trusted in Christ.

How great is his goodness, and how great is his beauty!—The LORD is good to all: and his tender mercies are over all his works. All thy works shall praise thee, O LORD; and thy saints shall bless thee. They shall speak of the glory of thy kingdom, and talk of thy power; to make known to the sons of men his mighty acts, and the glorious majesty of his kingdom.

PSA. 107. 8. *Ps.* 34. 8.—*Ps.* 31. 19. *Is.* 43. 21.—*Ep.* 1. 5, 6, 12. *Zec.* 9. 17.
—*Ps.* 145. 9-12.

Behold, we count them happy which endure.

We glory in tribulations: . . . knowing that tribulation worketh patience; And patience, experience; and experience, hope: And hope maketh not ashamed; because the love of God is shed abroad in our hearts by the Holy Ghost which is given unto us.—No chastening for the present seemeth to be joyous, but grievous: nevertheless afterward it yieldeth the peaceable fruit of righteousness unto them which are exercised thereby.—My brethren, count it all joy when ye fall into divers temptations; knowing this, that the trying of your faith worketh patience. But let patience have her perfect work, that ye may be perfect and entire, wanting nothing.— Blessed is the man that endureth temptation: for when he is tried, he shall receive the crown of life, which the Lord hath promised to them that love him.—Most gladly therefore will I rather glory in my infirmities, that the power of Christ may rest upon me. For when I am weak, then am I strong.

JAM. 5. 11. *Ro.* 5. 3-5.—*He.* 12. 11.—*Ja.* 1. 2-4, 12.—2 *Co.* 12. 9, 10.

Let us, who are of the day, be sober, putting on the breastplate of faith and love; and for an helmet, the hope of salvation.

Gird up the loins of your mind, be sober, and hope to the end for the grace that is to be brought unto you at the revelation of Jesus Christ.—Stand therefore, having your loins girt about with truth, and having on the breastplate of righteousness; above all, taking the shield of faith, wherewith ye shall be able to quench all the fiery darts of the wicked. And take the helmet of salvation, and the sword of the Spirit, which is the word of God.

He will swallow up death in victory; and the Lord GOD will wipe away tears from off all faces; and the rebuke of his people shall he take away from off all the earth: for the LORD hath spoken it. And it shall be said in that day, Lo, this is our God; we have waited for him, and he will save us: this is the LORD; . . . we will be glad and rejoice in his salvation.

Faith is the substance of things hoped for, the evidence of things not seen.

1 *THES.* 5. 8. 1 *Pe.* 1. 13.—*Ep.* 6. 14, 16, 17. *Is.* 25. 8, 9. *He.* 11. 1.

The children of Israel pitched before them like two little flocks of kids; but the Syrians filled the country.

Thus saith the LORD, because the Syrians have said, the LORD is God of the hills, but he is not God of the valleys; therefore will I deliver all this great multitude into thine hand, and ye shall know that I am the LORD. And they pitched one over against the other seven days; and so it was, that in the seventh day the battle was joined: and the children of Israel slew of the Syrians an hundred thousand footmen in one day.—Ye are of God, little children, and have overcome them; because greater is he that is in you, than he that is in the world.

Fear thou not; for I am with thee: be not dismayed; for I am thy God: I will strengthen thee; yea, I will help thee; yea, I will uphold thee with the right hand of my righteousness.

They shall fight against thee; but they shall not prevail against thee; for I am with thee, saith the LORD, to deliver thee.

1 *Ki.* 20. 27. 1 *Ki.* 20. 28, 29.—1 *Jno.* 4. 4. *Is.* 41. 10.—*Jer.* 1. 19.

I have laid help upon one that is mighty; I have exalted one chosen out of the people.

I, even I, am the Lord; and beside me there is no saviour.—There is one God, and one mediator between God and men, the man Christ Jesus.—There is none other name under heaven given among men, whereby we must be saved.

The mighty God.—Who made himself of no reputation, and took upon him the form of a servant, and was made in the likeness of men: and being found in fashion as a man, he humbled himself and became obedient unto death, even the death of the cross. Wherefore God also hath highly exalted him, and given him a name which is above every name.—We see Jesus, who was made a little lower than the angels for the suffering of death, crowned with glory and honour; that he by the grace of God should taste death for every man.—Forasmuch . . . as the children are partakers of flesh and blood, he also himself likewise took part of the same.

PSA. 89. 19. *Is.* 43. 11.—1 *Ti.* 2. 5.—*Ac.* 4. 12. *Is.* 9. 6. *Phi.* 2. 7-9.—*He.* 2. 9.—*He.* 2. 14.

Gather my saints together unto me, those that have made a covenant with me by sacrifice.

Christ was once offered to bear the sins of many; and unto them that look for him shall he appear the second time, without sin, unto salvation.—He is the mediator of the new testament, that by means of death, . . . they which are called might receive the promise of eternal inheritance.

Father, I will that they also, whom thou hast given me, be with me where I am.—Then he shall send his angels, and shall gather together his elect from the four winds, from the uttermost part of the earth, to the uttermost part of heaven.—If any of thine be driven out unto the outmost parts of heaven, from thence will the LORD thy God gather thee, and from thence will he fetch thee.

The dead in Christ shall rise first: then we which are alive and remain shall be caught up together with them in the clouds, to meet the Lord in the air: and so shall we ever be with the Lord.

PSA. 50. 5. *He.* 9. 28.—*He.* 9. 15. *Jno.* 17. 24.—*Mar.* 13. 27.—*De.* 30. 4. 1 *Thes.* 4. 16, 17.

Faithful in every good work, and increasing in the knowledge of God.

I beseech you, . . . brethren, by the mercies of God, that ye present your bodies a living sacrifice, holy, acceptable unto God, which is your reasonable service. And be not conformed to this world: but be ye transformed by the renewing of your mind, that ye may prove what is that good, and acceptable, and perfect, will of God.—As ye have yielded your members servants to uncleanness and to iniquity unto iniquity; even so now yield your members servants to righteousness unto holiness. In Christ Jesus neither circumcision availeth any thing, nor uncircumcision, but a new creature. And as many as walk according to this rule, peace be on them, and mercy.

Herein is my Father glorified, that ye bear much fruit; so shall ye be my disciples.—I have chosen you, and ordained you, that ye should go and bring forth fruit, and that your fruit should remain: that whatsoever ye shall ask of the Father in my name, he may give it you.

COL. 1. 10. *Ro.* 12. 1, 2.—*Ro.* 6. 19.—*Gal.* 6. 15, 16. *Jno.* 15. 8.— *Jno.* 15. 16.

I sought him, but I found him not.

Return unto the LORD thy God; for thou hast fallen by thine iniquity. Take with you words, and turn to the LORD: say unto him, Take away all iniquity, and receive us graciously.

Let no man say when he is tempted, I am tempted of God. But every man is tempted, when he is drawn away of his own lust, and enticed. Do not err, my beloved brethren. Every good gift and every perfect gift is from above, and cometh down from the Father of lights, with whom is no variableness, neither shadow of turning.

Wait on the Lord; be of good courage, and he shall strengthen thine heart: wait, I say, on the LORD.—It is good that a man should both hope and quietly wait for the salvation of the LORD.—Shall not God avenge his own elect, which cry day and night unto him, though he bear long with them?

Truly my soul waiteth upon God: from him cometh my salvation. My soul, wait thou only upon God; for my expectation is from him.

CANT. 3. 1. *Ho.* 14. 1, 2. *Ja.* 1. 13-17. *Ps.* 27. 14.—*La.* 3. 26.—*Lu.* 18. 7. *Ps.* 62. 1, 5.

He led them on safely.

I lead in the way of righteousness, in the midst of the paths of judgment.

Behold, I send an Angel before thee, to keep thee in the way, and to bring thee into the place which I have prepared.—In all their affliction he was afflicted, and the angel of his presence saved them: in his love and in his pity he redeemed them; and he bare them, and carried them all the days of old.

They got not the land in possession by their own sword, neither did their own arm save them: but thy right hand, and thine arm, and the light of thy countenance, because thou hadst a favour unto them.—So didst thou lead thy people, to make thyself a glorious name.

Lead me, O LORD, in thy righteousness because of mine enemies; make thy way straight before my face.—O send out thy light and thy truth: let them lead me; let them bring me unto thy holy hill, and to thy tabernacles. Then will I go unto the altar of God, unto God my exceeding joy: yea, upon the harp will I praise thee, O God my God.

PSA. 78. 53. *Pr.* 8. 20. *Ex.* 23. 20.—*Is.* 63. 9. *Ps.* 44. 3.—*Is.* 63. 14.
Ps. 5. 8.—*Ps.* 43. 3, 4.

Ye are washed, . . . ye are sanctified, . . . ye are justified.

The blood of Jesus Christ his Son cleanseth us from all sin.—The chastisement of our peace was upon him; and with his stripes we are healed.

Christ . . . loved the church, and gave himself for it; that he might sanctify and cleanse it with the washing of water by the word, that he might present it to himself a glorious church, not having spot, or wrinkle, or any such thing; but that it should be holy and without blemish.—To her was granted that she should be arrayed in fine linen, clean and white: for the fine linen is the righteousness of saints.—Let us draw near with a true heart in full assurance of faith, having our hearts sprinkled from an evil conscience, and our bodies washed with pure water.

Who shall lay any thing to the charge of God's elect? It is God that justifieth.—Blessed is he whose transgression is forgiven. Blessed is the man unto whom the LORD imputeth not iniquity, and in whose spirit there is no guile.

1 COR. 6. 11. *1 Jno.* 1. 7.—*Is.* 53. 5. *Ep.* 5. 25-27.—*Re.* 19. 8.—*He.* 10. 22.
Ro. 8. 33.—*Ps.* 32. 1, 2.

Godly sorrow worketh repentance not to be repented of.

Peter remembered the word of Jesus, which said unto him, Before the cock crow, thou shalt deny me thrice. And he went out, and wept bitterly.—If we confess our sins, he is faithful and just to forgive us our sins, and to cleanse us from all unrighteousness.—The blood of Jesus Christ his Son cleanseth us from all sin.

Mine iniquities have taken hold upon me, so that I am not able to look up; they are more than the hairs of my head: therefore my heart faileth me. Be pleased, O LORD, to deliver me: O LORD, make haste to help me.

Turn thou to thy God: keep mercy and judgment, and wait on thy God continually.

The sacrifices of God are a broken spirit: a broken and a contrite heart, O God, thou wilt not despise.—He healeth the broken in heart, and bindeth up their wounds.—He hath shewed thee, O man, what is good: and what doth the LORD require of thee, but to do justly, and to love mercy, and to walk humbly with thy God?

2 *COR.* 7. 10. *Mat.* 26. 75.—1 *Jno.* 1. 9.—1 *Jno.* 1. 7. *Ps.* 40. 12, 13. *Ho.* 12. 6. *Ps.* 51. 17.—*Ps.* 147. 3.—*Mi.* 6. 8.

Is it well with thee? And she answered, It is well.

We having the same spirit of faith.

As chastened, and not killed; as sorrowful, yet alway rejoicing; as poor, yet making many rich; as having nothing, and yet possessing all things.

We are troubled on every side, yet not distressed; we are perplexed, but not in despair; persecuted, but not forsaken; cast down, but not destroyed; always bearing about in the body the dying of the Lord Jesus, that the life also of Jesus might be made manifest in our body. For which cause we faint not, but though our outward man perish, yet the inward man is renewed day by day. For our light affliction, which is but for a moment, worketh for us a far more exceeding and eternal weight of glory; while we look not at the things which are seen, but at the things which are not seen.

Beloved, I wish above all things that thou mayest prosper and be in health, even as thy soul prospereth.

2 *Kl.* 4. 26. 2 *Co.* 4. 13. 2 *Co.* 6. 9, 10. 2 *Co.* 4. 8-10, 16-18. 3 *Jno.* 2.

Christ loved the church, and gave himself for it; that he might sanctify and cleanse it with the washing of water by the word.

Walk in love, as Christ also hath loved us, and hath given himself for us an offering and a sacrifice to God for a sweetsmelling savour.

Being born again, not of corruptible seed, but of incorruptible, by the word of God, which liveth and abideth for ever.—Sanctify them through thy truth: thy word is truth.—Except a man be born of water and of the Spirit, he cannot enter into the kingdom of God. —Not by works of righteousness which we have done, but according to his mercy he saved us, by the washing of regeneration, and renewing of the Holy Ghost.—Thy word hath quickened me.

The law of the LORD is perfect, converting the soul: the testimony of the LORD is sure, making wise the simple. The statutes of the LORD are right, rejoicing the heart: the commandment of the LORD is pure, enlightening the eyes.

EPH. 5. 25, 26. *Ep.* 5. 2. 1 *Pe.* 1. 23.—*Jno.* 17. 17.—*Jno.* 3. 5.—*Tit.* 3. 5.— *Ps.* 119. 50. *Ps.* 19. 7, 8.

Through him we both have access by one Spirit unto the Father.

I in them, and thou in me, that they may be made perfect in one.

Whatsoever ye shall ask in my name, that will I do, that the Father may be glorified in the Son. If ye shall ask any thing in my name, I will do it. And I will pray the Father, and he shall give you another Comforter, that he may abide with you for ever; even the Spirit of truth; whom the world cannot receive, because it seeth him not, neither knoweth him: but ye know him; for he dwelleth with you, and shall be in you.—There is one body, and one Spirit, even as ye are called in one hope of your calling; one Lord, one faith, one baptism, one God and Father of all, who is above all, and through all, and in you all.—When ye pray, say, Our Father which art in heaven.

Having therefore, brethren, boldness to enter into the holiest by the blood of Jesus, by a new and living way . . . let us draw near.

EPH. 2. 18. *Jno.* 17. 23. *Jno.* 14. 13, 14, 16, 17.—*Ep.* 4. 4-6. *Lu.* 11. 2. *He.* 10. 19, 20, 22.

Thou art my help and my deliverer; make no tarrying, O my God.

The steps of a good man are ordered by the LORD: and he delighteth in his way. Though he fall, he shall not be utterly cast down: for the LORD upholdeth him with his hand.—In the fear of the LORD is strong confidence: and his children shall have a place of refuge.—Who art thou, that thou shouldest be afraid of a man that shall die, and of the son of man which shall be made as grass; and forgettest the LORD thy maker?

I am with thee to deliver thee.—Be strong and of a good courage, fear not, nor be afraid of them: for the LORD thy God, he it is that doth go with thee; he will not fail thee, nor forsake thee.

I will sing of thy power; yea, I will sing aloud of thy mercy in the morning: for thou hast been my defence and refuge in the day of my trouble.—Thou art my hiding place; thou shalt preserve me from trouble; thou shalt compass me about with songs of deliverance.

PSA. 40. 17. *Ps.* 37. 23, 24.—*Is.* 51. 12, 13. *Je.* 1. 8.—
De. 31. 6. *Ps.* 59. 16.—*Ps.* 32. 7.

How wilt thou do in the swellings of Jordan?

For Jordan overfloweth all his banks all the time of harvest.

The priests that bare the ark of the covenant of the LORD stood firm on dry ground in the midst of Jordan, and all the Israelites passed over on dry ground, until all the people were passed clean over Jordan.

We see Jesus, who was made a little lower than the angels, for the suffering of death, crowned with glory and honour; that he by the grace of God should taste death for every man.

Though I walk through the valley of the shadow of death, I will fear no evil: for thou art with me; thy rod and thy staff they comfort me.—When thou passest through the waters, I will be with thee; and through the rivers, they shall not overflow thee.

Fear not; I am the first and the last: I am he that liveth, and was dead; and, behold, I am alive for evermore, Amen; and have the keys of hell and of death.

JER. 12. 5. *Jos.* 3. 15. *Jos.* 3. 17.—*He.* 2. 9. *Ps.* 23. 4.—*Is.* 43. 2.
Re. 1. 17, 18.

God is faithful, by whom ye were called unto the fellowship of his Son Jesus Christ our Lord.

Let us hold fast the profession of our faith without wavering; for he is faithful that promised.—God hath said, I will dwell in them, and walk in them; and I will be their God, and they shall be my people.—Truly our fellowship is with the Father, and with his Son Jesus Christ.—Rejoice, inasmuch as ye are partakers of Christ's sufferings; that, when his glory shall be revealed, ye may be glad also with exceeding joy.

That ye, being rooted and grounded in love, may be able to comprehend with all saints what is the breadth, and length, and depth, and height; and to know the love of Christ, which passeth knowledge, that ye might be filled with all the fulness of God.

Whosoever shall confess that Jesus is the Son of God, God dwelleth in him, and he in God.—And he that keepeth his commandments dwelleth in him, and he in him.

1 COR. 1. 9. He. 10. 23.—2 Co. 6. 16.—1 Jno. 1. 3.—1 Pe. 4. 13. Ep. 3. 17-19. 1 Jno. 4. 15.—1 Jno. 3. 24.

We are his workmanship.

They brought great stones, costly stones, and hewed stones, to lay the foundation of the house.—The house, when it was in building, was built of stone made ready before it was brought thither: so that there was neither hammer nor axe nor any tool of iron heard in the house, while it was in building.

Ye also, as lively stones, are built up a spiritual house.—Built upon the foundation of the apostles and prophets, Jesus Christ himself being the chief corner stone; in whom all the building fitly framed together groweth unto an holy temple in the Lord: in whom ye also are builded together for an habitation of God through the Spirit.—Which in time past were not a people, but are now the people of God.

Ye are God's building.—Therefore if any man be in Christ, he is a new creature: old things are passed away; behold, all things are become new.—Now he that hath wrought us for the selfsame thing is God, who also hath given unto us the earnest of the Spirit.

EPH. 2. 10. 1 Ki. 5. 17.—1 Ki. 6. 7. 1 Pe. 2. 5.—Ep. 2. 20-22.— 1 Pe. 2. 10. 1 Co. 3. 9.—2 Co. 5. 17.—2 Co. 5. 5.

Sanctify them through thy truth: thy word is truth.

Now ye are clean through the word which I have spoken unto you.—Let the word of Christ dwell in you richly in all wisdom.

Wherewithal shall a young man cleanse his way? by taking heed thereto according to thy word. With my whole heart have I sought thee: O let me not wander from thy commandments.

When wisdom entereth into thine heart, and knowledge is pleasant unto thy soul: discretion shall preserve thee, understanding shall keep thee.

My foot hath held his steps, his way have I kept, and not declined. Neither have I gone back from the commandment of his lips; I have esteemed the words of his mouth more than my necessary food.—I have more understanding than all my teachers: for thy testimonies are my meditation.—If ye continue in my word, then are ye my disciples indeed; and ye shall know the truth, and the truth shall make you free.

JOHN 17. 17. *Jno.* 15. 3.—*Col.* 3. 16. *Ps.* 119. 9, 10. *Pr.* 2. 10, 11.
Job 23. 11, 12.—*Ps.* 119. 99.—*Jno.* 8. 31, 32.

Fellow citizens with the saints.

Ye are come unto mount Sion, and unto the city of the living God, the heavenly Jerusalem, and to an innumerable company of angels, to the general assembly and church of the firstborn, which are written in heaven, and to God the Judge of all, and to the spirits of just men made perfect.

These all died in faith, not having received the promises, but having seen them afar off, and were persuaded of them, and embraced them, and confessed that they were strangers and pilgrims on the earth.—Our conversation (*Gr.* citizenship) is in heaven; from whence also we look for the Saviour, the Lord Jesus Christ: who shall change our vile body, that it may be fashioned like unto his glorious body, according to the working whereby he is able even to subdue all things unto himself.—The Father, . . . hath delivered us from the power of darkness, and hath translated us into the kingdom of his dear Son.

As strangers and pilgrims, abstain from fleshly lusts, which war against the soul.

EPH. 2. 19. *He.* 12. 22, 23. *He.* 11. 13.—*Phi.* 3. 20, 21.—*Col.* 1. 12, 13.
1 *Pe.* 2. 11.

Thy thoughts are very deep.

We . . . do not cease to pray for you, and to desire that ye might be filled with the knowledge of his will in all wisdom and spiritual understanding.—That ye, being rooted and grounded in love, may be able to comprehend with all saints what is the breadth, and length, and depth, and height; and to know the love of Christ, which passeth knowledge, that ye might be filled with all the fulness of God.

O the depth of the riches both of the wisdom and knowledge of God! how unsearchable are his judgments, and his ways past finding out! My thoughts are not your thoughts, neither are your ways my ways, saith the LORD. For as the heavens are higher than the earth, so are my ways higher than your ways, and my thoughts than your thoughts.—Many, O LORD my God, are thy wonderful works which thou hast done, and thy thoughts which are to us-ward: they cannot be reckoned up in order unto thee: if I would declare and speak of them, they are more than can be numbered.

PSA. 92. 5. *Col.* 1. 9.—*Ep.* 3. 17-19. *Ro.* 11. 33.—*Is.* 55. 8, 9.—*Ps.* 40. 5.

Whatsoever a man soweth, that shall he also reap.

They that plow iniquity, and sow wickedness, reap the same.—They have sown the wind, and they shall reap the whirlwind.—He that soweth to his flesh shall of the flesh reap corruption.

To him that soweth righteousness shall be a sure reward.—He that soweth to the Spirit shall of the Spirit reap life everlasting. And let us not be weary in well doing: for in due season we shall reap, if we faint not. As we have therefore opportunity, let us do good unto all men, especially unto them who are of the household of faith.

There is that scattereth, and yet increaseth; and there is that withholdeth more than is meet, but it tendeth to poverty.—The liberal soul shall be made fat: and he that watereth shall be watered also himself.—He which soweth sparingly shall reap also sparingly; and he which soweth bountifully shall reap also bountifully.

GAL. 6. 7. *Job* 4. 8.—*Ho.* 8. 7.—*Gal.* 6. 8. *Pr.* 11. 18.—*Gal.* 6. 8-10. *Pr.* 11. 24, 25.—*2 Co.* 9. 6.

He stayeth his rough wind in the day of the east wind.

Let us fall now into the hand of the LORD; for his mercies are great.—I am with thee, saith the LORD, to save thee: . . . I will correct thee in measure, and will not leave thee altogether unpunished.—He will not always chide: neither will he keep his anger for ever. He hath not dealt with us after our sins; nor rewarded us according to our iniquities. For he knoweth our frame; he remembereth that we are dust.—I will spare them, as a man spareth his own son that serveth him.

God is faithful, who will not suffer you to be tempted above that ye are able; but will with the temptation also make a way to escape, that ye may be able to bear it.—Satan hath desired to have you, that he may sift you as wheat: but I have prayed for thee, that thy faith fail not.

Thou hast been a strength to the poor, a strength to the needy in his distress, a refuge from the storm, a shadow from the heat, when the blast of the terrible ones is as a storm against the wall.

ISA. 27. 8. *2 Sa.* 24. 14.—*Je.* 30. 11.—*Ps.* 103. 9, 10, 14.—*Mal.* 3. 17.
1 *Co.* 10. 13.—*Lu.* 22. 31, 32. *Is.* 25. 4.

I believed not the words, until I came, and mine eyes had seen it; and, behold, the half was not told me.

The queen of the south shall rise up in the judgment with this generation, and shall condemn it: for she came from the uttermost parts of the earth to hear the wisdom of Solomon; and, behold, a greater than Solomon is here.—We beheld his glory, the glory as of the only begotten of the Father, full of grace and truth.

My speech and my preaching was . . . in demonstration of the Spirit and of power: that your faith should not stand in the wisdom of men, but in the power of God. But as it is written, Eye hath not seen, nor ear heard, neither have entered into the heart of man, the things which God hath prepared for them that love him. But God hath revealed them unto us by his Spirit: for the Spirit searcheth all things, yea, the deep things of God.

Thine eyes shall see the King in his beauty.—We shall see him as he is.—In my flesh I shall see God.—I shall be satisfied.

1 KINGS 10. 7. *Mat.* 12. 42.—*Jno.* 1. 14. 1 *Co.* 2. 4, 5, 9, 10. *Is.* 33. 17.—
1 *Jno.* 3. 2.—*Job* 19. 26.—*Ps.* 17. 15.

By their fruits ye shall know them.

Little children, let no man deceive you: he that doeth righteousness is righteous, even as he is righteous.—Doth a fountain send forth at the same place sweet water and bitter? Can the fig tree, my brethren, bear olive berries? either a vine, figs? so can no fountain both yield salt water and fresh. Who is a wise man and endued with knowledge among you? let him shew out of a good conversation his works with meekness of wisdom.—Having your conversation honest among the Gentiles: that, whereas they speak against you as evildoers, they may by your good works, which they shall behold, glorify God in the day of visitation.

Either make the tree good, and his fruit good; or else make the tree corrupt, and his fruit corrupt: for the tree is known by his fruit.—A good man out of the good treasure of the heart bringeth forth good things: and an evil man out of the evil treasure bringeth forth evil things.

What could have been done more to my vineyard, that I have not done in it?

MAT. 7. 20. 1 *Jno.* 3. 7.—*Ja.* 3. 11-13.—1 *Pe.* 2. 12. *Mat.* 12. 33.—
Mat. 12. 35. *Is.* 5. 4.

I will make the place of my feet glorious.

Thus saith the LORD, The heaven is my throne, and the earth is my footstool.

Will God in very deed dwell with men on the earth! Behold, heaven and the heaven of heavens cannot contain thee; how much less this house which I have built!

Thus saith the LORD of hosts, Yet once, it is a little while, and I will shake the heavens, and the earth, and the sea, and the dry land; and I will shake all nations, and the desire of all nations shall come: and I will fill this house with glory, saith the LORD of hosts. The glory of this latter house shall be greater than of the former, saith the LORD of hosts.

I saw a new heaven and a new earth: for the first heaven and the first earth were passed away; and there was no more sea. And I heard a great voice out of heaven, saying, Behold, the tabernacle of God is with men, and he will dwell with them, and they shall be his people, and God himself shall be with them, and be their God.

ISA. 60. 13. *Is.* 66. 1. 2 *Ch.* 6. 18. *Hag.* 2. 6, 7, 9. *Re.* 21. 1, 3.

When I sit in darkness, the Lord shall be a light unto me.

When thou passest through the waters, I will be with thee; and through the rivers, they shall not overflow thee: when thou walkest through the fire, thou shalt not be burned; neither shall the flame kindle upon thee. For I am the LORD thy God, the Holy One of Israel, thy Saviour.—I will bring the blind by a way that they knew not; I will lead them in paths that they have not known: I will make darkness light before them, and crooked things straight. These things will I do unto them, and not forsake them.

Yea, though I walk through the valley of the shadow of death, I will fear no evil: for thou art with me; thy rod and thy staff they comfort me.—What time I am afraid, I will trust in thee. In God I will praise his word, in God I have put my trust; I will not fear what flesh can do unto me.—The LORD is my light and my salvation; whom shall I fear? the LORD is the strength of my life; of whom shall I be afraid?

MIC. 7. 8. *Is.* 43. 2, 3.—*Is.* 42. 16. *Ps.* 23. 4.—*Ps.* 56. 3, 4.—*Ps.* 27. 1.

One God, and one mediator between God and men, the man Christ Jesus.

Hear, O Israel: The LORD our God is one LORD.—A mediator is not a mediator of one, but God is one.

We have sinned with our fathers, we have committed iniquity, we have done wickedly. Our fathers understood not thy wonders in Egypt; they remembered not the multitude of thy mercies. . . . Therefore he said that he would destroy them, had not Moses his chosen stood before him in the breach, to turn away his wrath, lest he should destroy them.

Wherefore, holy brethren, partakers of the heavenly calling, consider the Apostle and High Priest of our profession, Christ Jesus; who was faithful to him that appointed him, as also Moses was faithful in all his house.

He is the mediator of a better covenant, which was established upon better promises. I will be merciful to their unrighteousness, and their sins and their iniquities will I remember no more.

1 *TIM.* 2. 5. *De.* 6. 4.—*Gal.* 3. 20. *Ps.* 106. 6, 7, 23. *He.* 3. 1-3. *He.* 8. 6, 12.

Him that cometh to me I will in no wise cast out.

It shall come to pass, when he crieth unto me, that I will hear; for I am gracious.—I will not cast them away, neither will I abhor them, to destroy them utterly, and to break my covenant with them: for I am the LORD their God.—I will remember my covenant with thee in the days of thy youth, and I will establish unto thee an everlasting covenant.

Come now, and let us reason together, saith the LORD: though your sins be as scarlet, they shall be as white as snow; though they be red like crimson, they shall be as wool.—Let the wicked forsake his way, and the unrighteous man his thoughts: and let him return unto the LORD, and he will have mercy upon him; and to our God, for he will abundantly pardon.—Lord, remember me when thou comest into thy kingdom. And Jesus said unto him, Verily I say unto thee, To day shalt thou be with me in paradise.

A bruised reed shall he not break, and the smoking flax shall he not quench.

JOHN 6. 37. *Ex.* 22. 27.—*Le.* 26. 44.—*Eze.* 16. 60. *Is.* 1. 18.—*Is.* 55. 7.— *Lu.* 23. 42, 43. *Is.* 42. 3.

His dear Son.

Lo a voice from heaven, saying, This is my beloved Son, in whom I am well pleased.—Behold my servant, whom I uphold; mine elect, in whom my soul delighteth.—The only begotten Son, which is in the bosom of the Father.

In this was manifested the love of God toward us, because that God sent his only begotten Son into the world, that we might live through him. Herein is love, not that we loved God, but that he loved us, and sent his son to be the propitiation for our sins. And we have known and believed the love that God hath to us. God is love.

The glory which thou gavest me I have given them; that they may be one, even as we are one: I in them, and thou in me, that they may be made perfect in one; and that the world may know that thou hast sent me, and hast loved them, as thou hast loved me.—Behold, what manner of love the Father hath bestowed upon us, that we should be called the sons of God.

COL. 1. 13. *Mat.* 3. 17.—*Is.* 42. 1.—*Jno.* 1. 18. 1 *Jno.* 4. 9, 10, 16. *Jno.* 17. 22-24.—1 *Jno.* 3. 1.

Praying in the Holy Ghost.

God is a Spirit: and they that worship him must worship him in spirit and in truth.—We . . . have access by one Spirit unto the Father.

O my Father, if it be possible, let this cup pass from me: nevertheless not as I will, but as thou wilt.

The Spirit . . . helpeth our infirmities: for we know not what we should pray for as we ought: but the Spirit itself maketh intercession for us with groanings which cannot be uttered. And he that searcheth the hearts knoweth what is the mind of the Spirit, because he maketh intercession for the saints according to the will of God.—This is the confidence that we have in him, that, if we ask any thing according to his will, he heareth us.—When he, the Spirit of truth, is come, he will guide you into all truth.

Praying always with all prayer and supplication in the Spirit, and watching thereunto with all perseverance and supplication.

JUDE 20. *Jno.* 4. 24.—*Ep.* 2. 18. *Mat.* 26. 39. *Ro.* 8. 26, 27.—
1 *Jno.* 5. 14.—*Jno.* 16. 13. *Ep.* 6. 18.

There is a hope of a tree, if it be cut down, that it will sprout again, and that the tender branch thereof will not cease.

A bruised reed shall he not break.—He restoreth my soul.

Godly sorrow worketh repentance to salvation not to be repented of: but the sorrow of the world worketh death.—No chastening for the present seemeth to be joyous, but grievous: nevertheless, afterward it yieldeth the peaceful fruit of righteousness unto them which are exercised thereby.

Before I was afflicted I went astray: but now have I kept thy word.—After all that is come upon us for our evil deeds, and for our great trespass, seeing that thou our God hast punished us less than our iniquities deserve, and hast given us such deliverance as this.

Rejoice not against me, O mine enemy: when I fall, I shall arise; when I sit in darkness, the LORD shall be a light unto me. He will bring me forth to the light, and I shall behold his righteousness.

JOB 14. 7. *Is.* 42. 3.—*Ps.* 23. 3. 2 *Co.* 7. 10.—*He.* 12. 11. *Ps.* 119. 67.—
Ezra 9. 13. *Mi.* 7. 8, 9.

Whoso hearkeneth unto me shall dwell safely, and shall be quiet from fear of evil.

LORD, thou hast been our dwelling place in all generations.— He that dwelleth in the secret place of the most High shall abide under the shadow of the Almighty.—His truth shall be thy shield and buckler.

Your life is hid with Christ in God.—He that toucheth you toucheth the apple of his eye.—Fear ye not, stand still, and see the salvation of the LORD. The LORD shall fight for you, and ye shall hold your peace.—God is our refuge and strength, a very present help in trouble. Therefore will not we fear.

Jesus spake unto them, saying, Be of good cheer; it is I; be not afraid.—Why are ye troubled? and why do thoughts arise in your hearts? Behold my hands and my feet, that it is I myself: handle me, and see ; for a spirit hath not flesh and bones, as ye see me have.—I know whom I have believed, and am persuaded that he is able to keep that which I have committed unto him against that day.

PROV. 1. 33. *Ps.* 90. 1.—*Ps.* 91. 1.—*Ps.* 91. 4. *Col.* 3. 3.—*Zec.* 2. 8.— *Ex.* 14. 13, 14.—*Ps.* 46. 1, 2. *Mat.* 14. 27.—*Lu.* 24. 38, 39.—*2 Ti.* 1. 12.

My kingdom is not of this world.

This man, after he had offered one sacrifice for sins for ever, sat down on the right hand of God; from henceforth expecting till his enemies may be made his footstool.—Hereafter shall ye see the Son of man sitting on the right hand of power, and coming in the clouds of heaven.

He must reign, till he hath put all enemies under his feet.

Thanks be to God, which giveth us the victory through our Lord Jesus Christ.—He raised him from the dead, and set him at his own right hand in the heavenly places, far above all principality, and power, and might, and dominion, and every name that is named, not only in this world, but also in that which is to come: and hath put all things under his feet, and gave him to be the head over all things to the church, which is his body, the fulness of him that filleth all in all.—He shall shew who is the blessed and only Potentate, the King of kings, and Lord of lords.

JNO. 18. 36. *He.* 10. 12, 13.—*Mat.* 26. 64. **1** *Co.* 15. 25. **1** *Co.* 15. 57.— *Ep.* 1. 20-23.—*1 Ti.* 6. 15.

My mother and my brethren are these which hear the word of God, and do it.

Both he that sanctifieth and they who are sanctified are all of one: for which cause he is not ashamed to call them brethren: saying, I will declare thy name unto my brethren; in the midst of the church will I sing praise unto thee.—In Jesus Christ neither circumcision availeth any thing, nor uncircumcision; but faith which worketh by love.—Ye are my friends, if ye do whatsoever I command you. Blessed are they that hear the word of God, and keep it.

Not every one that saith unto me, Lord, Lord, shall enter into the kingdom of heaven; but he that doeth the will of my Father which is in heaven.—My meat is to do the will of him that sent me.

If we say that we have fellowship with him, and walk in darkness, we lie, and do not the truth.—Whoso keepeth his word, in him verily is the love of God perfected; hereby know we that we are in him.

LUKE 8. 21. *He.* 2. 11, 12.—*Ga.* 5. 6.—*Jno.* 15. 14.—*Lu.* 11. 28.
Mat. 7. 21.—*Jno.* 4. 34. 1 *Jno.* 1. 6.—1 *Jno.* 2. 5.

NOVEMBER 24

EVENING

What doest thou here, Elijah?

He knoweth the way that I take.—O LORD, thou hast searched me, and known me. Thou knowest my downsitting, and mine uprising; thou understandest my thought afar off. Thou compassest my path, and my lying down, and art acquainted with all my ways. Whither shall I go from thy spirit? or whither shall I flee from thy presence? If I take the wings of the morning, and dwell in the uttermost parts of the sea; even there shall thy hand lead me, and thy right hand shall hold me.

Elias was a man subject to like passions as we are.—The fear of man bringeth a snare: but whoso putteth his trust in the LORD shall be safe.—Though he fall, he shall not be utterly cast down: for the LORD upholdeth him with his hand.—A just man falleth seven times, and riseth up again.

Let us not be weary in well doing: for in due season we shall reap, if we faint not.—The spirit indeed is willing, but the flesh is weak.—Like as a father pitieth his children, so the LORD pitieth them that fear him.

1 KINGS 19. 9. *Job* 23. 10.—*Ps.* 139. 1-3, 7, 9, 10. *Ja.* 5. 17.—*Pr.* 29. 25.—*Ps.* 37. 24.—*Pr.* 24. 16. *Ga.* 6. 9.—*Mat.* 26. 41.—*Ps.* 103. 13, 14.

Being made free from sin, ye became the servants of righteousness.

Ye cannot serve God and Mammon.—When ye were the servants of sin, ye were free from righteousness. What fruit had ye then in those things whereof ye are now ashamed? for the end of those things is death. But now being made free from sin, and become servants to God, ye have your fruit unto holiness, and the end everlasting life.

Christ is the end of the law for righteousness to every one that believeth.

If any man serve me, let him follow me; and where I am, there shall also my servant be: if any man serve me, him will my Father honour.—Take my yoke upon you, and learn of me: for I am meek and lowly in heart: and ye shall find rest unto your souls For my yoke is easy, and my burden is light.

O LORD our God, other lords beside thee have had dominion over us: but by thee only will we make mention of thy name.— I will run the way of thy commandments, when thou shalt enlarge my heart.

ROM. 6. 18. *Mat.* 6. 24.—*Ro.* 6. 20-22. *Ro.* 10. 4. *Jno.* 12. 26.— *Mat.* 11. 29, 30. *Is.* 26. 13.—*Ps.* 119. 32.

Whosoever shall call on the name of the Lord shall be saved.

Manasseh did that which was evil in the sight of the LORD, after the abominations of the heathen, and he reared up altars for Baal. And he built altars for all the host of heaven in the two courts of the house of the LORD.—And he made his son pass through the fire, and observed times, and used enchantments, and dealt with familiar spirits and wizards: he wrought much wickedness in the sight of the LORD, to provoke him to anger.—And when he was in affliction, he besought the LORD his God, and humbled himself greatly before the God of his fathers, and prayed unto him: and he was intreated of him, and heard his supplication.

Come now, and let us reason together, saith the LORD: though your sins be as scarlet, they shall be as white as snow; though they be red like crimson, they shall be as wool.—The Lord is long-suffering to us-ward, not willing that any should perish.

ACTS 2. 21. 2 *Ki.* 21. 1, 2, 3, 5, 6.—2 *Ch.* 33. 12, 13, *Isa.* 1. 18.— 2 *Pe.* 3. 9.

The Lord delighteth in thee.

Thus saith the LORD that created thee, . . . Fear not: for I have redeemed thee, I have called thee by thy name; thou art mine.— Can a woman forget her sucking child, that she should not have compassion on the son of her womb? yea, they may forget, yet will I not forget thee. Behold, I have graven thee upon the palms of mine hands: thy walls are continually before me.

The steps of a good man are ordered by the LORD: and he delighteth in his way.—My delights were with the sons of men.— The LORD taketh pleasure in them that fear him, in those that hope in his mercy.—They shall be mine, saith the LORD of hosts, in that day when I make up my jewels; and I will spare them, as a man spareth his own son that serveth him.

You, that were sometime alienated and enemies in your mind by wicked works, yet now hath he reconciled in the body of his flesh through death, to present you holy and unblameable and unreproveable in his sight.

ISA. 62. 4. *Is.* 43. 1.—*Is.* 49. 15, 16. *Ps.* 37. 23.—*Pr.* 8. 31.—*Ps.* 147. 11.— *Mal.* 3. 17. *Col.* 1. 21, 22.

The sorrow of the world worketh death.

When Ahithophel saw that his counsel was not followed, he saddled his ass, and arose, and gat him home to his house, to his city, and put his household in order, and hanged himself, and died. —A wounded spirit who can bear?

Is there no balm in Gilead? is there no physician there? why then is not the health of the daughter of my people recovered?— The LORD hath anointed me to preach good tidings unto the meek: he hath sent me to bind up the broken-hearted, to comfort all that mourn; to appoint unto them that mourn in Zion, to give unto them beauty for ashes, the oil of joy for mourning, the garment of praise for the spirit of heaviness.—Come unto me, all ye that labour and are heavy laden, and I will give you rest. Take my yoke upon you, and learn of me; for I am meek and lowly in heart: and ye shall find rest unto your souls. For my yoke is easy, and my burden is light.

Philip preached unto him Jesus.—He healeth the broken in heart, and bindeth up their wounds.

2 *COR.* 7. 10. 2 *Sa.* 17. 23.—*Pr.* 18. 14. *Je.* 8. 22.—*Is.* 61. 1-3.— *Mat.* 11. 28-30. *Ac.* 8. 35.—*Ps.* 147. 3.

The glory which thou gavest me I have given them.

I saw . . . the Lord sitting upon a throne, high and lifted up, and his train filled the temple. Above it stood the seraphims. And one cried unto another, and said, Holy, holy, holy, is the LORD of hosts; the whole earth is full of his glory.—These things said Esaias, when he saw his glory, and spake of him.—Upon the likeness of the throne was the likeness . . . of a man above upon it. As the appearance of the bow that is in the cloud in the day of rain, so was the appearance of the brightness round about. This was the appearance of the likeness of the glory of the LORD.

I beseech thee, shew me thy glory. And he said, Thou canst not see my face: for there shall no man see me, and live.—No man hath seen God at any time; the only begotten Son, which is in the bosom of the Father, he hath declared him.—God, who commanded the light to shine out of darkness, hath shined in our hearts, to give the light of the knowledge of the glory of God in the face of Jesus Christ.

JOHN 17. 22. *Is.* 6. 1-3.—*Jno* 12. 41.—*Eze.* 1. 26, 28. *Ex.* 33. 18, 20.—
Jno. 1. 18.—*2 Co.* 4. 6.

My son, if sinners entice thee, consent thou not.

She took of the fruit thereof, and did eat, and gave also unto her husband with her; and he did eat.—Did not Achan the son of Zerah commit a trespass in the accursed thing, and wrath fell on all the congregation of Israel? and that man perished not alone in his iniquity.

Thou shalt not follow a multitude to do evil.

Wide is the gate, and broad is the way, that leadeth to destruction, and many there be which go in thereat.

None of us liveth to himself.—Brethren, ye have been called unto liberty; only use not liberty for an occasion to the flesh, but by love serve one another.—Take heed lest by any means this liberty of your's become a stumblingblock to them that are weak. When ye sin so against the brethren, and wound their weak conscience, ye sin against Christ.

All we, like sheep, have gone astray; we have turned every one to his own way; and the Lord hath laid on him the iniquity of us all.

PROV. 1. 10. *Ge.* 3. 6.—*Jos.* 22. 20. *Ex.* 23. 2. *Mat.* 7. 13. *Ro.* 14. 7.—
Ga. 5. 13.—*1 Co.* 8. 9, 12. *Isa.* 53. 6.

As the body without the spirit is dead, so faith without works is dead also.

Not every one that saith, . . . Lord, Lord, shall enter into the kingdom of heaven; but he that doeth the will of my Father which is in heaven.—Holiness, without which no man shall see the Lord.—Add to your faith virtue; and to virtue knowledge; and to knowledge temperance; and to temperance patience; and to patience godliness; and to godliness brotherly kindness; and to brotherly kindness charity. For if these things be in you, and abound, they make you that ye shall neither be barren nor unfruitful in the knowledge of our Lord Jesus Christ. But he that lacketh these things is blind, and cannot see afar off, and hath forgotten that he was purged from his old sins. Wherefore the rather, brethren, give diligence to make your calling and election sure: for if ye do these things, ye shall never fall.

By grace are ye saved through faith; and that not of yourselves; it is the gift of God: not of works, lest any man should boast.

JAMES 2. 26. *Mat.* 7. 21.—*He.* 12. 14.—*2 Pe.* 1. 5-10. *Ep.* 2. 8, 9.

NOVEMBER 28

EVENING

As the children are partakers of flesh and blood, he also himself likewise took part of the same; that he might deliver them who through fear of death were all their lifetime subject to bondage.

O death, where is thy sting? O grave, where is thy victory? Thanks be to God, which giveth us the victory through our Lord Jesus Christ.—For which cause we faint not; but though our outward man perish, yet the inward man is renewed day by day.

We know that if our earthly house of this tabernacle were dissolved, we have a building of God, an house not made with hands, eternal in the heavens. Therefore we are always confident, knowing that, whilst we are at home in the body, we are absent from the Lord. We are willing rather to be absent from the body, and to be present with the Lord.

Let not your heart be troubled: ye believe in God, believe also in me. In my Father's house are many mansions: if it were not so, I would have told you. I go to prepare a place for you.

HEB. 2. 14, 15. *1 Cor.* 15. 55, 57.—*2 Co.* 4. 16. *2 Co.* 5. 1, 6-8. *Jno.* 14. 1-3.

We shall be satisfied with the goodness of thy house.

One thing have I desired of the LORD, that will I seek after; that I may dwell in the house of the LORD all the days of my life, to behold the beauty of the LORD, and to enquire in his temple.

Blessed are they which do hunger and thirst after righteousness: for they shall be filled.—He hath filled the hungry with good things; and the rich he hath sent empty away.

He satisfieth the longing soul, and filleth the hungry soul with goodness.—I am the bread of life: he that cometh to me shall never hunger; and he that believeth on me shall never thirst.

How excellent is thy lovingkindness, O God! therefore the children of men put their trust under the shadow of thy wings. They shall be abundantly satisfied with the fatness of thy house; and thou shalt make them drink of the river of thy pleasures. For with thee is the fountain of life: in thy light shall we see light.

PSA. 65. 4. Ps. 27. 4. Mat. 5. 6.—Lu. 1. 53. Ps. 107. 9.—Jno. 6. 35.
Ps. 36. 7-9.

Do ye now believe?

What doth it profit, my brethren, though a man say he hath faith, and have not works? can faith save him? Faith, if it hath not works, is dead, being alone.

By faith Abraham, when he was tried, offered up Isaac: and he that had received the promises offered up his only begotten son. Accounting that God was able to raise him up, even from the dead.—Was not Abraham our father justified by works, when he had offered Isaac his son upon the altar? Ye see then how that by works a man is justified, and not by faith only.

Whoso looketh into the perfect law of liberty, and continueth therein, he being not a forgetful hearer, but a doer of the work, this man shall be blessed in his deed.

By their fruits ye shall know them. Not every one that saith unto me, Lord, Lord, shall enter into the kingdom of heaven; but he that doeth the will of my Father which is in heaven.—If ye know these things, happy are ye if ye do them.

JOHN 16. 31. Ja. 2. 14, 17. He. 11. 17-19.—Ja. 2. 21, 24. Ja. 1. 25.
Mat. 7. 20, 21.—Jno. 13. 17.

The Lord of peace himself give you peace always by all means. The Lord be with you all.

Peace, from him which is, and which was, and which is to come. —The peace of God, which passeth all understanding, shall keep your hearts and minds through Christ Jesus.

Jesus himself stood in the midst of them, and saith unto them, Peace be unto you.—Peace I leave with you, my peace I give unto you: not as the world giveth, give I unto you. Let not your heart be troubled, neither let it be afraid.

The Comforter . . . even the Spirit of truth. The fruit of the Spirit is love, joy, peace.—The Spirit itself beareth witness with our spirit, that we are the children of God.

My presence shall go with thee, and I will give thee rest. And he said unto him, If thy presence go not with me, carry us not up hence. For wherein shall it be known here that I and thy people have found grace in thy sight? is it not in that thou goest with us?

2 *THES.* 3. 16. *Re.* 1. 4.—*Phi.* 4. 7. *Lu.* 24. 36.—*Jno.* 14. 27. *Jno.* 15. 26.— *Ga.* 5. 22.—*Ro.* 8. 16. *Ex.* 33. 14-16.

We glory in tribulations.

If in this life only we have hope in Christ, we are of all men most miserable.

Beloved, think it not strange concerning the fiery trial which is to try you, as though some strange thing happened unto you: but rejoice, inasmuch as ye are partakers of Christ's sufferings; that, when his glory shall be revealed, ye may be glad also with exceeding joy.—Sorrowful, yet alway rejoicing.

Rejoice in the Lord alway: and again I say, rejoice.—They departed from the presence of the council, rejoicing that they were counted worthy to suffer shame for his name.

The God of hope fill you with all joy and peace in believing.

Although the fig tree shall not blossom, neither shall fruit be in the vines; the labour of the olive shall fail, and the fields shall yield no meat; the flock shall be cut off from the fold, and there shall be no herd in the stalls: Yet I will rejoice in the LORD, I will joy in the God of my salvation.

ROM. 5. 3. 1 *Co.* 15. 19. 1 *Pe.* 4. 12, 13.—2 *Co.* 6. 10. *Ph.* 4. 4.— *Ac.* 5. 41. *Ro.* 15. 13.—*Hab.* 3. 17, 18.

A man shall be as a hiding place from the wind, and a covert from the tempest.

Forasmuch . . . as the children are partakers of flesh and blood, he also himself likewise took part of the same.—The man that is my fellow, saith the LORD of hosts.—I and my Father are one.

He that dwelleth in the secret place of the most High shall abide under the shadow of the Almighty.—There shall be a tabernacle for a shadow in the daytime from the heat, and for a place of refuge, and for a covert from storm and from rain.—The LORD is thy shade upon thy right hand. The sun shall not smite thee by day, nor the moon by night.

When my heart is overwhelmed: lead me to the rock that is higher than I.—Thou art my hiding place; thou shalt preserve me from trouble.—Thou hast been a strength to the poor, a strength to the needy in his distress, a refuge from the storm, a shadow from the heat, when the blast of the terrible ones is as a storm against the wall.

ISA. 32. 2. *He.* 2. 14.—*Zec.* 13. 7.—*Jno.* 10. 30. *Ps.* 91. 1.—*Is.* 4. 6.— *Ps.* 121. 5, 6. *Ps.* 61. 2.—*Ps.* 32. 7.—*Is.* 25. 4.

Behold, I create new heavens and a new earth.

The new heavens and the new earth, which I will make, shall remain before me, . . . so shall your seed and your name remain.

We, according to his promise, look for new heavens and a new earth, wherein dwelleth righteousness.

I saw a new heaven and a new earth: for the first heaven and the first earth were passed away; and there was no more sea. And I John saw the holy city, new Jerusalem, coming down from God out of heaven, prepared as a bride adorned for her husband. And I heard a great voice out of heaven saying, Behold, the tabernacle of God is with men, and he will dwell with them, and they shall be his people, and God himself shall be with them, and be their God. And God shall wipe away all tears from their eyes; and there shall be no more death, neither sorrow, nor crying, neither shall there be any more pain: for the former things are passed away. And he that sat upon the throne said, Behold, I make all things new.

ISA. 65. 17. *Is.* 66. 22. *2 Pe.* 3. 13. *Re.* 21. 1-5.

Ye have an unction from the Holy One, and ye know all things.

God anointed Jesus of Nazareth with the Holy Ghost and with power.—It pleased the Father that in him should all fulness dwell. —Of his fulness have all we received, and grace for grace.

Thou anointest my head with oil.—The anointing which ye have received of him abideth in you, and ye need not that any man teach you: but as the same anointing teacheth you of all things, and is truth, and is no lie, and even as it hath taught you, ye shall abide in him.

The Comforter, which is the Holy Ghost, whom the Father will send in my name, he shall teach you all things, and bring all things to your remembrance, whatsoever I have said unto you.

The Spirit also helpeth our infirmities: for we know not what we should pray for as we ought: but the Spirit itself maketh intercession for us with groanings which cannot be uttered.

1 *JOHN* 2. 20. *Ac.* 10. 38.—*Col.* 1. 19.—*Jno.* 1. 16. *Ps.* 23. 5.—1 *Jno.* 2. 27. *Jno.* 14. 26. *Ro.* 8. 26.

Having our hearts sprinkled from an evil conscience.

If the blood of bulls and of goats, and the ashes of an heifer sprinkling the unclean, sanctifieth to the purifying of the flesh: How much more shall the blood of Christ, who through the eternal Spirit offered himself without spot to God, purge your conscience from dead works to serve the living God.—The blood of sprinkling, that speaketh better things than that of Abel.

We have redemption through his blood, the forgiveness of sins, according to the riches of his grace.

When Moses had spoken every precept to all the people according to the law, he took the blood of calves and of goats, with water, and scarlet wool, and hyssop, and sprinkled both the book, and all the people. Moreover he sprinkled . . . with blood both the tabernacle, and all the vessels of the ministry. And almost all things are by the law purged with blood; and without shedding of blood is no remission.

HEB. 10. 22. *He.* 9. 13, 14.—*He.* 12. 24. *Ep.* 1. 7. *He.* 9. 19, 21, 22.

I would seek unto God, and unto God would I commit my cause.

Is anything too hard for the LORD?—Commit thy way unto the LORD; trust also in him; and he shall bring it to pass.—Be careful for nothing; but in every thing by prayer and supplication, with thanksgiving, let your requests be made known unto God. —Casting all your care upon him, for he careth for you.

Hezekiah received the letter from the hand of the messengers, and read it: and Hezekiah went up unto the house of the LORD, and spread it before the LORD. And Hezekiah prayed unto the LORD.

It shall come to pass, that before they call, I will answer; and while they are yet speaking, I will hear.—The effectual fervent prayer of a righteous man availeth much.

I love the LORD, because he hath heard my voice and my supplications. Because he hath inclined his ear unto me, therefore will I call upon him as long as I live.

JOB 5. 8. *Ge.* 18. 14.—*Ps.* 37. 5.—*Phi.* 4. 6.—1 *Pe.* 5. 7. *Is.* 37. 14, 15. *Is.* 65. 24.—*Ja.* 5. 16. *Ps.* 116. 1, 2.

Our bodies washed with pure water.

Thou shalt . . . make a laver of brass, . . . and thou shalt put it between the tabernacle of the congregation and the altar, and thou shalt put water therein. For Aaron and his sons shall wash their hands and their feet thereat: when they go into the tabernacle of the congregation, they shall wash with water, that they die not; . . . they shall wash their hands and their feet, that they die not.—Your body is the temple of the Holy Ghost which is in you.—If any man defile the temple of God, him shall God destroy; for the temple of God is holy, which temple ye are.

In my flesh shall I see God: whom I shall see for myself, and mine eyes shall behold, and not another.—There shall in no wise enter into it any thing that defileth.—Thou art of purer eyes than to behold evil, and canst not look on iniquity.—I beseech you, therefore, brethren, by the mercies of God, that ye present your bodies a living sacrifice, holy, acceptable unto God, which is your reasonable service.

HEB. 10. 22. *Ex.* 30. 18-21. 1 *Co.* 6. 19.—1 *Co.* 3. 17. *Job* 19. 26, 27.— *Re.* 21. 27.—*Ha.* 1. 13.—*Ro.* 12. 1.

Where shall wisdom be found?

If any of you lack wisdom, let him ask of God, that giveth to all men liberally, and upbraideth not; and it shall be given him. But let him ask in faith, nothing wavering.—Trust in the LORD with all thine heart; and lean not unto thine own understanding. In all thy ways acknowledge him, and he shall direct thy paths.— The only wise God.—Be not wise in thine own eyes.

Ah, Lord God! behold, I cannot speak: for I am a child. But the Lord said unto me, Say not, I am a child: for thou shalt go to all that I shall send thee, and whatsoever I command thee thou shalt speak. Be not afraid of their faces: for I am with thee to deliver thee, saith the LORD.

Whatsoever ye shall ask the Father in my name, he will give it you. Hitherto have ye asked nothing in my name: ask, and ye shall receive, that your joy may be full.—All things whatsoever ye shall ask in prayer, believing, ye shall receive.

JOB 28. 12. *Ja*. 1. 5, 6.—*Pr*. 3. 5, 6.—1 *Ti*. 1. 17.—*Pr*. 3. 7. *Je*. 1. 6-8. *Jno*. 16. 23, 24. *Mat*. 21. 22.

I would not live alway.

And I said, O that I had wings like a dove! for then would I fly away, and be at rest. I would hasten my escape from the windy storm and tempest.

In this we groan, earnestly desiring to be clothed upon with our house which is from heaven. For we that are in this tabernacle do groan, being burdened: not for that we would be unclothed, but clothed upon, that mortality might be swallowed up of life.— Having a desire to depart, and to be with Christ; which is far better.

Let us run with patience the race that is set before us. Looking unto Jesus the author and finisher of our faith; who, for the joy that was set before him, endured the cross, despising the shame, and is set down at the right hand of the throne of God. For consider him that endured such contradiction of sinners against himself, lest ye be wearied and faint in your minds.

Let not your heart be troubled, neither let it be afraid.

JOB 7. 16. *Ps*. 55. 6, 8. 2 *Co*. 5. 2, 4.—*Ph*. 1. 23. *He*. 12. 1-3. *Jno*. 14. 27.

It is good for me that I have been afflicted; that I might learn thy statutes.

Though he were a Son, yet learned he obedience by the things which he suffered.—We suffer with him, that we may be also glorified together. For I reckon that the sufferings of this present time are not worthy to be compared with the glory which shall be revealed in us.

He knoweth the way that I take: when he hath tried me, I shall come forth as gold. My foot hath held his steps, his way have I kept, and not declined.

Thou shalt remember all the way which the LORD thy God led thee these forty years in the wilderness, to humble thee, and to prove thee, to know what was in thine heart, whether thou wouldest keep his commandments, or no. Thou shalt also consider in thine heart, that, as a man chasteneth his son, so the LORD thy God chasteneth thee. Therefore thou shalt keep the commandments of the LORD thy God, to walk in his ways, and to fear him.

PSA. 119. 71. *He.* 5. 8.—*Ro.* 8. 17, 18. *Job* 23. 10, 11. *De.* 8. 2, 5, 6.

By strength shall no man prevail.

Then said David to the Philistine, Thou comest to me with a sword, and with a spear, and with a shield: but I come to thee in the name of the Lord of hosts, the God of the armies of Israel, whom thou hast defied. And David put his hand in his bag, and took thence a stone, and slang it. So David prevailed over the Philistine with a sling and with a stone.

There is no king saved by the multitude of an host: a mighty man is not delivered by much strength. Behold, the eye of the Lord is upon them that fear him, upon them that hope in his mercy.—Both riches and honour come of thee, and thou reignest over all; and in thine hand is power and might; and in thine hand it is to make great, and to give strength unto all.

I glory in my infirmities, that the power of Christ may rest upon me. Therefore I take pleasure in infirmities, in reproaches, in necessities, in persecutions, in distresses for Christ's sake: for when I am weak, then am I strong.

1 *SAM.* 2. 9. 1 *Sa.* 17. 45, 49, 50. *Ps.* 33. 16, 18.—1 *Ch.* 29. 12. 2 *Co.* 12. 9, 10.

It is God which worketh in you.

Not that we are sufficient of ourselves to think any thing as of ourselves; but our sufficiency is of God.—A man can receive nothing, except it be given him from heaven.—No man can come to me, except the Father which hath sent me draw him: and I will raise him up at the last day.—And I will give them one heart, and one way, that they may fear me for ever.

Do not err, my beloved brethren. Every good gift and every perfect gift is from above, and cometh down from the Father of lights, with whom is no variableness, neither shadow of turning. Of his own will begat he us with the word of truth, that we should be a kind of firstfruits of his creatures.

For we are his workmanship, created in Christ Jesus unto good works, which God hath before ordained that we should walk in them.

LORD, thou wilt ordain peace for us: for thou also hast wrought all our works in us.

PHI. 2. 13. *2 Co.* 3. 5.—*Jno.* 3. 27. *Jno.* 6. 44.—*Je.* 32. 39. *Ja.* 1. 16-18. *Ep.* 2. 10. *Is.* 26. 12.

The spirit indeed is willing, but the flesh is weak.

In the way of thy judgments, O LORD, have we waited for thee; the desire of our soul is to thy name, and to the remembrance of thee. With my soul have I desired thee in the night; yea, with my spirit within me will I seek thee early.

I know that in me, (that is, in my flesh) dwelleth no good thing: for to will is present with me; but how to perform that which is good I find not. For I delight in the law of God after the inward man: but I see another law in my members, warring against the law of my mind, and bringing me into captivity to the law of sin which is in my members.—The flesh lusteth against the Spirit, and the Spirit against the flesh: and these are contrary the one to the other: so that ye cannot do the things that ye would.

I can do all things through Christ which strengtheneth me.— Our sufficiency is of God.—My grace is sufficient for thee.

MAT. 26. 41. *Is.* 26. 8, 9. *Ro.* 7. 18, 22, 23.—*Gal.* 5. 17. *Ph.* 4. 13.— *2 Co.* 3. 5.—*2 Co.* 12. 9.

He hath made him to be sin for us, who knew no sin; that we might be made the righteousness of God in him.

The LORD hath laid on him the iniquity of us all.—Who his own self bare our sins in his own body on the tree, that we, being dead to sins, should live unto righteousness: by whose stripes ye were healed.—As by one man's disobedience many were made sinners, so by the obedience of one shall many be made righteous.

After that the kindness and love of God our Saviour toward man appeared, not by works of righteousness which we have done, but according to his mercy he saved us, by the washing of regeneration, and renewing of the Holy Ghost; which he shed on us abundantly through Jesus Christ our Saviour; that being justified by his grace, we should be made heirs according to the hope of eternal life.—There is therefore now no condemnation to them which are in Christ Jesus, who walk not after the flesh, but after the Spirit.

The LORD our Righteousness.

2 *COR.* 5. 21. *Is.* 53. 6.—1 *Pe.* 2. 24.—*Ro.* 5. 19. *Tit.* 3. 4-7.—*Ro.* 8. 1. *Je.* 23. 6.

I will be as the dew unto Israel.

The meekness and gentleness of Christ.

A bruised reed shall he not break, and the smoking flax shall he not quench.

The Spirit of the Lord is upon me, because he hath anointed me to preach the gospel to the poor; he hath sent me to heal the brokenhearted, to preach deliverance to the captives, and recovering of sight to the blind, to set at liberty them that are bruised, to preach the acceptable year of the Lord. And he began to say unto them, This day is this scripture fulfilled in your ears. And all bare him witness, and wondered at the gracious words which proceeded out of his mouth.

And the Lord turned, and looked upon Peter, and Peter remembered the word of the Lord, how he had said unto him, Before the cock crow, thou shalt deny me thrice. And Peter went out and wept bitterly.

He shall feed his flock like a shepherd: he shall gather the lambs with his arm, and carry them in his bosom, and shall gently lead those that are with young.

HOS. 14. 5. 2 *Co.* 10. 1. *Is.* 42. 3. *Lu.* 4. 18, 19, 21, 22. *Lu.* 22. 61, 62. *Is.* 40. 11.

DECEMBER 8

By love serve one another.

Brethren, if a man be overtaken in a fault, ye which are spiritual, restore such an one in the spirit of meekness; considering thyself, lest thou also be tempted. Bear ye one another's burdens, and so fulfil the law of Christ.

Brethren, if any of you do err from the truth, and one convert him; let him know, that he which converteth the sinner from the error of his way shall save a soul from death, and shall hide a multitude of sins.—Seeing ye have purified your souls in obeying the truth through the Spirit unto unfeigned love of the brethren, see that ye love one another with a pure heart fervently.—Owe no man any thing, but to love one another: for he that loveth another hath fulfilled the law.—Be kindly affectioned one to another in brotherly love; in honour preferring one another.—Yea, all of you be subject one to another, and be clothed with humility: for God resisteth the proud, and giveth grace to the humble.

We . . . that are strong ought to bear the infirmities of the weak, and not to please ourselves.

GAL. 5. 13. *Ga.* 6. 1, 2. *Ja.* 5. 19, 20.—1 *Pe.* 1. 22.—*Ro.* 13. 8.—*Ro.* 12. 10. —1 *Pe.* 5. 5. *Ro.* 15. 1.

DECEMBER 8

The dust shall return to the earth as it was.

It is sown in corruption; it is sown in dishonour; it is sown in weakness; it is sown a natural body.—The first man is of the earth, earthy.

Dust thou art, and unto dust shalt thou return.—One dieth in his full strength, being wholly at ease and quiet. And another dieth in the bitterness of his soul, and never eateth with pleasure. They shall lie down alike in the dust, and the worms shall cover them.

My flesh . . . shall rest in hope.—Though after my skin worms destroy this body, yet in my flesh shall I see God.—The Lord Jesus Christ shall change our vile body, that it may be fashioned like unto his glorious body, according to the working whereby he is able even to subdue all things unto himself.

LORD, make me to know mine end, and the measure of my days, what it is; that I may know how frail I am.—So teach us to number our days, that we may apply our hearts unto wisdom.

ECCLES. 12. 7. 1 *Co.* 15. 42-44.—1 *Co.* 15. 47.—*Gen.* 3. 19.— *Job* 21. 23, 25, 26. *Ps.* 16. 9.—*Job* 19. 26.—*Ph.* 3. 20, 21. *Ps.* 39. 4.—*Ps.* 90. 12.

To do justice and judgment is more acceptable to the Lord than sacrifice.

He hath shewed thee, O man, what is good; and what doth the LORD require of thee, but to do justly, and to love mercy, and to walk humbly with thy God?—Hath the LORD as great delight in burnt offerings and sacrifices, as in obeying the voice of the LORD? Behold, to obey is better than sacrifice, and to hearken than the fat of rams.—To love him with all the heart, and with all the understanding, and with all the soul, and with all the strength, and to love his neighbour as himself, is more than all whole burnt offerings and sacrifices.

Therefore turn thou to thy God: keep mercy and judgment, and wait on thy God continually.—Mary . . . sat at Jesus' feet, and heard his word. One thing is needful: and Mary hath chosen that good part, which shall not be taken away from her.

It is God which worketh in you both to will and to do of his good pleasure.

PROV. 21. 3. *Mi.* 6. 8.—1 *Sa.* 15. 22.—*Mar.* 12. 33. *Ho.* 12. 6.—
Lu. 10. 39, 42. *Phi.* 2. 13.

The spirit shall return unto God who gave it.

The LORD God formed man of the dust of the ground, and breathed into his nostrils the breath of life; and man became a living soul.—There is a spirit in man; and the inspiration of the Almighty giveth them understanding.—The first man Adam was made a living soul.—The spirit of man that goeth upward.

Whilst we are at home in the body, we are absent from the Lord. We are confident, . . . and willing rather to be absent from the body, and to be present with the Lord.—With Christ; which is far better.—I would not have you to be ignorant, brethren, concerning them which are asleep, that ye sorrow not, even as others which have no hope. For if we believe that Jesus died and rose again, even so them also which sleep in Jesus will God bring with him.

I go to prepare a place for you. And if I go and prepare a place for you, I will come again, and receive you unto myself; that where I am, there ye may be also.

ECCLES. 12. 7. *Ge.* 2. 7.—*Job* 32. 8.—1 *Co.* 15. 45.—*Ec.* 3. 21.
2 *Co.* 5. 6, 8.—*Ph.* 1. 23.—1 *Thes.* 4. 13, 14.—*Jno.* 14. 2, 3.

No man is able to pluck them out of my Father's hand.

I know whom I have believed, and am persuaded that he is able to keep that which I have committed unto him against that day.—The Lord shall deliver me from every evil work, and will preserve me unto his heavenly kingdom.—We are more than conquerors through him that loved us. For I am persuaded, that neither death, nor life, nor angels, nor principalities, nor powers, nor things present, nor things to come, nor height, nor depth, nor any other creature, shall be able to separate us from the love of God, which is in Christ Jesus our Lord.—Your life is hid with Christ in God.

Hath not God chosen the poor of this world rich in faith, and heirs of the kingdom which he hath promised to them that love him?

Our Lord Jesus Christ himself, and God, even our Father, which hath loved us, and hath given us everlasting consolation and good hope through grace, comfort your hearts, and stablish you in every good word and work.

JOHN 10. 29. 2 *Ti.* 1. 12.—2 *Ti.* 4. 18.—*Ro.* 8. 37-39.—*Col.* 3. 3. *Ja.* 2. 5
2 *Thes.* 2. 16, 17.

The perfect law of liberty.

Ye shall know the truth, and the truth shall make you free. Verily, verily, I say unto you, Whosoever committeth sin is the servant of sin. If the Son therefore shall make you free, ye shall be free indeed.

Stand fast therefore in the liberty wherewith Christ hath made us free, and be not entangled again with the yoke of bondage. For, brethren, ye have been called unto liberty; only use not liberty for an occasion to the flesh, but by love serve one another. For all the law is fulfilled in one word, even in this; Thou shalt love thy neighbour as thyself.—Being then made free from sin, ye became the servants of righteousness.—For the woman which hath an husband is bound by the law to her husband so long as he liveth; but if the husband be dead, she is loosed from the law of her husband.

The law of the Spirit of life in Christ Jesus hath made me free from the law of sin and death.—I will walk at liberty: for I seek thy precepts.

JAMES 1. 25. *Jno.* 8. 32-34, 36. *Ga.* 5. 1, 13, 14.—*Ro.* 6. 18.—*Ro.* 7. 2.
Ro. 8. 2.—*Ps.* 119. 45.

Let not your good be evil spoken of.

Abstain from all appearance of evil.—Providing for honest things, not only in the sight of the Lord, but also in the sight of men.—For so is the will of God, that with well doing ye may put to silence the ignorance of foolish men.

But let none of you suffer as a murderer, or as a thief, or as an evildoer, or as a busybody in other men's matters. Yet if any man suffer as a Christian, let him not be ashamed; but let him glorify God on this behalf.

Brethren, ye have been called unto liberty; only use not liberty for an occasion to the flesh, but by love serve one another.—Take heed lest by any means this liberty of yours become a stumbling-block to them that are weak.—Whoso shall offend one of these little ones which believe in me, it were better for him that a millstone were hanged about his neck, and that he were drowned in the depth of the sea.—Inasmuch as ye have done it unto one of the least of these my brethren, ye have done it unto me.

ROM. 14. 16. 1 *Thes.* 5. 22.—2 *Co.* 8. 21.—1 *Pe.* 2. 15. 1 *Pe.* 4. 15, 16.
Ga. 5. 13.—1 *Co.* 8. 9.—*Mat.* 18. 6.—*Mat.* 25. 40.

Awake thou that sleepest, and arise from the dead, and Christ shall give thee light.

It is high time to awake out of sleep: for now is our salvation nearer than when we believed.—Therefore let us not sleep, as do others; but let us watch and be sober. For they that sleep sleep in the night: and they that be drunken are drunken in the night. But let us, who are of the day, be sober, putting on the breastplate of faith and love; and for an helmet, the hope of salvation.

Arise, shine; for thy light is come, and the glory of the Lord is risen upon thee. For behold darkness shall cover the earth, and gross darkness the people, but the Lord shall arise upon thee, and his glory shall be seen upon thee.

Wherefore gird up the loins of your mind, be sober, and hope to the end for the grace that is to be brought unto you at the revelation of Jesus Christ.—Let your loins be girded about, and your lights burning; and ye yourselves like unto men that wait for their lord.

EPH. 5. 14. *Ro.* 13. 11.—1 *Thes.* 5. 6-8. *Is.* 60. 1, 2. 1 *Pe.* 1. 13.—
Lu. 12. 35, 36.

The Lord is in the midst of thee.

Fear thou not; for I am with thee: be not dismayed; for I am thy God: I will strengthen thee; yea, I will help thee; yea, I will uphold thee with the right hand of my righteousness. Strengthen ye the weak hands, and confirm the feeble knees. Say to them that are of a fearful heart, Be strong, fear not: behold, your God will come with vengeance, even God with a recompence; He will come and save you.—The LORD thy God in the midst of thee is mighty; he will save, he will rejoice over thee with joy; he will rest in his love, he will joy over thee with singing.—Wait on the LORD: be of good courage, and he shall strengthen thine heart.

I heard a great voice out of heaven, saying, Behold, the tabernacle of God is with men, and he will dwell with them, and they shall be his people, and God himself shall be with them, and be their God. And God shall wipe away all tears from their eyes; and there shall be no more death, neither sorrow, nor crying, neither shall there be any more pain.

ZEPH. 3. 15. *Is.* 41. 10.—*Is.* 35. 3, 4.—*Zep.* 3. 17.—*Ps.* 27. 14. *Re.* 21. 3, 4.

Wherefore criest thou unto me? speak unto the children of Israel, that they go forward.

Be of good courage, and let us behave ourselves valiantly for our people, and for the cities of our God: and let the LORD do that which is good in his sight.—We made our prayer unto our God, and set a watch against them day and night.

Not every one that saith unto me, Lord, Lord, shall enter into the kingdom of heaven; but he that doeth the will of my Father which is in heaven.—If any man will do his will, he shall know of the doctrine, whether it be of God.—Then shall we know, if we follow on to know the LORD.

Watch and pray, that ye enter not into temptation.—Watch ye, stand fast in the faith, quit you like men, be strong.—Not slothful in business; fervent in spirit; serving the Lord.

Strengthen ye the weak hands, and confirm the feeble knees. Say to them that are of a fearful heart, Be strong, fear not.

EXOD. 14. 15. 1 *Ch.* 19. 13.—*Ne.* 4. 9. *Mat.* 7. 21.—*Jno.* 7. 17.—*Ho.* 6. 3. *Mat.* 26. 41.—1 *Co.* 16. 13.—*Ro.* 12. 11. *Is.* 35. 3, 4.

Be strong in the grace that is in Christ Jesus.

Strengthened with all might, according to his glorious power.—As ye have therefore received Christ Jesus the Lord, so walk ye in him: rooted and built up in him, and stablished in the faith, as ye have been taught, abounding therein with thanksgiving.—Trees of righteousness, the planting of the LORD, that he might be glorified.—Built upon the foundation of the apostles and prophets, Jesus Christ himself being the chief corner stone; in whom all the building fitly framed together groweth unto a holy temple in the Lord: in whom ye also are builded together for a habitation of God through the Spirit.

I commend you to God, and to the word of his grace, which is able to build you up, and to give you an inheritance among all them which are sanctified.—Being filled with the fruits of righteousness, which are by Jesus Christ, unto the glory and praise of God.

Fight the good fight of faith.—In nothing terrified by your adversaries.

2 *TIM.* 2. 1. *Col.* 1. 11.—*Col.* 2. 6, 7.—*Is.* 61. 3.—*Ep.* 2. 20-22.
Ac. 20. 32.—*Phi.* 1. 11. 1 *Ti.* 6. 12.—*Phi.* 1. 28.

Thou renderest to every man according to his work.

Other foundation can no man lay than that is laid, which is Jesus Christ. If any man's work abide which he hath built thereupon, he shall receive a reward. If any man's work shall be burned, he shall suffer loss: but he himself shall be saved; yet so as by fire.—We must all appear before the judgment seat of Christ; that every one may receive the things done in his body, according to that he hath done, whether it be good or bad.

When thou doest alms, let not thy left hand know what thy right hand doeth: that thine alms may be in secret: and thy Father which seeth in secret himself shall reward thee openly.—After a long time the lord of those servants cometh, and reckoneth with them.

Not that we are sufficient of ourselves to think any thing as of ourselves; but our sufficiency is of God.—LORD, thou wilt ordain peace for us: for thou also hast wrought all our works in us.

PSA. 62. 12. 1 *Co.* 3. 11, 14, 15.—2 *Co.* 5. 10. *Mat.* 6. 3, 4.—*Mat.* 25. 19.
2 *Co.* 3. 5.—*Is.* 26. 12.

Make his praise glorious.

This people have I formed for myself; they shall shew forth my praise.—I will cleanse them from all their iniquity, whereby they have sinned against me; and I will pardon all their iniquities, whereby they have sinned, and whereby they have transgressed against me. And it shall be to me a name of joy, a praise and an honour before all the nations of the earth.—By him therefore let us offer the sacrifice of praise to God continually, that is, the fruit of our lips giving thanks to his name.

I will praise thee, O Lord my God, with all my heart: and I will glorify thy name for evermore. For great is thy mercy toward me: and thou hast delivered my soul from the lowest hell.— Who is like unto thee, O Lord, . . . glorious in holiness, fearful in praises, doing wonders?—I will praise the name of God with a song, and will magnify him with thanksgiving.—They sing the song of Moses the servant of God, and the song of the Lamb, saying, Great and marvellous are thy works, Lord God Almighty.

PSA. 66. 2. *Is.* 43. 21.—*Jer.* 33. 8, 9.—*He.* 13. 15. *Ps.* 86. 12, 13.— *Ex.* 15. 11.—*Ps.* 69. 30.—*Re.* 15. 3.

By nature the children of wrath, even as others.

We ourselves also were sometime foolish, disobedient, deceived, serving divers lusts and pleasures, living in malice and envy, hateful, and hating one another.—Marvel not that I said unto thee, Ye must be born again.

Job answered the Lord, and said, Behold, I am vile: what shall I answer thee? I will lay mine hand upon my mouth.—The Lord said unto Satan, Hast thou considered my servant Job, that there is none like him in the earth, a perfect and an upright man, one that feareth God, and escheweth evil?

Behold, I was shapen in iniquity; and in sin did my mother conceive me.—David . . . to whom also he gave testimony, and said, I have found David the son of Jesse, a man after mine own heart, which shall fulfil all my will.

I obtained mercy, . . . who was before a blasphemer, and a persecutor, and injurious.

That which is born of the flesh is flesh; and that which is born of the Spirit is spirit.

EPH. 2. 3. *Tit.* 3. 3.—*Jno.* 3. 7. *Job* 40. 3, 4.—*Job* 1. 8. *Ps.* 51. 5.— *Ac.* 13. 22.—1 *Ti.* 1. 13. *Jno.* 3. 6.

Bear ye one another's burdens, and so fulfil the law of Christ.

Look not every man on his own things, but every man also on the things of others. Let this mind be in you, which was also in Christ Jesus: who . . . took upon him the form of a servant.— Even the Son of man came not to be ministered unto, but to minister, and to give his life a ransom for many.—He died for all, that they which live should not henceforth live unto themselves, but unto him which died for them, and rose again.

When Jesus . . . saw her weeping, and the Jews also weeping which came with her, he groaned in the spirit, and was troubled. Jesus wept.—Rejoice with them that do rejoice, and weep with them that weep.

Be ye all of one mind, having compassion one of another, love as brethren, be pitiful, be courteous: not rendering evil for evil, or railing for railing: but contrariwise blessing; knowing that ye are thereunto called, that ye should inherit a blessing.

GAL. 6. 2. *Phi.* 2. 4, 5, 7.—*Mar.* 10. 45.—2 *Co.* 5. 15. *Jno.* 11. 33, 35.— *Ro.* 12. 15. 1 *Pe.* 3. 8, 9.

Son, go work to day in my vineyard.

Thou are no more a servant, but a son; and if a son, then an heir of God through Christ.

Reckon ye . . . yourselves to be dead indeed unto sin, but alive unto God through Jesus Christ our Lord. Let not sin therefore reign in your mortal body, that ye should obey it in the lusts thereof. Neither yield ye your members as instruments of unrighteousness unto sin; but yield yourselves unto God, as those that are alive from the dead, and your members as instruments of righteousness unto God.—As obedient children, not fashioning yourselves according to the former lusts in your ignorance: but as he which hath called you is holy, so be ye holy in all manner of conversation; because it is written, Be ye holy; for I am holy.— Sanctified, and meet for the master's use, and prepared unto every good work.

Therefore, my beloved brethren, be ye stedfast, unmoveable, always abounding in the work of the Lord, forasmuch as ye know that your labour is not in vain in the Lord.

MAT. 21. 28. *Ga.* 4. 7. *Ro.* 6. 11-13.—1 *Pe.* 1. 14, 15.—2 *Ti.* 2. 21. 1 *Co.* 15. 58.

Having loved his own which were in the world, he loved them unto the end.

I pray for them: I pray not for the world, but for them which thou hast given me; for they are thine. And all mine are thine, and thine are mine; and I am glorified in them. I pray not that thou shouldest take them out of the world, but that thou shouldest keep them from the evil. They are not of the world, even as I am not of the world.

As the Father hath loved me, so have I loved you: continue ye in my love.—Greater love hath no man than this, that a man lay down his life for his friends. Ye are my friends, if ye do whatsoever I command you.—A new commandment I give unto you, That ye love one another; as I have loved you, that ye also love one another.

He which hath begun a good work in you will perform it until the day of Jesus Christ.—Christ . . . loved the church, and gave himself for it; that he might sanctify and cleanse it with the washing of water by the word.

JOHN 13. 1. *Jno.* 17. 9, 10, 15, 16. *Jno.* 15. 9.—*Jno.* 15. 13, 14.—
Jno. 13. 34. *Phi.* 1. 6.—*Ep.* 5. 25, 26.

The deep things of God.

Henceforth I call you not servants; for the servant knoweth not what his lord doeth: but I have called you friends; for all things that I have heard of my Father I have made known unto you.—It is given unto you to know the mysteries of the kingdom of heaven.

We have received, not the spirit of the world, but the Spirit which is of God; that we might know the things that are freely given to us of God.

For this cause I bow my knees unto the Father of our Lord Jesus Christ, of whom the whole family in heaven and earth is named, that he would grant you, according to the riches of his glory, to be strengthened with might by his Spirit in the inner man; that ye, being rooted and grounded in love, may be able to comprehend with all saints what is the breadth, and length, and depth, and height; and to know the love of Christ, which passeth knowledge, that ye might be filled with all the fulness of God.

1 *COR.* 2. 10. *Jno.* 15. 15.—*Mat.* 13. 11. 1 *Co.* 2. 12. *Ep.* 3. 14-19.

Quicken us, and we will call upon thy name.

It is the Spirit that quickeneth.—The Spirit also helpeth our infirmities: for we know not what we should pray for as we ought: but the Spirit itself maketh intercession for us with groanings which cannot be uttered. And he that searcheth the hearts knoweth what is the mind of the Spirit, because he maketh intercession for the saints according to the will of God.—Praying always with all prayer and supplication in the Spirit, and watching thereunto with all perseverance.

I will never forget thy precepts: for with them thou hast quickened me.—The words that I speak unto you, they are spirit, and they are life.—The letter killeth, but the spirit giveth life.—If ye abide in me, and my words abide in you, ye shall ask what ye will, and it shall be done unto you.—This is the confidence that we have in him, that, if we ask any thing according to his will, he heareth us.

No man can say that Jesus is the Lord, but by the Holy Ghost.

PSA. 80. 18. *Jno.* 6. 63.—*Ro.* 8. 26, 27.—*Ep.* 6. 18. *Ps.* 119. 93.— *Jno.* 6. 63.—*2 Co.* 3. 6. *Jno.* 15. 7.—*1 Jno.* 5. 14. *1 Co.* 12. 3.

Have no fellowship with the unfruitful works of darkness, but rather reprove them.

Be not deceived: evil communications corrupt good manners.

Know ye not that a little leaven leaveneth the whole lump? Purge out therefore the old leaven. I wrote unto you in an epistle not to company with fornicators. Yet not altogether with the fornicators of this world, or with the covetous, or extortioners, or with idolators; for then must we needs go out of the world. I have written unto you not to keep company, if any man that is called a brother be a fornicator, or covetous, or an idolater, or a railer, or a drunkard, or an extortioner; with such an one no not to eat. —That ye may be blameless and harmless, the sons of God, without rebuke, in the midst of a crooked and perverse nation, among whom ye shine as lights in the world.

In a great house there are not only vessels of gold and of silver, but also of wood and of earth; and some to honour, and some to dishonour.

EPH. 5. 11. *1 Co.* 15. 33. *1 Co.* 5. 6, 7, 9-11.—*Phi.* 2. 15. *2 Ti.* 2. 20.

Let us come boldly unto the throne of grace that we may obtain mercy, and find grace to help in time of need.

Be careful for nothing; but in every thing by prayer and supplication with thanksgiving let your requests be made known unto God. And the peace of God, which passeth all understanding, shall keep your hearts and minds through Christ Jesus.—Ye have not received the spirit of bondage again to fear; but ye have received the Spirit of adoption, whereby we cry, Abba, Father.

I said not unto the seed of Jacob, Seek ye me in vain.—Having therefore, . . . boldness to enter into the holiest by the blood of Jesus, by a new and living way, which he hath consecrated for us, through the veil, that is to say, his flesh; and having an high priest over the house of God; let us draw near with a true heart in full assurance of faith, having our hearts sprinkled from an evil conscience, and our bodies washed with pure water.—We may boldly say, The Lord is my helper, and I will not fear what man shall do unto me.

HEB. 4. 16. *Phi.* 4. 6, 7.—*Ro.* 8. 15. *Is.* 45. 19.—*He.* 10. 19, 22.—*He.* 13. 6.

DECEMBER 18

EVENING

Ye shall know the truth, and the truth shall make you free.

Where the Spirit of the Lord is, there is liberty.—The law of the Spirit of life in Christ Jesus hath made me free from the law of sin and death.—If the Son . . . shall make you free, ye shall be free indeed.

Brethren, we are not children of the bondwoman, but of the free. Knowing that a man is not justified by the works of the law, but by the faith of Jesus Christ, even we have believed in Jesus Christ, that we might be justified by the faith of Christ, and not by the works of the law: for by the works of the law shall no flesh be justified.

Whoso looketh into the perfect law of liberty, and continueth therein, he being not a forgetful hearer, but a doer of the work, this man shall be blessed in his deed.—Stand fast therefore in the liberty wherewith Christ hath made us free, and be not entangled again with the yoke of bondage.

JOHN 8. 32. 2 *Co.* 3. 17.—*Ro.* 8. 2.—*Jno.* 8. 36. *Ga.* 4. 31.—*Ga.* 2. 16.
Ja. 1. 25.—*Ga.* 5. 1.

Unto the upright there ariseth light in the darkness.

Who is among you that feareth the LORD, that obeyeth the voice of his servant, that walketh in darkness, and hath no light? let him trust in the name of the LORD, and stay upon his God.— Though he fall, he shall not be utterly cast down: for the LORD upholdeth him with his hand.—The commandment is a lamp, and the law is light.

Rejoice not against me, O mine enemy: when I fall, I shall arise; when I sit in darkness, the LORD shall be a light unto me. I will bear the indignation of the LORD, because I have sinned against him, until he plead my cause, and execute judgment for me: he will bring me forth to the light, and I shall behold his righteousness.

The light of the body is the eye: if therefore thine eye be single, thy whole body shall be full of light. But if thine eye be evil, thy whole body shall be full of darkness. If therefore the light that is in thee be darkness, how great is that darkness!

PSA. 112. 4. *Is.* 50. 10.—*Ps.* 37. 24.—*Pr.* 6. 23. *Mi.* 7. 8, 9.
Mat. 6. 22, 23.

He shall feed his flock like a shepherd: he shall gather the lambs with his arm, and carry them in his bosom, and shall gently lead those that are with young.

I have compassion on the multitude, because they continue with me now three days, and have nothing to eat: . . . I will not send them away fasting, lest they faint in the way.—We have not an high priest which cannot be touched with the feeling of our infirmities.

They brought young children to him, and he took them up in his arms, put his hands upon them, and blessed them.

I have gone astray like a lost sheep; seek thy servant.—The Son of man is come to seek and to save that which was lost.—Ye were as sheep going astray; but are now returned unto the Shepherd and Bishop of your souls.

Fear not, little flock; for it is your Father's good pleasure to give you the kingdom.—I will feed my flock, and I will cause them to lie down, saith the Lord GOD.

ISA. 40. 11. *Mat.* 15. 32.—*He.* 4. 15. *Mar.* 10. 13, 16. *Ps.* 119. 176.—
Lu. 19. 10. 1 *Pe.* 2. 25. *Lu.* 12. 32.—*Eze.* 34. 15.

He hath chosen us in Him before the foundation of the world.

That we should be holy and without blame before him in love.

God hath from the beginning chosen you to salvation through sanctification of the Spirit and belief of the truth: whereunto he called you, . . . to the obtaining of the glory of our Lord Jesus Christ.—Whom he did foreknow, he also did predestinate to be conformed to the image of his Son, that he might be the firstborn among many brethren. Moreover whom he did predestinate, them he also called: and whom he called, them he also justified: and whom he justified, them he also glorified.—Elect according to the foreknowledge of God the Father, through sanctification of the Spirit, unto obedience and sprinkling of the blood of Jesus Christ.

A new heart also will I give you, and a new spirit will I put within you: and I will take away the stony heart out of your flesh, and I will give you a heart of flesh.—God hath not called us unto uncleanness, but unto holiness.

EPH. 1. 4. *Ep.* 1. 4. 2 *Thes.* 2. 13, 14.—*Ro.* 8. 29, 30.—1 *Pe.* 1. 2. *Eze.* 36. 26.—1 *Thes.* 4. 7.

If the Lord would make windows in heaven might this thing be?

Have faith in God.—Without faith it is impossible to please God.—With God all things are possible.

Is my hand shortened at all, that it cannot redeem? or have I no power to deliver?

My thoughts are not your thoughts, neither are your ways my ways, saith the LORD. For as the heavens are higher than the earth, so are my ways higher than your ways, and my thoughts than your thoughts.—Prove me now herewith, saith the LORD of hosts, if I will not open you the windows of heaven, and pour you out a blessing, that there shall not be room enough to receive it.

Behold, the LORD's hand is not shortened, that it cannot save; neither his ear heavy, that it cannot hear.—LORD, it is nothing with thee to help, whether with many or with them that have no power.

We should not trust in ourselves, but in God which raiseth the dead.

2 *KINGS* 7. 2. *Mar.* 11. 22.—*He.* 11. 6.—*Mat.* 19. 26. *Is.* 50. 2 *Is.* 55. 8, 9. —*Mal.* 3. 10. *Is.* 59. 1.—2 *Ch.* 14. 11. 2 *Co.* 1. 9.

The days of thy mourning shall be ended.

In the world ye shall have tribulation.—The whole creation groaneth and travaileth in pain together until now. And not only they, but ourselves also, which have the firstfruits of the Spirit, even we ourselves groan within ourselves, waiting for the adoption, to wit, the redemption of our body.—We that are in this tabernacle do groan, being burdened: not for that we would be unclothed, but clothed upon, that mortality might be swallowed up of life.

These are they which came out of great tribulation, and have washed their robes, and made them white in the blood of the Lamb, Therefore are they before the throne of God, and serve him day and night in his temple: and he that sitteth on the throne shall dwell among them. They shall hunger no more, neither thirst any more; neither shall the sun light on them, nor any heat. For the Lamb which is in the midst of the throne shall feed them, and shall lead them unto living fountains of waters; and God shall wipe away all tears from their eyes.

ISA. 60. 20. *Jno.* 16. 33.—*Ro.* 8. 22, 23.—*2 Co.* 5. 4. *Re.* 7. 14-17.

Master, carest thou not that we perish?

The LORD is good to all: and his tender mercies are over all his works.

Every moving thing that liveth shall be meat for you; even as the green herb have I given you all things.—While the earth remaineth, seed-time and harvest, and cold and heat, and summer and winter, and day and night, shall not cease.

The LORD is good, a strong hold in the day of trouble; and he knoweth them that trust in him.—God heard the voice of the lad: and the angel of God called to Hagar out of heaven, and said unto her, What aileth thee, Hagar? fear not; for God hath heard the voice of the lad where he is. And God opened her eyes, and she saw a well of water; and she went, and filled the bottle with water, and gave the lad drink.

Take no thought, saying, What shall we eat? or, what shall we drink? for your heavenly Father knoweth that ye have need of all these things.—Trust . . . in the living God, who giveth us richly all things to enjoy.

MARK 4. 38. *Ps.* 145. 9. *Ge.* 9. 3.—*Ge.* 8. 22. *Na.* 1. 7.—*Ge.* 21. 17, 19. *Mat.* 6. 31, 32.—*1 Ti.* 6. 17.

Your work of faith.

This is the work of God, that ye believe on him whom he hath sent.

Faith, if it hath not works, is dead, being alone.—Faith worketh by love.—He that soweth to his flesh, shall of the flesh reap corruption; but he that soweth to the Spirit shall of the Spirit reap life everlasting.—We are his workmanship, created in Christ Jesus unto good works, which God hath before ordained that we should walk in them.—Who gave himself for us, that he might redeem us from all iniquity, and purify unto himself a peculiar people, zealous of good works.

We are bound to thank God always for you, brethren, as it is meet, because that your faith groweth exceedingly, and the charity of every one of you all toward each other aboundeth. Wherefore also we pray always for you, that our God would count you worthy of this calling, and fulfil all the good pleasure of his goodness, and the work of faith with power.—It is God which worketh in you both to will and to do of his good pleasure.

1 THES. 1. 3. Jno. 6. 29. Ja. 2. 17.—Ga. 5. 6.—Ga. 6. 8.—Ep. 2. 10.— Tit. 2. 14. 2 Thes. 1. 3, 11.—Phi. 2. 13.

Where is the promise of his coming?

Enoch . . . the seventh from Adam, prophesied of these, saying, Behold, the Lord cometh with ten thousands of his saints, to execute judgment upon all.—Behold, he cometh with clouds; and every eye shall see him, and they also which pierced him; and all kindreds of the earth shall wail because of him.

The Lord himself shall descend from heaven with a shout, with the voice of the archangel, and with the trump of God: and the dead in Christ shall rise first: then we which are alive and remain shall be caught up together with them in the clouds, to meet the Lord in the air: and so shall we ever be with the Lord.

The grace of God that bringeth salvation hath appeared to all men, teaching us that, denying ungodliness and worldly lusts, we should live soberly, righteously, and godly, in this present world; looking for that blessed hope, and the glorious appearing of the great God and our Saviour Jesus Christ.

2 PE. 3. 4. Jude 14. 15.—Re. 1. 7. 1 Thes. 4. 16, 17. Tit. 2. 11-13.

Let him take hold of my strength, that he may make peace with me.

I know the thoughts that I think toward you, saith the LORD, thoughts of peace, and not of evil.—There is no peace, saith the LORD, unto the wicked.

In Christ Jesus ye who sometime were far off are made nigh by the blood of Christ. For he is our peace.

It pleased the Father that in him should all fulness dwell: and having made peace through the blood of his cross, by him to reconcile all things unto himself.—Christ Jesus: whom God hath set forth to be a propitiation through faith in his blood, to declare his righteousness for the remission of sins that are past: . . . that he might be just, and the justifier of him which believeth in Jesus.—If we confess our sins, he is faithful and just to forgive us our sins, and to cleanse us from all unrighteousness.

Trust ye in the LORD for ever, for in the LORD JEHOVAH is everlasting strength.

ISA. 27. 5. *Je.* 29. 11.—*Is.* 48. 22. *Ep.* 2. 13, 14. *Col.* 1. 19, 20.—
Ro. 3. 24-26.—1 *Jno.* 1. 9. *Is.* 26. 4.

God hath given to us eternal life, and this life is in his Son.

As the Father hath life in himself; so hath he given to the Son to have life in himself. As the Father raiseth up the dead, and quickeneth them; even so the Son quickeneth whom he will.

I am the resurrection, and the life: he that believeth in me, though he were dead, yet shall he live: and whosoever liveth and believeth in me shall never die.—I am the good shepherd: the good shepherd giveth his life for the sheep. I lay down my life, that I might take it again. No man taketh it from me, but I lay it down of myself. I have power to lay it down, and I have power to take it again. This commandment have I received of my Father.—No man cometh unto the Father, but by me.—He that hath the Son, hath life; and he that hath not the Son of God, hath not life.—For ye are dead, and your life is hid with Christ in God. When Christ, who is our life, shall appear, then shall ye also appear with him in glory.

1 *JNO.* 5. 11. *Jno.* 5. 26, 21. *Jno.* 11. 25, 26.—*Jno.* 10. 11, 17, 18.
Jno. 14. 6.—1 *Jno.* 5. 12.—*Col.* 3. 3, 4.

If ye live after the flesh, ye shall die: but if ye through the Spirit do mortify the deeds of the body, ye shall live.

Now the works of the flesh are manifest which are these; Adultery, fornication, . . . and such like : of the which I tell you before, as I have also told you in time past, that they which do such things shall not inherit the kingdom of God. But the fruit of the Spirit is love, joy, peace, longsuffering, gentleness, goodness, faith, meekness, temperance: against such there is no law. And they that are Christ's have crucified the flesh with the affections and lusts. If we live in the Spirit, let us also walk in the Spirit.

The grace of God that bringeth salvation hath appeared to all men, teaching us that, denying ungodliness and worldly lusts, we should live soberly, righteously, and godly, in this present world; looking for that blessed hope, and the glorious appearing of the great God and our Saviour Jesus Christ; who gave himself for us, that he might redeem us from all iniquity.

ROM. 8. 13. *Ga.* 5. 19, 21-25. *Tit.* 2. 11-14.

Then said the princes of the Philistines, What do these Hebrews here?

If ye be reproached for the name of Christ, happy are ye: for the spirit of glory and of God resteth upon you: on their part he is evil spoken of, but on your part he is glorified. But let none of you suffer as a murderer, or as a thief, . . . or as a busybody in other men's matters.

Let not . . . your good be evil spoken of.—Having your conversation honest among the Gentiles.

Be ye not unequally yoked together with unbelievers: for what fellowship hath righteousness with unrighteousness? and what communion hath light with darkness? Ye are the temple of the living God. Wherefore come out from among them, and be ye separate, saith the Lord, and touch not the unclean thing.

Ye are a chosen generation, a royal priesthood, an holy nation, a peculiar people: that ye should shew forth the praises of him who hath called you out of darkness into his marvellous light.

1 *SAM.* 29. 3. 1 *Pe.* 4. 14, 15. *Ro.* 14. 16.—1 *Pe.* 2. 12. 2 *Co.* 6. 14, 16, 17. 1 *Pe.* 2. 9.

The kindness and love of God our Saviour toward man appeared.

I have loved thee with an everlasting love.

In this was manifested the love of God toward us, because that God sent his only begotten Son into the world, that we might live through him. Herein is love, not that we loved God, but that he loved us, and sent his Son to be the propitiation for our sins.

When the fulness of the time was come, God sent forth his Son, made of a woman, made under the law, to redeem them that were under the law, that we might receive the adoption of sons.—The Word was made flesh, and dwelt among us, (and we beheld his glory, the glory as of the only begotten of the Father), full of grace and truth.—Great is the mystery of godliness: God was manifest in the flesh.

As the children are partakers of flesh and blood, he also himself likewise took part of the same; and through death he might destroy him that had the power of death, that is, the devil.

TIT. 3. 4. *Je.* 31. 3. 1 *Jno.* 4. 9, 10. *Ga.* 4. 4, 5.—*Jno.* 1. 14.—1 *Ti.* 3. 16.
He. 2. 14.

Thanks be unto God for his unspeakable gift.

Make a joyful noise unto the LORD, all ye lands. Serve the LORD with gladness; come before his presence with singing. Enter into his gates with thanksgiving, and into his courts with praise: be thankful unto him, and bless his name.—For unto us a child is born, unto us a son is given: and the government shall be upon his shoulder: and his name shall be called Wonderful, Counsellor, The mighty God, The everlasting Father, The Prince of Peace.

He . . . spared not his own Son, but delivered him up for us all.—Having yet . . . one son, his wellbeloved, he sent him.

Oh that men would praise the LORD for his goodness, and for his wonderful works to the children of men!—Bless the LORD, O my soul: and all that is within me, bless his holy name.

My soul doth magnify the Lord, and my spirit hath rejoiced in God my Saviour.

2 *COR* 9. 15. *Ps.* 100. 1, 2, 4.—*Isa.* 9. 6, 7. *Ro.* 8. 32.—*Mar.* 12. 6.
Ps. 107. 21.—*Ps.* 103. 1. *Lu.* 1. 46, 47.

Be ye stedfast, unmoveable, always abounding in the work of the Lord.

Ye know that your labour is not in vain in the Lord.—As ye have . . . received Christ Jesus the Lord, so walk ye in him: rooted and built up in him, and stablished in the faith, as ye have been taught, abounding therein with thanksgiving.—He that shall endure unto the end, the same shall be saved.—That on the good ground are they, which in an honest and good heart, having heard the word, keep it, and bring forth fruit with patience.

By faith ye stand.

I must work the works of him that sent me, while it is day: the night cometh, when no man can work.

He that soweth to his flesh shall of the flesh reap corruption; but he that soweth to the Spirit shall of the Spirit reap life everlasting. And let us not be weary in well doing: for in due season we shall reap, if we faint not. As we have therefore opportunity, let us do good unto all men, especially unto them who are of the household of faith.

1 COR. 15. 58. *1 Co.* 15. 58.—*Col.* 2. 6, 7.—*Mat.* 24. 13.—*Lu.* 8. 15. *2 Co.* 1. 24. *Jno.* 9. 4. *Ga.* 6. 8-10.

He is able . . . to save them to the uttermost that come unto God by him.

I am the way, the truth, and the life: no man cometh unto the Father, but by me.—Neither is there salvation in any other: for there is none other name under heaven given among men, whereby we must be saved.

My sheep hear my voice, and I know them, and they follow me: and I give unto them eternal life; and they shall never perish, neither shall any man pluck them out of my hand.—He which hath begun a good work in you will perform it until the day of Jesus Christ.—Is any thing too hard for the LORD!

Now unto him that is able to keep you from falling, and to present you faultless before the presence of his glory with exceeding joy, to the only wise God our Saviour, be glory and majesty, dominion and power, both now and ever. Amen.

HEB. 7. 25. *Jno.* 14. 6.—*Ac.* 4. 12. *Jno.* 10. 27, 28. *Ph.* 1. 6.—*Gen.* 18. 14. *Jude* 24, 25.

We look not at the things which are seen, but at the things which are not seen: for the things which are seen are temporal; but the things which are not seen are eternal.

Here have we no continuing city.—Ye have in heaven a better and an enduring substance.

Fear not, little flock; for it is your Father's good pleasure to give you the kingdom.

Now for a season, if need be, ye are in heaviness through manifold temptations.—There the wicked cease from troubling; and there the weary be at rest.

We that are in this tabernacle do groan, being burdened.—God shall wipe away all tears from their eyes; and there shall be no more death, neither sorrow, nor crying, neither shall there be any more pain: for the former things are passed away.

The sufferings of this present time are not worthy to be compared with the glory which shall be revealed in us.—Our light affliction, which is but for a moment, worketh for us a far more exceeding and eternal weight of glory.

2 COR. 4. 18. *He.* 13. 14.—*He.* 10. 34. *Lu.* 12. 32. 1 *Pe.* 1. 6.—*Job* 3. 17.
2 *Co.* 5. 4.—*Re.* 21. 4.—*Ro.* 8. 18.—2 *Co.* 4. 17.

He is our peace.

God was in Christ, reconciling the world unto himself, not imputing their trespasses unto them; for he hath made him to be sin for us, who knew no sin; that we might be made the righteousness of God in him.—Having made peace through the blood of his cross, by him to reconcile all things unto himself. And you that were sometime alienated and enemies in your mind by wicked works, yet now hath he reconciled in the body of his flesh through death, to present you holy and unblameable and unreproveable in his sight.—Blotting out the handwriting of ordinances that was against us, which was contrary to us, and took it out of the way, nailing it to his cross.—Having abolished in his flesh the enmity, even the law of commandments contained in ordinances; for to make in himself of twain one new man, so making peace.

Peace I leave with you, my peace I give unto you: not as the world giveth, give I unto you. Let not your heart be troubled, neither let it be afraid.

EPH. 2. 14. 2 *Co.* 5. 19, 21.—*Col.* 1. 20-22.—*Col.* 2. 14. *Ep.* 2. 15.
Jno. 14. 27.

Thy sins be forgiven thee.

I will forgive their iniquity, and I will remember their sin no more.—Who can forgive sins but God only?

I, even I, am he that blotteth out thy transgressions for mine own sake, and will not remember thy sins.—Blessed is he whose transgression is forgiven, whose sin is covered. Blessed is the man unto whom the LORD imputeth not iniquity.—Who is a God like unto thee, that pardoneth iniquity?

God for Christ's sake hath forgiven you.—The blood of Jesus Christ his Son cleanseth us from all sin. If we say that we have no sin, we deceive ourselves, and the truth is not in us. If we confess our sins, he is faithful and just to forgive us our sins, and to cleanse us from all unrighteousness.

As far as the east is from the west, so far hath he removed our transgressions from us.—Sin shall not have dominion over you: for ye are not under the law, but under grace. Being then made free from sin, ye became the servants of righteousness.

MARK 2. 5. *Jer.* 31. 34.—*Mar.* 2. 7. *Is.* 43. 25.—*Ps.* 32. 1, 2.—*Mi.* 7. 18. *Ep.* 4. 32.—1 *Jno.* 1. 7-9. *Ps.* 103. 12.—*Ro.* 6. 14, 18.

We would see Jesus.

O LORD, we have waited for thee; the desire of our soul is to thy name, and to the remembrance of thee.

The LORD is nigh unto all them that call upon him, to all that call upon him in truth.

Where two or three are gathered together in my name, there am I in the midst of them.—I will not leave you comfortless: I will come to you.—Lo, I am with you alway, even unto the end of the world.

Let us run with patience the race that is set before us, looking unto Jesus the author and finisher of our faith.

Now we see through a glass, darkly; but then face to face.—Having a desire to depart, and to be with Christ; which is far better.

Beloved, now are we the sons of God; and it doth not yet appear what we shall be: but we know that, when he shall appear, we shall be like him; for we shall see him as he is. And every man that hath this hope in him purifieth himself, even as he is pure.

JOHN 12. 21. *Is.* 26. 8. *Ps.* 145. 18. *Mat.* 18. 20.—*Jno.* 14. 18.— *Mat.* 28. 20. *He.* 12. 1, 2. 1 *Co.* 13. 12.—*Ph.* 1. 23. 1 *Jno.* 3. 2, 3.

Understanding what the will of the Lord is.

This is the will of God, even your sanctification.—Acquaint now thyself with him, and be at peace: thereby good shall come unto thee.—This is life eternal, that they might know thee the only true God, and Jesus Christ, whom thou hast sent.—We know that the Son of God is come, and hath given us an understanding, that we may know him that is true, and we are in him that is true, even in his Son Jesus Christ. This is the true God, and eternal life.

We . . . do not cease to pray for you, and to desire that ye might be filled with the knowledge of his will in all wisdom and spiritual understanding.—The God of our Lord Jesus Christ, the Father of glory, . . . give unto you the spirit of wisdom and revelation in the knowledge of him: the eyes of your understanding being enlightened; that ye may know what is the hope of his calling, and what the riches of the glory of his inheritance in the saints, and what is the exceeding greatness of his power to us-ward who believe.

EPH. 5. 17. 1 *Thes.* 4. 3.—*Job* 22. 21.—*Jno.* 17. 3.—1 *Jno.* 5. 20. *Col.* 1. 9.—
Ep. 1. 17-19.

Draw nigh to God, and he will draw nigh to you.

Enoch walked with God.—Can two walk together, except they be agreed?—It is good for me to draw near to God.

The LORD is with you, while ye be with him: and if ye seek him, he will be found of you: but if ye forsake him, he will forsake you. When they in their trouble did turn unto the LORD GOD of Israel, and sought him, he was found of them.

For I know the thoughts that I think toward you, saith the LORD, thoughts of peace, and not of evil, to give you an expected end. Then shall ye call upon me, and ye shall go and pray unto me, and I will hearken unto you. And ye shall seek me, and find me, when ye shall search for me with all your heart.

Having therefore, brethren, boldness to enter into the holiest by the blood of Jesus, by a new and living way, . . . and having an high priest over the house of God; let us draw near with a true heart in full assurance of faith.

JAMES 4. 8. *Ge.* 5. 24.—*Am.* 3. 3.—*Ps.* 73. 28. 2 *Ch.* 15. 2, 4. *Je.* 29. 11-13.
He. 10. 19-22.

Blameless in the day of our Lord Jesus Christ.

You, that were sometime alienated and enemies in your mind by wicked works, yet now hath he reconciled in the body of his flesh through death, to present you holy and unblameable and unreproveable in his sight: if ye continue in the faith grounded and settled, and be not moved away from the hope of the gospel.— That ye may be blameless and harmless, the sons of God, without rebuke, in the midst of a crooked and perverse nation, among whom ye shine as lights in the world.

Wherefore, beloved, seeing that ye look for such things, be diligent that ye may be found of him in peace, without spot, and blameless.—Sincere and without offence till the day of Christ.

Now unto him that is able to keep you from falling, and to present you faultless before the presence of his glory with exceeding joy, to the only wise God our Saviour, be glory and majesty, dominion and power, both now and ever.

1 *COR.* 1. 8. *Col.* 1. 21-23.—*Phi.* 2. 15. 2 *Pe.* 3. 14.—*Phi.* 1. 10.
Jude 24, 25.

He will keep the feet of his saints.

If we say that we have fellowship with him, and walk in darkness, we lie, and do not the truth: but if we walk in the light, as he is in the light, we have fellowship one with another, and the blood of Jesus Christ his Son cleanseth us from all sin.—He that is washed needeth not save to wash his feet, but is clean every whit.

I have taught thee in the way of wisdom; I have led thee in right paths. When thou goest, thy steps shall not be straitened; and when thou runnest, thou shalt not stumble. Enter not into the path of the wicked, and go not in the way of evil men. Avoid it, pass not by it, turn from it, and pass away. Let thine eyes look right on, and let thine eyelids look straight before thee. Ponder the path of thy feet, and let all thy ways be established. Turn not to the right hand nor to the left: remove thy foot from evil.

The Lord shall deliver me from every evil work, and will preserve me unto his heavenly kingdom: to whom be glory for ever and ever. Amen.

1 *SAM.* 2. 9. 1 *Jno.* 1. 6, 7.—*Jno.* 13. 10. *Pr.* 4. 11, 12, 14, 15, 25-27.
2 *Ti.* 4. 18.

The Lord thy God bare thee, as a man doth bear his son, in all the way that ye went, until ye came into this place.

I bare you on eagles' wings, and brought you unto myself.—In his love and in his pity he redeemed them; and he bare them, and carried them all the days of old.—As an eagle stirreth up her nest, fluttereth over her young, spreadeth abroad her wings, taketh them, beareth them on her wings: so the LORD alone did lead him.

Even to your old age I am he; and even to hoar hairs will I carry you: I have made, and I will bear; even I will carry, and will deliver you.—This God is our God for ever and ever: he will be our guide even unto death.

Cast thy burden upon the LORD, and he shall sustain thee.— Take no thought for your life, what ye shall eat, or what ye shall drink; nor yet for your body, what ye shall put on. For your heavenly Father knoweth that ye have need of all these things.

Hitherto hath the LORD helped us.

DEUT. 1. 31. *Ex.* 19. 4.—*Is.* 63. 9.—*De.* 32. 11, 12. *Is.* 46. 4.—*Ps.* 48. 14. *Ps.* 55. 22.—*Mat.* 6. 25, 32. 1 *Sa.* 7. 12.

There remaineth yet very much land to be possessed.

Not as though I had already attained, either were already perfect: but I follow after, if that I may apprehend that for which also I am apprehended of Christ Jesus.

Be ye therefore perfect—Giving all diligence, add to your faith virtue; and to virtue knowledge; and to knowledge temperance; and to temperance patience; and to patience godliness; and to godliness brotherly kindness; and to brotherly kindness charity.

I pray, that your love may abound yet more and more in knowledge and in all judgment.

Eye hath not seen, nor ear heard, neither have entered into the heart of man, the things which God hath prepared for them that love him. But God hath revealed them unto us by his Spirit.

There remaineth . . . a rest for the people of God.—Thine eyes shall see the King in his beauty: they shall behold the land that is very far off.

JOSH. 13. 1. *Ph.* 3. 12. *Mat.* 5. 48.—2 *Pe.* 1. 5-7. *Ph.* 1. 9. 1 *Co.* 2. 9, 10. *He.* 4. 9.—*Isa.* 33. 17.

NOTES

NOTES

NOTES

NOTES

NOTES

NOTES

NOTES

NOTES

NOTES

NOTES

NOTES

THE CHRISTIAN LIBRARY

Classics of the Christian faith in deluxe, hardcover, gold stamped, gift editions. These beautifully crafted volumes are in matching burgundy leatherette bindings so you can purchase a complete set or pick and choose. All books are complete and unabridged and are printed in good readable print. **Only $7.95 each!**

ABIDE IN CHRIST, Andrew Murray
BEN-HUR: A TALE OF THE CHRIST, Lew Wallace
CHRISTIAN'S SECRET OF A HAPPY LIFE,
Hannah Whitall Smith
CONFESSIONS OF ST. AUGUSTINE
DAILY LIGHT, Samuel Bagster
EACH NEW DAY, Corrie ten Boom
FOXE'S CHRISTIAN MARTYRS OF THE WORLD,
John Foxe
GOD AT EVENTIDE, A.J. Russell
GOD CALLING, A.J. Russell
GOD. OF ALL COMFORT, Hannah Whitall Smith
GOD'S SMUGGLER, Brother Andrew
HIDING PLACE, THE, Corrie ten Boom
HIND'S FEET ON HIGH PLACES, Hannah Hurnard
IMITATION OF CHRIST, THE, Thomas A. Kempis
IN HIS STEPS, Charles M. Sheldon
MERE CHRISTIANITY, C.S. Lewis
MY UTMOST FOR HIS HIGHEST, Oswald Chambers
PILGRIM'S PROGRESS, John Bunyan
POWER THROUGH PRAYER/PURPOSE IN PRAYER,
E.M. Bounds
QUIET TALKS ON PRAYER, S.D. Gordon
SCREWTAPE LETTERS, C.S. Lewis
WHO'S WHO IN THE BIBLE, Frank S. Mead

Available wherever books are sold.

or order from:

Barbour and Company, Inc.
164 Mill Street   Box 1219
Westwood, New Jersey 07675

If you order by mail add $2.00 to your order for shipping.
Prices subject to change without notice.